KT-229-700

Current Approaches
to Phonological Theory

CONTRIBUTORS

Stephen R. Anderson,
*University of California at
Los Angeles*

Daniel A. Dinnsen,
Indiana University

Patricia Jane Donegan,
Ohio State University

Fred R. Eckman,
*University of Wisconsin at
Milwaukee*

John Goldsmith,
Indiana University

James W. Harris,
*Massachusetts Institute of
Technology*

Joan B. Hooper,
*State University of New York at
Buffalo*

Kathleen Houlihan,
University of Minnesota

Fred W. Householder,
Indiana University

Gregory K. Iverson,
University of Iowa

S. D. Joshi,
Poona University

Jonathan Derek Kaye,
Université du Québec à Montréal

Paul Kiparsky,
*Massachusetts Institute of
Technology*

William R. Leben,
Stanford University

James D. McCawley,
University of Chicago

Gerald A. Sanders,
University of Minnesota

Sanford A. Schane,
University of California at San Diego

David Stampe,
Ohio State University

Linda R. Waugh,
Cornell University

Current Approaches to Phonological Theory

Edited by Daniel A. Dinnsen

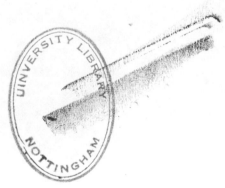

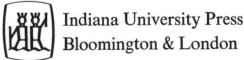

Indiana University Press
Bloomington & London

Copyright © 1979 Indiana University Press
All rights reserved

No part of this book may be reproduced or utilized in any form
or by any means, electronic or mechanical, including photocopying
and recording, or by any information storage and retrieval system,
without permission in writing from the publisher. The Association
of American University Presses' Resolution on Permissions constitutes
the only exception to this prohibition.

Manufactured in the United States of America

Library of Congress Cataloging in Publication Data

Main entry under title:
Current approaches to phonological theory.
Based on papers and discussions from the Conference on
the Differentiation of Current Phonological Theories held
at Indiana University, Bloomington, Sept. 30–Oct. 1, 1977.
Bibliography: p. 317

1. Grammar, Comparative and general–Phonology–
Congresses. I. Dinnsen, Daniel A. II. Conference on
Indiana University, 1977.
P215.CB   414   78–3241
ISBN 0–253–31596–4   1 2 3 4 5 83 82 81 80 70

To my parents with thanks and to
my son, Ross, with the wish
that I might be to him all that
they have been to me.

Contents

Introduction   ix

I. **Theoretical Approaches**
1. On the Subsequent Development of the 'Standard Theory' in Phonology / *Stephen R. Anderson*   2
2. Atomic Phonology / *Daniel A. Dinnsen*   31
3. Functionally-constrained Phonology / *Kathleen Houlihan* and *Gregory K. Iverson*   50
4. Equational Rules and Rule Functions in Phonology / *Gerald A. Sanders*   74
5. Substantive Principles in Natural Generative Phonology / *Joan B. Hooper*   106
6. The Study of Natural Phonology / *Patricia J. Donegan* and *David Stampe*   126
7. The Phonological Component as a Parsing Device / *William R. Leben*   174
8. The Aims of Autosegmental Phonology / *John Goldsmith*   202
9. Siddha and Asiddha in Pāṇinian Phonology / *S. D. Joshi* and *Paul Kiparsky*   223

II. **Review Article**
10. How Different Are They? / *Fred W. Householder*   252

III. **Remarks and Replies**
11. On Arguing about Phonological Theories / *Fred R. Eckman*   266
12. On the Alleged Correlation of Markedness and Rule-function / *Jonathan Derek Kaye*   272
13. Some Observations on "Substantive Principles in Natural Generative Phonology" / *James W. Harris*   281

14. Comments / *James D. McCawley*   294
15. Nonsegmental Phonology / *Sanford A. Schane*   303
16. Remarks on Markedness / *Linda R. Waugh*   310

Bibliography   317

Introduction

This volume addresses some of the new and developing approaches to phonological theory with a view toward comparing and differentiating them. The impact of generative phonology ('standard theory') as articulated most notably by Chomsky and Halle (1968) in their monumental work *The Sound Pattern of English* has been dominant and immeasurable in terms of directing phonological research and defining issues. Since the advent of generative phonology, considerable interest and activity have been centered on elaborating or constraining the 'standard theory' in a variety of ways. This activity has been so extensive in some instances that quite a number of apparently distinct theoretical approaches have emerged. On superficial grounds, it is clear that there are, at least, intended differences among these approaches. The terminology and descriptive devices are certainly different in some sense, and positions on certain issues also vary. However, it has not been especially clear what any of these differences may mean in the larger contexts of developing correct models of phonological systems and explaining why these systems are the way they are. That is, it is not always clear which assumptions are held constant and are shared, what different empirical predictions are embodied in the various proposals, or whether the newly devised formalism actually excludes any language-types. In short, there have been no serious systematic, coherent comparison and differentiation of these various approaches. Moreover, it has become virtually impossible to evaluate these approaches. It is accordingly most difficult to discern real progress in the field.

In response to this situation, a project was undertaken that would result in this volume. As the first step, on September 30–October 1, 1977, the Conference on the Differentiation of Current Phonological Theories (held at Indiana University, Bloomington.) convened some of the major figures in current phonological theory and the leading proponents of some of the more popular and/or provocative theoretical approaches. The conference was to address the following questions:

1) What specific issues or problems have given rise to each new theoretical approach to force a departure from 'standard theory'?
2) How do the new approaches differ from one another?
3) What aspects of these differences are formal/empirical?
4) Are there any bases for judging one theory or approach to be superior to another?

Nine papers were presented, each of which sketched a particular theoretical approach in terms of the conference charge. Discussion followed each paper including remarks from the invited discussants and other conferees. As part of the final session, Professor Fred Householder was called upon to review the positions represented at the conference by criticizing them where appropriate and by defining the areas of common ground so that we might gain some perspective on the field currently.

The conference, then, represented only the initial phase of the project, i.e., a preliminary forum for the statement of positions, an occasion to discern areas of overlap, conflict, and divergence. I think it is fair to say that there was some disappointment on the part of many conferees concerning the general absence of confrontation during the conference. In fact, it was observed that an unusual level of politeness was evident throughout the proceedings. The absence of more intense confrontation is, however, explainable on several counts. For many, unfortunately, this was the first convenient occasion to hear a more or less coherent presentation of others' research. Also, one of the significant conclusions that surely surfaces from this project is that most of us are working on specific but distinct problems, the solutions to which, for the most part, are mutually compatible. As for the politeness that seemed to prevail—well, in part it may be the beginning of a new social grace introducing itself to the field, but I doubt it. Whatever public display of politeness there may have been was not especially evident in the exchanges that took place in the weeks following the conference. This opened the second phase of the project, i.e., reflection, revision, and restatement for the purpose of publication. The authors of the nine presented papers were permitted to revise their papers, taking into account the discussions from the conference. The discussants were invited to submit short papers summarizing their remarks from the conference. It was at this point that confrontation was somewhat more feasible, intense, and productive. Much of the resultant confrontation is reflected in this volume; and, of course, some of it is not, for various reasons. This volume, thus, represents an introduction to current phonological theory in terms of a comparison and differentiation of the various approaches that constitute it and should serve as a general statement reflecting some of the significant research interests and problems in the field today.

The volume is organized into three sections. The first (and main) section includes articles on each of the theoretical approaches to be considered. Householder's review article constitutes the second section of the volume. The third section comprises short articles prepared by the conference discussants which critique the various theoretical approaches or provide a general perspective on the issues and controversies at present.

Section I is opened by Anderson's contribution which sets the stage by reviewing some of the recent developments within generative phonology leading to what might be termed 'revised standard theory.' The next three papers, mine on Atomic phonology, Houlihan and Iverson's on Functionally-constrained phonology and Sanders' on Equational phonology, have in common an interest in developing a theory of phonology more highly constrained than standard theory (possibly more than any other theory discussed here). All three proposals severely constrain what a rule of grammar can be. Equational phonology and Functionally-constrained phonology are closely linked at least in terms of some of the claims made. Kaye in his paper in Section III argues against the correctness of Houlihan and Iverson's (and by implication against Sanders') claims. Hooper develops in her article a particular aspect of Natural generative phonology by advancing a principle of analysis for morphologically- motivated alternation, i.e., a characterization of a 'natural morphological process.' Harris counters in his paper with a detailed critique of Hooper's proposal. The Donegan and Stampe article presents, in my judgment, the most impressive statement to date of Natural phonology and further refines their position on rule ordering. Leben, in his contribution, reviews and extends 'upside-down' phonology. Goldsmith's article sketches an 'autosegmental' approach to phonology which extends standard theory in the characterization of phonological representation somewhat along the lines of Firthian 'prosodies.' The final article in this section by Joshi and Kiparsky elucidates some of the principles of Pāṇinian phonology, particularly as regards rule ordering, and relates these principles to proposals in the current literature.

Stepping back from any individual contribution in this volume, a few general points emerge. First, and perhaps most comforting, is the re-affirmation of the enormous and transcendent contributions to phonological theory of such giants in the field as Jakobson, Trubetzkoy and Halle. Their influence is undeniably profound in all contemporary work. The second point would be that fundamentally the various approaches are not that different (with the possible exception of Natural phonology). While specifics may differ, many of the essential bases of generative phonology remain. Thus it should not be surprising that the diversity of generally non-overlapping problems would be met by proposals that are generally compatible and presumably could be integrated into a unified theory. Some less isolationism and more interchange might obtain in the field if we could recognize our common ground and build together; and at the same time, we appear to be in need of some *radical* rethinking for the sake of fresh insights.

I would like to take this opportunity to acknowledge the contribution of those who have participated in this project in its various phases. The entire project was supported by funds from the National Science Foundation, the American Council of Learned Societies, the Indiana University Linguistics Club, and both the Department of Linguistics and Office of Research and Graduate Development here. This project never would have gotten off the ground had it not been for the I.U. Linguistics Club. The Club provided the initial underwrite, its facilities and people-power. As it was, the total budget approached $12,000 and would have been considerably higher without the Club's help. Our success in securing the needed funding owes to the guidance provided by the local organizing committee including T. A. Sebeok, David Pisoni, Linda Schwartz, and Fred Householder. We also benefited in this regard from the comments and suggestions provided by W. P. Lehmann, Paul Chapin, and Robert Woodley.

I am indebted to all the contributors to the volume for their participation in and support of the conference and for their cooperation and goodwill throughout.

On a personal level, I want to note that my greatest debt is to the conference staff, Lucia Hammar, Carmen Lozano, and Edith Maxwell, who saw this project through its entirety in a highly competent, versatile and successful fashion. They involved themselves in all aspects of the project including the initial organizing, proposal writing, correspondence, conference arrangements, editing, etc. They anticipated needs and problems and executed the appropriate tasks while insulating me as much as possible from the burdensome details. The extent to which I have retained any sanity, I owe to them; any apparent diminished capacity on my part is inherently mine.

I would like to add a special note of acknowledgment for the contributions made by two particular individuals. Charles Ferguson wrote to each of the volume's contributors in advance of the conference, inviting us to make use of the Phonology Archive at Stanford University. I speak not only for myself when I say that the capabilities and the contribution of the Archive as a research tool are immeasurably helpful. The other person I want to thank is Robert Stockwell, who was the only senior scholar in attendance at the conference who came at his own expense. This is particularly noteworthy because Bob found it so (on several occasions) in his remarks at the conference. I am indebted to him, as we all should be, for having the courage and spirit to inject the pessimistic view that we may not be doing what we are supposed to be doing. His remarks reaffirmed the charge of the conference and ultimately contributed to a more vigorous volume.

Daniel A. Dinnsen

February, 1978

PART ONE

THEORETICAL APPROACHES

On the Subsequent Development of the 'Standard Theory' in Phonology

Stephen R. Anderson

The major problem facing one who would present and defend a 'Revised Standard Theory' in phonology is whether such an animal has any existence apart from that of a dragon to serve as the target for the lances of a variety of knights-errant. We can probably all agree that the 'Standard Theory' itself is represented in the enormously rich collection of problems, proposals, and projects of Chomsky and Halle (1968); but as opposed to the situation in syntax, it would be hard to identify a position which represents a substantive and coherent development of these ideas in a reasonably direct line and which is subscribed to by any substantial group of phonologists. Most of the schools current in phonological discussion seem to arise by the rejection or radical revision of some basic tenet of the standard theory rather than by continuous development from and within it. Nonetheless, I will attempt to identify below some of the central ideas of the standard theory in response to which subsequent phonological discussion has developed, and to indicate particular problem areas within which some consensus seems possible. Inevitably, given the state of the field, this discussion will have a rather idiosyncratic character (particularly with respect to the conclusions that are presented as established).

1. THE CHARACTER OF THE STANDARD THEORY

The central innovation of the theory of Chomsky and Halle (1968) over pre-generative discussions is undoubtedly the extent to which it attempted to make explicit the principles relating phonological to phonetic

representation. The existence and association of two levels of sound
structure had of course been generally accepted at least since the works
of de Saussure and Baudouin de Courtenay (with some idiosyncratic
exceptions, such as Bloomfield's rejection of the significance of phonetic
representations). Phonological (or 'phonemic') structure was generally
accepted as a representation of the sound properties of an utterance that
distinguish it from others and establish its position in a network of inter-
relations within a particular language as opposed to phonetic structure,
which identifies an utterance in the range of possible language-inde-
pendent human vocalizations. While the degree of abstractness of the
relation between these two was subject to considerable variation across
theories, Chomsky and Halle's position on this issue was certainly
within the range of those accepted by previous writers.

The unique contribution of the standard theory of generative phonology, then, was not in the character of the phonological representations it proposed (though these did indeed represent a break with
the ideas of their immediate predecessors in the structuralist tradition),
or even in the extent to which the character of these representations was
made explicit and a goal of scientific inquiry (which was also a characteristic of the structuralist tradition, especially in America), but rather
in the theory's concentration on making explicit the principles governing
the association of phonological with phonetic representation, conceived
as a system of rules or algorithm for converting one into the other in a
series of steps. The theory required the individual rules to be specified
with a formal precision quite unprecedented in discussions of phonological structure (which had concentrated on the character of the representations themselves). Further, since the rules of such a description are
in principle interdependent (as distinct from those in, e.g., American
structuralist or 'autonomous phonemic' descriptions), their potential interactions have to be specified with comparable precision.

In this conception, then, a phonological theory is first and foremost
an explicit, notational system of description specifying a) the formal
character of phonological and phonetic representations; b) the formal
character of the individual components of the operation mapping one
representation onto the other (the 'rules'); and c) an effective procedure
for applying the set of rules so as to effect the required mapping, involving both a definition of what it means to 'apply' a rule to a representation and a specification of the ways in which the rules can interact.

The standard theory of generative phonology also aspired to another
goal, however: in addition to providing an explicit descriptive frame-

work for the formulation of phonological descriptions, the theory also wished to address the problem of providing an account of how one out of a range of possible descriptions is to be chosen and justified as 'correct' for a given range of data. The notational system, that is to say, ought to facilitate the direct, formal comparison of alternative accounts of the same set of facts.

It is important to note that this latter project, the achieving of 'explanatory adequacy,' is logically quite distinct from the project of description; but in the proposals of Chomsky and Halle (1968) they often seem to have become inextricably merged. Since in the standard theory a phonological theory is a notational system, over expressions in which an evaluation metric can be defined, questions of notation come quickly and apparently inevitably to involve descriptive and explanatory concerns.

Much theoretical discussion since the publication of SPE, including a number of the positions represented in this volume, has been based on the explanatory concerns of that theory, under the assumption that the purely descriptive problems have already been (or at least could trivially be) solved. The strategy of workers in the field has been to propose radical limitations on the class of possible phonological rules or on the internal complexity of grammars which will have the effect of insuring that at worst only a very few accounts will be available for any given set of data. In the course of this development of the concerns of phonological theory, many interesting proposals have been made and much has been learned about the limits of linguistic structure. Considerations of the phonetic content and motivation of rules especially make it clear that a formal notational system in which all possible expressions are directly comparable is at the very least far in the future.

Indeed, the famous last chapter of Chomsky and Halle (1968) recognizes and addresses this problem, to which we will return below in section 5. There is little doubt that phonetic substance plays an important role in determining and justifying the choice of grammars, because it is basic to the nature of language. This is, in an important sense, however, completely foreign to the essential thrust of the standard theory, which aims to construct a formal descriptive system in which any expression is at least potentially a rule of a natural language.

Given the observed tendency of languages to incorporate at least some 'crazy rules' (rules whose synchronic phonetic motivation is apparently lacking), and of restructuring and other forms of language change to produce such rules, it would probably be utopian to expect phonetic substance to serve directly as the basis for a system of descriptive phonology. In constructing a descriptive system, then, the formal approach of the standard theory undoubtedly still makes sense, so long as we realize that issues of explanation still remain to be considered.

At any rate, while the descriptive issues have been less emphasized in recent discussion than the more 'glamorous' ones of explanation, there are still problems that arise within and proceed from these formal and mundane aspects of the standard theory. The character of these problems suggests that this is an appropriate place to begin in the search for a Revised Standard Theory.

2. NOTATIONAL CONVENTIONS

The set of abbreviatory conventions proposed in SPE form one of the central problem areas for investigation within the standard theory of phonology. A consideration of the rather interesting history of these conventions and their role in the theory will serve to indicate both some of the character of the 'notationalist' program and some of the directions of subsequent work.

In early work in generative phonology (as summarized, e.g., in Chomsky and Halle 1965), abbreviatory conventions such as curly brackets, parentheses, Greek-letter variables, etc. were justified as aspects of the evaluation metric for descriptions, rather than as a part of the descriptive system itself. The fully expanded set of primitive rules was taken to be the grammar, and the notational conventions were assigned the task of assessing certain aspects of the internal coherence of the system of these primitive rules. Each notational convention, that is, was justified by the claim that certain (purely formal, in terms of the rest of the notational system) resemblances between rules are highly valued, and contribute to ameliorating the complexity of a set of primitive rules within which they obtain.

The notational conventions soon came to be employed for another purpose, however. Chomsky (1967) suggested that, in addition to their evaluatory function, notational conventions such as those of Greek-letter variables and parentheses also defined subclasses of rules within which systematic deviations from otherwise valid organizing principles of grammars could be localized. By associating simultaneous and disjunctive (as opposed to sequential, conjunctive) ordering with rules displaying these formal resemblances, such a move considerably enriches the content of the claim of significance for these abbreviatory conventions. In the process, however, purely descriptive issues (what grammars are possible?) came to be merged with issues of explanation (what grammars are preferred?) in a way that has been taken much further in later work, much of which is represented in the other contributions to this conference.

Along with this shift in the content of the notational conventions of phonological theory there took place a corresponding shift in the sort of justification offered for a given proposed notational device. For example, the first discussion of Greek-letter variable rules (in Halle 1962) proposed this device as a "descriptive device for the treatment of assimilation", in order to remedy the obvious loss of generality in a formulation which required, e.g., nasal assimilation to labials, dentals, and velars to be performed by separate rules. Arguing that sets of rules of this type are in fact descriptively common, but would be counterintuitively clumsy to express in the primitive notation, Halle suggested that the device of feature counting (the fundamental mechanism by which formal expressions were to be assessed for complexity) be supplemented by a special provision for those rule-sets meeting the formal conditions of the proposed notation. Essentially the same justification as Halle's is offered by Bach (1968) for the introduction of a notational device for 'neighborhood' or 'mirror-image' rules. The basic support offered for a proposed notation as part of the evaluation function was to demonstrate that a given formal resemblance between rules recurs in the grammars of a number of diverse languages, together with an appeal to the intuition (of other linguists) that the resemblance in question is not an accidental one.

The discussion of Chomsky (1967), however, introduced a new basis for justifying notational proposals: besides showing that some formal resemblance is a recurrent one in the languages of the world, one could also demonstrate that some aspect of the internal organization of grammars is associated with all (and only?) sets of rules displaying the resemblance in question. Chomsky thus argues that Greek-letter variables, besides defining a relationship of significance for the evaluation of descriptions, also define the class of 'exchange rules' for which simultaneous rather than sequence application is required. Similarly, the discussion in Anderson (1974) argues that (at least in the domain of phonological, as opposed to phonetic rules) the mirror-image notation defines a class of rule-sets which must be applied disjunctively rather than conjunctively. Such a descriptive justification for a convention is quite different in kind, and subject to rather different sorts of confrontation with the facts of natural languages, than the fundamentally evaluative justifications offered in most early work.

Another sort of justification for notational proposals also has a fundamentally descriptive basis, and was first suggested by Kiparsky (1968b). Kiparsky argued that rules abbreviable into a single schema could be shown to function as a unit in historical change, as when the entire schema is simplified, re-ordered, lost, etc. If rules function as a unit in this way, of course, it is not unreasonable to conclude that there is an important sense in which they are a unit in a synchronic description of the language in question, and hence that a theory which provided no way of expressing this unity would fail to achieve descriptive adequacy independent of explanatory concerns.

An example of the interaction of these concerns in relation to a specific notational device is furnished by a consideration of the 'curly brackets' notation. This notation, which allows shared material in two adjacent rules to be 'factored out' and counted only once as contributing to the complexity of the total grammar, was originally justified by its contribution to the evaluation function: it allowed the coherence of a set of partially identical rules to be taken into account. It was considered self-evident in early works on generative phonology that sets of rules demonstrating such partial overlap were more natural or expected, and hence to be evaluated more highly, than arbitrary sets of primitive rules of the same basic complexity.

An attack was made on the significance of the curly brackets notation by McCawley (1970), who observed that the purely formal sense of shared material embodied in this device allows for a wide range of surely spurious simplifications. McCawley argued that the use of the notation generally allowed the concealment of flaws in an analysis, and that in every case where it appeared to be applicable, either the analysis required further refinement (so as to result in a formulation in which the supposedly collapsible rules were in fact treated as the same rule) or there was in fact no significant generalization to be captured.

It is not, in fact, possible to defend the use of curly brackets by an appeal to the internal organization of sets of rules to which they can be applied. This is because, unlike the cases of parentheses and Greek-letter variables, which are associated with exceptional disjunctive application of rules, curly brackets are associated with conjunctive application: precisely the mode of interaction of rules having nothing in common at all. Thus, one might take this fact as a sort of argument ex silentio for McCawley's position.

In some cases, however, evidence from historical change is available to confirm the significance of the collapsing performed by curly brackets. Consider the discussion of consonant gradation in Finnish in Anderson (1974). There it is shown that consonant gradation in fact involves two distinct sub-rules, one applying to geminate stops and one applying to single stops preceded by a sonorant (consonant or vowel). The separateness of these two rules is confirmed by, among other things, the distribution of exceptions in the language; and hence McCawley's position (given the evidence against a refinement of the anlysis which reduces the two to a single case) implies that there must be no generalization involved in the rule pair. Aside from the clearly counter-intuitive nature of this conclusion (linguists' intuitions being, as shown in Anderson 1977, more reliable as descriptions of linguists than of language), there is clear historical evidence against it. According to Collinder (1969), the gradation rule originally applied only in the position between a stressed and an unstressed syllable. In Modern Finnish, however, there is no such restriction; and what is significant for our purposes, the limitation has been lost equally from both cases of gradation. Similarly, in related languages such as Estonian and, more distantly, Lappish (as well as Finnish itself, to a small extent) subsequent phonological change has rendered the gradation environment opaque and the rule has been partially or completely morphologized. The crucial point, again, is that the replacement of phonological by morphological conditioning has proceeded identically for the two subcases of gradation. In considering the historical and comparative data concerning gradation, it is difficult to avoid the conclusion that changes have taken place in a single collapsed schema (which still abbreviates two distinct rules, however) rather than separately in two unrelated rules.

Such an argument would seem to establish the significance of a device for collapsing related but non-identical rules in a grammar, even in the absence of a special type of interaction among the rules so collapsed. On the other hand, a purely formal approach to the question of which rules potentially fall under this collapsing is bound to lead to problems. Consider a language containing a limited intervocalic voicing process, affecting only the dental stop /t/; and also a process of assibilation of /t/ before high front vowels:

$$(1) \quad \text{a.} \quad t \longrightarrow d \: / \: V \underline{\quad\quad} V$$
$$ \text{b.} \quad t \longrightarrow s \: / \: \underline{\quad\quad} i$$

By the definition of the curly brackets notation, the two rules in (1) would have to be collapsed to the single schema in (2):

$$(2) \qquad t \longrightarrow \begin{Bmatrix} d \: / \: V \underline{\quad\quad} V \\ s \: / \: \underline{\quad\quad} i \end{Bmatrix}$$

Now imagine that a change takes place, by which intervocalic voicing is extended to the other stops (/p,k/). If the collapsing of (1) into (2) truly represents a synchronic unity between the two rules, we would expect this extension of intervocalic voicing to entail a similar extension of spirantization, causing /p,k/ to become /f,x/ before high front vowels. In fact, we can probably agree that such an extension of spirantization as a consequence of the extension of intervocalic voicing is exceedingly unlikely, and (subject to the reservation noted above about the validity of linguists's intuitions about what languages could possibly be like) would probably wish to deny that the collapsing in (2) is valid or significant.

We must then ask ourselves what it is that makes collapsing valid for the rules of Finnish gradation, but invalid for the hypothetical case just considered. We might conclude that collapsibility, rather than being a mechanical effect captured by formal similarities in an explicit nota-tion, is rather an idiosyncratic and variable property of particular gram-mars: the Finnish rules collapse, the others don't, tout court.

It is probably possible to improve on that conclusion, however, but only by going beyond the notational program of the standard theory. In that theory the form of the rules themselves, in an appropriate expres-sion, is all that is relevant to determining the applicability of the col-lapsing operations: this is precisely what is meant by the name 'nota-tional conventions'. If we consider the function of the rules, however (in what are at present the intuitive, pre-systematic terms of traditional phonetics), we can distinguish between the two cases. The two rules involved in Finnish gradation are both weakening processes (degemina-tion of double stops, voicing or sonorization of single stops) while the intervocalic voicing and assibilation of (1) belong to quite unrelated categories (in the sense of having unrelated motivations or phonetic explanations) in traditional terms. We might suggest, then, that col-lapsing be limited to adjacent rules which are related in terms of their substance, function, phonetic motivation, etc. Of course, in order to make such a notion other than arbitrary, we must examine the tradi-tional categories of phonetic explanation and attempt to make them (or whatever should replace them) as precise as possible. As we will note again below in section 5, however, it may well be only through such a return to the traditional concerns of the study of phonetic explanation that the goals of explanation espoused by phonologists can be approached.

The conclusion that the formal approach to phonological description which is at the heart of the standard theory must be, at the least, supplemented by an appeal to functional considerations is further confirmed by the discussion of the principle of disjunctive ordering which has taken place since the publication of SPE. A number of cases have been discussed in the literature which indicate the need for disjunctive application of rules under circumstances in which no principled notational resemblance such as that captured by the parentheses notation, etc., obtains. A principle which was probably first employed by Pāṇini has been argued for by several writers (Anderson 1969, 1974; Kiparsky 1972; Koutsoudas, Sanders, and Noll 1974). Roughly, this could be stated as, "When two rules conflict, apply the more specific to the exclusion of the less specific." That is to say, when two rules would yield different results, if one of the rules applies to a proper subset of the forms to which the other applies, the more specific rule takes precedence over the more general, 'elsewhere' rule.

Not only does there seem to be a need for such a principle to govern the internal organization of grammars, but it also appears that this principle subsumes the cases in which the parentheses notation can be unambiguously shown to be associated with disjunctive ordering. If true, this conclusion would not of course establish the non-significance of the parentheses notation: this notation could still be shown to be of importance by an argument similar to that given above for the curly brackets notation. The argument for the significance of this notation which originates with Chomsky (1967), however, would have been shown to be incorrect. Disjunctive ordering appears to be associated with an independent principle, rather than with schematization by any particular notation.

The interest for our concerns at this point, however, lies in the fact that, in order to state the principle on which disjunctive ordering appears to depend, it is necessary to give some substance to the clause "when two rules conflict." Practically any pair of rules in a grammar can be seen to do different things, and it is not of course simply this that is meant. Rather, we are concerned with cases in which the rules involved are somehow comparable. It would be strange to speak of, say, a rule of penultimate stress assignment and a rule of velar softening as 'conflicting,' although they do of course yield different modifications of the input string. Since a general stress assignment rule can apply to any form in the language, while velar softening only applies to forms meeting a specific condition, the most mindless form of the principle we have discussed would seem to predict that stress is not assigned to forms that undergo velar softening in such a language! Obviously, the sort of case which interests us is one in which, say, a rule of antepenul-

timate stress assignment applies to some specific class of forms and precludes the application of the general rule of penultimate stress applicable
to the rest of the language. Stress assignment in distinct positions obviously constitutes a significant sort of 'conflict' in a way the hypothetical
case of stress and velar softening does not. Similarly, in an example discussed in Anderson (1969, 1974), lengthening (with concomitant lowering) of vowels in open syllables conflicts with shortening of vowels in
a certain subset of open syllables in Middle English.

The formulation of a principle of disjunctive ordering, then, requires
that we give precise sense to the notion of 'conflicting rules,' and this in
turn appears to require an appeal to the same substantive, functional
considerations that we argued above were important to a proper understanding of schematization by the curly brackets convention (or some
suitable alternative). From this we can conclude that the purely formal
program of notational conventions of Chomsky and Halle (1968) leads
naturally to such issues of phonological substance and function, which
take us beyond the standard theory and constitute an important revision
of it.

Another area in which the problems originally posed in the standard
theory of notational conventions lead to an extension of that theory is
the recognition of a distinction between morphological rules and phonological rules. In the program of SPE, essentially all operations on sound
structures are performed by phonological rules, which in turn are freely
allowed to contain morphological conditions without entailing a significant difference between rules that do and rules that do not involve
such non-phonological information.

Subsequent work, however, suggests that the distinction between
morphological and other rules is of significance, and must be made in
order to carry out the program of defining notational conventions. In
connection with the analysis of the synchronic reflex of the Great Vowel
Shift in Modern English, Chomsky and Halle had to deal with the question of whether 'exchange rules,' performing an interchange of two
phonological elements in some uniform environment, are possible operations in a grammar. They conclude that such rules do exist, but that
they can be precisely localized as rules abbreviable by the device of Greek-
letter variables. Accordingly, Chomsky (1967) proposed that part of
the definition of this notation ought to be a principle that rules so abbreviable apply simultaneously rather than sequentially.

More extensive examination of real (and purported) cases of exchange rules by Anderson and Browne (1973) confirms the existence of
such examples, but suggests an important limitation on them: apparently,

all genuine exchange rules contain significant morphological conditions. This is in fact rather intuitive: rules which are purely phonological in character are generally fairly close to their phonetic motivation, and it is hard to imagine that some environmental conditions which motivate the replacement of *A* by *B* could simultaneously motivate the replacement of *B* by *A*. Rules involving morphological environments, however, are to just that extent removed from a phonetic motivation. Accordingly, there is no reason to expect that an exchange arising under such circumstances should be especially unlikely.

The principle of simultaneous application for exchange rules, then, is apparently limited to morphologically conditioned rules, and accordingly suggests the significance of a typological distinction between such rules (which class must, of course be properly defined in a motivated way) and purely phonological rules. A similar conclusion is suggested by a consideration of rules involving variables (or some other device, such as the X_o notation of Chomsky and Halle 1968) which can range over arbitrarily long strings. In Anderson (1974) it is argued (on the basis of a stress assignment rule from Tahitian) that where several distinct but overlapping interpretations of such a variable are possible in conformance with the rest of the rule's structural description, only the longest of these should be taken. This principle is quite close to the spirit of the other convention(s) for disjunctive ordering, and seems to be supported for a variety of cases (cf. also Howard 1972).

This conclusion regarding variable terms in phonological rules, however, does not seem to extend to morphologically conditioned rules. In Acoma, for example (cf. Miller 1965), there is a rule of accent ablaut, which applies when certain suffixes are added to a word. There is apparently no phonological characterization of the relevant class of affixes, and the rule must thus be considered to be conditioned by an arbitrary morphological property (at least from a synchronic standpoint). The effect of the rule is to replace the tonal accents of all vowels in the affected word by a 'high' accent:

(3)   V $\longrightarrow$ [+High Tone] / _____ X [+ABLAUT]
(where X contains no #)

The formulation of this rule is no doubt imprecise, but the important point to note is that, if the above interpretation of variables were correct, it would apply only to the leftmost vowel of the word, rather than to all vowels as desired. If we assume that the interpretation given above for phonological variables does not apply in morphologically conditioned rules, however, the correct result can be obtained.

Another example supporting the same conclusion comes from the languages of the Abkhaz-Abaza group of Northwest Caucasian languages. In these languages, we find a dissimilation rule of roughly the following type: when a verb prefix with the shape /r/ (marking 3rd person plural) precedes a stem which begins with /r/, or one which is preceded by the prefix /r/ marking causative formations, it is replaced by /d/.

$$(4) \quad /r/ \longrightarrow /d/ \quad / \left[\underline{} \right]_{3rd\ pl\ pfx} X\ [_{stem}\ r$$

Again, the formulation of this rule could doubtless be refined (we assume that the causative prefix forms part of a 'stem' when added to a 'root', and that some boundary delimits this stem from the other prefix material). What is important however is the fact that any amount of other material may intervene between the prefix affected and the beginning of the stem (the Abkhaz-Abaza verb allows a large number of positions for prefixes marking various functions), and also the fact that the rule is obviously morphologically (rather than purely phonologically) conditioned.

We can now ask what happens when more than one /r/ prefix appears in the same verb. Given the interpretation of phonological variables which seems valid for phonological rules per se, it would seem that only the leftmost prefix should dissimilate. From the underlying form /y+r+r+r+ba+d/ "it-them-they-cause-see-aorist, they showed them it" we get (ignoring predictable inserted vowels) [yddrbad], showing that in fact both prefixes are affected. Note, incidentally, that the presence of two /r/ prefixes alone is not sufficient to provoke dissimilation: from /y-r-a-r-h°-d/ "it-them-to-they-tell-aorist, they told it to them" we get simply [yrarh°d], with no dissimilation of one /r/ by the other. From this evidence we conclude that this rule, too, must not involve the interpretation of variables proper to phonological rules in the pure sense.

In addition to the properties surveyed above, other formal distinctions seem to mark off the morphologically conditioned rules of a grammar from the purely phonological rules (for some discussion of this issue, cf. Anderson, 1975). The recognition of a typological distinction between morphological and phonological rules, while it is not a part of the standard theory, clearly follows directly from the range of problems which that theory poses as central; and indeed the greatly increased attention paid to the properties of morphology in recent discussion is a major area in which the standard theory has been revised since the publication of SPE.

3. THE INTERNAL ORGANIZATION OF GRAMMARS

To the questions of how rules interact with one another and of how they apply to a form, the standard theory proposes a fairly straight-forward set of answers. A rule is 'applied' by scanning the form for all places where its structural description is met, and performing all of the indicated changes simultaneously. The rule does not then re-apply to the result of this process. On the other hand, it can easily be seen that in some cases rules do have to apply to the results of applying other rules; and for this reason the main mode of rule interaction in the standard theory is application in conjunctive sequence. The rules are assumed to be organized in a (single) linear list, and applied by performing whatever changes result from the first rule on the list, then applying the second rule to the result of this process, and so on until the end of the list is reached.

One complication in this clear picture is introduced by the device of the transformational cycle in phonology proposed in SPE. Some of the rules are assumed to be applied cyclically, in that this sub-list of rules is applied in sequence to the innermost layer of constituent structure, then re-applied to the next layer of structure, etc. (For details, cf. Chomsky and Halle 1968.)

All of these aspects of the internal organization of grammars have been seriously questioned in recent years, and few of the standard theory's positions on these issues enjoy general acceptance currently. The device of the transformational cycle has seemed particularly dubious, especially since the cases in which it was apparently motivated seemed to be confined to rules involving the assignment of stress (cf. Brame 1974 for some discussion). No clear cases of segmental rules which must be applied cyclically have apparently been found, though some candidates have been proposed (particularly by Kisseberth, 1972). It is particularly plausible that stress rules should have this character: the cycle is after all a way of making a rule's application dependent on internal constituent structure, and the demarcative function of stress in many languages makes its association with constituent structure quite intuitive. It is not clear that the cycle is the correct way to capture this relationship, however, since it does not seem to extend to other sorts of rules in the way we might expect of a fundamental property of the organization of grammars.

In fact, the problems surrounding the cycle have resulted in proposals by Liberman and Prince (1977) for a different representation of stress than has generally been assumed. Liberman and Prince's approach provides a particularly elegant way of integrating the dependence of stress on syntactic structure with other properties of stress in a way that obviates the use of cyclic rules of stress assignment. For this reason, it appears at present that the device of the cycle can be completely dispensed with and we will therefore ignore it in the remainder of this discussion.

Turning to the question of whether the rules of a grammar should be represented as organized into a linear list, we can distinguish two aspects of the problem which have received a great deal of discussion in the literature: a) the question of whether the interactions of rules can in general be represented as a linear ordering; and b) the question of whether the ordering (whether linear or not) is a language-particular property of grammars ("extrinsic ordering") or can rather be predicted by a set of general principles of linguistic theory ("intrinsic ordering," though this expression also has a narrower and more precise sense for which it should perhaps be reserved). These two questions are, to varying degrees, subject to empirical examination, in the sense of presenting analyses of particular languages whose individual rules in isolation can be determined and then observing how they must be assumed to interact in order to yield the correct set of forms. We can also ask whether the ordering relations that are observed are consistent with the hypothesis of overall linear ordering, and whether it is possible to relate all (significant) types of rule interaction to a single consistent set of predictive principles.

It will perhaps come as no surprise to some readers of these remarks that my own opinion on the issue of linearity is quite clear. It seems undeniable that there exist cases in the phonologies of natural languages in which one or more of the defining properties of a linear order is violated (antisymmetry, irreflexivity, or transitivity). A range of such cases was discussed in Anderson (1974), and others have appeared (sometimes in the literature) since then. It is of course possible to argue about the details of specific examples, and there is no doubt that some of the cases discussed in this connection require refinements or revisions of the original analysis, sometimes so as to remove the particular example from the class of those supporting non-linear orderings. But other examples remain, and indeed there is reason to believe, based on our knowledge of the processes involved in language history, that synchronic grammars *ought* to contain violations of linear ordering (cf. Anderson, 1977).

The example of *u*-umlaut in Icelandic, and its interaction with other rules of the grammar, forms a central part of the argument in Anderson (1974) and will suffice for our discussion here. Essentially, the violation of linearity involved (which has been left unimpugned by subsequent discussion, as far as I can tell) arises from the fact that in order to derive [jökli] from underlying /jak+ül+e/ it is necessary to apply umlaut before syncope; but in order to derive [kötlüm] from underlying /katil+üm/ it is necessary to apply syncope before umlaut. An account of these orderings within a synchronic grammar, based on a synchronic analog of the principles of feeding and bleeding orders first invoked by Kiparsky in discussing historical change (cf. Kiparsky 1968b) was suggested, but regardless of the correctness of that account (in which I still believe, although logically that account forms a quite separate issue, related to predictability of ordering rather than to non-linearity) the violation of linear ordering seems firmly established. Some authors have suggested that this conclusion could be avoided by establishing underlying /jök+ül/ as the stem for 'glacier' rather than /jak+ül/, and thus abandoning the derivation of [ö] from /a/ by umlaut in these forms; but this possibility was raised and (to my mind) conclusively eliminated on the basis of evidence from the highly structured metrical system of Old Icelandic skaldic verse (cf. Anderson 1972). The violation of linearity, which has apparently been part of the grammar of Icelandic for more than a millenium, seems well established; and in light of other examples from a variety of languages, not isolated. We can only conclude, it seems, that the claim of the standard theory that ordering relationships are linear must be replaced with a richer set of possibilities.

Some linguists have seen the possibility of non-linear ordering relationships as completely absurd and 'counter-intuitive.' The intuition involved here is again that of linguists about formal systems, and there are good reasons to expect these intuitions (as opposed to the sorts of cognitive processes that underlie language) to favor linear orderings. A sober consideration of the facts of natural languages, however, seems to require the conclusion that these intuitions are mistaken (cf. Anderson 1977).

With respect to the question of whether all orderings can be predicted from a single coherent set of universal principles, the question is somewhat less clear. In principle, it is probably not possible to disprove the claims of those who assert the existence of such a set of principles. After all, someone may come forward with a correct proposal tomorrow. Such as we know about ordering relationships, however, does not appear to give much hope to those who await this. One of the best established predictive principles, for example, is that of the preference of languages for 'feeding' orders. Despite the overwhelming predominance of feeding orders over counter-feeding orders, however, it is difficult to deny that at least a small number of cases of the counter-feeding sort exist. To return to Icelandic *u*-umlaut, there is another rule in the language which inserts certain epenthetic *u* vowels; this rule could feed *u*-umlaut, but fails to do so. There is no other obvious principle to explain this fact; it is presumably due to the fact that the epenthesis rule appears comparatively late in the history of Icelandic, well after the umlaut rule was well established, and its appearance at 'the end of the grammar' after (and in counter-feeding relationship to) umlaut thus has a historical but not a synchronic explanation. Some discussion of this issue will be found in the exchange between Iverson (1976) and Anderson (1976a, 1976b); the result of that interchange would appear to be agreement that in at least some cases (despite some disagreement on just which stages of what language are the ones concerned) epenthesis has failed to feed umlaut when such a relationship was possible; and this would appear to go some ways toward establishing that some cases of "extrinsic' ordering are unavoidable.

Another generally valid principle of rule interaction suggests that morphological rules precede rather than follow phonologically conditioned ones, at least in the general case. In Anderson (1975) evidence was presented, however, that natural languages sometimes contain violations of this principle as well, though many fewer examples of this sort can be found than there are cases which support its general validity. Aronoff (1976) attempted to refine the hypothesis by suggesting that a given morphological rule either precedes all of the phonological rules or follows all of them; but examples discussed by Chung and Anderson (to appear) show that indeed morphological rules and phonological rules can be fully intermixed in principle (though of course the situation in most languages is much simpler than that). Further examples which appear to demonstrate the difficulties of the position that all ordering relationships are predictable are given by Vago (1977a).

What are we to make of the apparent fact that we know of a number of principles (preference for feeding orders, minimizing opacity, the precedence of morphological over phonological rules, etc.) which have a high degree of generality, but which fail in specific instances? In Anderson (1974) a hierarchical arrangement of such principles was suggested, but as the number and complexity of principles with some apparent explanatory value increases, this seems less and less likely to be worked out in practice. Yet we surely do not wish to discard such principles entirely on the basis of isolated counterexamples, any more than we wish to discard from the grammar of a given language every rule which has even a single exception.

It seems to me that the situation is in some ways parallel to that in which the neogrammarian movement found itself at the beginning of this century. The close and detailed studies of sound change which had been carried out in those terms had suggested some broadly explanatory principles of language change (especially the pair 'Lautgesetz' and 'Analogie'), and it is undeniable that the understanding of linguistic change was immensely increased thereby. Nonetheless, the conflict among these principles was such that it was quite impossible to achieve a predictive sort of explanation, in the sense of providing principles that would determine whether one or the other would prevail in a given change.

If we distinguish the ex post facto understanding of a linguistic fact which a given principle can provide from the ability of that principle to predict beforehand what the facts will be, we can I think find a proper value to set on principles such as those that have been suggested for rule interaction. When we find a particular sort of interaction in a given language, we can suggest that it is motivated by, or implements, or whatever, a tendency to reduce opacity, e.g., or to maximize feeding orders, etc. When we say that, we have, it seems to me, made some progress in understanding the facts as they are, though not in the sense of showing that they could not be otherwise. We might perhaps describe a theory which provided a set of principles meeting this requirement as achieving a level of 'Exegetic adequacy' (as opposed to explanatory adequacy in the predictive sense). The work on ordering relationships and their bases which has proceeded out of the standard theory in various directions gives good grounds for hoping that such a level of exegetic adequacy is attainable in this domain, but does not encourage the further hope for a predictive account, which would eliminate the need for 'extrinsic orderings' in the grammars of natural languages.

The other issue raised by the standard theory in the domain of the internal organization of grammars is that of how to apply a rule to a form. In the general case, of course, this is trivially resolved; the difficulties arise in cases in which the same rule is potentially applicable at a number of places in the same form, in overlapping environments. The literature dealing with this question has become quite extensive in recent years (including proposals by Johnson 1970; Howard 1972; Anderson 1974; Vago 1977b; and an excellent summary of issues in Kenstowicz and Kisseberth 1977). By now it has come to be generally accepted that the simple algorithm of simultaneous application proposed (for want of any reason at that time to think otherwise, it should be emphasized) by Chomsky and Halle (1968) is inadequate to deal with all of the cases that have been discussed. There are primarily two contenders for an effective algorithm to incorporate all of the examples to date: a revised form of the simultaneous theory, as proposed by Anderson (1974), or a 'directional' theory as proposed originally by Johnson (1970) and developed further by others.

The revised simultaneous theory of Anderson (1974) is based on an algorithm which is rather difficult to summarize, given its complexity. This is, of course, no objection to it in principle, since it is to be assigned the status of a metatheoretic construct, rather than as a rule to be stated in the grammars of particular languages. Its principal virtue is probably the fact that it allows the same principles which appear to govern the interaction of different rules to be invoked to give an account of the interaction of multiple applications of the same rule. There is also at least one example, an accentual rule from Acoma, for which it appears to provide the only viable account; though the isolation and complexity of this example make it rather insecure as evidence in the absence of further support.

This algorithm is capable of generating a variety of patterns of surface interactions of multiple applications of a single rule; there are, however, some patterns which it cannot describe, and which it must thus claim are non-occurring in natural languages. One of these is the case which is in fact simplest for the standard theory algorithm: the case in which every potential application of the rule is realized. For reasons which are too complex to go into here, an example in which three or more overlapping potential applications of a rule all undergo it would serve to falsify this theory (under some modestly restrictive assumptions about the type of rule involved).

It is not in fact at all easy to find examples which falsify this theory in this way. In part, this is because the examples with which we are concerned are of considerable complexity, and it is hard to find any evidence which bears on these questions at all. Some examples which appear to have the necessary character turn out on further analysis to require a revision of the rules involved which removes them from the class of counterexamples (some cases of this sort are discussed in Anderson 1974); and of course a number of examples exist which are perfectly consistent with the claims of the theory. It now appears, however, that there are some genuine counterexamples to the revised simultaneous application algorithm, and that it must be abandoned.

An example of the required sort is furnished by a rule of vowel shortening in Fula, a West Atlantic language. In this language, a suffix containing a basic long vowel shortens that vowel before another (basic) long vowel. Thus the suffix /-i:-/ appears as long in *njog-ii-mi* "I grasped, will grasp" but as short in *njog-i-maa-mi* "I grasped, will grasp you." The rule involved has the right character to provide a criterial example, and thus we can ask what happens when a form contains a sequence of four (or more) basic long vowel suffixes. If all of these (except the last, of course, which is not followed by a long vowel) shorten, the revised simultaneous theory is unable to describe this fact; and unfortunately that is precisely the case. In the form /suud+etee+noo+moo+ɗaa/ we have the required conditions; and the surface form of this word *cuuɗetenomoɗaa* "he was hidden from you/you were hidden from him" shows that all but the last vowel in the sequence do indeed shorten (this form was provided me by Mr. Yero Syllah, a native speaker of the Futa Toro dialect who is currently preparing a phonological description of Fula).

The Fula shortening rule, then, forces us to abandon the revised simultaneous application theory, at least as a general and universal claim. The same conclusion is supported by Kenstowicz and Kisseberth (1977), in their discussion of the Slovak Rhythmic law, which appears to be another counterexample contrary to the discussion of this case given in Anderson (1974). Furthermore, Vago (1977b) has suggested the possibility of an account of the Acoma accent loss rule which eliminates this as the single case apparently supporting the revised simultaneous theory.

If this theory cannot be maintained, then, and the claim of the standard theory cannot either, does this mean that the theory of directional rules is confirmed? This theory is certainly capable of accounting for the great bulk of the data, including essentially all the cases that have been discussed in the literature. There is one case, however, which would appear to pose problems for this theory as well and thus to suggest that the answer to the problem of rule application is not yet at hand in a general form.

Many languages have patterns of stress assignment or, conversely, syllable reduction which affect every other syllable of a word or of some subsequence within a word. In general, such processes can be described by means of a variety of application algorithms, but there is one instance in which this is not clear: the case of a rule which deletes every other vowel within the relevant sequence. Potawatomi, for example (cf. Hockett, 1948) has a rule which applies to a sequence of syllables containing the vowel *u* and deletes the first, third, fifth, etc., of these (this account is slightly simplified, but not enough to alter the bearing of the example on our problem). Now let us imagine a directional account of this fact. Suppose the rule applies from left to right: in that case it will first examine the leftmost occurrence of *u* and delete that, and then move on to the next. But now the (originally second) *u* it encounters is the first of a sequence, and thus the rule must apparently delete it too. This mode of application will clearly delete *all u*'s, contrary to what is desired.

Suppose, on the other hand, the rule applies from right to left. But now the first vowel that is considered will be the rightmost of a sequence, and in order to determine whether this is an odd- or an even-numbered vowel, it must look all the way to the left end of the sequence, contrary to the spirit at least of the directional theory. There does not seem to be a satisfactory account of these facts within that theory, without resorting to ad hoc devices such as some diacritic alternating stress or other feature (not realized phonetically) which is assigned to all syllables to be (or not to be) deleted before the deletion actually takes place, obviously an undesirable alternative.

The structure of this example appears to be such that the determination of which vowels are odd-numbered and which even should be made all at once, since once some are deleted the relations within the sequence have been changed. This example can of course be accommodated quite well by the revised simultaneous theory, but we have seen above that that theory is not able to account for other sets of facts.

It may well be that there is an adequate account of examples such as the Potawatomi case, which seems to indicate a simultaneous theory of some sort, within the theory of directional rules. We should also allow for the possibility, however, that current discussion has simply misconceived the terms of this problem raised by the standard theory, and that a totally new approach to the facts that have entered into discussions of it thus far is called for. It may also be the case that there simply is no interesting (or at any rate completely general) solution: there may be some elements of language-particular specification in the interpretation of how to apply rules of this type to a given form. At any rate, discussion of this problem has been a major area in which phonologists have attempted to revise and extend the standard theory.

4. THE STRUCTURE OF REPRESENTATIONS IN PHONOLOGY

The standard theory's view of the internal structure of phonological and phonetic representations is an appealingly straightforward and homogeneous one. At all levels of representation, these have the structure basically of a simple two dimensional array traditionally treated as a matrix. This array is divided into sequential elements of uniform size (segments) with no additional hierarchical structure; each segment is a simultaneous specification for each of the features provided by universal phonetic theory. It is assumed that the matrix is provided with a simultaneous proper bracketing as a result of syntactic and lexical structure, though this bracketing is really of interest only insofar as it controls the operation of the transformational cycle, which as we have seen above may well be unnecessary. Additional structure is provided by the assumption that morphemes, words, and phonological phrases are delimited by boundary elements; these boundaries, however, are treated as quasi-segmental entities with their own internal feature structure. They do not so much provide a (hierarchical) structure to the string of phonological/phonetic segments per se as simply partition it: they are intercalated among the segments as entities of the same basic sort.

There are three aspects of this sort of structure that have been extensively discussed in the recent literature: a) the question of what boundary elements should be posited, what sort of internal structure a feature system for these should have, etc.; b) the question of whether some additional hierarchical structure, especially an organization of segments into syllables, is necessary and appropriate; and c) the question of whether (in one way of posing the problem) the segments themselves have internal structure, and whether a given feature specification always takes exactly one segment as its domain.

With regard to the first two of these questions, I have very little to say. Stanley (1972) provided an important re-study of the nature and inventory of boundaries in phonology, and other papers since have addressed this issue at least tangentially, but there do not presently appear to be distinct, substantive positions concerning boundaries that divide phonologists in the way other problems discussed above do.

The question of the role of syllabic structure in phonology also must be neglected here. This is, of course, not an issue arising particularly within the standard theory of generative phonology: it is rather a standard problem of traditional phonetics, though posed here in different formal terms. The problem of the syllable has been mostly examined from the perspective of 'non-standard' theories, especially that of Natural Generative Phonology (cf., for example, Hooper 1972 and Vennemann 1972b). Recent work by Kahn (1976) involves proposals for motivating and incorporating syllabic structure within the standard theory, but this discussion is still in an early stage as concerns its ultimate import for revisions in the theory. Perhaps the upcoming Symposium on Segment Organization and the Syllable, to be held in October, will clarify some of these issues.

A great deal of interest has appeared in recent years, however, in the problem of the integrity of the segment. The first basic questions in this area arose from the study of tone, where the pioneering work of Leben (1973) made it clear that the traditional assumptions concerning segmental structure were in need of revision. A basic point arises in the treatment of contour tones, where it can be shown clearly that a single tone-bearing segment (usually a vowel) must be associated with more than one tone feature (for a summary of this and related issues, cf. Anderson, forthcoming). On the other hand, the study of other areas of phonological structure, particularly the phonology of nasality, argues that a single specification for a single feature may also have as its domain more than a single segment (though perhaps not an integral number of segments): cf. Anderson (1976c). The general conclusion seems clear, then, that the assumption of uniform-sized segments (uniform from the point of view of all features, that is) must be abandoned.

Two more or less independent approaches have been made to this conclusion: the program of Autosegmental phonology, represented at this conference by Goldsmith's contribution, and the line taken by Anderson (1976c) which is quite close to the sort of phonetic description appearing in work by Pike (1943) and some American Structuralist accounts. There are obvious superficial differences between these two approaches, but there are also obvious similarities of principle, and it is not clear at present that there are empirical grounds for distinguishing between the two. Some discussion of this issue will be found in Goldsmith's paper at this conference and we will not go into it further.

Discussion of these problems has reached general agreement on the proposition that feature specifications need not take as their domain precisely one segment: single segments (in the usual phonetic sense; of course precisely the problem we are dealing with here raises fundamental difficulties with the notion of "segment") may have more than one specification for the same feature, sequenced in some way, and a single specification may take more than one segment as its domain. This substantial enrichment of the notion of phonological/phonetic representation opens up a wide range of problems and possibilities which are only beginning to be explored.

The study of tonal patterns, for example, has suggested that in many cases such patterns extending over substantial stretches of an utterance may be made up of only a very few elements. This, in turn, raises the question of whether other phonological processes of similar appearance may best be treated in a similar way. An obvious candidate for such a status is the process of vowel harmony: one might well propose that, instead of specifying each vowel of the word for the harmonic features, there is only one specification, taking as its domain the entire word (or whatever stretch constitutes an appropriate scope for the harmony). Just this sort of analysis has been proposed by Clements (1976b, 1976c). It appears at present that the arguments for treating harmony in this way rather than as a segmental assimilation do not carry conviction (cf. Anderson, forthcoming, for discussion of this controversy), but the issue can hardly be considered resolved. In any event, there are undoubtedly other cases, outside the domain of tone, for which such a 'prosodic' (as opposed to assimilatory) approach to intersegmental identities is appropriate. Some facts concerning nasals appear to have this character (cf. Anderson 1976), and the search for others is a particularly exciting area of current research.

Another particularly promising line of research follows from the fact that, if the sort of structure we envision here is appropriate for phonological representations, it should be the case that rules of the phonology of particular languages can manipulate it; and the properties of such rules remain to be examined. To turn again to the phonology of tone, we can consider the proposals of Hyman and Schuh (1974). They distinguish between rules of tonal assimilation and rules of tone spreading; rules of the latter sort are precisely the sort whose formal properties require discussion, since they involve not simple changes in feature values, like garden variety rules, but rather extensions and/or contractions of the scope of a feature value.

Rules of this sort seem particularly suggestive in the context of the problem of diphthongization, as discussed in an important paper by Andersen (1972). He distinguishes two stages in diphthongization: the phonetic diphthongization, in which a single segment becomes internally complex by a polarization of one or more of its features and a phonemic diphthongization, by which such a complex segment is reinterpreted as a sequence of two (or more) segments. In the development of diphthongs from tense vowels in English, Icelandic, and many other languages, for example, we could distinguish stages a) in which, e.g., /o:/ is a single, homogenous segment; b) in which /o:/ remains a single segment, but comes to be realized phonetically with a rise in tongue height at its offset; and c) in which /o:/ has been reinterpreted as the sequence /ow/ (at some level of structure, not necessarily underlyingly):

(5) a.

syll	cons	high	back	low	rnd
+	−	−	+	−	+

b.

syll	cons	high	back	low	rnd
+	−	− +	+	−	+

c.

syll	cons	high	back	low	rnd
+ −	− −	− +	+ +	− −	+ +

The two processes of phonetic diphthongization and phonemic reinterpretation of complex segments seem to yield a more interesting account of the process of diphthongization than do the hitherto accepted processes of glide formation, etc. involved in previous generative discussion. Once we admit such processes (whose essence is the manipulation they perform on the domains of feature specifications, not their values) other areas of potential application are opened up.

It seems possible, for instance, that by recognizing such rules we can propose a constraint that phonological rules never insert epenthetic segments. Epenthesis would then be treated as a sequence of internal diphthongization, followed by phonemic re-interpretation, followed perhaps by some segmental modifications. This is clearly a reasonable approach to a large number of segment-insertion processes that have been suggested in the literature (consider, for example, the appearance of epenthetic stop consonants between nasals and following obstruents in English, discussed in these terms in Anderson, 1976c). Other cases that might not seem to be of the same sort are probably amenable to such a treatment as well, however. Consider the development of epenthetic *e* before clusters of *s* plus consonant in Spanish. We can suggest, following Hooper (1976), that this process has its origin in a revision of the syllable structure canon of Spanish, by which such clusters were prohibited. As a result of this change, the *s* of such clusters was expelled from its original syllable and came to form a syllable of its own. Thus (marking syllable boundaries with .), *sta.re* becomes *ṣ.ta.re*. We can now assume that such 'syllabic' *s*'s undergo diphthongization with respect to the feature [±syllabic], becoming [ṣs]; subsequently, syllabic *ṣ* (or perhaps more generally syllabic obstruents) are replaced with a more natural vowel [e], yielding modern *estar*. Such a history is of course largely conjectural, but if validated in some interesting cases it would suggest the existence of a constraint forbidding 'structure building' rules in phonology other than through the processes of internal phonetic diphthongization followed by subsequent re-interpretation.

We should note at this point that such a constraint would only apply to phonological rules, and not to rules with morphologically conditioned environments. Most of the modern Algonquian languages, for example, have a rule which inserts a *t* between a possessive prefix and a following vowel-initial stem. Such a rule obviously involves morphological conditioning; since there is no reason to believe it was ever phonetically motivated, there is no reason to expect a constraint of the form we are considering to have applied to it. This is of course another example of the utility of the distinction between phonological and morphological rules discussed above in making precise the domain of theoretical principles in phonology.

Processes of the sort we have been discussing can also be invoked, it appears, to exclude another type of formal operation in phonology: compensatory lengthening. While it is not certain that all putative cases of this classic category of phonological change can be so analyzed, preliminary investigation (cf. DeChene and Anderson, 1977) suggests that compensatory lengthening can generally be treated as a combination of sonorization to a glide of the element to be lost, followed by monophthongization of the resultant vowel plus glide sequence—the inverse of the diphthongization process dealt with above.

We conclude, then, that the enrichment of phonological structure involved in feature specifications having either more or less than a whole 'segment' as their domain raises a number of interesting possibilities for phonology. A significant number of traditional phonological process types may well turn out to be more insightfully (and restrictedly) formulated in these terms than in the terms of previous purely segmental operations.

5. THE RELATION OF DESCRIPTION TO EXPLANATION

In the last chapter of Chomsky and Halle (1968), a number of problems are cited with the strictly formal approach of the standard theory. These all center around the fact that such an approach completely neglects the phonetic content and function of phonological representations and rules. An approach is suggested, based loosely on ideas of Trubetzkoy and Jakobson, which will allow some of these notions to be brought within the notational approach to phonology that characterizes the rest of their work.

It is more than a little ironic that Chomsky and Halle characterize the earlier Prague approach to markedness by stating that "[A]fter a promising start, the exploration of these problems was not continued, largely because it seemed impossible to surmount the conceptual difficulties that stemmed from the taxonomic view of linguistics, which was all but universally accepted at that time. The attempts to break out of the confines of this view [. . .] elicited little positive response and almost no interest among contemporary workers, and the notion of markedness is hardly mentioned in the phonological literature of the 1940's and 1950's." (Chomsky and Halle 1968:402). While it would certainly be difficult to attribute a 'taxonomic view of linguistics' to Chomsky and Halle's work, it is striking that their attempts to surmount the limitations inherent in a purely formal approach to phonology by developing a theory of phonological substance elicited virtually the same lack of response as did the earlier proposals of Trubetzkoy and Jakobson. To the best of my knowledge, not a single phonological description published since 1968 has attempted to carry out the program of incorporating marking conventions, and (while occasional favorable references to the idea of having such a theory appear in the literature) virtually no discussion and development of their ideas can be found.

The basic idea of the markedness proposal involves the observation that some configurations (of features or of segments) are more to be expected (perhaps in a contextually determined way) than others. These (putatively universal) facts are expressed in a set of marking conventions, considered to be part of linguistic theory and thus stated once and for all rather than being part of the grammar of a particular language.

Now just as the notational conventions which capture the degree of coherence of a description are treated as fundamentally part of the procedure for evaluating grammars, so the marking conventions are treated as an aspect of the evaluation metric, and their function is to render forms conforming to the universally expected conditions less 'costly' than forms which violate them.

This notion of natural configuration is then to be extended to capture the notion of natural rule in a fairly straightforward way: rules producing expected configurations are to be rendered less costly, while those that produce configurations violating these conditions are to become more costly. This is to be achieved by assigning each marking convention an added function: it is also to serve as a 'linking rule', applying to the output of every phonological rule in a derivation to perform corrective therapy on the output of the rule unless explicitly prevented (at some added cost) from so altering the otherwise expected result. Thus, those aspects of a rule's effects which are 'natural' or 'expected' need not be stated in the rule at all (and are thus rendered cost-free) since they will come about by the operation of the (universal) marking conventions; while any aspect of a rule's operation which violates expectation, or indeed which simply fails to enforce it, requires overt statement and a consequent increase in cost.

It is clear then that such an approach is completely consistent with the rest of the program of the standard theory, as it attempts to bring aspects of phonological substance under the scope of a formal treatment in terms of the notation for the expression of phonological processes.

Unfortunately, there are a number of problems with this approach which become apparent upon examination. Some of these are largely mechanical (though not insignificant), and relate to the fact that even highly natural rules are still rules of the grammar, with their own idiosyncratic statements, limitations, exceptions, interactions with other rules, etc. This point is developed to some extent by Anderson (1974) and by Stampe (1973a). It would appear that it is simply not possible to extract all of the naturalness from a phonological description and state it once and for all in linguistic metatheory, simply because each language's implementation of such naturalness is potentially different, and the line between natural and unnatural processes is a continuum rather than a dichotomy.

A more serious limitation of the SPE approach to markedness comes from the fact that it is based on a theory of natural configurations, rather than on natural processes. Thus, it might be possible to state that clusters of obstruents heterogeneous in voicing are unexpected ('marked'), but whether a given language eliminates them by progressive assimilation (as in English inflectional endings), regressive assimilation (as in, e.g., Russian), bidirectional assimilation to one preferred value (as in Swedish), or by breaking them up or simplifying them (as in some other languages) cannot be predicted from this statement alone. Thus, all of these ways of achieving the state in which all obstruent clusters are homogeneous in voicing must be treated as completely language-particular. Aside from the fact that this leaves the unmarkedness of voicing assimilation (or whatever replaces it) completely unstated, it also fails to capture the fact that regressive assimilation is far and away the most expected way of achieving the desired configurations, apparently, although all of the other possibilities are in a sense rules of 'voicing assimilation' too.

This limitation is an essential feature of the SPE proposal, since that proposal is simply an attempt to extend the notion of natural configuration (which has a straightforward interpretation in terms of a notation and an evaluation applied to that notation) to encompass the notion of natural rule as well. On such an approach, it is inevitable that anything having to do with the preferred or natural way of achieving a given natural configuration, or any phonetically motivated natural process which creates configurations that are (in isolation) unnatural (such as syncope rules which increase cluster complexity) must stand outside the theory. Thus, at best, even with a theory of marking conventions and linking rules a great deal of the original program of taking account of phonological substance still remains to be carried out elsewhere in the theory.

Partially in recognition of such problems, Chomsky and Halle suggest that the theory of markedness would have to be supplemented by a theory of 'plausible' phonological processes. Such a notion in fact comes quite close to the sort of substantive typology of phonological processes which we have suggested at various points above is necessary elsewhere in phonology (to define the possibilities of rules schematization, disjunctive order, and other properties of the organization of a grammar). Such a theory of plausible processes might well distinguish, say, weakening processes such as degemination, voicing of obstruents, spirantization of stops, replacements of fricatives by *h,* etc. as a unitary class, associating particular environments favoring such weakenings with this class, and imposing substantive constraints on (precisely) rules which fall into this category. Such a theory might well give us a way to bridge the gap between formal phonological statements and constraints and phonetic substance, by providing a way of incorporating aspects of phonetic explanation into phonological theory in an appropriately limited way (limited, that is, to the class of processes to which the explanation in question is applicable).

It would appear that phonological theory must also recognize a systematic statement of the distinctions among (sub-phonemic or) phonetic rules, phonological rules, morphological rules, and quasi-systematic relations among forms within the lexicon. Such a distinction (or at least the distinction between phonological and morphological rules) has already been argued for above (and more extensively in Anderson 1975). It corresponds closely to the ideas of Baudouin de Courtenay (1895), who gives a similar classification of processes.

It is Baudouin de Courtenay's discussion, in fact, that points up what is probably the most important use for such a classification of process types, when he treats the conditions under which phonetic rules become phonologized, phonological rules become opaque and subsequently morphologized or lexicalized. Given a) a substantive typology of phonetically motivated rule types, each narrowly and specifically constrained; and b) an account of the conditions under which rules classified along another dimension (that of phonetic, phonological, morphological, etc.) can change their status along that dimension, we might well come quite close to a theory of grammar that is as explanatory as is intrinsically possible, in terms of our present notion of the nature of language. Concrete application of this approach to the specific problem of understanding "compensatory lengthening" can be seen in DeChene and Anderson (1977). Such a theory should not, of course, be expected to meet the condition of complete predictability, but rather the more limited notion of 'exegetic adequacy' suggested above. The very fact that a single linguistic system can apparently evolve in any one of several ways (as shown by the existence of a variety of descendents of a single ancestral language) would seem to argue that a perfectly predictive theory of language is impossible in principle, in any event. Such an exegetically adequate theory as suggested above, then, may well constitute both a more reasonable and an achievable approach to the reconciliation of problems of explanation while giving proper attention to those of description, the basic paradox approached through the notion of markedness in the standard theory.

CHAPTER TWO

Atomic Phonology

Daniel A. Dinnsen

1. The purpose of this paper is to review the developing theory of atomic phonology and differentiate it from other, competing theories of phonology.

The theory of atomic phonology maintains that all linguistic variation requiring distinctly varied formulations of phonological rules is predictable from a set of atomic rules and universal principles of grammar. Within this theory, there is a crucial distinction between atomic and non-atomic rules. Atomic rules are entirely independent rules of grammar which are presumed to be the most basic, most specific rules that can be motivated on empirical grounds. For any given atomic rule, then, there could be no more specific nor equally specific and independent rule effecting a same or otherwise related structural change. Atomic rules thus specify all the necessary initial conditions from which any correct variation on that process for any natural language can be predicted by universal principles. Non-atomic rules are dependent on atomic rules. The dependence on atomic rules derives from the requirement that non-atomic rules are all and only those rules which are complements of atomic rules or complements of their complements. The complement relation may be defined as follows:[1]

(1) Two rules are complements, and thus in a complement relation, if just those commonly shared (identical) features in the structural descriptions of the two rules are sufficient to define precisely the same set of input representations defined by the two rules jointly.

This relation is exemplified by the following two rules:

(2) $\begin{bmatrix} - \text{sonorant} \\ - \text{continuant} \end{bmatrix} \longrightarrow [- \text{voice}] / \underline{\hspace{1cm}} \#$

(Stop obstruents are voiceless word-finally.)

(3) $\begin{bmatrix} - \text{sonorant} \\ + \text{continuant} \end{bmatrix} \longrightarrow [- \text{voice}] / \underline{\hspace{1cm}} \#$

(Continuant obstruents are voiceless word-finally.)

These two rules are complements since just the commonly shared features in their structural descriptions, i.e., [−sonorant] #, equivalently characterize the set of input representations defined by the combined effects of the two rules. However, the following hypothetical rule is not a possible complement of either rule (2) or (3):

(4) $\begin{bmatrix} - \text{sonorant} \\ - \text{anterior} \\ - \text{coronal} \end{bmatrix} \longrightarrow [- \text{voice}] / \underline{\hspace{1cm}} \#$

(Velar obstruents are voiceless word-finally.)

The features common to rules (4) and (2) or (3), i.e. [− sonorant] #, do not define the same set of input representations as the pair of rules (2) and (4) or the pair of rules (3) and (4). For example, the class of segments actually defined by rules (2) and (4) would be all stop ob-struents and velar fricatives in word-final position. Since such a class excludes at least word-final dental and labial fricatives, it clearly cannot be considered equivalent to the class of all word-final obstruents and thus does not constitute a complement relation.

By assuming that rule (2) is the atomic rule for Terminal Devoicing, it is claimed that rule (2) is a possible, independently verifiable rule of grammar that can be motivated empirically as, for example, in Fer-rarese Italian, Turkish, and certain Greek dialects (cf. Dinnsen and Eckman 1977). It also follows that rule (3) is a non-atomic rule and as such is not a possible independently occurring rule of grammar. The claim is, then, that rule (3) will be without any empirical support as an independent rule. This is a particular instance of one of the central claims of atomic phonology, and that is that no two languages will differ solely by the postulation of an atomic rule for one language with an-other language evidencing the complement rule as an equally independent and necessary rule of grammar. Rule (3), being a dependent rule, can be evidenced, however, if and only if there is also evidence motivating rule (2). Such empirical findings as, for example, in German and Catalan (cf. Dinnsen and Eckman 1977), motivate the distinct, more general formulation of Terminal Devoicing stated in (5):

(5) [− sonorant] ⟶ [− voice] / _____ #

(All obstruents are voiceless word-finally.)

Rule (5) derives from the conventional conflation of the atomic rule (2) with its non-atomic complement rule (3). Rule (5) is thus predicted to be a possible correct variation on the Terminal Devoicing process. What this illustrates is that within a theory of atomic phonology, rule formulations may vary or differ from the atomic rule only to the extent that that variation follows from the relationship of rules in a complement relation. It is this same constraint that excludes the hypothetical rule (4) as a possible rule or variation of the Terminal Devoicing process. Specifically, since rule (4) is not a possible complement of the atomic rule (2), no relationship can be established between the two rules. Since the atomic rule contains no restrictions based on point of articulation features, it follows that no rule effecting Terminal Devoicing will ever need to incorporate point of articulation features. The apparent absence of any well motivated rule of Terminal Devoicing formulated in terms of point of articulation features bears out the predictions of atomic phonology (cf. Anwar 1974).

One point which perhaps requires further comment is a point which frequently arises in discussions over the characterization of complement rules. And that is, it might appear to some that the construct 'complement rule' reduces to rules that simply differ in the coefficient specification of a single feature. This is certainly true in the case of rules (2) and (3) above. In fact, any two rules that differ solely in the coefficient specification of a single binary feature will be complements. But, what is not true is that all complement rules differ in the coefficient specification of just one feature. To see this, consider the following two rules which account for certain vocalic alternations in various Swiss German dialects (cf. Robinson 1976; Keel 1976, 1977):

(6) $\begin{bmatrix} V \\ - high \\ + back \\ - long \end{bmatrix} \longrightarrow [+ low] / \_\_\_ \begin{bmatrix} + sonorant \\ + consonant \\ - nasal \\ - lateral \end{bmatrix}$

(o ⟶ ɔ / _____ r)

$$(7) \quad \begin{bmatrix} V \\ -\text{high} \\ +\text{back} \\ -\text{long} \end{bmatrix} \longrightarrow [+\text{low}] \, / \underline{\quad\quad} \begin{bmatrix} -\text{sonorant} \\ +\text{consonant} \\ +\text{coronal} \end{bmatrix}$$

(o ⟶ ɔ in the environment before coronal obstruents.)

These two rules are complements despite the fact that they differ in more than one feature specification. The focus of each rule is, of course, identical; and while the determinants differ explicitly in the coefficient specification of the feature [sonorant], they also differ in other respects. That is, rule (6) explicitly requires specification for the features [nasal] and [lateral] while rule (7) does not. Similarly, rule (7) explicitly requires a specification for the feature [coronal] while rule (6) does not. These two rules do, however, have more features common to their structural descriptions than may be initially evident and that permit their characterization as complements. That is, in this language, r's are redundantly [+ coronal], and obstruents are redundantly [− nasal, − lateral]. Therefore, since the features common to the determinants of both rules are actually [+ consonant, − nasal, − lateral, + coronal], i.e., lower in the environment before coronal obstruents and r, and since this is precisely the same set of contexts defined by the two rules, they are quite properly complements. These two rules are incidentally conflatable as rule (8)— the well known rule of lowering for the Schaffhausen dialect (cf. Robinson 1976: 148; Kiparsky 1968b):

$$(8) \quad \begin{bmatrix} V \\ -\text{high} \\ +\text{back} \\ -\text{long} \end{bmatrix} \longrightarrow [+\text{low}] \, / \underline{\quad\quad} \begin{bmatrix} +\text{consonant} \\ +\text{coronal} \\ -\text{nasal} \\ -\text{lateral} \end{bmatrix}$$

(o ⟶ ɔ in the environment before coronal obstruents and r.)

This discussion of the lowering rules also reveals some of the implications of atomic phonology for the characterization of linguistic change by means of rule simplification or generalization (cf. Dinnsen 1976a). That is, atomic phonology maintains that all cases of rule simplification are derivable by means of the independently necessary mechanism of rule addition—but rule addition of a highly limited sort, namely complement rule addition. In this particular instance, the rule lowering o before r, i.e., rule (6), can be established as the atomic rule (cf. Robinson 1976; Keel 1976, 1977). Subsequently and in other dialects rule (7) was added lowering o before coronal obstruents. Given the same degree of applicability for the two rules, they can be conflated as the generalized rule (8). Rule (8) also serves to illustrate that not all cases of a generalized rule will differ from the atomic rule or some predecessor rule in only one feature specification. While the feature [sonorant] is lost from the formulation of rule (8), the feature [coronal] must be added.

The discussion above is intended to demonstrate that there are examples of complement rules that differ in more than one feature. It may be suspected, however, that after consulting the redundant or implied features, the rules then do differ in only one feature. To dispel this view, consider the following highly plausible rules:

(9)
$$\begin{bmatrix} V \\ + \text{back} \\ - \text{low} \end{bmatrix} \longrightarrow [- \text{tense}] / \underline{\hspace{1cm}} CC$$

(Non-low back vowels are lax in closed syllables.)

(10)
$$\begin{bmatrix} V \\ - \text{back} \\ - \text{low} \end{bmatrix} \longrightarrow [- \text{tense}] / \underline{\hspace{1cm}} CC$$

(Non-low front vowels are lax in closed syllables.)

In a language where roundness is a redundant property of non-low vowels, these two rules would differ in the coefficient specifications of both the features [back] and [round]; yet these rules are complements since the commonly shared features of the rules, namely non-low vowels in closed syllables, define precisely the same set of input representations defined by the two rules jointly.

This discussion, thus, suggests that the characterization of "complement rule" given in (1) does not reduce simply to any statement that counts the number or type of differences in feature specifications.

2. The inclusion of the construct "complement rule" in a theory of phonology has many significant empirical consequences, as has been argued in earlier papers. For example, it is generally recognized that rules are added to grammars as optional rules (Kiparsky 1971; Norman 1973). If rule generalization is a special case of rule addition as predicted by a theory of atomic phonology, one would expect that in the course of rule simplification certain component parts or expansions of the generalized rule should evidence optionality corresponding to complement rules. These predictions are also borne out in Keel (1976), Keel and Shannon (1976), and Dinnsen (1976a).

3. Moreover, within standard theory, rule generalization is characterized by two formally distinct mechanisms, i.e., generalization by feature loss and generalization by Greek letter variables. There is, however, absolutely no empirical basis whatever for distinguishing these types of simplification. Within a theory of atomic phonology both types of simplification are derived in the same way—by complement rule addition (cf. Dinnsen 1976a). It is thus not surprising that the two putative types of simplification are empirically indistinguishable.

4. The theory of atomic phonology also provides for the principled exclusion of certain rule formulations which within the standard theory are judged to constitute linguistically significant generalizations but which are otherwise empirically indefensible. This exclusion follows from the general requirement that any rule R is a possible rule of grammar if and only if R is atomic or is in a complement relation with an atomic rule. For example, in Dinnsen (1977a) it was argued that the well known rule of French Truncation proposed by Schane (1968a) abbreviates two rules which cannot possibly be related within atomic phonology.

(11) French Truncation

$$\begin{bmatrix} \alpha \text{ consonant} \\ -\alpha \text{ vocalic} \end{bmatrix} \longrightarrow \emptyset \ / \ \_\_\_\_ \ [- \text{segment}] \ [\alpha \text{ consonant}]$$

(In word-final position, true consonants are truncated before consonants and liquids, vowels are truncated before vowels and glides, and liquids and glides are never truncated.)

The Truncation rule abbreviates the following two sub-rules:

(12) a. $\begin{bmatrix} + \text{consonant} \\ - \text{vocalic} \end{bmatrix} \longrightarrow \emptyset \ / \ \_\_\_\_ \ [- \text{segment}] \ [+ \text{consonant}]$

b. $\begin{bmatrix} - \text{consonant} \\ + \text{vocalic} \end{bmatrix} \longrightarrow \emptyset \ / \ \_\_\_\_ \ [- \text{segment}] \ [- \text{consonant}]$

The exclusion of the French Truncation rule follows from the non-complement character of its two sub-rules in (12). The sub-rules in (12) are not in a complement relation since the features common to their structural descriptions define a set of input representations not specified by the two rules. A consideration of only the commonly shared features in the two sub-rules would suggest the following rule formulation:

(13) [+ segment] $\longrightarrow \emptyset \ / \ \_\_\_\_ \ [- \text{segment}] \ [+ \text{segment}]$

Rule (13) is clearly not equivalent to Truncation in terms of potential input representations. Rule (13) would, for example, specify incorrectly the deletion of consonants before vowels and glides, the deletion of vowels before consonants, and the deletion of liquids and glides. It should, therefore, be clear that atomic phonology excludes in a principled manner the Truncation rule as a possible account of any natural language fact.

The correctness of this exclusion is supported by Schane's (1974) reanalysis which does not involve the conflation of non-complement rules. The numerous empirical reasons offered by Schane for rejecting the earlier analysis are summarized in Dinnsen (1977a:12).

5. The construct 'complement rule' has similar constraining effects for such other descriptive devices as the so-called 'neighborhood convention' or mirror-image rules (cf. Bach 1968, Anderson 1974, Langacker 1969). A mirror-image rule schematically represented as (14) abbreviates the two rules (14a and b):

(14) A → B % C _____ D
    a.   A→B/C _____ D
    b.   A→B/D _____ C

The claim embodied in this device is that it is linguistically significant for a language to evidence two rules with symmetric determinants and which are identical in all other respects. It is argued in Dinnsen (1977a), however, that there is no empirical justification whatever for relating rules abbreviated as mirror-image rules and further that within the theory of atomic phonology such empirically indefensible relationships are excluded on principled grounds.

The general arguments against mirror-image rules can be stated succinctly as follows:

(15) a. In some cases, the sub-rules of mirror-image rules cannot be independently motivated (Norman 1976).
    b. In others, the conjunctive vs. disjunctive application of the sub-rules is unpredictable (Norman 1976, Anderson 1974, Miller 1976).
    c. Yet other cases reduce to 'non-rules' (Harms 1973, Norman 1976).
    d. There is apparently no evidence of an implicational relation between any of the sub-rules in a mirror-image relation.
    e. There is apparently no evidence of the sub-rules of any putative mirror-image rule simplifying in precisely the same way at the same time.
    f. And finally, it may even be that the structural description of

certain putative mirror-image rules is non-mirror-image or 'constant' (cf. Miller 1976).

To illustrate how atomic phonology excludes in principle mirror-image rules, consider, for example, the rule of Spanish glide formation proposed by Harris (1969:33) as a "first approximation of the correct rules":[2]

(16) $\begin{bmatrix} + \text{ syllabic} \\ - \text{ stress} \end{bmatrix} \longrightarrow [- \text{ syllabic}] \ \% \ \underline{\hspace{1cm}} [+ \text{ syllabic}]$

(Effectively an unstressed vowel becomes a glide adjacent to a stressed vowel, and the first of two unstressed vowels becomes a glide.)

This rule abbreviates the following two ordered sub-rules:

(17) $\begin{bmatrix} + \text{ syllabic} \\ - \text{ stress} \end{bmatrix} \longrightarrow [- \text{ syllabic}] \ / \ \underline{\hspace{1cm}} [+ \text{ syllabic}]$

(18) $\begin{bmatrix} + \text{ syllabic} \\ - \text{ stress} \end{bmatrix} \longrightarrow [- \text{ syllabic}] \ / \ [+ \text{ syllabic}] \underline{\hspace{1cm}}$

The commonly shared features of these two sub-rules would define the following rule:

(19) $\begin{bmatrix} + \text{ syllabic} \\ - \text{ stress} \end{bmatrix} \longrightarrow [- \text{ syllabic}] \ / \ [+ \text{ syllabic}] \underline{\hspace{1cm}} [+ \text{ syllabic}]$

(An unstressed vowel between vowels becomes a glide.)

Rule (19) clearly does not define the same set of input representations as (17) and (18) thus failing to establish a complement relationship between the two rules. Rule (16) is therefore correctly excluded as a possible rule of grammar within the theory of atomic phonology.

6. The construct 'complement relation' also contributes to the explanation of certain aspects of the historical phenomena known as 'drag chains.' A drag chain is a complex series of related sound shifts which serve the function of filling vacated slots in a phoneme inventory. Within a standard theory framework, drag chains have been characterized as a special case of simplification utilizing Greek letter variables (King 1969a). For example, in the historical development of Corsican (Rohlfs 1966), three such sound shifts are evident.[3] During stage I, short voiced stops spirantized. During stage II, short voiceless stops voiced. And finally, long voiceless stops shortened (Rohlfs 1966:323).[4] This drag chain may be schematized as follows:

(20) ð ⟵ d ⟵ t ⟵ t:

To see that this is indeed a special case of simplification, note the following rule formulations:

(21) Stage I

$$\begin{bmatrix} - \text{son} \\ - \text{cont} \\ + \text{voice} \\ - \text{long} \end{bmatrix} \longrightarrow [+ \text{cont}] \: / \: [- \text{cons}] \underline{\hspace{1cm}} [+ \text{son}]$$

$$([b,d,g] \longrightarrow [\beta, \eth, \gamma])$$

(22) Stage II

$$\begin{bmatrix} - \text{son} \\ - \text{cont} \\ - \text{long} \\ \alpha\text{voice} \end{bmatrix} \longrightarrow \begin{bmatrix} + \text{voice} \\ \alpha\text{cont} \end{bmatrix} / \: [- \text{cons}] \underline{\hspace{1cm}} [+ \text{son}]$$

$$([b,d,g] \longrightarrow [\beta, \eth, \gamma] \text{ and } [p,t,k] \longrightarrow [b,d,g])$$

(23) Stage III

$$\begin{bmatrix} - \text{son} \\ - \text{cont} \\ \alpha\text{long} \\ \beta\text{voice} \end{bmatrix} \longrightarrow \begin{bmatrix} - \alpha\text{voice} \\ \beta\text{cont} \\ - \text{long} \end{bmatrix} / \: [- \text{cons}] \underline{\hspace{1cm}} [+ \text{son}]$$

$$([b,d,g] \longrightarrow [\beta,\eth,\gamma], [p,t,k] \longrightarrow [b,d,g],$$
$$[p\text{:},t\text{:},k\text{:}] \longrightarrow [p,t,k])$$

There is, however, another logically possible sound shift which seemingly corresponds to a drag chain and which can be characterized in a standard theory framework as a simplification, i.e., short voiced stops spirantize and long voiceless stops voice. The rule for such a 'drag chain' would be formulated as follows:

(24)

$$\begin{bmatrix} - \text{son} \\ - \text{cont} \\ \alpha\text{voice} \\ - \alpha\text{long} \end{bmatrix} \longrightarrow \begin{bmatrix} - \text{long} \\ + \text{voice} \\ \alpha\text{cont} \end{bmatrix} / \: [- \text{cons}] \underline{\hspace{1cm}} [+ \text{son}]$$

$$([b,d,g,] \longrightarrow [\beta,\eth,\gamma] \text{ and } [p\text{:},t\text{:},k\text{:}] \longrightarrow [b,d,g])$$

Such a drag chain, while possible within standard theory, appears to be unattested in any natural language history. However, its unattested character must be regarded as an accident in standard theory. The standard theory thus fails to explain why certain drag chains can be evidenced and why certain others cannot. Atomic phonology, on the other hand, provides a principled explanation of this fact. That is, the characterization of especially stages II and III of the Corsican drag chain entail rule formulations which abbreviate rules in a complement relation whereas the characterization of the presumably unattested drag chain (24) entails a rule formulation abbreviating rules not in a complement relation. Rule (24) is thus properly excluded as a possible rule of grammar. For further discussion of yet other drag chains and their characterization within atomic phonology, see Walsh (1976a,b).

The preceding discussions should serve to review some of the essential claims of atomic phonology, the problems and issues that it addresses, and how it differs from standard theory. The remainder of this paper will attempt to distinguish atomic phonology from other presumably competing theories.

7. One of the fundamental claims of Natural Generative Phonology as developed by Hooper (1976) is that naturalness constraints on phonemic systems are the same as those on phonological rules.

(25) We need not separate the notion of naturalness in phonemic systems from the naturalness of rules. (Hooper 1976:136)

This same position is also identifiable in Natural Phonology as indicated in the following statement from [Donegan] Miller (1972:165):

(26) What should emerge from this paper, at least, is that the principles governing possible phonological inventories can be identified with the processes themselves, and thus, ultimately, with the intrinsic character of the human speech capacity.

The distinguishing claim of atomic phonology is that the constraints on rule formulations are relatively independent of constraints on inventories. These two claims are substantively different and can be evaluated on empirical grounds.

Hooper (1976:136–37) proposes the following rule as a natural constraint on both phonemic systems and phonological rules:

$$(27) \quad \begin{bmatrix} -\text{ sonorant} \\ <+\text{ continuant} > \end{bmatrix} \longrightarrow \begin{cases} [+\text{ voice}] \, / \, V \underline{\quad\quad} V \\ [-\text{ voice}] \end{cases} \quad \begin{matrix} \text{(a)} \\ \text{(b)} \end{matrix}$$

The '<+continuant>' specification in this rule means, as stated by Hooper,

(28) The rule may affect only fricatives, or it may affect all ob-

struents, but it may not affect ONLY stops (except trivially where a language has only stops).

. . . if stops undergo a context sensitive process involving voicing, fricatives do as well.

The predictions which follow from rule (27) for phonemic inventories appear to recapitulate some of the implicational restrictions on inventories proposed by Jakobson (1942) and would appear to be correct. However, as a constraint on phonological rules, rule (27) makes incorrect predictions. (27) predicts, for example, that there could be no language with the following characteristics:

(29) a. A voice contrast in obstruent stops and fricatives with the contrast neutralized in word-final stops only.
    b. No voice contrast in obstruents with only certain stops voiced intervocalically.

The fact is, however, that Ferrarese Italian evidences precisely the characteristics of (29a) and Korean evidences those of (29b). For discussion of the Italian and Korean facts, see Dinnsen and Eckman (1977) and references therein.

Rule (27) also predicts that there should be languages evidencing the following characteristics:

(30) a. Voicing is contrastive, but the contrast is neutralized in favor of [+voice] intervocalically (part (a) only).
    b. Voicing is contrastive, but the contrast is neutralized in fricatives only in favor of [+voice] intervocalically (part (a) with [+continuant]).

Hooper fails, however, to cite any known language evidencing the characteristics stated in (30). It appears, moreover, that languages like (30a) and (30b) are completely without empirical attestation (cf. Dinnsen and Eckman 1977). It is interesting, too, that the inadequacies of Hooper's proposal cannot evidently be remedied by reformulating (27) with the specification <−continuant>. While such a reformulation would correctly provide for languages like (29a and b), it would fail to account for languages like Old English evidencing the effects of an intervocalic fricative voicing rule. The reformulation would moreover be inconsistent with the previously established constraints on phonemic systems. The end result for Hooper's theory or any other theory failing to recognize the distinction between constraints governing inventories and rule formulations is that such theories either make false predictions or predictions that are without empirical support.

Within atomic phonology where this distinction is recognized, a correct account of the facts of voicing and devoicing is available. That is, languages like Ferrarese Italian are accounted for by the postulation of rule (2) as the atomic rule for Terminal Devoicing. Korean is accounted for by the postulation of an intervocalic voicing rule restricted to unaspirated stops (cf. Dinnsen and Eckman 1977). The unattested character of those languages in (30) is explained by the universal constraining principle (31).

> (31) All intervocalic voicing rules are allophonic (Dinnsen and Eckman 1977).[5]

The same principle explains the apparent restriction on the intervocalic voicing rule of Old English. That is, Old English evidences a voice contrast in obstruent stops only and an alternation between voiced fricatives medially and voiceless fricatives finally. While it would appear that intervocalic voicing in Old English is restricted to fricatives, the rule can be formulated generally to voice all obstruents between vowels with the universal principle permitting the rule to apply only to the extent that its effect is allophonic, that is, to fricatives.

The postulation of atomic rules for Devoicing and Intervocalic voicing and the inclusion of such universal principles as (31) constitutes a strong empirical claim by predicting the principled exclusion of, at least, the following language-types:

> (32) a. (30a)
> b. (30b)
> c. A language with a voice contrast in both stops and fricatives and an alternation between voiced fricatives medially and voiceless fricatives finally (a rule devoicing fricatives finally).
> d. A language with no voice contrast in obstruents and an alternation between voiced fricatives medially and voiceless fricatives finally (a rule voicing fricatives medially).

The exclusion of the logically possible language-types (32a and b) follows from principle (31) since the rules would have a neutralizing effect. The logically possible language-types cited in (32c and d) are excluded since each would require the postulation of a non-atomic rule with no associated atomic rule.

8. There are a number of descriptive devices from various theories
which would seem to parallel the role of the 'complement relation' in
atomic phonology, but which in fact make different empirical claims. The
descriptive devices of interest here include (a) the 'natural process' notation [!+F] ([Donegan] Miller 1972, Donegan and Stampe 1977a), (b)
the simplex-feature hypothesis (Sanders 1974b), (c) hierarchies (Chen
1973, Foley 1972, Zwicky 1972a).

The 'natural process' notation [!+F] of Natural Phonology could conceivably be incorporated into the Intervocalic Voicing rule expressing
some of the same implicational claims as an atomic rule along with
the principle of rule complementation. The Voicing rule could be
formulated roughly as follows:[6]

(33) $\begin{bmatrix} - \text{ sonorant} \\ !-\text{continuant} \end{bmatrix} \longrightarrow [+ \text{ voice}] \, / \, V \underline{\quad} V$

     (where [!−continuant] is read "especially stops")

The prediction is that fricatives may or may not undergo the rule, but
if they do, stops must also undergo it. Both Natural Phonology and atomic
phonology make the same empirical prediction in this particular instance. However, Natural Phonology fails to account for a related language fact where atomic phonology provides a principled explanation of
that fact. Specifically, Natural Phonology cannot explain the apparent
restriction of the Old English intervocalic voicing rule to fricatives, unless it incorporates universal principles such as (31) governing the application of phonological rules. In atomic phonology, this apparent restriction is but a consequence of the universal principle governing the
application of a generalized voicing rule.

The preceding discussion can also be related to the simplex-feature
hypothesis proposed by Sanders (1974b). In its strong form, this
hypothesis excludes reference to a positively specified class in one instance and the negative specification of that same class in some other
instance. For example, intervocalic voicing would presumably be characterized as follows:

(34) $\begin{bmatrix} \text{OBS} \\ \text{STOP} \end{bmatrix} \longrightarrow [\text{VOICE}] \, / \, V \underline{\quad} V$

Such a characterization permits reference to obstruent stops or to
all obstruents by the loss of the feature STOP. To this extent, there is
overlap between the predictions of atomic phonology and the simplex-

feature hypothesis. However, in the case of the simplex-feature hypothesis, just as in the preceding discussion, there is no explanation for the apparent restriction on the Old English rule voicing fricatives—unless the universal principle (31) governing certain rule applications is incorporated.

Appeal to implicational hierarchies has long been evident in many theories of phonology, and atomic phonology is no exception.[7] It is, however, the contention of atomic phonology that the form and configuration of any defensible hierarchy is inferable/derivable from an atomic rule and the associated principle of rule complementation. Furthermore, since different processes will require the postulation of different atomic rules, it follows necessarily that any inferential hierarchy will be process-dependent.

The schematization of the Corsican drag chain, for example, given in (20) represents an implicational hierarchy. The implication is that if long voiceless stops weaken, then so do all the segments arranged to the left. The validity of this implication is not in question here. Rather, the questions should be raised relative to this phenomenon: "Why does the weakening of long voiceless stops imply the weakening of specifically short voiceless stops and not some other set of segments, and why does the weakening of short voiceless stops imply specifically the weakening of short voiced stops?" Put differently: "Why couldn't the hierarchy be arranged differently with a different set of implications such as the following?"

(35) ð ⟵ d ⟵ t: ⟵ t

The answer seems to be that hierarchies can only establish implicational relations between classes which are in a complement relation.

Consider the hierarchy proposed by Chen (1973) for vowel nasalization where vowels are assigned an integer value along a height continuum as follows:

(36) Vowel Height

Low	Mid	High
1	2	3

A formalism is developed by Chen such that the nasalization of any vowel with a relatively high integer value implies the nasalization of all vowels with a lesser value. Precisely this configuration of the hierarchy is inferable from the postulation of an atomic rule for vowel nasalization defined on low vowels and the successive extension of the rule by complementation (cf. Dinnsen 1976a).

In short, implicational hierarchies of this sort do not appear to be necessary and independent of the constraints on rule formulation. On the contrary, they are totally derivable within atomic phonology. The argument for an independent construct 'hierarchy' in phonological theory must lie in the establishment of a universal process-independent hierarchy governing the formulation of all rules in all languages. The prospects of such a development are clearly remote. A case in point is the comprehensive dialect study by Keel (1977) of the extensive variation from the Swiss German rule lowering [o to ɔ] in various phonological contexts. In his study, it is demonstrated that all the dialects lower at least before [r], supporting the postulation of rule (6) noted earlier as the atomic rule. Keel notes, however, that an implicational hierarchy can be inferred that is capable of characterizing this variation. The hierarchy may be formulated as follows:

(37)

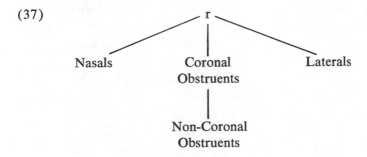

Some of the variation that this hierarchy represents may be summarized as follows: [o] lowers to [ɔ]

(38) a. before r and only r, or
      b. before r and nasals, or
      c. before r and coronal obstruents, or
      d. before r and laterals, or
      e. before r and all obstruents.

The implicational restrictions that obtain are the following: If [o] lowers to [ɔ]

(39) a. before non-coronal obstruents, then it also lowers before coronal obstruents and r.
      b. before nasals, then it also lowers before r.
      c. before laterals, then it also lowers before r.
      d. before coronal obstruents, then it also lowers before r.

Precisely these implicational restrictions and thus the hierarchy in (37) follow from the postulation of rule (6) as the atomic rule and the identification of those rules in a complement relation with (6) or with some rule that is itself a complement of (6) (cf. Keel 1977).

Aside from the fact that atomic phonology is capable of deriving the empirically correct set of implicational restrictions on the vowel lowering rule, this case has special significance inasmuch as the empirically well-supported hierarchy in (37) violates the often cited (e.g., Householder 1974 and references therein), purportedly universal hierarchy given below:

(40) VOWELS — GLIDES — [r] — [l] — [n] — [m] — [ŋ] —
       FRICATIVES — STOPS

The violation obtains relative to the implications expressed in (40) between [r] and presumably obstruents such as fricatives. That is, if (40) is a valid process-independent hierarchy, it should follow for the vowel lowering process that if [o] lowers before obstruents and [r], then it should also lower before nasals and laterals. The fact is, however, that no implicational relation can be established between obstruents and nasals or between obstruents and laterals as regards the lowering of [o] since there are dialects that lower before all obstruents and [r] without lowering before nasals or laterals (Keel 1977:63,73,82,89).

The point here is that different processes will evidence different implicational restrictions supporting the process-dependent character of such restrictions and that any such implicational restrictions (hierarchies) are derivable from the postulation of an atomic rule and the identification of rules in a complement relation with the atomic rule.

9. A few words are in order concerning functional constraints on rule formulations as set forth in Houlihan and Iverson (1977) and in their contribution to this volume. While we are all interested to some extent in determining the correct constraints on rules, Houlihan and Iverson's particular program differs significantly from that of atomic phonology. That is, their interests so far have been limited to constraining on principled grounds what a given phonological rule type may *produce*. Atomic phonology, on the other hand, maintains in general the weaker position that the structural change of any given phonological rule must be stated axiomatically in the atomic rule. The contentions of atomic phonology appear at least to be consistent with the facts, where Functionally Constrained Phonology does not.

Houlihan and Iverson advance the following constraint and corollary as bidirectionals:

(41) Markedness Constraint. Phonologically-conditioned neutralization rules convert relatively marked segments into relatively unmarked segments.
Corollary. Phonologically-conditioned rules which produce exclusively segments that are marked relative to the input segments are allophonic.

This constraint clearly excludes the possibility of a neutralization rule producing exclusively marked segments. However, the facts of a particular vocalic alternation in the Western dialect of Catalan suggest that this constraint is too strong by virtue of incorrectly excluding a defensible rule of grammar. The Western dialect evidences a neutralization of the distinction between [a] and [e] in favor of [e] when in word-final, unstressed, closed syllables (cf. Moll 1952:102).[8] The following data illustrate the alternation between [a] and [e]:

(42) [káza] 'house'   [kázes] 'houses'
      [sistéma] 'system' [sistémes] 'systems'
      [kɔ́rða] 'rope'   [kɔ́rðes] 'ropes'

This alternation is equally productive in verbs (cf. Moll 1952: 224–25, 237). The rule accounting for this alternation is neutralizing since there is a contrast between [e] and [a] in open syllables and [e] does not alternate in the same contexts:

(43) [méstre] 'teacher' [méstres] 'teachers'
      [máre] 'mother'   [máres] 'mothers'

Assuming, then, that [a] is relatively less marked than [e], Western Catalan evidences a neutralization rule which produces only marked segments—thus casting doubt on the correctness of such constraints as the Markedness Constraint. Additional counterexamples to the Markedness Constraint are presented in Jonathan Kaye's contribution to this volume.

10. In conclusion, following this review of atomic phonology and the discussions of how it differs from some of the other competing theories, it should at least be evident that atomic phonology constitutes some strong claims constraining phonological systems. It is true, too, that atomic phonology is not as highly constrained in certain areas as some

of the other theories. However, in those cases where the weaker position has been adopted, this presumably is warranted on empirical grounds. In any case, it is hoped that the basic tenets and claims of atomic phonology are sufficiently explicit to permit its empirical differentiation from the other theories and that any choice between competing theories can be an empirical one.

Naturally, as atomic phonology is a new and developing theory, many questions remain open. For example, the question of rule ordering is left entirely open. Rule order and rule formulations are not wholly independent. In fact, it must be clear now to anyone involved in the recent rule ordering controversy that the question of how rules apply relative to one another cannot reasonably be pursued in the absence of severe constraints on what constitutes an admissible rule formulation. It seems that the debate over rule ordering has reached an impasse primarily because, for any given analysis supporting some hypothesis on rule ordering, an alternative analysis involving different rule formulations is available which supports an opposing hypothesis. The discovery of atomic rules would substantially limit the range of possible analyses by establishing clear cases of necessary and independent rule formulations against which competing hypotheses about rule interactions could be tested.

Another area which remains largely open is the principled determination of atomic rules. All that is available at present is a methodological principle for identifying atomic rules. This principle is, however, strictly empirical, and thus, the claims derivable from it are clearly vulnerable to empirical disconfirmation. Inasmuch as many of the atomic rules correspond with what others would refer to as 'natural rules', it may be fruitful to pursue 'phonetic explanations' for at least some atomic rules. At present, however, the character of phonetic explanations is sufficiently nebulous that this particular avenue does not permit a totally satisfactory principled determination of atomic rules. The explanation of atomic rules may, of course, lie in other areas as well. Until these explanatory bases are more accessible, the methodological basis for determining atomic rules will at least encourage extensive typological investigations which would in the final analysis be pertinent to the evaluation of any theory of phonology.

NOTES

I am especially indebted to Thomas Walsh for his numerous and valuable discussions with me about many of the issues raised in this paper. I have also

plaining the distribution of certain rule types among the world's languages. The second way in which this definition differs from standard views of neutralization is that it will characterize insertion and deletion rules as either neutralizing or non-neutralizing only if "in the input to the rule" is taken to mean "existing at some level of derivation before the rule applies," which is apparently what Kiparsky intended, rather than to mean "satisfies the structural description of the rule." Although preliminary investigations suggest that the constraints developed here are also applicable to insertion and deletion rules, we have limited the scope of this paper to a consideration of feature-changing rules.

The definition in (1) determines the status of a rule by inspecting the rule's form and its input, but it does not predict which types of rules can be neutralizing and which cannot. However, it can be observed that certain types of rules are always neutralizing and that certain other types are always allophonic. Thus, the rules which devoice final obstruents in German, Russian, and Sanskrit are all neutralization rules, as are the rules which deaspirate final stops in Sanskrit, Korean, and Marathi. Examples illustrating the operation of these types of rules are given in (2) and (3).

(2)   Final devoicing of obstruents

    a. German (Moulton 1962)

Singular	*Plural*	
Ta[t]	Tä[t]e	'deed'
Ra[t]	Rä[d]er	'wheel'

    b. Russian (Trager 1934:340)

Nom. Sg.	*Gen. Sg.*	
[pop]	[papá]	'priest'
[rap]	[rabá]	'slave'

    c. Sanskrit (Whitney 1879)

Nom Sg.	*Acc. Sg.*	
[marut]	[marutam]	'wind'
[pa:t]	[pa:dam]	'foot'

(3)   Final deaspiration of stops

    a. Sanskrit (Whitney 1879)

Nom. Sg.	*Acc. Sg.*	
[stup]	[stubham]	'praising'
[pat]	[patham]	'road'

   b. Korean (Informant)[1]
     Citation   *Objective*
     [nat]   [nadɯl]   'a grain'
     [nat]   [natʰɯl]   'piece'

   c. Marathi (Informant)
     [tap]   'fever'   [tapala]   'to the fever'
     [top]   'cannon'   [tophela]   'to the cannon'
     [vad]   'discussion' [vadala]   'to the discussion'
     [dud]   'milk'   [dudhala]   'to the milk'

The devoicing of obstruents in these examples is neutralizing because it eliminates the contrast between voiced and voiceless obstruents, i.e., there are both voiced and voiceless obstruents in the inputs to the devoicing rules but only voiceless ones in their outputs. Similarly, the deaspiration of stops in these examples is neutralizing because there are both aspirated and unaspirated stops in the inputs to the deaspiration rules but only unaspirated ones in their outputs.

Other types of rules, however, are always allophonic. Thus, the rules which voice intervocalic obstruents in Corsican, Korean, and Old English are all allophonic, as are those which aspirate initial voiceless stops in English, German, and Swahili. Examples illustrating the operation of these types of rules are given in (4) and (5).

(4) Intervocalic voicing

   a. Corsican (Dinnsen and Eckman 1977)
     [peδe]   'foot'   [u beδe]   'the foot'
     [tengu] 'I have'   [u dengu]   'I have it'
     [sakku] 'bag'   [u zakku]   'the bag'

   b. Korean "plain" stops
     Citation   *Objective*
     [tap]   [tabɯl]   'answer'
     [pok]   [pogɯl]   'fortune'
     [nat]   [nasɯl]   'sickle'

   c. Old English fricatives (Campbell 1959:179–81)
     [stæf]   [stavas]   'staff'   (sg./pl.)
     [snāθ]   [snīδan]   'cut'   (pret./inf.)
     [čēas]   [čēozan]   'choose'   (pret./inf.)

(5) Initial aspiration

    a. English   b. German

       [pʰ]ort   [tʰ]at   'deed'

       re[pʰ]ort   ge[tʰ]an 'done'

       s[p]ort   S[t]aat   'state'

    c. Swahili (Tucker and Ashton 1942:89–90)

       [kʰaháwa]   'coffee'

       [msitʰúni]   'in the forest'

       [msítu]   'forest'

In these examples, intervocalic voicing never neutralizes a contrast between voiced and voiceless obstruents. In Korean, the only voiced stops in the language are those in intervocalic position, or more precisely, those occurring between voiced segments (Martin 1951:524). They correspond to, and alternate with, lax voiceless unaspirated stops in other positions. Thus, these voiced stops are analyzed as underlying lax voiceless unaspirated ones that are voiced by a rule of intervocalic voicing. This rule is allophonic because it is the only source of voiced stops in the language. The situation in Old English is similar, where the only voiced fricatives in the language are those in voiced environments (Campbell 1959:20). They are derivable from underlying voiceless fricatives by an allophonic intervocalic voicing rule. However, in Corsican, there are voiced stops that contrast with voiceless ones in word-initial position. But these voiced stops are spirantized in exactly the same environment in which the voiceless stops are voiced, as can be seen in (6) below. Thus, the intervocalic voicing rule is allophonic, because at the time that it applies, spirantization has already taken place, and there are no voiced stops in the input to the rule.[2]

(6) Corsican intervocalic spirantization (Dinnsen and Eckman 1977)

    [bokka] 'mouth'   [a βokka] 'the mouth'

    [dente] 'tooth'   [u δente]   'the tooth'

    [gola]   'throat'   [di γola]   'of throat'

Similarly, initial aspiration rules never neutralize a contrast between aspirated and unaspirated stops. In languages with such rules, voiceless aspirated stops are in complementary distribution with corresponding voiceless unaspirated ones and are derived from them by the rule that aspirates stops word-initially and syllable-initially in word-medial stressed syllables, which is the only source of these aspirated stops. Since there are no aspirated stops in the input to the rule, the aspiration rule is allophonic.

Within current phonological theories, however, there is no reason why devoicing and deaspiration rules could not be allophonic. Nothing suggests, for example, that we should not find a language otherwise like German but whose underlying voiced obstruents are devoiced word-finally by an allophonic rule, or a language otherwise like Sanskrit but whose underlying aspirated stops are deaspirated word-finally by an allophonic rule. By the same token, nothing in current phonological theory excludes rules like intervocalic voicing and initial aspiration from the class of neutralization rules. There is no reason to expect, for example, that we should not find a language with a contrast between voiced and voiceless obstruents, like English, that neutralizes this contrast intervocalically by a voicing rule, or a language with a contrast between aspirated and unaspirated stops, like Sanskrit, that neutralizes this contrast word-initially by an aspiration rule. But there are no such languages. In order to explain their absence, we must first turn to the typology of phonological markedness.

The distinction we draw between marked and unmarked segments is a generally accepted one, and is derived from well-known implicational universals of phonological systems. According to these universals, a segment X is considered to be 'marked' with respect to a segment Y just in case the presence of X in a given language implies the presence of Y but the presence of Y does not imply the presence of X in that language. Examples of such implicational universals are given in (7).

(7) Selected Implicational Universals

    a. The presence of voiced stops implies the presence of voiceless stops, but not vice versa (Jakobson 1969:70).

    b. The presence of voiced fricatives implies the presence of voiceless fricatives, but not vice versa (Jakobson 1969:70).

    c. The presence of fricatives implies the presence of stops, but not vice versa (Jakobson 1969:51).

    d. The presence of aspirated stops implies the presence of unaspirated stops, but not vice versa (Jakobson 1969:14).

    e. The presence of a bilabial nasal implies the presence of a dental or alveolar nasal, but not vice versa (Ferguson 1963: 56–7).

f. The presence of mid vowels implies the presence of high vowels, but not vice versa (Jakobson 1969:56).

g. The presence of voiceless vowels implies the presence of voiced vowels, but not vice versa (Greenberg 1969:156).[3]

Given the implicational universals cited in (7), the relative markedness of the segment types they refer to is determined as in (8).

(8) Relative Markedness

a. Voiced stops are marked with respect to voiceless stops.
b. Voiced fricatives are marked with respect to voiceless fricatives.
c. Fricatives are marked with respect to stops.
d. Aspirated stops are marked with respect to unaspirated stops.
e. The bilabial nasal is marked with respect to the dental or alveolar nasal.
f. Mid vowels are marked with respect to voiced vowels.
g. Voiceless vowels are marked with respect to voiced vowels.

While implicational universals such as those in (7) must obviously refer to inventories of phonetic segments, the assumption that they hold for phonemic inventories as well offers a principled basis for establishing phonological representations. Thus, if a language has corresponding marked and unmarked segments in complementary distribution, e.g., aspirated and unaspirated voiceless stops in English, the question of which should be posited as the underlying phoneme will be resolved in favor of the unmarked member of the pair. In English, then, the unmarked, unaspirated stops are basic, while their marked, aspirated counterparts are derived by rule. If a language has corresponding marked and unmarked segments in contrast, on the other hand, both are accorded phonemic or underlying status.

Since the relative markedness of a pair of segment types can be determined from typologically based implicational universals, and since these universals hold at both the phonemic and the phonetic levels, it follows that any rule which converts marked segments (e.g., voiced or aspirated stops) into unmarked ones (e.g., voiceless or unaspirated stops) must be a neutralization rule. This follows because a language has phonemic marked segments only if they contrast with unmarked ones, and such a rule neutralizes this contrast. Our definition of markedness thus warrants the generalization stated in (9).

(9) Any rule which converts marked segments into unmarked segments must be a neutralization rule.

Hence, rules like final devoicing and final deaspiration, which convert marked into relatively unmarked segments, are necessarily neutralization rules. There are no languages like German in which final devoicing is allophonic or languages like Sanskrit in which final deaspiration is allophonic, nor could there be, because no languages have the kinds of marked underlying systems which would be required in order for these rules to have purely allophonic effects.

Thus, all rules which produce relatively unmarked segments must be neutralization rules. It is not obvious, however, that all neutralization rules produce unmarked segments. Yet this generalization also appears to be true, at least for the class of well-motivated, phonologically-conditioned rules. In addition to the rules of final devoicing and deaspiration discussed above, which clearly do produce unmarked segments, consider the neutralization rules given in (10).

(10) Neutralization Rules

    a. Neutralization of mid and high vowels to high vowels in word-final unstressed syllables in Portuguese (Mattoso Câmara 1972:34);

    b. Neutralization of /s/, /č/, and /t/ to [t] in syllable-final position in Korean (Moon 1974);

    c. Neutralization of /m/ and /n/ to [n] in word-final position in Finnish (Collinder 1969:10); and

    d. Neutralization of /l/ and /n/ to [n] word-initially in Korean (Shibatani 1973:98).

In each case noted in (10), contrasts are neutralized in favor of the unmarked member of the opposition. There appear to be no languages in which purely phonologically-conditioned rules always neutralize similar contrasts to the marked member. For example, there are no languages that consistently neutralize voiced and voiceless obstruents to voiced obstruents, or aspirated and unaspirated stops to aspirated stops. Neither are there languages with neutralization rules like those in (11).

(11) Non-occurring Neutralization Rules

    a. Neutralization of mid and high vowels to mid vowels.

    b. Neutralization of /s/, /č/, and /t/ to [s] or to [č].

    c. Neutralization of /m/ and /n/ to [m].
    d. Neutralization of /l/ and /n/ to [l].

There are, however, some rules which do appear to neutralize contrasts to a marked member. Examples of such rules are given in (12) and will be discussed in turn.

(12) Rules Producing Marked Segments

    a. Merger of /t/ and /d/ to the tap [ɾ] between stressed and unstressed syllabic segments in English;
    b. Merger of unstressed vowels to [ə] in English;
    c. Merger of /s/ and /t/ to [s] before a morpheme boundary followed by [i] in Finnish (Kiparsky 1976);
    d. Merger of plain and palatalized consonants to palatalized consonants before /e/ in Russian (Jones and Ward 1969: 198–99);
    e. Voicing assimilation to a following voiced or voiceless obstruent in Russian (Jones and Ward 1969:197–98); and
    f. Nasal assimilation to the place of articulation of a following consonant in Spanish (Harris 1969:8–18).

Of these rules, (12a) and (12b) are not regarded as neutralization rules by definition (1) above. Rather, they are considered allophonic rules which merge segments to some new segment not present in the input to the rule. Taps in English can be derived from their 'unreduced' counterparts /t/ and /d/, with which they alternate in slow or formal styles of speech in words like *latter* and *ladder*. Thus, there is no reason to grant phonemic status to the tap in English, and the tapping rule is allophonic because there are no taps in the input to the rule.[4]

Similarly, schwas in English can be derived from their 'unreduced' counterparts, the range of full vowels. Some schwas alternate with full vowels, as is illustrated by alternations of the type found in pairs like *telegraph* and *telegraphy*. Other non-alternating schwas in unstressed syllables are in complementary distribution with the slightly longer and lower vowel that occurs only in stressed syllables and is transcribed with the wedge [ʌ] in words like *cut* and *rut*. Non-alternating schwas in unstressed syllables, then, can be derived from /ʌ/ by the same rule that derives alternating schwas from their full-vowel counterparts. In this analysis, a word like *above* is phonemically /ʌbʌ́v/, as is shown in (13) below, and its phonetic form [əbʌ́v] is derived by the vowel reduction rule that merges most unstressed vowels to schwa. Schwa is therefore not a phoneme of American English, and the vowel reduction rule is allophonic because there are no schwas in the input to the rule.[5]

(13) /ʌbʌ́v/ ——→ [əbʌ́v] *above*

Rules (12c) and (12d) are both rules of questionable status. They do meet the definition of neutralization in (1) because there are morpheme-final non-derived /s/'s that occur before /i/ in Finnish and there are non-derived palatalized consonants before front vowels in Russian. However, both rules are severely restricted as to the environments in which they apply, and both rules are opaque in that there are phonetic representations that meet the conditions for the rules but have not undergone them.

Specifically, the Finnish rule converting /t/ into /s/ before morpheme-initial or derived /i/ accounts for alternations such as those in the singular paradigm of 'hand', shown in (14a). As Skousen (1975:70–71) makes clear, however, the purported /t/ to /s/ rule is anything but a valid generalization about Finnish surface phonology. Thus, the suffix *-i* 'repetitive' does not induce assibilation, and neither does the suffix *-isi* 'conditional', shown in (14b) and (14c). Similarly exceptional are the suffix *-jä* 'agentive' and the onomatopoeic suffix *-ise,* shown in (14d) and (14e). A Finnish rule of t ——→ s / ＿＿ i, if it exists at all, does therefore not quality as purely phonologically-conditioned.

(14) Finnish Assibilation (Skousen 1975:70–71)
    a. käsi (nom.) kätena (ess.) käteen (ill.) kätta (part.) 'hand'
    b. /-i/:   sota   'war'   soti   'to wage war'
    c. /-isi/:   tunte   'to feel'   tuntisi   'would feel'
    d. /-jä/:   tunte   'to feel'   tuntija   'expert'
    e. /-ise/: kitise   'to creak'   lotise   'to splash'

The rule in Russian that changes unmarked plain consonants into marked palatalized consonants before the mid front vowel /e/ effects a neutralization of the contrast between plain and palatalized consonants, as can be seen from the forms in (15a). Before the high front vowel /i/, however, the palatalization rule only applies to velar consonants, where its effect is strictly allophonic (Jones and Ward 1969). After non-velar consonants, /i/ is realized as its central allophone [ɨ], as is shown by the alternations of the suffix /-ij/ in (15b). Thus, palatalization of consonants in Russian must be restricted to apply only before the mid front vowel /e/, except in the case of velar consonants, where it also applies before the high front vowel /i/.

Palatalization before /e/ is not a productive phonological rule, however, in that it fails to apply in a large number of foreign words. In his investigation of the rates of assimilation of borrowings in Russian, Holden (1976:143) states that "dental consonants before *e* in borrowings show little if any movement toward palatalization in the course of assimilation," although velar and labial consonants do palatalize in some borrowings. Examples of non-palatalized consonants in the palatalization environment in loanwords are given in (15c). Palatalization before /e/ fails to apply in certain types of native words as well. The /e/ in the first syllable of *etot* 'this' does not condition palatalization of preceding consonants in prefixes, as is shown in (15d), where the /v/ in *v etom gorod'e* remains non-palatalized. In addition, palatalization does not apply to consonants before /e/ in acronyms, as is shown in (15e). Finally, consonants do not palatalize before /e/ in the names of the letters of the alphabet, as is shown in (15f).

We conclude, then, that palatalization of consonants in Russian is not a thoroughly productive phonological rule because it fails to apply to loanwords and to certain types of native words in the language.

(15) Russian Palatalization (Jones and Ward 1969)[6]

a.

Nom. Sg.	*Loc. Sg.*	*Gen. Sg.*	
[zal]	[zal'ɛ]	[zala]	'hall'
[st'il']	[st'il'ɛ]	[st'il'a]	'style'

b.

Masc. Nom. Sg.	*Fem.Nom. Sg.*	
[d'ik'ij]	[d'ikaja]	'wild'
[glupɨj]	[glupaja]	'stupid'
[s'in'ij]	[s'in'aja]	'blue'

c.

[konsomɛ]	'consommé'
[tɛmbr]	'timbre'
[mʌdél']	'model'
[zɛró]	'zero'

d. v etom ([vɛtəm]) gorod'e 'in this city'

e.

[nép]	'NEP'	(New Economic Policy)
[ɛsér]	'SR'	(Socialist Revolutionary)

f.

[pɛ]	'p'	(letter)
[bɛ]	'b'	(letter)

The last two rules cited in (12), rules (12e) and (12f), are quite general rules which do change unmarked segments to marked ones. (12e) changes some unmarked voiceless obstruents to marked voiced ones, and (12f) changes some unmarked alveolar nasals to marked labial, alveopalatal, and velar ones. However, both of these rules also have the opposite effect. That is, they both also change marked segments to unmarked ones. Such rules, then, do not falsify the claim that all neutralization rules produce unmarked segments, because they do in fact produce unmarked segments. It just so happens that they produce marked segments as well. Assimilatory rules that would disconfirm this claim would be those that produced only marked segments, but with the improbable exception of rules like (12c) and (12d), there are no such rules that have a neutralizing effect.

More specifically, alongside rules which assimilate voicing in obstruents to the value for voice found in an immediately following obstruent, as in Russian, we find neutralization rules which guarantee a uniform value for voice in obstruent clusters by devoicing the entire cluster, as in Swedish. But we never find the third logical possibility, a neutralization rule which only voices obstruents in a cluster. These three possibilities are schematized in (16), where the non-occurring rule type in (16c) is marked with an asterisk.

(16) Logically Possible Voicing Assimilation Rules

a. $[-\text{sonorant}] \longrightarrow [\alpha\text{voice}] / \underline{\qquad} \begin{bmatrix} -\text{sonorant} \\ \alpha\text{voice} \end{bmatrix}$

Russian (Unbegaun 1957:13)

rub'ec	rupca	'scar'	(nom.sg./gen. sg.)
plav'it'	plafk'ij	'fuse'	(inf./adj.)
pros'it	proz'by	'request'	(3rd. sg. pres./nom.pl.)
otodrat'	oddirat'	'to tear off'	(imperf./perf.)

b. $[-\text{sonorant}] \longrightarrow [-\text{voice}] / \begin{bmatrix} -\text{sonorant} \\ -\text{voice} \end{bmatrix}$

Swedish (Linell, et al. 1971:104)

Inf.	*Pret.*	*Past P.*	*Supine*	
(/-a)	(/-de)	(/-d/)	(/-t/)	
höra	hörde	hörd	hört	'hear'
köpa	köpte	köpt	köpt	'buy'
bygga	byggde	byggd	by[kk]t	'build'

c. *$[-\text{sonorant}] \longrightarrow [+\text{voice}] / \begin{bmatrix} -\text{sonorant} \\ +\text{voice} \end{bmatrix}$

On the basis of the above observations, we propose that phonological rules are constrained in such a way that neutralization rules must produce unmarked segments. We call this constraint the Markedness Constraint, which is stated in (17).

(17) Markedness Constraint: Phonologically-conditioned neutralization rules convert relatively marked segments into relatively
unmarked segments.

The Markedness Constraint obviously excludes a host of possible rules from the grammars of natural languages, namely, all rules defined as neutralizing by (1) whose outputs are always relatively more marked than their inputs.

This constraint does not preclude the existence of rules which do produce exclusively marked segments relative to their inputs, however; it just maintains that such rules are not neutralizing, but rather are allophonic. Thus, the cases of intervocalic voicing and initial aspiration cited in (4) and (5) all represent instances of rules which produce exclusively marked segments, and each of them is allophonic. The same is true of the rules given in (18).

(18) Allophonic Rules
    a. Devoicing of vowels in voiceless environments in Comanche,
       Japanese, Serbo-Croatian, and other languages (Greenberg
       1969).
    b. Devoicing of certain word-final sonorant consonants in Rus-
       sian, French, and Icelandic (Jones and Ward 1969:189,
       Deferrari 1954, Einarsson 1945:24).
    c. Spirantization of voiced stops post-vocalically and after cer-
       tain consonants in Spanish (Harris 1969:37–40).
    d. Change of /n/ to [ŋ] syllable-finally in certain dialects of
       Spanish (Canfield 1962:70–71).
    e. Change of /s/ to [h] syllable-finally in certain dialects of
       Spanish (Canfield 1962:83–84).

These phenomena, and countless others like them, are all accounted for by the obvious corollary to the Markedness Constraint stated in (19).

(19) Corollary: Phonologically-conditioned rules which produce exclusively marked segments from relatively unmarked ones are
allophonic.

Related to (19) is the corollary to (9) above, which is that any rule which is not a neutralization rule does not convert marked segments into unmarked ones. This corollary, together with (19), will insure that all rules that produce only marked segments are allophonic rules and that all allophonic rules produce only marked segments.

It should be noted that the Markedness Constraint differs from the proposals concerning the relationship between neutralization and markedness made by Trubetzkoy (1969). Trubetzkoy claimed that the relative markedness of a pair of phonemes in a privative opposition could be determined by the representative of the archiphoneme occurring in the position of neutralization. That is, he defined unmarked segments as those that are found in the position of neutralization. By appealing to implicational universals, however, we define relative segmental markedness independently of phonological neutralization and claim that the product of neutralization is unmarked because neutralization rules are constrained so as to produce unmarked segments, not construed so as to define them.

Our understanding of "neutralization," moreover, is quite different from the sense in which Trubetzkoy used the term. For Trubetzkoy, neutralization included those cases in which a contrast is actually eliminated as well as cases in which a contrast is simply absent. Thus, neutralization could be either dynamic, involving the merger of morphemes (e.g., German *Rad* 'wheel' = *Rat* 'advice' through final devoicing), or static, involving no such merger (e.g., the English contrast between voiced and voiceless stops is suspended after /s/, as in *spit,* but no ambiguity results since alternations do not support a /sp/ - /sb/ contrast).

The distinction between the two positions is important, because many static phenomena characterized as neutralizing by Trubetzkoy are actually allophonic in our view. Consider the following quotation.

> In German the opposition *s-š* is neutralized before consonants. The archiphoneme is represented root-initially by *š,* root-medially and finally by *s.* [And] . . . the opposition between "sharp" *s* and "soft" *z* is neutralized root-initially as well as morpheme-finally, the archiphoneme being represented by "soft" *z* initially, and "sharp" *s* finally.
>
> (Trubetzkoy 1969:82)

But while alternations exist which justify positing an underlying /s/-/z/-/š/ contrast in medial and final position in German, as can be seen in (20a) below, no such alternations can be found in morpheme-initial position, where only [z] occurs prevocalically and [š] preconsonantally, as can be seen in (20b).

(20) German Sibilant Consonants

    a. *weiss*   [vais]   'white'   (nom. sg./obl.)

       weisse   [vaisə]

       weis   [vais]   'wise'   (prefix/adj.)

       weise   [vaizə]

       Busch   [buš]   'bush'   (sg./pl.)

       Büsche   [büšə]

    b. *sagen*   [za:gən]   'say'   (inf./part.)

       gesagt   [gəza:kt]

       sprechen [šprexən] 'speak' (inf./part.)

       gesprochen [gəšproxən]

This defectiveness of distribution may well justify positing only /s/ morpheme-initially, along with rules which convert /s/ into the relatively more marked [z] and [š], but since no morpheme-initial /z/ or /š/ would then be found in the inputs to these rules, they would be allophonic by definition (1). There is thus neither contrast nor neutralization among these initials in German. (Of course, if one had posited /z/ and /š/ to begin with as the initials of *sagen* and *sprechen,* respectively, no rules would be involved at all, neutralizing or otherwise.)

Thus far, we have suggested that there is a direct correlation between the neutralizing status of a rule and the relative markedness of its input and output. Thus for the class of well-motivated phonologically-conditioned rules, two of four logically possible configurations of rule status and output are excluded in principle, namely, neutralization rules which produce exclusively marked segments, and allophonic rules which produce unmarked ones. These exclusions are indicated by an asterisk in (21).

OUTPUT

(21) S T A T U S		Marked	Unmarked
	Allophonic		*
	Neutralizing	*	

We maintain that the Markedness Constraint is a functional principle of phonology which explains why a particular rule may be found in one language but not in another. Whether a rule consistent with this constraint actually *is* found in some language is doubtless due to various factors bearing on the language's history and phonetic naturalness. But phonetic naturalness alone, for example, is not sufficient to explain why one language maintains a rule of intervocalic stop voicing and another does not. Our explanation is that the phenomenon per se is "phonetically natural" for all languages. But the only languages that can exploit the natural phonetic tendency toward intervocalic voicing are languages like Korean, and unlike English, for which inclusion of such a rule does not conflict with the Markedness Constraint. That is, Korean voices intervocalic stops because the production of these relatively marked segments is accomplished through an allophonic rule. English does not because, if it did, the same rule producing relatively marked voiced stops would effect a neutralization with the set of phonemic voiced stops, and this neutralization would violate the Markedness Constraint.

Now let us consider some of the theoretical implications of this hypothesis and its interaction with other theories that have been proposed.

A theory incorporating the Markedness Constraint claims that permissible phonological rules can be distinguished from impermissible ones by considering only the interaction between a rule's function, i.e., whether it is neutralizing or not, and the relative markedness of the input and output of the rule. The Markedness Constraint itself thus does not consider the positions within a word or syllable in which particular rules apply. Moreover, the relative markedness of segment types is determined only by reference to typological universals governing phonetic and phonemic systems, quite irrespective of the positions in which various segment types are found to occur.

Other recent phonological theories have proposed that phonological rules be constrained in terms of the types of changes they may produce in particular environments. In the theory of Natural Generative Grammar, proposed by Vennemann (1971 and 1972a) and by Hooper (1974), all segments in a language are arranged on a hierarchy according to their relative strength. Furthermore, all rules are constrained in such a way that those which apply in syllable-initial position must be strengthening rules, and those which apply in syllable-final position must be weakening rules. In the Simplex-Feature Hypothesis proposed by Sanders (1974b), distinctive features are unary or simplex, rather than binary or complex, and all phonological rules involve either the insertion of features or segments or the deletion of features or segments. In this theory, all rules which apply in word-initial position must be insertion rules and all rules which apply in word-final position must be deletion rules.

In both of these theories, a particular rule changing a segment type

X to a segment type Y is considered either a strengthening or a weakening rule (in Natural Generative Grammar) or an insertion or deletion rule (in the Simplex-Feature Hypothesis) and is restricted accordingly as to the position in which it may apply. Both theories, then, correctly predict that rules like aspiration rules, considered as either strengthening or insertion, may apply only word- or syllable-initially and rules like deaspiration, considered as either weakening or deletion, may apply only word- or syllable-finally. However, neither theory can handle situations in which a rule changing segment type X to Y in some environment exists in one language and the opposite rule, changing segment type Y to X in the same environment, exists in another. Of course, such situations could be accommodated in these theories if relative strength and the choice of distinctive features were a language-specific matter, but then neither theory would have any empirical content.

Situations such as the one just described do exist in natural languages, however. Consider the types of rules described in (22) below:

(22) Rules effecting opposite changes

    a. i. Raising of unstressed mid vowels to high vowels in word-final syllables in Portuguese (Mattoso Câmara 1972:34) and raising of word-final /e/ to /i/ in Finnish (Collinder 1969:10).

       ii. Lowering of phrase-final high vowels to mid vowels in Tagalog (Bloomfield 1917) and lowering of high vowels to mid vowels word-finally and before uvulars in Western Greenlandic Eskimo (Schultz-Lorentzen 1945).

    b. i. Change of word-final /m/ to [n] in Finnish (Collinder 1969:10) and change of root-final /m/ to [n] when word-final in Sanskrit (Whitney 1879:47).

       ii. Change of word-final /n/ to [ŋ] syllable- and word-finally in many dialects of Spanish in both America and Spain (Canfield 1962:70–71).

In (22a) and (22b), examples are given of rules in certain languages effecting a change from segment type X to segment type Y and of rules in other languages effecting the opposite change under essentially identical conditions. Pairs of rules like these appear to constitute counterexamples to the two theories of phonology mentioned above, since if one type of change is weakening in word-final position, the opposite type must be strengthening in the same position, or if one type of change involves the deletion of particular features in word-final position, the opposite type must involve the insertion of those features in the same position.

However, a theory incorporating the Markedness Constraint predicts that we should find situations exactly like the ones described in (22). Examination of the languages involved shows that the rules in (22ai) and (22bi) are neutralization rules and that those in (22aii) and 22bii) are allophonic rules. Since we have already seen that high vowels are unmarked with respect to mid vowels and dental nasals are unmarked with respect to labial or velar nasals, the neutralization rules in (22ai) and (22bi) change marked segments to relatively unmarked ones and the allophonic rules in (22aii) and (22bii) change unmarked segments to relatively marked ones. Thus, these examples provide support for the Markedness Constraint over the theory of Natural Generative Grammar and the Simplex-Feature Hypothesis.

While we have argued that neither of these two theories alone, without recognizing some equivalent of the Markedness Constraint, can predict the variety of different types of rules that are found in natural languages, it is also true that the Markedness Constraint alone does not disallow certain types of rules that apparently do not occur in natural languages. With respect to rules of particular types, the Markedness Constraint restricts the function the rule may have, but does not restrict the positions in which it may occur with that particular function. Consider the schema in (23), which gives examples of some types of rules conditioned by position that would be allowed by the Markedness Constraint, where asterisks are used to indicate rules that are not known to occur in natural languages:

(23) Rules allowed by the Markedness Constraint

	Neutralizing	Non-neutralizing
Word-initial	*Deaspiration	Aspiration
Intervocalic	*Devoicing	Voicing
	*Stop formation	Spirantization
Word-final	Devoicing	Voicing
	Vowel raising	Vowel lowering

It can be seen from (23) that the Markedness Constraint, because it does not refer to position in a word or syllable, allows certain types of rules for which there is no empirical support, in particular, rules like initial deaspiration in a language like Hindi, with a contrast between aspirated and unaspirated stops, and intervocalic devoicing in a language like English, with a contrast between voiced and voiceless obstruents. It appears, then, that in addition to incorporating the Markedness Constraint, an adequate theory of phonology must restrict phonological rules by referring to position. Either the theory of Natural Generative Grammar or the Simplex-Feature Hypothesis, appropriately revised and combined with the Markedness Constraint, might provide such a theory. But the type of situation outlined in (23) can also be explained by a principle of language which restricts neutralization rules to final position, of words or perhaps of syllables, and allows allophonic rules to apply in any position, either initially, medially, or finally. It is as yet unclear whether assimilation rules, in general, are subject to the same constraints as are non-assimilatory rules, or what the types of constraints are on rules affecting vowels, where the level of stress appears to be more relevant than the position in a syllable. But, based on the cases we have examined at this point, at least, it appears that allophonic rules apply in all positions within a word or syllable while neutralization rules apply only in word- or syllable-final position.

An additional comment is in order here concerning the types of rules found in the positions listed in (23). According to the Markedness Constraint, any obstruent voicing rule must be an allophonic rule, because it changes relatively unmarked voiceless obstruents into relatively marked voiced ones. Still consistent with the Markedness Constraint, though, as well as with the preceding observation on the positions to which neutralization is restricted, such an allophonic rule could apply anywhere within a word. Voicing of obstruents, in this view, then, would be expected to occur in word-final position as well as in intervocalic position, although most other phonological theories have claimed that only final devoicing of obstruents, and not final voicing, are permissible phonological processes. However, a recent study by Steyaert (1977) provides evidence for just such a rule of final voicing in the Siouan language of Dakota.[7] Steyaert shows that voiced and voiceless obstruents contrast only morpheme-initially in Dakota, but that intervocalically within morphemes stops are voiceless and fricatives are voiced, while word-finally stops are voiced and fricatives are voiceless. Even though the facts here regarding stops are contrary to expectations based on notions of phonetic naturalness, it does appear that Dakota must be analyzed as having a rule of word-final voicing of stops. Further, this rule is allophonic, since there are no contrasts involving voicing that are neutralized by application of the rule.[8] If this analysis of Dakota is correct, the language provides a counterexample to many theories of phonology which disallow final voicing of obstruents. However, a theory which incorporates the Markedness Constraint disallows final voicing only if it is neutralizing, but allows such a rule if it is allophonic. As uncommon as this situation appears to be, we take the existence of allophonic rule of final voicing of stops in Dakota to provide strong support for the proposals suggested in this paper.

Historical linguistics constitutes another proving ground for the Markedness Constraint. All things being equal, the Markedness Constraint precludes the possibility of any phonologically-conditioned neutralization rule becoming allophonic or of any allophonic rule becoming neutralizing. It is not the case that all things always are equal, however, and one can imagine circumstances in which change in a language's phonemic system may precipitate change in the status of its phonological rules, or circumstances in which a rule's output itself changes so as to alter its markedness value, i.e., the marked output of an allophonic rule might simplify somewhat, resulting in neutralization with other segments in the language.

While we know of no clear-cut cases where these kinds of changes have taken place without also (perhaps necessarily) destroying the purely phonological nature of the rules involved, it is certainly true that synchronically non-general, morphologized neutralization rules are found in most if not all natural languages, and such rules typically produce relatively marked segments. Since they are not purely phonologically-conditioned, however, these rules do not fall within the purview of the Markedness Constraint, which would otherwise disallow neutralization to marked segments. Yet such rules are always assumed to have originated as phonetically-conditioned, general rules, and there is no reason to suspect that the relatively marked output of a morphologized process like umlaut in the Germanic languages, for example, was any less marked at an earlier stage. However, there *is* reason to doubt the neutralizing character of this earlier rule.

In fact, the consensus is universal that, in its earliest manifestations, the Germanic umlaut rule which fronted vowels (without unrounding them) before an *i* or *j* in the following syllable was strictly allophonic (cf. Anderson 1974:288; Twaddell 1938). The umlaut of *u* to *ü* and *o* to *ö,* though producing relatively marked segments, was not neutralizing because umlaut itself was the only source of front rounded vowels in early Germanic. As King (1969a:92–101) has shown, like Twaddell (1938) before him, the point at which umlaut does become neutralizing is precisely the point at which the rule loses its phonetic conditioning through other developments, e.g., the reduction of umlaut-inducing vowels to schwa or null. Thus, while an Old High German (OHG) alternation between the singular and plural for 'worm', shown in (24a) below, was allophonic because [ü] appeared only before [i] or [j] in the following syllable, the corresponding Middle High German (MHG) alternation, shown in (24b), was phonemic, because [ü] had come to appear in a host of unpredictable environments (e.g., in MHG [übəl]<[OHG][übil] 'evil').

(24)   Germanic Umlaut

     a. OHG: [wurm]   (sg.)   [würmi]   (pl.)   'worm'
     b. MHG: [wurm]   (sg.)   [würmə]   (pl.)   'worm'

That is, [ü] had become phonemicized, and a MHG rule accounting for umlaut in the plural of 'worm' now resulted in the neutralization of unmarked /u/ with marked /ü/. Such a rule would have to refer to morphosyntactic properties like "PLURAL", however, because /u/ did not generally front before schwa (cf. MHG [gutə]obl. 'good').

This sequence of events is well known, of course, but we suggest that it typifies the way in which some neutralization rules which produce marked segments may arise in a language. Indeed, given our assumptions about the markedness of underlying representations, according to which a marked element is posited only if the corresponding unmarked one is also posited, the ONLY way in which such neutralization rules can come into existence is through the morphologization of allophonic rules. For once a phonemic contrast between marked and unmarked segments has been established, the Markedness Constraint will prevent the introduction of any general rule which converts the latter into the former.

The Markedness Constraint is thus fully consistent with these kinds of historical developments, although, like the discipline of historical linguistics in general, it cannot predict when or if they will occur. However, it can explain some heretofore puzzling phenomena. In the case of OHG umlaut, for example, not only was *u* converted to *ü* and *o* converted to *ö,* which were purely allophonic changes, but *a* was converted to *e,* as in *gast* singular versus *gesti* plural, 'guest'. Since an *e* vowel was already extant in early Germanic, it would seem that the umlaut of *a* to *e,* a relatively more marked segment, constituted a neutralization even during the period when umlaut was phonetically conditioned.

But the facts are otherwise. Based on meticulous rime and borrow-
ing studies, handbooks such as Braune (1967:27–28) (cf. also Twaddell
1938) are very clear on the point that the *e* from umlaut was a closer,
higher vowel consistently distinguished from original *e* (normalized as
ë), which was a more open, lower vowel. While there is no dispute that
the two were different, and that umlaut of *a* to *e* hence did not constitute
a neutralization in OHG, there is no reason at all, save one, that the
umlauted vowel should have risen to a point higher than original *ë*. That
one reason, we suggest, was to preserve the allophonic character of
umlaut by avoiding the neutralization, prohibited in principle by the
Markedness Constraint, of umlauted *a* with the relatively more marked *ë*.[9]

In summary, we have proposed that the Markedness Constraint and its
corollary, together with the consequences of our definition of segmental
markedness and its corollary, constrain phonologically-conditioned rules
to the effect that (1) all neutralization rules produce unmarked segments, (2) all rules that produce unmarked segments are neutralization rules, (3) all allophonic rules produce exclusively marked segments, and (4) all rules which produce exclusively marked segments
are allophonic rules. Given these constraints, it can be determined
by examining the structural change of a particular rule and the phonemic
system of a given language whether that rule may be a rule of that
language. We have further claimed that a theory incorporating the
Markedness Constraint is a more adequate theory of phonology than
ones which only constrain particular types of rules as to the environments in which they may apply, although we have noted that some
type of restriction appears to be needed regarding the positions in a
word in which neutralization rules may apply. Finally, we have shown
how instances of historical change are consistent with, and governed
by, the Markedness Constraint, which also gives a principled account
of certain previously unexplained developments in, for example, the
history of Germanic umlaut.[10]

NOTES

We would like to thank Daniel A. Dinnsen, Larry W. Martin, Gerald A.
Sanders, and Tom Walsh for their helpful comments during the preparation
of this paper. We are also indebted to Ashley Hastings, Hong Im Iverson,

Indira Junghare, Anatoly Liberman, and Per Linell for their contributions to the data included here.

1. These data also show the effect of the phonological process in Korean that voices intervocalic stops, discussed further below. The three series of stops in Korean in word-initial position are described as lax voiceless unaspirated, or slightly aspirated (e.g., [p]), tense voiceless unaspirated (e.g., [p']), and voiceless aspirated (e.g., [pʰ]), but intervocalically the lax voiceless unaspirated series appears as voiced. Word-finally, and syllable-finally, these contrasts are neutralized and only voiceless unreleased stops occur (Moon 1974).

2. Both of these aspects of consonant gradation in Corsican, the spirantization of voiced stops and the voicing of voiceless stops, can be conflated with the use of angled brackets as follows:

$$\begin{bmatrix} -\text{sonorant} \\ <+\text{voice}> \end{bmatrix} \longrightarrow \begin{bmatrix} +\text{voice} \\ <+\text{continuant}> \end{bmatrix} / \text{V}\_\_\_\_\text{V}$$

The first expansion of this schema is the spirantization rule, which is allophonic because there are no voiced non-strident fricatives corresponding to those produced by the rule before the rule applies. The second expansion is the voicing rule, which now also is seen to be allophonic, since there are no voiced stops in the input to the rule. This example shows that it is individual subrules of a rule schema that must be considered in determining whether a rule is neutralizing or not.

3. Greenberg (1969:162) further notes, in his synchronic universal (4): "To every voiceless vowel in any language there is a corresponding voiced vowel of the same quality, but not necessarily vice versa."

4. Moreover, Ladefoged (1975:147) notes that the rule which merges /t/ and /d/ is part of a more general tapping process in English that applies to all alveolar stops, including the nasal /n/. In the case of the nasal, the result is a nasal tap, as in the word *tanner,* which, like the oral tap, is not present in the input to the rule. Further, as was pointed out to us by Larry W. Martin, tapping may be one aspect of an even more general phenomenon of consonantal "weakening" between stressed and unstressed syllabics. This "weakening" results in the shortening of all consonants, and even in the reduction of /b/ to [β] and /g/ to [γ] as in neighbor [néyβɾ] and *wagon* [wǽɣn̩].

5. In British English, on the other hand, minimal pairs can be found between [ə] and [ʌ], as in [kʰət] 'curt' and [kʰʌt] 'cut' (Ladefoged 1975:71–72). But here too [ə] must be viewed as a derived segment, in this case from /ʌr/ or perhaps from a rhotacized /ʌʳ/, because stressed [ə] is in complementary distribution with initial and intervocalic [r] and [ɾ] as in [rɛd] 'red' and [bɛɾi] 'berry'. Thus, despite the superficial contrast between [ə] and [ʌ], it is still the case that every stressed [ə] is uniquely identifiable as phonemic /ʌr/ (or /ʌʳ/) and is derivable from such a representation through a general rule of preconsonantal and syllable-final /r/-loss (or derhotacization), a rule which is necessary for British English in any event.

6. The allophonic variation of the front mid vowel /e/ in Russian can be seen in the data in (15). According to Jones and Ward (1969:40–44), /e/

in stressed syllables is realized as [e] before palatalized consonants. In other environments, /e/ is realized as a raised [ɛ̂] after palatalized consonants and as [ɛ] word-initially and after non-palatalized consonants. In unstressed syllables the /e/ phoneme is "reduced" in various ways, depending on the dialect (Jones and Ward 1969:44–6).

7. The dialect of Dakota investigated in Steyaert (1977) is that spoken on the Santee reservation in northeastern Nebraska.

8. Steyaert claims that the rule of word-final voicing of stops is neutralizing because there are voiced stops in word-final position that do not alternate with intervocalic voiceless ones. However, we maintain that the rule is allophonic and that these non-alternating final stops are phonemically voiceless, since there is no reason for positing a phonemic contrast between voiced and voiceless obstruents in any position other than morpheme-initial. Under our analysis, there are no voiced stops in the input to the word-final voicing rule, and the rule is therefore allophonic.

9. Comparative Germanic linguistics offers another familiar sound change, which might appear to run counter to the Markedness Constraint. This is the case of Verner's Law, which had the effect of voicing the Proto-Germanic (PGmc) fricatives /f θ h/ to [β δ γ] whenever the immediately preceding syllable in the same word was unstressed. This resulted in merger with the PGmc reflexes of Proto-Indo-European /bh dh gh/, which, according to the very thorough reconstruction of Moulton (1954), had the allophones [β δ γ] in postvocalic environments, [b d g] elsewhere. But if we follow Moulton's persuasive phonemic analysis for PGmc, in which /b d g/ are basic and [β δ γ] are derived, Verner's Law remains consistent with the Markedness Constraint. This is so because, even though a PGmc form like *[faδár] 'father' is phonemically ambiguous (/fadár/ or /faθár/), no neutralization of the form as defined in (1) is involved, i.e., the merger that takes place between /d/ and /θ/ is not to either member of the opposition, but to the third elecent, [δ]. Verner's Law is thus "allophonic" for the same reason as the tapping of American English /t/ and /d/ to [ɾ] is.

10. Discussion after the presentation of this paper revealed several potential counter-examples to the predictions of the Markedness Constraint. In particular, Jonathan Kaye cited a variety of apparently quite general yet neutralizing palatalization rules from diverse Amerindian languages, rules which produce only segments that are marked relative to their inputs and which therefore constitute *prima facie* falsification of the Markedness Constraint.

The individual cases cited bear further investigation, of course, although we have no reason to believe the facts are other than what Kaye presented. If these rules are found to be general, phonologically-conditioned neutralization rules, then the status of the Markedness Constraint will be called into question. However, we believe that the Markedness Constraint represents a true generalization about the vast majority of phonological rules and therefore that it cannot be easily abandoned. In order to accommodate these apparent counter-examples, we suggest two directions of further research. First, the interaction between historical change and the Markedness Constraint must be investigated in more detail. In the Germanic umlaut example discussed above, we considered the situation in which the loss of the conditioning environment of an allophonic rule results in the rule becoming a morphologically-conditioned one and simultaneously produces a change in the phonemic system of the language, altering the rule's status from allophonic to neutralizing. The palatalization rules described by Kaye are examples of independent changes in the phonemic system of a language which turn an allophonic rule into a neutralizing one, apparently without causing the rule to become morphologically conditioned. Additional cases of this type must be investigated before any principles governing this situation can be proposed. Second, the status of assimilation rules with respect to the Markedness Constraint must be further investigated. Non-assimilatory rules, i.e., feature-changing rules conditioned by boundaries, syllable structure, the presence or absence of stress, etc., pose no problems for the Markedness Constraint, while certain types of assimilatory rules, such as the palatalization rules under discussion, apparently do. Again, we believe that the majority of assimilation rules are consistent with the Markedness Constraint, but only further research will reveal whether there are definable conditions under which the Markedness Constraint is systematically suspended with respect to specific types of assimilatory rules.

CHAPTER FOUR

Equational Rules and
Rule Functions in Phonology

Gerald A. Sanders

1. INTRODUCTION

Natural languages are cultural instruments for the symbolic association
of sounds and meanings for purposes of effective communication by the
members of human societies. Like all other instrumental objects, therefore, it is the functions or purposive goals of languages that determine
their essential properties and their range of possible variation and change.
The science of linguistics, which takes natural language as its subject
matter,[1] must consequently provide theories, metatheories, and metalanguages which are capable of expressing lawlike descriptive and explanatory generalizations not only about the forms and formal structures
of the objects in its domain, but also about their functions and functional
structures, and the systematic relationships that hold between these two
types of structure. Like biology, economics, anthropology, and all other
sciences that deal with the characteristics of physical or cultural instruments, linguistics can adequately account for its subject matter only by
determining the precise nature of these operant relationships between
form and function. One of the most important tasks for a theory of
language, therefore, is the principled differentiation of those characteristics of languages that are naturally determined by their natural communicative function from those characteristics that are underdetermined
by this function and thus free to vary arbitrarily within functionally
established limits from language to language.

The hypothesis of Equational Grammar (Sanders 1971, 1972) constitutes a partial differentiation of this sort. This hypothesis asserts that
all the variable, or functionally underdetermined, characteristics of
natural languages are due exclusively to differences in the particular sets

74

of naturally arbitrary symbolic equivalence relations that are linguistically institutionalized in one language community or another. Languages can differ, for example, as to whether 'young male human' and *boy* are symbolically equivalent or not, or whether word-final voiced and voiceless obstruents are equivalent or not. Languages cannot differ, according to this hypothesis, in any ways other than this—and in particular not in any ways that involve differences in the inferential or derivational functions and functional interactions of the symbolic equivalences of different languages. The equationality hypothesis thus claims that all non-universal rules of grammar are simple symmetric principles of equivalence or non-equivalence, and that all constraints on the proper use of such principles for purposes of inference, association of particular meanings with their expressions, proving theorems about words and sentences, or whatever must be fully determined by strictly universal principles of natural language function.

Evidence and arguments in support of this claim have been presented in various recent publications, including not only my own studies on equational grammar itself, but also my paper "On the notions 'optional' and 'obligatory' in linguistics" (1974a), and the large body of works on Universally Determined Rule Application, which deal particularly with the prediction of appropriate rule-ordering interactions in phonological derivations.[2] One purpose of the present paper will be to provide additional phonological support for the equationality hypothesis on the basis of evidence concerning the functions of phonological processes and the phonological equivalence rules that underlie them. For the most part, however, I will consider the equationality hypothesis itself here to be a sufficiently well-confirmed principle of natural-language grammar, and will be concerned solely with determining the precise nature of the relationships that hold between the forms of equational phonological rules and their directed uses in derivations. My primary goal will be the discovery and expression of the underlying principles of grammatical function that determine these particular derivational uses of grammatical rules from the structures and functions of the whole grammars that include them.

The hypothesis of equational grammar can be appropriately viewed both as a theoretical claim or empirical hypothesis about natural languages, and as a general metatheory, model, or metalanguage for all descriptions and analyses of such languages. We will actually maintain that the equationality principle is more highly valued than its contrary or contradictory hypotheses under both of these interpretations. The distinc-

tion, nevertheless, is an important one to bear in mind here, since failure
to distinguish between theories and empirical hypotheses, on the one
hand, and models or metalanguages, on the other, is one of the primary
sources of counterproductive inquiry and argumentation in linguistics.
Thus, for example, one cannot usefully try to compare the standard three-
level phonological model of American structuralism with any of the
various multiple-level models of standard generative phonology on any
possible factual grounds, since these are not distinct theories generating
different factual claims about natural languages, but rather different
metalanguages for the description of such languages—and thus subject
to evaluation only on the basis of such practical and essentially non-
empirical criteria as clarity, economy, perspicuity, and appropriateness
of expressive powers.

2. EQUATIONAL GRAMMAR AND ITS IMPLICATIONS

2.1   The basic principles and applications of Equational Grammar
have been described and fairly thoroughly exemplified in my paper,
"On the symmetry of grammatical constraints" (1971), and in the monograph titled *Equational Grammar* (1972). It was proposed and argued
in these studies that the axioms and theorems of natural-language grammars are intrinsically equational in content and function. All linguistically significant facts about the words, sentences, and other linguistic
objects constituting a particular language were shown to be expressible,
as suggested in (1), by interpreted instances of the general theorem
schema $A = b,$ where A is a terminal semantic representation, a string
of elements with distinct interpretations into non-null observation statements about the meanings of linguistic expressions, and b is a terminal
phonetic representation, a string of elements with distinct interpretations into non-null observation statements about the sounds or pronunciations of linguistic expressions.

(1) (a) $A = b$ ([A, b] is a *well-formed* linguistic
                                object; A *is a meaning of* b; b *is an*
                                expression of A)

     (b) $A = b;\ A = c$ (b and c are *synonymous*)

     (c) $A = b;\ C = b$ (b is *ambiguous* (where A and C are
                                not identical))

A *valid proof* for any theorem of the form (A = b) can be appropriately defined simply as a finite sequence of equations of the form (A = b, ..., b = b) or (A = b, ..., A = A), such that the equivalence of all equations in the sequence follows deductively from the axioms and rules of inference of some given theory. A proof that terminates in an equation between identical phonetically interpreted representations is called a *phonetically-directed proof* or *phonetically-directed derivation*. A proof terminating in an identity equation between semantically-interpreted representations is called a *semantically-directed proof* or *semantically-directed derivation*. It has been shown (Sanders 1972) that validity is decidable for any finite equation sequence and any finite theory; it has also been shown that if a theorem (A = b) has a valid proof at all, then it will have at least one valid proof that is phonetically-directed and at least one that is semantically-directed.

Moreover, for the effective proof of all true theorems of this sort, it was shown that the only language-specific linguistic principles, or rules of grammar, that are required are simple equations asserting or denying the symmetrical relations of symbolic equivalence between linguistic representations. All non-universal grammatical principles, in other words, are appropriately expressible as instances of the equational statement schemata in (2), and are appropriately interpretable into law-like linguistic generalizations in accordance with these schemata.

(2) (a)   A = B   (There is a set of one or more linguistic objects in the language such that for each object it can be appropriately represented both as XAY and XBY.)

    (b)   A ≠ B   (It is not the case that A = B; i.e., there is no linguistic object in the language which can be appropriately represented both as XAY and XBY.)

Equivalence statements, instances of the affirmative equation schema (2a), express ordinary affirmative rules of grammar. Non-equivalence statements, instances of the negative schema (2b), express well-formedness constraints, or prohibitive rules of grammar. Examples of the major types of equivalence and non-equivalence rules are given in (3) and (4).

(3) *Equivalence Rules*
    (a) *Redundancy rules; adjunction-deletion of constants*
        [NASAL] = [NASAL, VOICED]
        [HUMAN] = [HUMAN, ANIMATE]

(b) *Lexical and ordering rules; intermodal substitution*
[YOUNG, MALE, HUMAN] = [[LAB, OBST,
VCD] [VOC, BK] [VOC]]
[[ADJ], [NOUN]] = [ADJ] & [NOUN]

(c) *Idempotency rules; identity adjunction-deletion*
[NASAL] [CONS, X] = [NASAL, X] [CONS, X]
[X, NP, Y] = [NP, [X, NP, Y]]

(4) *Non-Equivalence Rules*
[SEG] [SEG] [SEG] ≠ [CONS] [CONS] [CONS]
[PRO, CLITIC] & [PRO, CLITIC] ≠ [1ST PERS] &
[2ND PERS]

Language-specific equivalence rules will constitute at least part of
the necessary axiomatic basis for the proof of grammatical theorems
under all metatheoretical assumptions about linguistic description, both
equational and non-equational alike. The need for axiomatic assertions
of language-specific non-equivalence, on the other hand, which express
global and prohibitive constraints only, has not been as definitively established. For present purposes, in any event, we can assume the more
restricted version of equational grammar, without language-specific non-
equivalence statements, and all subsequent discussions will be based on
this more restricted version.

An equational grammar, then, is a finite set of symmetrical equivalence
statements of the form A = B, (2a). Each such statement justifies by
the principle of equal substitutability a pair of converse directed inferences, or transformations, or derivational processes, of the forms (5a)
and (5b).

(5) (a) A $\longrightarrow$ B
    (b) B $\longrightarrow$ A

The basic hypothesis of Equational Grammar asserts that all empirically
significant constraints on the derivational uses of such directed inferences
are determined from their governing equivalence rules by some set of
strictly universal principles of grammatical function.[3] It asserts, in other
words, that the grammars of natural languages can differ only in the
particular sets of representational equivalence relations they postulate.

The metalanguage of Equational Grammar thus generates a much
more restricted and more homogeneous set of possible grammars, or
phonological components of grammars, than those generated by any of
the various standard or non-standard metalanguages of generative

phonology, including among others those particular versions proposed or exemplified in Chomsky (1967), Halle (1962), Chomsky and Halle (1968), Kiparsky (1971), Anderson (1974), and Vennemann (1971). All such non-equational metalanguages generate grammars which specify axiomatically not only a particular set of representational equivalence relations but also a particular set of inferential constraints on the directed use of these equivalences in the justification of derivational substitutions, on the optionality or obligatoriness of such directed substitutions, and on the relative order in which these substitutions can be appropriately made. These metalanguages, in other words, permit grammars to differ not only in their posited equivalence relations, or *rules,* but also in the extrinsic directionality, optionality, and ordering constraints that are imposed on their derivational functions. The set of distinct grammars so generated will be vastly larger and more diverse, therefore, than that generated by any otherwise comparable equational metalanguage, which can permit grammars to differ only in their representational equivalence rules, and not in any of their derivational uses or functions.[4]

2.2 The natural basis and primary implications of the equationality hypothesis can be seen quite easily. The equational nature of grammar can be shown to follow directly from the essentially equational characteristics of languages and of the linguistic objects that comprise them. Viewed extensionally, a language is just an infinite set of linguistic objects, and each such object—that is, each word, phrase, sentence, or discourse of a language—is just a conventional association, or symbolic equivalence pairing, between the meaning of that expression and its sound (or other publicly perceptible type of expression). Since sounds and meanings are totally different types of entities—sharing no physical, spatial, or temporal characteristics whatever—any use of a directed or non-symmetrical relation between the members of a sound-meaning pairing would be wholly redundant. Each linguistic expression, then, can be appropriately represented as a symmetrically related pairing, or equation, of the form $(A = b)$, where the interpretation of A is a set of observation statements about the meaning of that expression, and the interpretation of b is a set of observation statements about its sound, or pronunciation.[5]

Grammars can be viewed as the intentions of languages, the systems or general principles that are necessary and sufficient to establish or determine the particular infinite sets of sound-meaning pairings that constitute their various culturally variable extensions. It is in their grammatical or intentional aspect, of course, that languages appear most obviously instrumental in character. Something can be considered to be a grammar, in fact, only if it has the function of finitely establishing, determining, or generating some unbounded set of sound-meaning pairings that could be efficiently used for purposes of communication by the members of some possible human society. This function is achieved, of course, for any given grammar and given language if and only if the grammar provides a sufficient non-universal basis for specifying or identifying exactly those pairings of sounds and meanings that are available for communicative use by the speakers of that language.

To specify a pairing between the interpretations of A and b in the sound-meaning pair (A, b) is simply to provide a *proof* of the theorem $(A = b)$. To specify all such pairings for a given language, and thereby achieve the function of a grammar of that language, it is thus necessary merely to provide a finite basis for the proof of some particular infinite set of theorems of this type.

Every proof of a linguistic theorem has a well-defined function too—namely, the deductive derivation of a terminal representation in one interpretable alphabet—phonetic or semantic—from a terminal representation in the other interpretable alphabet. Phonetically-directed proofs or derivations thus have the inherent function of deriving fully-specified terminal phonetic representations from terminal semantic ones; and semantically-directed proofs or derivations have the converse function of deriving terminal semantic representations from terminal phonetic ones. The structure of any particular proof, then, will be partially determined or delimited in advance of any appeal to particular rules by its particular derivational function—just as the structure of any grammar will be partially determined or delimited by its essential function as a basis for determining the validity and truth of theorems about sound-meaning associations.

It is, therefore, not a matter of chance or arbitrary convention, for example, that the successive lines of a non-redundant proof of any grammatical theorem will each be progressively closer in their approximation to a well-formed terminal representation in one mode and progressively less like a terminal representation in the other mode. Thus the most general metaprinciple of grammatical function, which I have called Maximalization of Terminal Specificity (Sanders 1971:234–35), the basis for all other universal constraints on rule application, can be seen to follow directly from the natural function of grammars as instruments for the proof of sound-meaning equivalences. This principle of Terminal Maximalization asserts in essence simply that a grammatical rule $(A = B)$

can be appropriately used to justify the derivational inference of representations of the form XBY from those of the form XAY if and only if XBY is a closer approximation than XAY to a well-formed terminal representation in the given terminal alphabet of the given derivation. It follows, therefore, from the natural function of grammatical derivations as instruments for the specification of sound-meaning pairings that the appropriate directed use of any particular equational rule in any particular derivation should always be fully predictable from the content of that rule, the mode of terminality of the derivation, and the rule-independent characteristics of all terminal representations in that mode. It is the power of the equationality hypothesis to motivate and direct the search for such universals of phonetic and semantic well-formedness that constitutes one of its most important metatheoretical and heuristic advantages over all non-equational models for linguistic description and explanation.

The specification of terminal well-formedness is partly determined by simple vocabulary and interpretability considerations alone. Such determination is effected in a particularly natural and straightforward way for those metalanguages that are consistent with the general hypothesis of Simplex-Feature representation (Sanders 1974). The Simplex-Feature hypothesis asserts in essence that all linguistic representations and rules, whether equational or not, must consist of finite strings of unanalyzable content or relational elements like NASAL, ANIMATE, X, &, and Ø, that every constant except Ø has a single, distinct, non-null interpretation into a distinct observation statement either about meaning or about articulation, and that every terminal, or empirically interpretable, representation of a linguistic object must consist wholly of constants that are interpretable into observation statements of the same type or mode, i.e., all semantic or all phonetic. It is clear, therefore, that for any model incorporating the Simplex-Feature hypothesis, terminal semantic representations and terminal phonetic representations will be completely distinct, the former consisting of strings of semantically interpretable elements, including the semantic relational element for simple grouping or association, the latter consisting of strings of phonetically interpretable elements, including the phonetic relational element for linear ordering. It follows, then, that the directed uses of any rule that is capable of justifying the substitution of elements of one interpretable type for elements of the other will be intrinsically determined for all derivations of either directionality.

The vast majority of rules in any grammar are of precisely this sort. These are the lexical rules of the language, which specify the direct pairings between the distinctive phonological and non-phonological repre-

sentations of individual morphemes, and its quasi-lexical rules of ordering, which specify direct equivalences between the groupings of individual constituent types into constructions and the relative orderings of
those constituent types. It is logically impossible for a representation in
one terminal alphabet to be derived from a representation in the other
terminal alphabet unless all applicable lexical rules and ordering rules
are used to justify substitutions of elements in the former alphabet for
elements in the latter, since in no other way can elements not in the
intended terminal alphabet be eliminated. The only possible way for
lexical rules to be applied, in other words, is to justify the substitution of
phonological representations for non-phonological ones in phonetically-
directed derivations and the substitution of non-phonological representations for phonological ones in semantically-directed derivations.

The directed use of rules is intrinsically determined in this fashion not
only for all ordinary context-free lexical rules like that indicated in (6a),
but also for all context-sensitive rules of lexicalization, like those in (6b),
and all of the various types of quasi-lexical rules of morphologically
conditioned phonological alternation, like those illustrated in (6c).

(6) (a) [YOUNG, MALE, HUMAN] = [[LAB, VCD, OBST]
             [VOC, BACK] [VOC]]

    (b) [OX] & [PLURAL] = [OX] & [*en*]
        [HIT] & [PAST] = [HIT] & Ø

    (c) *guws* & PLURAL = *giys*
        liy [LAB, OBST, CNT, DIACRITIC] & [PLURAL] =
             liy [LAB, OBST, CNT, VCD] & [PLURAL]
        bend & [PAST] = *bent*
        [X [VOC] Y] & [PLURAL] = [X [VOC, FRONT] Y]

Thus all such rules have the inherent capacity to justify the elimination
of phonetically uninterpretable elements (like PLURAL, PAST, and
DIACRITIC) in favor of phonetically interpretable ones during the
course of phonetically-directed derivations and the elimination of semantically uninterpretable elements (like LAB, VCD, and FRONT) in
favor of semantically interpretable ones in semantically-directed derivations. Given the function of grammatical derivations in general, therefore, as expressed by the principle of Terminal Maximalization, these are
the only *possible* directed uses of these rules.

It also follows from the Maximalization of Terminality principle that
all phonetic or semantic redundancy rules, like those in (7), can be appropriately used for derivational purposes only to justify the addition of

elements in the vocabulary of the final representation in a derivation and
to justify the deletion of elements from the alphabet of its initial representation.

(7) [VOC, BACK] = [VOC, BACK, ROUND]
     [HUMAN] = [HUMAN, ANIMATE]

For the vast majority of grammatical rules, therefore, the only facts
about terminal well-formedness and relative degrees of terminality that
are necessary for the complete prediction of their derivational uses are
facts about which elements have phonetic interpretations and which have
semantic interpretations—facts that are given by the rules of interpretation of whatever grammatical metalanguage is being employed. Nearly all
of the really significant questions about rule function in grammatical
derivations, however, revolve around non-elementary, or relational, characteristics of terminal representations. For example, in Sanders (1972),
it was suggested that among non-phonological representations semantic
terminality increases as the amount of internal grouping or bracketing
of constituents decreases; and that for phonological representations,
phonetic terminality increases, other things being equal, with increased
element identity between adjacent segments. Other relational principles
of relative terminality will be discussed in detail subsequently, with particular reference to Houlihan and Iverson's (1977) segmental markedness constraint, and other related principles of rule function in phonology.
It will been seen from these considerations that there are indeed certain
highly significant relational characteristics of phonetic well-formedness
which may make it possible in all cases to correctly predict the relative
terminality relations of equivalent phonological representations and
hence the appropriate derivational uses of all rules that express phonological equivalences.

3. PHONOLOGICAL PROCESSES AND THEIR FUNCTIONAL DETERMINATION

We will now turn to certain major representative types of phonological
rules with the aim of determining the precise nature of the underlying
principles of grammatical function that govern their directed uses in linguistic inference or derivation. We will thus be trying to find out exactly
what relations hold between the forms and functions of phonological
equivalence rules, and between the functions of particular derivational

processes and the more general functions of the whole grammars that justify them.

The first subsection, which deals with apocope, will use this process as a basis for illustrating in some detail the general framework and pattern for the discovery and development of functional laws. The following subsections will then be chiefly concerned with certain other major types of phonological processes as a basis for testing and refining the particular functional laws that have been suggested. Throughout we will attempt to restrict our investigations to maximally clear cases of general phonological processes where both the facts and the governing equational rules can be maximally well established.

3.1 *Apocope and Paragoge. Apocope* is the loss of word-final vowels or consonants. *Paragoge* is the addition of sounds in final position. These two processes are derivational converses, therefore, constituting the two possible directed or inferential uses of equivalence rules of the type schematized in (8).

(8) W [SEGMENT, X]   # = W Ø #

It follows from the Equationality Hypothesis, then, that for any given instance of this schema the specified equivalence statement can be used to justify apocope, or final deletion, only in derivations terminating in one mode of terminal representation—phonetic or semantic—and to justify paragoge, or final addition, only in derivations terminating in the other terminal mode. And it must be the case, moreover, that the empirically correct derivational uses can be made to follow in every instance from some set of true law-like generalizations about linguistic structure or function. I will attempt to show now how this might be achieved with respect to apocope and paragoge, on the basis of certain fundamental laws of grammatical function that may serve to determine the correct derivational uses of many other types of phonological rules as well.

There are a number of well-known patterns of morpheme alternation in various languages that can be derivationally accounted for most naturally by the assumption of a phonetically-directed process of apocope, or loss of segments in word- or possibly syllable-final positions. For example, in Samoan, where consonants can occur only in syllable-initial prevocalic positions (Pratt 1911:4), there are systematic patterns, as illustrated in (9), where consonants at the ends of morphemes alternate with nulls when the morphemes are word-final.

(9)	sulu	(light)	suluia	(be lighted)
	po	(slap)	poia	(be slapped)
	nuti	(crush)	nutiia	(be crushed)
	tau	(fight)	taulia	(be fought)
	puna	(spring up)	punalia	(be sprung up)
	inu	(drink)	inumia	(be drunk)
	lago	(lean against)	lagomia	(be leaned against)
	alo	(paddle)	alofia	(be paddled)
	tago	(take hold of)	tagofia	(be taken hold of)
	una	(pinch)	unafia	(be pinched)
	ula	(smoke)	ulafia	(be smoked)
	ula	(joke)	ulagia	(be joked)
	no	(borrow)	nogia	(be borrowed)
	fau	(tie together)	fausia	(be tied together)
	tagi	(cry)	tagisia	(be cried)
	ini	(pinch)	initia	(be pinched)
	na	(conceal)	natia	(be concealed)

Since the meaning 'passive' and the form *ia* are perfectly covariant here, and since the active form of any verb is fully predictable from its corresponding passive form, but not vice versa, a natural and empirically defensible grammatical analysis of Samoan verb forms will be one which treats the final consonants of alternating verb stems as distinctive characteristics of their associated stem morphemes, and specifies are predictable phonetically-directed loss, or null phonetic manifestation, of these consonants by a general rule of null-equivalence for consonants in word-final positions.[6]

In other words, for Samoan it is reasonable to assume a general process of phonetically-directed apocope, which is expressible by directed rule as in (10).

(10) W [CNS,X]   # Y ⟶ W Ø # Y

This derivational rule is justified by the representational equivalence statement (11),

(11) W [CNS, X]   # Y = W Ø # Y

from which it follows that Ø can be legitimately substituted for any subrepresentation of the form [CNS, X] in lines of the form W[CNS, X] # Y in otherwise well-constructed derivations, or proofs of linguistic theorems, for languages of which (11) is true. It also follows from this equation, of course, that the opposite substitution, as expressed by the directional rule (12), is a derivationally legitimate substitution too.

(12) W Ø # Y ⟶   W [CNS, X] # Y

The facts of Samoan are consistent with both of these inverse substitution rules, (10) and (12), but only if (10) is considered to be the only appropriate use of rule (11) in phonetically-directed derivations and (12) is considered to be its only appropriate use in semantically-directed derivations. By the hypothesis of equational grammar, these constraints on the derivational use of (11) must follow, like all other constraints on the use of grammatical rules, from strictly universal principles of linguistic structure and function in conjunction with the particular set of strictly symmetrical assertions of equivalence or non-equivalence which constitute the only equationally permissible grammars of particular languages.

The required restriction here follows in the required fashion from the overriding functional principle of linguistics—Maximalization of Terminality—and the empirical generalization (13), that, other things being equal, words of the form [X] are phonetically more optimal, or communicatively more valuable as terminal phonetic structures, than words of the form [X & CONSONANT].

(13) For any otherwise equivalent representations [W X # Y] and [W X [CNS] # Y] in any natural language, [W X # Y] is phonetically more optimal than [W X [CNS] # Y].

This generalization, like all other such assertions of differential communicative value, effectiveness, or efficiency for human systems of communication, is subject to both observational and experimental tests of various sorts, including tests of productive and receptive discrimination, measurements of physical time and energy expenditures in production and reception, word-confusion indices in sentence repetition and memory tasks and in spontaneous speech, errors by first- and second-language learners, etc. This type of evidence is necessarily indirect, of course, since the only real test of relative communicative value would require the controlled investigations of two otherwise identical human communities whose languages differ only in the particular characteristic whose relative value is at issue. Nevertheless, there are many relatively clear cases, like the present one, where indirect evidence, even of an informal and largely anecdotal sort, seems sufficient to support reasonably strong belief in the truth of the hypothesis in question.

The outlines of a general theory of grammatical function are first indicated in skeletal fashion by these clear cases of differential communicative value. The preliminary theory then serves as a basis for discovering
and explicating other, initially unclear values for human communicational
systems.

It is also possible to extend a theory of linguistic function by the
discovery of new characteristics or kinds of terminal value if such values
are found to be correlated with other more easily found or more easily
observed characteristics of languages. One such correlation at least does
appear to hold—the correlation between relative terminality and typological markedness.

Typological markedness relations are definable independently of any
facts about the morphological alternations or phonological rules of any
particular language and hence, *a fortiori,* of any empirical constraints
on the ways such rules are appropriately used in the construction of
particular derivations in any particular language. Thus A is *typologically
unmarked* relative to B (and B is marked relative to A) if and only if
every language that has B also has A and there is at least one language
that has A but not B. There seems to be a regular correlation, however,
between the relative typological markedness of two representations and
the logically quite independent relation of relative terminality that holds
between them in the derivations of particular sentences in particular
languages.

Thus there is found to be a logically non-necessary correlation between
derivational terminality and typological markedness, such that the phonetically more terminal (or more optimally phonetic) of two equivalent
representations in a language will be the one that is typologically unmarked relative to the other. For example, in German voiceless word-
final obstruents are phonetically more terminal in derivations than their
voiced word-final counterparts. And voiceless word-final obstruents are
unmarked relative to voiced word-final obstruents, since every language
which has the latter (e.g., English, Dakota) also has the former while
there are some languages (e.g., German, Thai) that have the former
but not the latter.

Examples like this are in fact consistent with the existence of a biconditional correlation between relative terminality and unmarkedness. This
is expressed by the empirical law of Unmarked Terminality stated in
(14).

(14) *Unmarked Terminality:* For any language L and any [seg-
mentally distinct, morphophonemically-related[7]] representations

X and Y, such that X =Y in L, X is phonetically more terminal
than Y if and only if X is phonetically unmarked (typologically)
relative to Y—i.e., there exist languages with X and Y and
with X but not Y, but no languages with Y but not X.

The evident correlation here between typological markedness and
relative terminality in derivations appears to be essentially only a somewhat generalized version of the segmental markedness constraints on
the functions of phonological rules proposed by Houlihan and Iverson
in their paper "Phonological Markedness and Neutralization Rules"
(1977). These constraints, which are put to a fairly extensive test both
in their original paper and in the one presented at this conference, assert
that "Phonologically-conditioned neutralization rules produce unmarked
segments" (1977:14), and that "Phonologically-conditioned rules which
produce exclusively marked segments are allophonic" (1977:15). Except for a few minor differences, mostly non-substantive, Houlihan and
Iverson's constraints seem essentially related as the segmental counterparts of the representational constraints on derivational function determined by Maximalization of Terminality and the Law of Unmarked
Terminality.

The precise nature of this relationship will become more clear, hope-
fully, as we consider more of the complete range of types of phonological
processes. Here it is sufficient to point out that functional constraints,
like Houlihan and Iverson's, or like those of Kisseberth (1970), Kiparsky
(1973b), and others, stand merely as *ad hoc* excrescences in the context
of *Sound Pattern of English* and all other such non-equational metalanguages for grammars, but play a fundamental and completely essential
role with respect to equational metalanguages. Thus, in contrast to the
standard models where the uses of phonological rules—the direction,
obligatoriness, and relative order of the derivational substitutions justified
by them—can be merely stipulated rule by rule and language by language
without any need at all for *universal* principles of appropriate rule function, equational grammars *require* such functional principles to achieve
even their simplest purpose of providing correct descriptions of the
pronunciations of words and sentences in particular languages. The
equationality hypothesis thus engenders an otherwise absent *need* for
universal principles of rule function, and thereby provides a *reason* for
their discovery and precise formulation, and hence for the explicit revela-
tion of the highly significant linguistic generalizations that they embody.

In our discussion of apocope and paragoge thus far we have seen that there are some natural languages with morphemic alternations between consonants and null such that the substitution of null for a consonant is appropriate if and only if the derivation is phonetically terminated and the substitution of a consonant for null is appropriate if and only if the derivation is semantically terminated. Thus it follows from the equationality hypothesis that since there is at least one language that has phonetically-directed apocope of consonants and semantically-directed paragoge, it must be the case that *all* languages make the *same* uses of the rule in question, and hence that there can be no languages with *phonetically*-directed *paragoge* of consonants or *semantically*-directed *apocope*. This prediction seems correct, since in such languages every word would end in a consonant and there would be some morphemes that end in a vowel in non-final positions but end in a null-equivalent consonant finally. There appear to be no viable natural languages like this. In fact, when phonetically paragogic consonants have been claimed at all—as for Mongolian by Poppe (1970) or for certain Italian dialects by Rohlfs (1966)—there are no morpheme alternations or regular patterns of any sort involved, and no basis at all for the assumption of any general rule-governed phonological process of paragoge. The known facts about apocope and paragoge are thus consistent with the hypothesis of equational grammar and provide further substantiation for it.

It has been seen here that the specific universal principle which specifies the appropriate derivational uses of equations justifying the apocopation or counter-apocopation of consonants would follow directly by Maximalization of Terminality from the functional law of Unmarked Terminality, which entails that for any equivalent representations (here words of the form [#X#] and [#X [CNS]#]) the phonetically most terminal ([#X#]) is the one that is phonetically unmarked relative to the other. It is as if the goal or target of all phonetically directed derivations and rule applications were the achievement of terminal phonetic representations which are maximally rich in phonetic characteristics that are typologically unmarked. It has also been seen, moreover, that there is a general correlation between the relative unmarkedness of phonetic characteristics, as determined simply by their presence or absence in the languages of the world, and their relative communicative value or efficiency for purposes of effective expression of meanings in human systems of verbal communication.

There are thus three wholly distinct variables here, each logically independent of the others, and determinable from a logically independent body of factual observations:

(1) *relative terminality*—determined language by language on the basis of the facts about the particular morpheme alternations, phonetic inventories, and phonotactic generalizations of each language;

(2) *relative unmarkedness*—determined for the set of all known human languages on the basis of the occurrence and co-occurrence of particular phonetic characteristics in the members of this set;

(3) *relative communicative value*—determined for the set of all possible human systems of verbal communication on the basis of the physical, social, and psychological efficiency of particular characteristics for ease and accuracy of use, learning, and cultural transmission.

It would thus be an empirical fact of the utmost significance if these three independent and independently determinable variables are actually correlated with each other in any way. And all indications thus far suggest that they are in fact correlated, and that they are correlated, moreover, in a quite direct and systematic way.

The evident triple correlation here is expressed in its strongest form by the Law of Unmarked Terminal Value, (15).

(15) *Unmarked Terminal Value:* For any language L and any (segmentally distinct, morphophonemically related) representations X and Y, such that X = Y in L, X is phonetically more terminal than Y if and only if X is phonetically unmarked relative to Y and if and only if X is a communicatively more valuable phonetic structure than Y.

This law appears to hold for a number of reasonably clear sets of facts about natural languages. Much of the remainder of this paper will involve further tests of (34) and its constituent sub-laws.

If these laws are true, it will be noted, then it obviously cannot be because *typological* characteristics *cause* one representation to be simpler or communicatively more valuable than another, or phonetically more terminal in particular derivations of particular languages. Nor could it be the case that such relative terminality characteristics cause one representation to be terminally more valuable than another or, alone, typologically unmarked relative to another. Instead, the direction of causation here would presumably have to be *from* relative communicative values to *both* terminality *and* markedness characteristics. The causal connection, moreover, would have to be by way of some extremely general cultural law of optimum availability of efficient means. I discussed the necessity for such a link generally with respect to linguistic universals in my paper on the typology of elliptical coordinations (Sanders 1976), where

I showed that the correlation that exists between the relative ease of decoding of a type of elliptical coordination and its relative typological unmarkedness can be explained if and only if there is a law to the effect that nothing complex or difficult can be available to a language (or culture) unless all things that are simpler and easier are also available to it. Although we will have nothing more to say here concerning matters of analysis or explanation at this level of generality, it is appropriate, nevertheless, to keep these fundamental matters of cultural adaptation and instrumental efficiency in mind as a general background for all particular investigations of grammatical rule function that may be carried out.

3.2 *Prothesis and Apheresis.* The traditional term *prothesis* is generally used to refer to the phonetically directed addition of a specified vowel at the beginning of words that would otherwise begin with a sequence of consonants not normally permitted in word-initial positions. The standard example is of the type illustrated for Spanish in (16).

(16)

escala	'ladder'	*scala
esgrima	'fencing'	*sgrima
espada	'sword'	*spada
esbozo	'sketch'	*sbozo
esfera	'sphere'	*sfera
esmalte	'enamel'	*smalte
estado	'state'	*stado

Thus, since there are words and potential words in Spanish that begin with the sequences *esk, esp, est,* etc., but no words or potential words beginning with *sk, sp, st,* etc., the initial *e* is wholly redundant in words like *escala* or *estado* and can be predictably added in all phonetically-directed derivations of Spanish sentences and predictably deleted in all semantically-directed ones.[8] The grammar of Spanish, in other words, could appropriately be assumed to include redundancy-free lexical rules like those in (17) for all words of the type exemplified in (16), and a perfectly regular phonological equivalence rule of the form given in (18).

(17) *scala* = 'ladder'

(18) #s [CNS] X = # [VOC] s [CNS] X

where italicized letters abbreviate distinctive phonological representations and (VOC, Ø) is the distinctive representation of Spanish *e,* the simplest or most neutral of its vowels.[9]

Given this analysis of Spanish, then, and the facts that make it defensible, it follows from the equationality hypothesis that there can be no language for which rule (18) could be used to justify counter-prothesis, or apheresis, rather than prothesis in phonetically-directed derivations, or prothesis rather than apheresis in semantically-directed ones. In other words, given Spanish, the equationality hypothesis predicts that there can be no language like the *Counter-Spanish language illustrated in (19), a language having words beginning with clusters of *s* followed by a consonant, but no words in which such clusters are preceded by a word-initial neutral vowel.

(19) *Counter-Spanish*

scala	'ladder'	*escala
spada	'sword'	*espada
stado	'state'	*estado

The correct use of rule (18) for languages like Spanish and the exclusion of such use as would yield non-natural languages like *Counter-Spanish would be effected simply by a functional constraint against phonetically-directed apheresis or semantically-directed prothesis—either constraint following from the other by the principle of opposite use for opposite directionality.

And the delimitation of the set of natural languages determined by these constraints, like all of the other language-delimiting implications of the equationality hypothesis, would appear to be consistent with the inclusion of all known natural languages while correctly excluding many otherwise expectable non-natural ones. Thus as in the case of purported phonetically directed paragoge, all purported instances of phonetically-directed apheresis seem to be only apparent counterexamples to the general laws of use for null equivalence rules rather than real ones. All of the cited examples I have seen, in fact, refer not to any even moderately general rules, processes, or relations between phonological structures, but rather to certain purely non-derivational relationships that hold between the sporadic alternate pronunciations of certain words in different styles or dialects. For example, in *Webster's Third New International Dictionary,* apheresis is illustrated by "*round* for *around, coon* for *raccoon,* baby talk '*top* for *stop.*"[10]

It will be observed, moreover, that this constraint follows directly as we would expect from the overriding functional Law of Unmarked Terminality. Thus any language which has words of the form #sCX# (e.g., English) also has words of the form #VsCX# (or even #esCX#), and there are languages which have words of the latter type (e.g., Spanish) but no words of the former type. Structures of the form #VsCX# are thus phonetically unmarked relative to those of the form #sCX# and are phonetically more terminal, therefore, by the Law of Unmarked Terminality.

The facts about prothetic vowels in languages like Spanish are thus fully consistent with the functional laws of Unmarked Terminality and Terminal Optimality and the general principle of Equationality that underlies them.

It also follows from these laws, moreover, that phonetically directed prothesis should not be possible before prevocalic consonants in general, since this would require, contrary to Unmarked Terminality, that a typologically more marked structure of the form #VCVX# be phonetically more terminal in derivations than its relatively less marked equivalent of the form #CVX#.

It is thus predicted that there are no natural languages that have words beginning with predictable vowels but no words beginning with single consonants followed by vowels. This prediction certainly appears to be correct.

There can be prothetic consonants in languages as well as prothetic vowels, but apparently only under just those conditions that are demanded by the law of Unmarked Terminality—namely, where the prothetic consonant occurs immediately before an otherwise word-initial vowel, thereby satisfying the required correlation between the terminality and unmarkedness of #CVX# relative to #VX#—since all languages have words and syllables beginning with consonants, and some (e.g., Arabic, possibly Thai) have no words beginning with vowels.

It is also worth noting that wherever clear cases of consonantal prothesis can be found—as in Arabic, for example, or German or Thai—the prothetic consonant, as predicted in "The Simplex-Feature Hypothesis" (Sanders 1974b), seems always to be the simplest and most neutral of all consonants, glottal stop, which is represented in simplex-feature notation by the consonantally minimal representation [CONSONANTAL, Ø] or, perhaps, [OBSTRUENT, Ø].

In Egyptian Colloquial Arabic, for example, where syllables beginning with vowels are prohibited (Mitchell 1962), there are systematic morphological alternations between prevocalic syllable-initial glottal stop and non-syllable-initial null. Thus the morpheme meaning 'you' is *?inta* in *?inta kitábt* 'you wrote', where the otherwise morpheme-initial *i* would otherwise be in syllable-initial positions, but *inta* in *šúɣlak inta* 'your work', where the *i* would not otherwise be syllable-initial (*suɣ-la-kin-ta*). The required phonetically directed prothesis or epenthesis of glottal stop in Egyptian Arabic will be correctly determined by the law of Unmarked Terminality from the Egyptian Arabic phonological rule in (20), which correctly asserts that null and glottal stop can be symbolically equivalent in this language before otherwise syllable-initial vowels.

(20) $ [VOC] = $ [CNS] [VOC]   ($ V = $? V)

Additive use in phonetically-directed derivations and subtractive use in semantically-directed ones follows by the governing functional law from the fact that the properly including member of the equivalence pair represents a type of phonetic structure, consonant-initiated syllables, that is typologically unmarked relative to the properly included member, representing vowel-initiated syllable structures.

3.3 *Epenthesis and Syncope. Epenthesis* usually refers to the phonetically directed introduction of a neutral vowel into a sequence of consonants in such a way as to render a phonetically impermissible sequence of segments phonetically permissible. Thus, for example, in Egyptian Arabic, where sequences of three consonants are impermissible within phrases (Mitchell 1962:34), the neutral vowel *i* generally occurs as a conditioned alternant of null between the second and third members of an otherwise ill-formed sequence.[11] This is illustrated in (21).

(21) bint   'girl'
      mahmuud   'mahmoud'
      bi*ntima*hmuud   'mahmoud's daughters'
      /b-y-tkallm/   'present-imperfect-talk'
      [#*biyi*tka*llim*#]   'he is talking'

The appropriate introduction of epenthetic vowels in phonetically-directed derivations of Arabic sentences and their appropriate elimination in semantically-directed ones can be fully justified by the equivalence rule (22).

(22) [CNS] [CNS] [CNS] = [CNS] [CNS] [VOC] [CNS]   (CCC = CC*i*C)

Thus it correctly follows by the law of Unmarked Terminality that the longer, or including, member of the pair of structures equated here must be the phonetically more terminal one, since every language with phonetic structures of the form CCC (e.g., English) also has structures of the form CCVC, but some languages which have CCVC structures (e.g., Arabic, Yawelmani Yokuts) have no CCC structures.

The beneficial effects of phonetically-directed epenthesis like this in terms of achieving optimally well-formed phonetic representations are so obvious that this type of directed transformation or process has traditionally been employed as the classic example of phonological functionalism. Yet, in spite of this, no principled basis has been provided in the traditional theories, models, or metalanguages of phonology for explicating the functional naturalness of phonetically- but not semantically-directed epenthesis, or for predicting the specific functions of this type of rule by general principles which determine the functions of other types as well. The greater perspicuity and conceptual facilitation values of an equational metalanguage are thus seen to be particularly striking here. Moreover, given Arabic, the factual claim generated by this choice of metalanguage alone is correct, namely, that there is no natural language in which vowels alternate with null in such a way as to maximize the number of triconsonantal sequences occurring and minimize the number of CCVC sequences. The non-existence of such "Counter Arabic" languages alongside ordinary Arabic can be given no really natural or fully principled explanation in the context of non-equational models of linguistic description.

Syncope is the phonetically-directed loss of weak unstressed vowels in medial positions, typically following stressed syllables and when flanked by single consonants. A standard case is illustrated by the optional null-alternation of the post-tonic vowels in words like *Minneap(o)lis* and *happ(e)nings* as pronounced in many varieties of American English.

Though epenthesis can add vowels and syncope can delete them, these processes are clearly not converses of each other. This is because the governing conditions for the occurrence of epenthetic vowels are always fully stable in terms of their adjacent consonants and boundaries, while the governing conditions for vowel syncopation are stable only by making essential reference also to the *vowels* or *vocalic prosodies* of the adjacent syllables in the word or phrase.

All rules justifying vocalic epenthesis will thus be instances of the general rule schema (23), and all rules justifying syncope will be special cases of the entirely distinct general schema in (24).

(23) $X C \emptyset C Y = X C V C Y$ (where X and Y are free of vocalic reference)

$$(24) \quad (\acute{V}) \, X \, \emptyset \, Y \, (\acute{V}) = (\acute{V}) \, X \, V \, Y \, (\acute{V})$$

Since no equation can be an instance of both of these distinct rule schemata at once, there are true law-like generalizations about the appropriate derivational uses of each type—phonetically additive and semantically reductive for (23), semantically additive and phonetically reductive for (24)—which are fully consistent both with each other and with the general hypothesis of equational grammar itself.

A different and, to me, basically quite plausible general account of syncope is outlined by Semiloff-Zelasko in a paper called "Syncope and Pseudo-Syncope" (1973). She proposes, on various grounds that I will not attempt to describe or evaluate here, that all cases of "real" or "pure" syncope involve the deletion of "a weakly accented syllabic which has come to be alone in a syllable," and suggests further that this process "does not depend on the nature of adjacent consonants, except incidentally, insofar as syllabication depends in turn on consonant-types" (1973:603). She also points out that intervocalic consonants generally if not always syllabify with the more stressed of the surrounding vowels or with the one that follows if both are equally stressed or destressed. This type of analysis is shown to be appropriate to several instances of syncope in different languages, the most interesting evidence being from French, where Semiloff-Zelasko argues that the alternative patterns of syncope in different pronunciations of an expression correspond exactly to alternative ways of segmenting the expression into sequences of well-formed French syllables, with different schwas constituting full syllables and hence being subject to syncope under different syllabifications. This analysis seems to accommodate the *Minneap(o)lis* type of syncope in English too, since the prescribed syllabification for such words will evidently always yield a segmentation (e.g., mi-ni-yæp-ə-ləs) such that the potentially syncopational (schwa) vowel is isolated between syllable boundaries. The typical "optionality" of syncopation is also explained here by the existence of alternative segmentations into sequences of well-formed syllables (e.g., hæp-ə-niŋz vs. hæ-pə-niŋz).

If this type of analysis is correct, then syncope is a syllable-structure-based process that would follow simply from the general rule (25).

$$(25) \quad \$ \, V \, \$ = \$ \, \emptyset \, \$$$

The correct directed uses of this rule would then follow in a perfectly regular fashion by the general principle of Unmarked Terminality. Thus since a null flanked by boundaries obviously has the same phonetic interpretation as null—namely, nothing—and since all languages can have nothing in any position of any expression, while vowel-only syllables do not occur in some languages (e.g., Arabic), structures of the form $ Ø $ are typologically unmarked relative to any otherwise equivalent ones of the form $ V $ and are hence correctly predicted to be phonetically more terminal. It is thus correctly predicted that syncope is possible only in phonetically-directed derivations and counter-syncope only in semantically-directed ones.

We have seen now that for all of the processes involving segmental equivalences with null—prothesis, epenthesis, apocope, syncope—the distinct derivational functions of each process are correctly determined from the structural equivalence that justifies the process by a single overriding principle of grammatical function—the law of Unmarked Terminality. It also seems reasonably clear that all of these processes, and the equivalence rules that underlie them, are principles for accommodating the segmental structure of morphemes to the required syllabic structures of the words and phrases that include them. Even the Samoan rule for consonant apocope seems to be syllable-based in reality, as expressed in (26), and a precise counterpart of the vocalic syncope schema (25).

(26) $ C $ = $ Ø $

The basic functional consideration throughout may thus be the avoidance phonetically of the typologically marked "extra weak" syllable types V and C and the also marked "extra strong" types with margins consisting of more than one consonant. The simplest, most efficient, and least ambiguating remedies are clearly phonetically-directed deletion for the extra weak syllables and phonetically-directed neutral vowel insertion for the extra strong syllables. Structure and function, means and ends seem admirably balanced here to me, and admirably economical in their contribution to the overriding function of human communication.

3.4 *Final Simplification.* It is a well-known fact about human languages that the ends of words, phrases, and syllables are phonologically less complex and less highly differentiated than their beginnings. Thus there are many examples of contrasts being maintained initially in a language but not finally—for example, voice contrasts for obstruents in German, Russian, Thai, Dakota, or Vietnamese; or aspiration, affrication, and continuancy contrasts in Thai and Vietnamese. The reverse, moreover, seems never to obtain; there are no known languages, for example, in which there is a contrast between voiced and voiceless stops in word-final position but no contrast word-initially; the same is true for aspiration, continuancy, affrication, glottalization, and all other characteristics of manner and, evidently, position of articulation as well. It is part of the nature of human languages, in other words, that oppositions can be maintained initially and neutralized finally, but not the reverse.

It is the case, moreover, that in such instances of final neutralization what occurs in final position generally is the *simplest* member of the neutralization set—the member pronounced with the fewest and most easily executed independent articulatory gestures.[12] Thus when the voice opposition is neutralized finally, it is the voiceless obstruents that always occur in final positions, not the voiced ones. Similarly, it is the non-continuants that occur under final neutralization rather than the continuants, the non-affricates rather than the affricates, the non-aspirated stops rather than the aspirated ones, etc. A particularly striking illustration of this general pattern of final simplicity is provided by Thai, where in word-initial (and syllable-initial) positions there are oppositions based on continuancy (s vs. t, t^h, d, $č$, $č^h$), affrication ($č$, $č^h$ vs. t, t^h), voicing (d vs. t), and aspiration (t^h vs. t), and where all six of these initially distinctive obstruents are represented finally only by t, clearly the simplest of the six, being non-continuant, non-affricated, non-voiced, non-aspirated—and for good measure, and with equally good reason, non-released as well. The fact of final simplicity must thus be accommodated in any adequate description or characterization of natural language.

In the Simplex-Feature Hypothesis (Sanders 1974b), I suggested that all these facts about final simplicity are determined as consequences of a single functional principle governing the derivational uses of all rules about word-marginal null equivalences. This principle asserts simply that "in phonetically directed derivations, elements that are equivalent to null can be added but not deleted in word-initial positions, and can be deleted but not added in word-final positions" (Sanders 1974b:151).

The full set of typological generalizations determined by the marginality principle are indicated by the schematic abbreviation in (27), where p and b represent the simpler and more complex members, respectively, of any pair of obstruent sounds differing only in the absence or presence of voicing, aspiration, glottalization, affrication, etc.

(27) *Marginality Principle Typology*

Possible Language Types		Non-possible Language Types	
(a) $\#^p_b$ $^p_b\#$		(g) $\#^p_b$ $b\#$	
(b) $\#^p_b$ $p\#$		(h) $\#p$ $b\#$	
(c) $\#b$ $^p_b\#$		(i) $\#b$ $b\#$	
(d) $\#b$ $p\#$			
(e) $\#p$ $p\#$			
(f) $\#p$ $^p_b\#$			

The typological laws generated by Unmarked Terminality sort out the nine language types as indicated in (28).

(28) *Unmarked Terminality Typology*

Possible Language Types		Non-possible Languages Types	
(a) $\#^p_b$ $^p_b\#$		(c) $\#b$ $^p_b\#$	
(b) $\#^p_b$ $p\#$		(d) $\#b$ $p\#$	
(e) $\#p$ $p\#$		(g) $\#^p_b$ $b\#$	
(f) $\#p$ $^p_b\#$		(h) $\#p$ $b\#$	
		(i) $\#b$ $b\#$	

Unmarked Terminality thus agrees with the Marginality principle in predicting the non-existence of languages with final neutralization to the more complex member of a neutralization set rather than the simpler member—as in Type (g)—or with the more complex allophones of a phoneme in final positions rather than initially—as in Type (h)—or with complex sounds without their simpler counterparts at all—as in Type (i). But Unmarked Terminality would preclude the phonetically directed addition of voicing, etc., in initial positions as well as final ones, thereby excluding any languages of Types (c) and (d) also, both of which are allowed by the Marginality principle.

Concerning type (d), it seems to be the case that there are some languages of this type, but that their existence is due to allophonic rather than morphophonemic processes and thus not really contrary to Un-

marked Terminality at all. But the same situation obtains also in fact for
the much more interesting language types (g) and (h), which have been
indicated in (27) and (28) as excluded by both Marginality and Unmarked Terminality. One possible example of a type (h) language is
the variety of Central American or Caribbean Spanish which has the
pattern of nasal distribution illustrated in (29), with labials and linguals
in contrast and the two linguals in complementary distribution. (There
is also a phonemically distinct palatal lingual nasal, which is irrelevant,
though, to the present issue.)

(29) nada   'nothing' *ŋada   mano   'hand'   *maŋo
      madre   'mother'   cama   'bed'

      paŋ   'bread'   fiŋ 'end'   razoŋ   'reason'
      panes   'breads'   fines 'ends'   razones 'reasons'
      *pan   *fin   *razon

But the only rules in question here are clearly *redundancy rules,*
whose intrinsic function is always to justify the addition of the specified
redundant elements in derivations terminating in the alphabet to which
those elements belong, and to justify the deletion of the redundant elements in derivations of the opposite directionality. Principles like both
Marginality and Unmarked Terminality could thus be viewed as simply
irrelevant to the application of such intrinsically directed rules. Under this
intepretation, languages of type (h) would be possible under both principles, but only if, as in the Spanish case, the complex segment that is
derived word-finally stands in an allophonic relation to its simpler
counterpart rather than a morphophonemic one.

    This interpretation would also allow for a possible subclass of the
otherwise excluded type (g), a subclass including at least Dakota, a
language that has voiced rather than voiceless stops word-finally, but
always in an allophonic relationship to other non-morpheme-initial stops.
(For details, see Boas and Deloria 1941; and Steyaert 1976, 1977.)
In other words, exactly as in the case of Houlihan and Iverson's (1977)
segmental markedness constraint, the phonetically directed conversion
of a simpler or less marked structure into a more complex or more marked
one is precluded only in those cases where the conversion would have
the effect of neutralizing an otherwise operant contrast. Where no neutralization, or morphophonemic effect, could result, rule use so as to
increase complexity or markedness is permitted—and in fact required.

    It remains to be seen, of course, whether there are other languages of
types (g) and (h), and if so whether they in fact all belong to the same

analytic subtypes as Spanish and Dakota. Extensive systematic investigations of language typology are needed here now, as they are indeed in
all other areas of linguistics as well. But if such investigations should
provide continued support for Unmarked Terminality, the Marginality
constraint, or any combination of these and the various other functional
laws that have been discussed here, it would still be necessary, of course,
to specify how these various principles are causally or instrumentally related to each other and to the overriding functional imperatives of
viability and selective adaptation. The outlines of a partial synthesis of
this sort have been suggested earlier with optimal simplification of
articulatory and perceptual distinctions as the functional basis from
which both Unmarked Terminality and Terminal Optimality follow. The
constraints on final complexity and final contrasts should certainly also be
derivable from the same functional basis, the operant cultural metalaw for
all these derivations being the principle of optimal availability of efficient
means, or again "harder only if easier," which seems to govern the non-
linguistic instruments of human societies as well as the linguistic ones.

A complete and fully explicit expression of such a synthesis must obviously await the results of further typological research and extensive
testing of various particular hypotheses about grammatical rule functions.
I would like to conclude the present paper, nevertheless, by providing a
rough sketch at least or tentative working model of this synthesis in the
form of what appears thus far to be the most general of all possibly true
principles of phonological rule function in natural language grammar.
This principle is stated, as the law of Terminal Simplification, in (30).

(30) *Terminal Simplification:* For any natural language L, and any
pair of phonological representations WAY and WBY that are
equivalent in L, WAY is *phonetically more terminal than* WBY
if and only if either
(1) A is a redundantly specified *expansion* of B (i.e., A = XCZ,
B = XZ, and there are no lexical [underlying] representations for L of the form XCZ) or
(2) A is *simpler* than B (i.e., either (a) A = XZ and B = XCZ,
as in apocope, syncope, final simplification; or (b) A is
also a part of W and/or Y but not B, as in agreement or
assimilation, or (c) A = [C, D] and B = [C, X] [D, Z], as
in contraction).

It follows from this law that phonological rules can be used to justify
the phonetically-directed *addition* of features or (epenthetic and

prothetic) segments only if the added elements are wholly redundant, or else mere copies of certain elements in their environment. Under all other circumstances, rules can be used in phonetically-directed derivations only for the purpose of justifying *deletion* of features, segments (as in apocope or syncope), or boundaries between segments (as in contraction). The overriding function of phonological rules in general is thus suggested here to be the function of associating optimally distinct and redundancy-free morphemic representations with fully-specified pronunciations that are both optimally rich in redundancies and as easy to pronounce and understand as possible.

4. SUMMARY AND CONCLUSION

We have investigated certain fundamental issues here concerning the structure and function of natural language grammars, with particular reference to their various types of phonological rules and the various directed uses, or derivational processes, that are appropriately determined or justified by them. We have carried out these investigations in the context of the general metatheory of Equational Grammar, a model for linguistic description and analysis which limits the content of all grammars to lawlike rules about representational equivalences, and thus requires that all constraints on the derivational use of such rules be determined by strictly universal natural principles of grammatical function. As an empirical hypothesis, Equational Grammar thus claims that human languages can vary only in formal characteristics and not in functional ones, and hence predicts that there can be no pairs of languages that have the same equivalence rules but different constraints on their directed application or applicational interaction in derivations. All available evidence indicates that this claim and prediction is correct, and hence that the equationality hypothesis expresses a true synthetic generalization about natural languages that is denied by the traditional contrary or contradictory hypotheses of directed grammar. Moreover, simply as a metalanguage, or determinant of linguistic metalanguages, Equational Grammar has also been found to be consistently superior to its available non-equational alternatives, on grounds of clarity, conciseness, appropriateness of expressive power, and facilitation of ascent to higher levels of analysis and explanation. In fact, by elevating all grammatical rules to the status of lawlike generalizations—which cannot naturally be done for the rules of non-equational grammars—the equationality hypothesis makes it possible for all linguistic terms, concepts, and statements to be subject to the kind of rigorous interpretation and verification standards that have standardly been required in all other empirical sciences.

Our primary purpose here, however, has not been to establish either the truth or the utility of the equationality hypothesis itself. Our chief intention, rather, has been to investigate the specific derivational functions of certain major types of phonological rules, and to try to discover how the functions of these particular rules are governed and determined by the functions of the whole grammars that include them. We considered in particular the types of rules that justify apocope, syncope, prothesis, and epenthesis, and their semantically-directed converses. The empirically appropriate functions of such rules were found to be in general accordance not only with the general hypothesis of equational grammar itself and the general functional principle of Maximalization of Terminality, but also with the more specific functional laws of Unmarked Terminality and Terminal Optimality, as well as Houlihan and Iverson's Segmental Markedness constraint on phonological rule applications. On further investigation, though, with respect to facts about word-and syllable-final simplification processes and the converse uses of phonological redundancy rules, certain questions of adequacy were seen to arise with respect to each of these hypotheses about phonological functions, as well as the previously proposed marginality constraint on the adjunction and deletion of elements in word-initial and word-final positions. A tentative restatement or reanalysis or partial synthesis of the governing principles of phonological rule function was then suggested, based primarily on the proposed law of Terminal Simplification, from which the laws of Unmarked Terminality and Terminal Optimality may be derivable as theorems.

A large number of very interesting and very challenging questions remains to be investigated, of course, concerning the individuals and combined functions of phonological rules and their relations to the structures and functions of the whole grammars that include them. There is every reason to believe, though, that these questions will be just as amenable to productive inquiry and analysis as those which have been raised thus far, and that the most appropriate context for such inquiry and analysis, as for the study of grammatical structure and function in general, will continue to be the metatheoretical framework and climate established by the general hypothesis of equational grammar.

NOTES

I am grateful to Kathleen Houlihan, Gregory Iverson, and Linda Schwartz for helpful comments and discussion during the preparation of this paper.

1. This remains quite true, I believe, in spite of the many recent prescriptions to the contrary, chiefly by Chomsky and his close associates, who have often tried to redefine linguistics as the study of human linguistic behavior rather than the study of human language.

2. See, for example, Hastings (1974), Iverson (1974), Koutsoudas, Sanders, and Noll (1974), and the papers by Iverson, Koutsoudas, Norman, Ringen, and Sanders in Koutsoudas (ed.) (1976).

3. The type of directed-rule relation that Vennemann (1972a) calls "inversion" is not a converse relation (i.e., the relation holding between members of rule pairs of the form $A \longrightarrow B$ and $B \longrightarrow A$), and the existence of such inversion relations is in fact entirely consistent with the equationality hypothesis. Thus Vennemann (1972a:212) defines rule inversion as the relation which holds between pairs of rules of the form $A \longrightarrow B/D$ and $B \longrightarrow A/\bar{D}$, where the context $\bar{D}$ is the complement of context D. But it is clear that these two directed processes follow from two distinctively different equational rules, namely, $(A, D = B, D)$ and $(A, \bar{D} = B, \bar{D})$, and thus do not constitute converse uses of any single rule of grammar. Facts about rule inversion are thus irrelevant to any issues of present concern. The same is true, needless to say, for proposals, like that of Leben and Robinson (1977), which postulate semantically-directed uses of axiomatically directed rules rather than phonetically directed ones.

4. Thus for any given set of n equivalence pairs there are $2^n \times 2^n \times 2!$ possible non-equational grammars, but only 2^n possible equational grammars with both equivalence and non-equivalence rules, and only one possible equational grammar with equivalence rules alone. This at least shows quite clearly and dramatically where the burden of proof lies—with the richer and more complex metalanguage of non-equational grammar, and not with the much more restricted and economical metalanguage of equational grammar.

5. The upper case letters here stand for terminal semantic representations or the meanings that constitute their interpretations; the lower case italicized letters stand for terminal phonetic representations or the pronunciations that constitute their interpretations. These notational distinctions have no systematic significance whatever and are made use of here simply for purposes of expository convenience.

6. Kiparsky (1971), following Hale (1973), attempts to argue against this type of analysis in a quite parallel situation from Maori. The evidence he presents, however, seems to me to be clearly insufficient to justify the intended conclusion.

7. This law is not intended to apply to representations that differ only allophonically, or just in the presence or absence of elements that are completely redundant, or predictably present simply from the presence of other characteristics of their including structures.

8. The pattern of predictability here may even govern a few morpheme alternations. Harris (1969:141) cites *checoslovaco: eslovaco* in support of his own proposal of phonetically-directed *e*-prothesis for Spanish.

9. A more general version of (18), which would also incorporate the process of epenthesis before prefinal *s*, ... would be simply ($ *s* $ = $ [VOC] *s* $). See Saltarelli (1970) for outlines of a related type of epenthesis analysis for Spanish, and Harris (1970) for criticisms of Saltarelli's proposals.

10. Either apheresis refers to non-systematic derivationally unrelated variants like these, or it is explicitly defined more as a contraction of adjacent vowels than as an inverse of prothesis; for example, Marouzeau defines it in his *Lexique de la terminologie linguistique* as "suppression . . . d' un phonème ou groupe de phonèmes à l'initiale du mot, par exemple d'une voyelle après voyelle finalle du mot précédent," giving as an example English *I'm* for *I am*.

11. In a small number of situations an evidently epenthetic vowel has the quality *a* or *u* instead of *i*, perhaps as a result of assimilation to an adjacent vowel (or perhaps copying by a combined epenthesis copying process of the sort seen in Mohawk; for discussion see Postal 1968 and Sanders 1974b).

12. This should be compared with the related but nevertheless distinct characterization of the relation between neutralization and simplicity given by Trubetzkoy (1969).

CHAPTER FIVE

Substantive Principles in Natural Generative Phonology

Joan B. Hooper

While several versions of natural generative phonology (NGP) have been proposed (by Vennemann 1971, 1974b, Hooper 1975, 1976, Hudson 1975, Rudes 1976) these proposals differ only in the structure of lexical entries: they all agree on the matter that we will be concerned with here, the nature of generalizations that speakers construct. The major claim of natural generative phonology is that speakers construct only generalizations that are surface-true and transparent. This claim is supported by the facts of linguistic change, and by other types of independent evidence as has been shown in Vennemann (1972a, 1974a, 1974b, 1974c), Hooper (1974 and 1976), Skousen (1975), and Baxter (1975). An important property of surface-true generalizations is that they are all falsifiable in a way that the more abstract generalizations of generative phonology are not. Such generalizations, then, can provide a sound basis for the formulation of universal substantive principles of phonology and morphology.

Much of the discussion in NGP has been concerned with the formal properties of grammars. The thrust of the argumentation has been to show that certain formal principles of generative phonology, i.e., extrinsic rule order, systematic phonemic representation, are neither necessary nor desirable. More recent investigations cast doubt upon even older and more widely accepted formal principles, such as the basis of the phonemic principle, which is that a feature can be either contrastive or predictable, but not both (Hyman 1977 and Hooper 1977). A growing body of data shows that an interest in the way speakers analyze their language seems to lead inevitably to the study of substantive rather than formal principles of analysis, and substantive rather than purely structural evidence. The present paper is intended to demonstrate that NGP is an appropriate framework for the study of substantive principles, and to explain briefly what some of these principles might be.

1. RULE TYPES IN NGP

Rules that are surface true generalizations can be divided into at least two types on a formal basis and these two types of rules have quite different characteristics. On the one hand there are rules or processes whose statement contains only phonetic information—phonetically based features and the phonetically-motivated boundaries, syllable boundary and pause boundary. These are phonetically-motivated processes and will be referred to as P-rules or processes. On the other hand, there are rules whose statement requires, along with some phonetic reference, the reference to morphological, syntactic and lexical features. These will be referred to as MP-rules.

This formal distinction is very similar (although not identical to) the distinction Stampe (1973b) draws between natural processes and acquired rules. One characteristic of P-rules or processes (following Stampe) is that they are productive and unsuppressible. They apply in loan-word adaptation; they interfere with foreign language acquistion. Further they make a minimal structural change as compared to MP-rules, and finally, they are all "natural," that is, they are all phonetically-explainable synchronically.

Since P-rules are unsuppressible or automatic, it follows that they will not have exceptions. (This is more strongly maintained in NGP than in Stampe's theory, since in Stampe's theory a process can be suppressed or partially suppressed by the subsequent application of another process. Thus surface exceptions are allowed in Stampe's natural phonology, but not in NGP.) All P-rules are variable to some extent. They are responsible for specifying the shape of the phonetic representation, in which some degree of variation is associated with every feature. Variation should be thought of as the extent to which a feature is altered and not as a matter of whether a rule applies or not. For instance, consider the process of flapping in English and what is sometimes thought of as a separate and highly variable process, flap-deletion. These should not be thought of as two separate processes, one which produces [D] and one that produces Ø. Rather they are one and the same process, a weakening of ambi-syllabic alveolar stops, which produces not just [D] and Ø, but dozens of articulations varying in a continuum from [D] to Ø.

The extent to which the articulation is weakened, or the weakening is cur-
tailed, depends on a variety of factors, such as the social situation, the
tempo of speech, the degree of stress, and even certain lexical and
grammatical factors.

An important way of determining if a P-rule is still a live and productive process is by looking for exceptions to it. Therefore it is important
to be able to distinguish true exceptions from the variation inherent in
any productive process. But this is a straightforward matter since no
lexical item that presents the appropriate phonetic environment for a
process can be totally resistant to it. Consider an example: certain words,
e.g., *veto* and certain acronyms such as *NATO,* seem resistant to flapping.
But the resistance is not absolute: [víyDow] and [néyDow] are possible
pronunciations. Compare this to an MP-rule that has true exceptions.
Consider the alleged S-voicing rule of English, which gives the alternations in *con[s]erve* and *re[z]erve, con[s]ent, re[z]ent, [s]emblance,
re[z]emble.* Chomsky and Halle (1968) formulate a rule which voices
/s/ after a V and a prefix boundary. This rule has dozens of surface exceptions, e.g., *descent, recite, assemble,* none of which, in even the most
unguarded speech will ever undergo voicing to give **de[z]ent, *re[z]ite*
or **a[z]emble.* Nor will the weakening of the boundary in *re#sell,
re#sew, re#sand* ever yield a voiced fricative such as **re[z]ell,* etc. The
rule is unproductive, it is an MP-rule (if it is a rule at all), and it has
true unyielding exceptions.

In the rare cases where it appears that an unproductive rule applies
to a new form, such an application can still be distinguished from the
application of a P-rule or process. A possible example would be *monologuist* [g] becoming or varying with *monologist* [ǰ]. Notice how this differs
from the variation or change produced by a P-rule. The variation produced by a P-rule is a phonetic continuum: when flapping affects NATO,
a whole range of pronunciations from a full [tʰ] to a weak flap are possible. There is no phonetic continuum between *monologuist* [g] and
monologist [ǰ] in present-day English.

In contrast with P-rules or processes, MP-rules make larger structural changes on the whole (e.g., the k →s of *electric, electricity,* versus
the process k → kʸ of *coo* and *key*).[1] And, as we have seen, they very
often have exceptions. If they apply to new forms, it is in the way just
explained for *monologuist,* or it is under morphological conditioning.

All alternations that are the residue of unproductive processes are
not accounted for by MP-rules. Some alternations amount to no more
than lexical correspondences which become more remote as time passes.

These are alternations that go along with morphological processes that are no longer productive (Hooper 1976: Chapter 4). Examples are the English vowel shift and velar softening rules. Vennemann (1972a) has proposed that these lexical correspondences be described in via-rules, which do not change one form into another, but merely state the relation that holds between the forms both semantically and phonologically.

On the other hand, some alternations occur in paradigms among items that are very closely and productively related semantically. Alternations of this type seem to be governed by rules. These rules must refer to morphological, syntactic or lexical information. These are the MP-rules that we will be discussing in some detail below.

The True Generalization Condition is meant to apply to MP-rules just as it applies to P-rules. However, in order to restrict MP-rules to generalizations that are true about surface forms, it is necessary to conceive of surface representations as containing non-phonetic information, i.e., the morphological and lexical features that are necessary for a well-formed derivation. Such a conception is entirely natural and realistic, since both the speaker and the hearer are fully aware of all of these features. What the True Generalization Condition means for MP-rules is that all surface exceptions must be marked as exceptions, and that generalizations about morphology must be surface-true and not abstract.

One of the most significant results of viewing synchronic phonologies as consisting of rules and processes is the discovery that many languages have identical, or very similar, processes.[2] The contribution of Natural Phonology is the idea that all such processes are natural, and that certain universal principles can be developed to explain all processes (Stampe 1973b). For instance, studying processes in their productive and non-productive stages, the notion of a "minimal structural change" can be made more precise. The internal organization of syllables is understood to some degree, and principles governing syllable-related processes, e.g., syllable-final weakening, constraints on deletion processes, can be formulated. The processes of palatalization and vowel nasalization have been explored in terms of substantive principles (Chen 1973, 1974a). In short, great progress has been made recently in the investigation of natural processes of phonology, and in the development of substantive universal principles. Such principles will greatly simplify the analyst's task of identifying and formulating the processes of a language. In addition, we can hope for some explanations for the various processes that we observe. These explanations will be found in phonetics.

It is the proposal of this paper that a corresponding theory of natural morphology can be developed to explain the nature of MP-rules. Such a theory would consist of a set of general principles that govern the speaker's analysis of the morpho-syntactically motivated alternations of the language. These principles will be distinct from the principles that explain natural phonological processes, for the MP-rules are motivated by meaning, not by phonetics. In this paper, I will argue that the principles previously used in analyzing morpho-syntactically motivated alternations, the principles borrowed from phonological analysis, are largely inappropriate, and must be replaced by principles based on meaning.

2. MORPHOLOGY IN A NATURAL GENERATIVE GRAMMAR

Some general points about the way morpho-syntactically motivated rules are viewed in NGP must be made clear at the outset. Skousen (1975) and Hooper (1976) have presented a large number of examples that support the hypothesis that speakers, when presented with a choice, will prefer to construct a morphologically-motivated analysis over a purely phonological analysis. The reason is that the speaker-hearer's task is to associate sound and meaning, and we assume that the speaker does this in the most direct way possible, i.e., surface form to meaning.

Because morpho-syntactic alternations are taken by speakers to be a part of the sound-meaning correspondence, rather than motivated by phonetics, it is to be expected that such alternations are phonologically arbitrary in the synchronic grammar. (Of course, they have a phonologically non-arbitrary diachronic source, but the speakers don't know this.) Therefore, it is often a pointless exercise to seek phonologically motivated generalizations and explanations for MP-rules in a synchronic grammar.

Let me illustrate this point briefly using the well-worked examples of Spanish stem-vowel alternations in verbs. With a handful of exceptions excluded, there are three basic types of stem-vowel alternations, as shown in (1).

(1) (a)   First and second conjugation only
           o~ue   e~ie
           contár   sentár   infinitive
           cuénto   siénto   1st sg. pres.

(b) Third conjugation only

o~ue~u	e~ie~i	
dormír	mentír	infinitive
duérmo	miénto	1st sg. pres.
durmió	mintió	3rd sg. pret.

(c) Third conjugation only

	e~i	
- - -	pedír	infinitive
	pído	1st sg. pres.

It is lexically arbitrary which verbs have the alternations (since, of course, some verbs don't), but if a verb has vowel alternations, the alternation will be one of those in (1). Furthermore, which alternation it will be is partially determined by conjugation class.

In the models of lexical representation proposed by Vennemann (1974b) and Hudson (1975), all the allomorphs of a paradigm are listed in the lexicon. Harris (1978) has argued that this type of representation makes it appear arbitrary that all the stems that have vowel alternations have just *these* alternations. Since the alternants are listed for each verb separately, there could as well, along with the alternations in (1), be alternations of *i* with *u* (which these aren't), alternations of *o* with *e* (which these aren't), or any other logically possible combination of vowels and diphthongs alternating. Since these other conceivable alternations do not occur, a model which records the alternations in (1) in a separate list for each verb stem, is, in Harris' view, representing the fact that *only* the alternations in (1) occur as a synchronically arbitrary fact.

This observation is quite correct, and, furthermore, the observed effect of the model is precisely the desired effect. It is only an accident of history that there are not other alternations along with those in (1). It is an arbitrary fact about the sound-meaning correspondence that each verb stem that alternates alternates in just the way it does. It is about as synchronically explainable as the fact that the word in Spanish for *table* is *mesa,* and that this noun is feminine.

Let me hasten to add that the fact that stem-vowel alternations are limited to just those in (1) certainly makes Spanish morphology easier to master than if there were dozens of different types of alternations. This advantage is registered in a natural generative grammar of Spanish by the fact that there is only one rule for vowel alternations that must be learned, rather than dozens (see Hooper 1976:Chapter 8).

Along with the stem vowel alternations in (1) there is an alternation of second and third conjugation *theme* vowels. The alternants are the same as the front vowel alternants of (1b):

(2) e~ie~i

2nd conjugation	3rd conjugation	
comér	vivír	infinitive
comémos	vivímos	1st pl. pres.
comímos	vivímos	1st pl. pret.
comiéron	viviéron	3rd pl. pret.
cóme	víve	3rd sg. pres.

The selected forms shown in (2) are enough to show that the appearance of a particular vowel is determined morphologically (cf. *comémos* and *comímos*). However, since the same vowels alternate, albeit under different conditions, Brame and Bordelois (1974) argue that the alternations in (2) should be handled by the same rule(s) as the alternation in (1). Brame and Bordelois feel that an important generalization is being missed if these alternations are not treated as a unified process.

Notice that the only basis for relating the stem and theme vowel alternations is a phonological identity of alternates. From a morphological point of view, that is, from the point of view of what they signal in terms of meaning, there is no relation between the alternations. Since the alternations are, in any analysis, at least partially morphologically conditioned, and since the conditioning factors differ for the two alternations, there is no reason to consider the phonological identity of any significance.

Substantive evidence supports this point of view. Dialectal innovations in the two alternations effect quite different sorts of changes. The leveling of the stem vowel alternation involves the extension of the high vowel to all unstressed syllables, leaving the diphthong in all stressed syllables (Espinosa 1946, Boyd-Bowman 1960). In the theme vowel, the changes show a movement towards eliminating the distinction between second and third conjugation in the first person of the present indicative. In some dialects the *e* of second conjugation shows up in the third, e.g., *vivémos;* in others the *i* of the third conjugation appears in the second, e.g., *comímos* (Rosenblat 1946, Espinosa 1946, Boyd-Bowman 1960). These developments are quite unrelated: among other differences, we can note that stress is not a factor in the theme vowel change, while it clearly has an effect on the stem vowel change. These two alternations, despite the identity of alternates, are not synchronically related.

There are of course clear cases of phonological factors influencing MP-rules. We will mention some of these in the last section. Phonological factors are not, however, as important as has been claimed (implicitly or explicitly) in generative phonology and its predecessors (see for example Bloomfield 1933). Rather morphological factors should be considered the primary factors governing MP-rules, and phonological factors should be included only where the evidence clearly indicates this necessity.

In the following sections, we will discuss one important hypothesis concerning morphological analysis. Substantive evidence from linguistic change and from language acquisition will be presented to support this hypothesis. Before turning to this discussion, however, it is important to note a recurrent difficulty in dealing with morphology. Morphology is inherently messy. Since in morphology we study the arbitrary sound-meaning correspondence, we find an almost disconcerting tolerance of exceptions, irregularities and competing generalizations. This is true of synchronic and diachronic data alike. However, certain strong tendencies and general principles are evident, especially in the dynamic data. To develop a theory of morphology, we must isolate those principles and learn to apply them to synchronic analysis.

3. THE SEMANTIC TRANSPARENCY HYPOTHESIS

The type of research that is applicable to morphological analysis has been carried on in the past to a limited extent. Kuryłowicz (1949) and Mańczak (1957) have studied morphology in a diachronic perspective and have attempted to develop general principles that will explain the direction of analogical change. Both hypothesize that the direction of leveling is determined primarily by grammatical category (N.B., not by phonological factors), but they have different notions of how one determines the category to be favored in leveling. Kuryłowicz (1949, 1968) claims that leveling favors the basic form, which is the semantically neutral form. Mańczak's principles rely on frequency of use: he predicts that the form to survive leveling is the most frequent form.

Jakobson (1932, 1939) makes extensive use of markedness in analyzing morphological categories and their expression. Jakobson points out that "Morphology is rich in examples of alternate signs which exhibit an equivalent relation between their signantia and signata" (Jakobson

1965:352). A case in point is Greenberg's (1963) observation that in languages which regularly distinguish singular from plural forms, it is the plural which always carries an overt mark, an additional morpheme, while the singular is under no such requirement.[3]

These notions are formalized in Vennemann (1972a): "Usually in natural languages, a semantic derivation of secondary conceptual categories from primitive ones, tertiary from secondary ones, etc., is reflected by a parallel syntactic or morpho-phonological derivation" (p. 240). The following diagram illustrates the principle:

(3)

	Primitive Category	Secondary Category
Semantic Level	A	A + b
Level of Overt Manifestation	X	X + y

Here X is the sign for A, and y is some "mark" added to X which signifies membership in the secondary category $A + b$. Thus y may be the addition of a morpheme or the application of an MP-rule. Vennemann proposes this principle, named the Semantic Transparency Hypothesis by Baxter (1975), as a principle of synchronic analysis which also explains certain morphological changes, in particular "rule inversions." This justifies the inclusion of such a principle in a general theory, and its use in synchronic analysis, since linguistic change is viewed as emanating from the same source as the synchronic grammar—the speakers of the language.

The type of change governed by the Semantic Transparency Hypothesis (i.e., rule inversion) can be simply illustrated with an example from Spanish given in Baxter (1975). (See also Kuryłowicz 1968 and Malkiel 1974.) In early Romance, many verb stems were followed by a back vowel in first singular present indicative and the present subjunctive, and by a front vowel in the remainder of the present indicative, as shown in (4).

(4) Present Indicative
    Sg 1 taŋgo
      2 taŋgis
      3 taŋgit

    Present Subjunctive
    Sg 1 taŋgam
      2 taŋgas
      3 taŋgat

Under phonetic motivation, velars before front vowels became palatalized, and nasal consonants and /1/ coalesced with contiguous palatals to yield the palatal consonants [ñ] and [ʎ]. These changes give the alternations in (5).

(5) 3rd sg. present

Indicative	Subjunctive	Latin Infinitive	
tañe	taŋga	tangere	'touch'
fiñe	fiŋga	fingere	'feign'
koʎe	kolga	colligere	'collect'
uñe	uŋga	iungere	'yoke'
frañe	fraŋga	frangere	'break'

Given the unmarked status of the 3rd person singular present indicative, with respect to both the present subjunctive and the first person singular indicative, and given a base form containing a velar consonant, we have the following expression of the semantic relations:

(6)

Semantic Level	Primitive Category MOOD	Secondary Category MOOD + [subjunctive]
Level of Overt Manifestation	/tang(+e)/ Palatalization	/tang(+a)/
Phonetic	[tañe]	[taŋga]

With the phonetically motivated palatalization process applying in the indicative, the phonetic representations do not accurately reflect the semantic relation between the primitive and derived categories. The Semantic Transparency Hypothesis predicts a reanalysis of the paradigm by the speakers. The reanalysis would involve taking the phonetic realization of the primitive category as the basis for the secondary category.

(7)

Semantic Level	Primitive Category MOOD	Secondary Category MOOD + [subjunctive]
Level of Overt Manifestation	/tañ(+e)/	/tañ(+a)/ + velar-insertion
Phonetic	[tañe]	[taŋga]

It is important to note the covert nature of the change: given the phonetic forms, either analysis will work. The evidence for the reanalysis of the velar as the marker of subjunctive is massive. A large number of verbs that have no etymological source for a velar in the subjunctive or in the first person singular present indicative now have these forms marked in just this way. The following are some examples.

(8)		Infinitive	3rd sg. Pres. Ind.	3rd sg. Pres. Subj.	'Regular'
	'come'	venir	viene	venga	*[beña]
	'have'	tenir	tiene	tenga	*[teña]
	'leave'	salir	sale	salga	*[saʎa]
	'put'	poner	pone	ponga	*[pona]
	'fall'	caer	cae	caiga	[kaya]
	'hear'	oir	oye	oiga	[oya]
	'bring'	traer	trae	traiga	[traya]
	'be worth'	valer	vale	valga	[vaʎa]

The 'Regular' column shows what the development of the present subjunctive would have been given the application of phonetic processes only. The forms without asterisks are attested, either in Old Spanish or in dialects (Espinosa 1946). The forms without velars also occur in Portuguese, e.g., *vinha* [víña], *tenha* [téña] and *valhe* [vaʎa].

The forms in (8) suggest, then, that the analysis in (7), where the velar is taken as a marker of the secondary category, is correct. Unfortunately, in analogical change, it is never certain precisely which forms serve as the model for a change. Malkiel (1974) suggests a number of models for this change including the ones given here, as the pattern was clearly present and strong in the language. It is important to note also that some verbs where leveled in favor of forms containing no velar, e.g., *uñir* 'to yoke,' *tañer* 'to play' (a musical instrument), and others wavered for a period, e.g., *salgo, salo, valgo, valo*. Notice that the loss of the velar is a predictable result, since the velar represents suppletion in the representation of the present subjunctive: /+a/ for some second and third conjugation verbs, /+ga/ for others. The change that would contradict the analysis in (7), the one predicted by the phonological analysis in (6), is the restoration of the velar throughout the entire paradigm. It is precisely this possibility that never occurs.

A number of examples of this sort have been discussed recently. There is the famous Maori example discussed by Hale (1971), the case of French liaison, shown to be an inverted rule by Baxter (1975) and by Klausenberger (1976b), Latin rhotacism, analyzed as an inverted rule by Vennemann (1974b) and Klausenberger (1976a), not to mention the many examples presented by Skousen (1975), and the examples discussed in the original work by Vennemann. Although these cases are generally accepted as valid, I do not think their significance has been properly appreciated. These are not rare and scattered cases where morphological (instead of phonological) principles are seen in action. Rather in every case where substantive evidence is available we see the MP-rules are governed by the Semantic Transparancy Hypothesis. This principle is not, then, just a way of explaining a few cases of analogical change, but rather a general principle that should guide synchronic analyses of morphologically motivated alternations even where additional evidence is not available.

Because MP-rules are conditioned by semantic categories, it follows that the principles which guide their formulation should be based on semantics, not on phonology. The Semantic Transparency formula should replace principles of analysis that are based on phonology. Thus, for example, the most widely used method of determining the base form of a paradigm is to choose as the base form the allomorph from which all other allomorphs are phonologically predictable, i.e., the one in which there are no neutralized contrasts (or a "patched" form, lacking neutralization, if no one form contains all contrastive features). When this principle is applied to the formulation of P-rules, the correct results emerge, because P-rules can neutralize a contrast, but never undo one. The correct direction and even the correct conditioning environment are very often discovered by formulating a P-rule so that it applies to an underlying contrast and neutralizes it. (This, of course, does not imply that speakers use this principle, only that it is useful for linguists.)

The same principle, however, gives the wrong results for MP-rules, unless it happens that the form from which the others are predictable is the semantically unmarked form. All of the cases of rule inversion that have been uncovered show precisely this: that semantic principles override the criterion of predictability. However, the predictability principle seems difficult to give up: Kuryłowicz (1968) invokes it, Jakobson (1948:120–121) cites it as a basic principle for morphological analysis (following Bloomfield 1933, who proposes predictability in the name of simplicity), and Vennemann (1974b:139) lists it as a principle determining rule inversion.

Vennemann cites the example of the so-called loss of final devoicing in Yiddish as a case in which analogical leveling (and rule inversion) are determined by phonological predictability. In this case, however, there is no evidence that the alternation which is alleged to have been leveled ever actually existed. Sapir (1915) was one of the first to notice that certain dialects of Yiddish do not exhibit the voiced/voiceless alternation found in MHG and NHG. Thus the following North East Yiddish forms correspond to NHG forms:

(9) NE Yiddish   NHG

sg	pl		sg	pl
rod	reder	'wheel'	ra:t	rɛ:dər
tog	teg	'day'	ta:k	ta:gə
hoyz	hayzer	'house'	haws	hoyzər

Sapir proposed that the alternation had once existed in NE Yiddish, but had been leveled analogically. The direction of leveling in this case is towards the marked category. It can be explained as the restoration of an underlying form, since these paradigms must have a voiced obstruent underlying to keep them distinct from paradigms with voiceless obstruents throughout.

Sapir's evidence that the alternation once existed comes from a few forms in which devoicing has clearly applied: *mit* 'with', *af* 'upon', *op* 'down' < MHG *abe,* and *avek* 'away' (=NHG *weg*). Sadock (1973), however, points out that these forms can be matched with other non-alternating forms with *voiced* finals: *oyb* 'if', *iz* 'is', *az* 'as', and *biz* 'up to, until.' Both sets of forms can be explained if it is assumed that final devoicing applied, but was never a fully generalized process. There is then no reason to posit a stage in which the forms in (9) alternated, and no need to suppose an analogical leveling. This interpretation is further supported by noun forms that did indeed undergo devoicing, nouns ending originally in *nd* and *ld*. In some of these forms a voiceless stem-final obstruent is found in both singular and plural, although its original phonetic environment occurred only in the singular: *hant, hent* 'hand', *vant, vent* 'wall', *funt, funtn* 'pound', *bunt, buntn* (dim. *bintl*) 'bundle', *vint, vintn* 'wind', *fant, fantn* 'pledge'. These forms show leveling in favor of the unmarked category, not the phonologically predictable underlying form. Other stems in *-nd* retained the voiced obstruent throughout, just as the forms in (9) do.

Thus this case is not at all clear, because we do not know if the forms alleged to have been leveled ever in fact alternated. Given the a priori implausibility of phonological predictability as a criterion in morphological change, a very clear and well-documented case is needed.

If the Semantic Transparency Hypothesis is correct, then a number of phonological criteria traditionally used in morphological analysis are inappropriate. Besides the predictability criterion, other suspicious criteria are phonological naturalness and simplicity, symmetry of the underlying segment inventory, and the criterion of the independently necessary rule. Unfortunately, there is not space here to discuss these other principles. However, if my main point is clear, that morphological criteria are of primary importance for morphological analysis, then it will be clear that these other phonological criteria may well be irrelevant also.

4. LANGUAGE ACQUISITION AND THE SEMANTIC TRANSPARENCY HYPOTHESIS

The original rationale behind the Semantic Transparency Hypothesis as explained in Vennemann (1972a) is that it reflects a language acquisition strategy. The presumed strategy is that the basic category is learned first, and, when necessary, certain modifications of the form of this basic category are made to produce the secondary ones.

Of course, more work needs to be done on the acquisition of inflectional systems and MP-rules. Most studies in the acquisition of morphology deal with inflections rather than explicitly with allomorphy or MP alternations. One study, however, illustrates clearly the hypothesized strategy. Stoel-Gammon (1976) reports on the acquisition of certain paradigms in Brazilian Portuguese, in particular on verbal and adjectival paradigms that show (in the adult language) an alternation of the mid vowels [e] and [o] with the low vowels [ɛ] and [ɔ]. The following present tense verbal forms illustrate a very general pattern of alternation:

(10)		1st conj	2nd conj	3rd conj
	infinitives	l[e]vár	b[e]bér	v[e]stír
	Person			
	1st sg	l[ɛ]vo	b[é]bo	v[í]sto
	3rd sg	l[ɛ]va	b[ɛ]be	v[ɛ]ste
	1st pl	l[e]vámos	b[e]bémos	v[e]stímos
	infinitive	m[o]rár	m[o]vér	d[o]rmír
	1st sg	m[ɔ]ro	m[ó]vo	d[ú]rmo
	3rd sg	m[ɔ]ra	m[ɔ]ve	d[ɔ]rme
	1st pl	m[o]rámos	m[o]vémos	d[o]rmímos

In the first singular forms the stem vowel varies according to conjugation class, low for first conjugation, mid for second, and high for third. The third singular form always has the low vowel. The first plural form has a mid vowel, which could be predicted from the low vowel, since there is a phonetically-conditioned, productive neutralization of [e] and [o] with [ɛ] and [ɔ] in unstressed syllables.

In the analyses Stoel-Gammon discusses, the mid vowel is taken as underlying, and a lowering rule is postulated to derive third singular forms. In both analyses cited (Harris 1974 and Imanishi 1975), morphological information is included in the lowering rule. The directionality of the rule (i.e., lowering from underlying mid vowel, rather than raising from underlying low vowel) is decided on by Harris (1974) on the basis of the existence of certain related nouns and adjectives with mid vowels, as show in (11)

(11)   Verb (3 sg.)   Noun, adjective

      1st conjugation
      ap[ɛ́]la   'appeal'   ap[é]lo   'appeal'
      esc[ɔ́]va   'brush'   esc[ó]va   'brush'
      f[ɔ́]rca   'force'   f[ó]rca   'force'

      2nd conjugation
      b[ɛ́]be   'drink'   b[é]bedo   'drunk'
      p[ɛ́]rde   'lose'   p[é]rda   'loss'
      s[ɔ́]rve   'sip'   s[ó]rvo   'sip'

      3rd conjugation
      s[ɛ́]rve   'serve'   s[é]rvo   'servant'

In Hooper (1976) I have argued that derivational relations such as those between nouns, adjectives and verbs are often not productive relations, and may not be relevant to decisions about the base form of a paradigm. Since the rules in question are undoubtedly MP-rules, we expect only paradigm-internal factors to be at work. Furthermore, we expect semantic factors to be the major determining factors.

The language acquisition data Stoel-Gammon presents and her analysis of these data support these expectations. In longitudinal studies of several children, she finds that the third singular present indicative form is the first to be used and is substituted for all other forms. Then gradually, the child begins to mark person with a pronoun, an inflection or both. The first forms inflected for first person singular have the distinctive inflection -o, but the stem appears in the third person form, as the following examples show:

(12)

			adult
	3rd sg	1st sg	1st sg
2nd conjugation	b[ɛ]be	b[ɛ]bo	b[e]bo
	c[ɔ]rre	c[ɔ]rro	c[o]rro
3rd conjugation	v[ɛ]ste	v[ɛ]sto	v[i]sto
	d[ɔ]rme	d[ɔ]rmo	d[u]rmo

Stoel-Gammon analyzes the process as follows: "we can say that the child's rule would be something like: to form first person verbs, take the vowel off the end of the neutral form (the 3rd sg. -JBH) and add -*o*" (p. 6). Stoel-Gammon says that the child later produces the adult form by a rule which raises the vowel of the first singular form. In other words, she is describing a process by which the primitive category is taken as basic and the secondary categories derived from it.[4] Furthermore, the vowels that occur in related nouns and adjectives seem to have no relevance for the child's analysis.

The acquisition of the alternation in adjectives shows the same strategy. In the adjective paradigms alternations of mid and low vowels are as follows:

(13)

	Singular		Plural	
masculine	n[o]vo	gr[o]sso	n[ɔ]vos	gr[ɔ]ssos
feminine	n[ɔ]va	gr[ɔ]ssa	n[ɔ]vas	gr[ɔ]ssas

The choice of an underlying form for this alternation is phonologically arbitrary, since non-alternating adjectives with [o] and with [ɔ] also occur. Morphological criteria are unambiguous, however, and once again, these seem to be the criteria used by children.

Stoel-Gammon reports that in the first stage a single constant form is used, usually the masculine singular form. Next gender, but not number, is differentiated. In this stage "adjectives with vowel alternations in the masculine and feminine seem to be produced correctly, e.g., *vestido* n[o]vo, *camisa* n[ɔ]va" (Stoel-Gammon 1976:7). When the plural is learned, it appears as the suffix /+s/, and the vowel alternations between singular and plural do not appear right away. In fact, Stoel-Gammon indicated that the adult plural forms are sometimes not acquired until after the child has been in school several years. The forms for this stage are

(14)

	Singular		Plural	
masculine	n[o]vo	gr[o]sso	n[o]vos*	gr[o]ssos*
feminine	n[ɔ]va	gr[ɔ]ssa	n[ɔ]vas	gr[ɔ]ssas

The forms marked with * have a low vowel in the adult forms. These forms show that the child takes the primitive category (singular) as basic and derives the secondary category from it.

Another interesting point is suggested by these data. The various alternations involving [o] and [ɔ] may not be considered related by the child. The singular forms of the adjective have the adult vowels as soon as gender is differentiated, but the plural forms lag far behind. This suggests that the masculine/feminine relation is of a different sort than the singular/plural relation, an idea which is not too surprising from a semantic point of view. It further supports a point made earlier in this paper, that phonological identity of alternating segments does not necessarily indicate a single source and a single MP-rule for all instances of the alternation. Stoel-Gammon suggests (very cautiously) that the masculine and feminine may have separate underlying forms, while plural forms are produced by rule. This may, in fact, be the way such alternations need to be differentiated.

The acquisition data shows, then, that children do implement a strategy much like the Semantic Transparency Hypothesis. This does not necessarily mean that adult grammars are formulated on the same basis. However, until evidence appears which shows that the acquisition process includes a total revision of the child underlying forms and rules before adulthood, so that child and adult grammars differ radically, we can hypothesize that adult grammars, like child grammars, are based on the Semantic Transparency Hypothesis.

5. FURTHER PROBLEMS

Given the notorious irregularity of morphological form, it would be surprising if any principles of morphological analysis could be upheld as anything but general tendencies. For instance, it is not always the case that the neutral or unmarked category is the category expressed with the fewest overt markers (Jakobson 1939). If the Semantic Transparency Hypothesis is a strategy of analysis used by speakers, what is the response to a situation in which the primitive category is expressed by an overt marker and the secondary category by zero? A logical possibility would be the analysis of the secondary category by deletion, so that the "mark" of the secondary category is the application of an MP deletion rule. However, it seems highly implausible that a morphologically-conditioned alternation of a segment with zero would be accounted for by a deletion rule. The reason is that if a segment appears in one category but not in another, then that segment will be taken as the marker of the category it appears in. This follows directly from the premise that speakers account for the sound-meaning correspondence in the most direct way possible.

For instance, the English present tense forms would not be analyzed with the third singular form *talks* taken as basic, and the other forms derived by deletion of *s*. Kuryłowicz's solution seems better in such a case: "in derivations like nominative singular: other case forms, present: other tenses, indicative: other moods, third person singular: other persons, the formal surplus of the basic form may be ignored" (1968:75). In other words, he advocates an analysis which isolates a base form of the *stem*.

It seems appropriate here to defer judgment until more evidence is examined, for even the case of *talk/talks* is not clear. In varieties of English that have leveled the present tense forms, the base form with no third singular marker is often found, e.g., in Black English, but a generalized form *with* the third singular suffix for all persons also occurs, e.g., in Appalachian (Wolfram and Fasold 1974). In many varieties of English the present tense of the verb *say* is leveled to *says* (*sez*) ("and then I sez") when this verb is used for reporting conversation.[5]

Problems such as this one, then, need to be studied further. Even a brief look at morphological data reveals numerous problems of just this type that need to be approached through the study of historical and psycho-linguistic data. I will mention only two more very important problems.

The first concerns the roles played by phonological factors in morphological systems. Of course, a good deal of allomorphy is due to phonetically motivated processes, and the role of phonology here is indisputable. However, some alternations that are restricted to certain morphemes are also clearly based on phonological principles. Alternations of this sort preserve the general syllable structure conditions and phonotactic constraints of the language without obliterating the morphological markers. An example is the alternation in the English plural morpheme of /z/ with /ɨz/ and the past /d/ with /ɨd/. (The variants /s/ and /t/ are phonetically conditioned.) The barred *i* in these morphemes appears in order to separate the consonant of the suffix from a similar stem-final consonant (e.g. *kisses* [kIsɨz], *wanted* [wãtɨd]). Phonological information concerning the end of the stem is necessary, and a phonological generalization is made. Yet this alternation is restricted to these few morphemes. When in other instances two similar obstruents came together, their assimilation and degemination is allowed, as in *horseshoe* or *maddog*.

The extension of the velar subjunctives in the second and third conjugation in Spanish seems to follow some phonological pattern as well. The stems that acquired the velar ended originally in /n/, /ñ/, /l/, /ʎ/, /s/, a vowel, or a palatal glide. The extension in these environments is quite general if we include dialectal data, where, e.g., *vaya* (subjunctive) "go" is *vaiga, crea* (subjunctive) "believe" is *creiga,* and so on. This is a reasonably natural class of segments, but the question arises, why just this phonological class? The answer has to do with syllable structure again. Vowels, glides, nasals, liquids and /s/ happen to be just those segments that can end syllables in Spanish. Note that with the inserted velar, the stem-final segment becomes syllable-final. If the velar were inserted after an obstruent, or a cluster, an unacceptable syllable would result. (I should note, as does Baxter (1975: 192–193) that there is no reason why /r/ should not belong to this class. However, Baxter notes that a few examples have been found, e.g., Old Spanish *ferir, firgades, fiergan,* and the velar insert appears after /r/ in Old French dialects.) In this case, then, it seems to be the general syllable structure conditions of the language that determine the morphological class membership.

A second use of phonology and phonological shape in MP-rules is in the designation of morphological class membership. An example is the English strong verb class exemplified by *sing, sang* and *sung*. This is one of the few strong verb classes that attracts any new members. Among its newer members are *fling, flang, flung* and the alternate past form of *bring, brung*. It is clear why *bring* and *fling* are assigned to this class of alternating verbs: ending in a nasal, particularly a velar nasal, makes them seem to belong to this class.

Finally, there is an important question remaining concerning further sub-classification of rules with morphosyntactic conditioning. There seem to be two major types: those which govern alternations that are viewed primarily as suppletive, and are subject to leveling, and those which govern alternations that correlate with morphological categories, and are subject to analogical extension. This distinction is made by Klausenberger (1976a) and also attributed to Kruszewski (Klausenberger 1977). Rules of both types usually arise in the same manner, by morphologization of an originally phonetically-conditioned process, but we do not know how to predict which type of rule will arise from a given alternation.

While it is clear that there must be some reasonably strong correlation with morphological categories, this correlation need not be perfect. The problem can be approached now through historical data. When we understand which alternations speakers consider to be suppletive and which they consider to be a signal for a meaningful category, we will understand a great deal more about how speakers analyze morphology.

NOTES

I am grateful to Andy Baxter and Carol Stoel-Gammon for comments on an earlier version of this paper, and to the participants in the Conference, in particular David Stampe and Linda Waugh, for comments and suggestions concerning the points made here.

1. In some cases the SC made by a P-rule and an MP-rule are the same. For example, intervocalic voicing of obstruents is attested as a P-rule in some languages, as an MP-rule in others.

2. Of course, Trubetzkoy was interested in neutralization processes, and American structuralists studied natural process under the heading of "phonetic similarity" (Austin 1957), but in both of these paradigms the emphasis was on the phonemic inventory, not the processes themselves.

3. Of course, as Jakobson (1939) points out, and as we will see below, the zero mark does not always coincide with the neutral category.

4. See Simões and Stoel-Gammon (1977) for a discussion of some of the possible reasons that children acquire the primitive category first.

5. I am grateful to David Stampe for pointing out the relevance of *sez*.

CHAPTER SIX

The Study of
Natural Phonology

Patricia Jane Donegan and *David Stampe*

1. INTRODUCTION

Natural phonology is a modern development of the oldest explanatory theory of phonology. Its diverse elements evolved in nineteenth-century studies of phonetics and phonetic change (Sweet, Sievers), dialect variation (Winteler), child speech (Passy, Jespersen), and synchronic alternation (Kruszewski, Baudouin), and developed further, still without integration, in twentieth-century studies of dynamic phonetics (Grammont, Fouché) and phonological perception (Sapir, Jakobson). Its basic thesis is that the living sound patterns of languages, in their development in each individual as well as in their evolution over the centuries, are governed by forces implicit in human vocalization and perception.

In the modern version of the theory (Stampe 1969, 1973a),[1] the implicit phonetic forces are manifested through processes, in the sense of Sapir—mental substitutions which systematically but subconsciously adapt our phonological intentions to our phonetic capacities, and which, conversely, enable us to perceive in others' speech the intentions underlying these superficial phonetic adaptations. The particular phonological system of our native language is the residue of a universal system of processes reflecting all the language-innocent phonetic limitations of the infant. In childhood these processes furnish interim pronunciations which, until we can master the mature pronunciation of our language, enable us to communicate with parents, siblings, and other empathetic addressees. Gradually we constrain those processes which are not also applicable in the mature language. (In multilingual situations, as the languages are sorted out by the child, so are the processes, so that ultimately a different subset of the universal system governs each native language—cf. Major

126

1977.) From adolescence, usually, there is little further change, and the
residual processes have become the limits of our phonological universe,
governing our pronunciation and perception even of foreign, invented,
and spoonerized words, imposing a 'substratum' accent on languages we
subsequently learn, and labeling us as to national, regional, and social
origins. If we have failed to constrain any childhood process which
others do constrain, then we are said to have implemented a regular
phonetic change. This innovation may be imitated, ridiculed, or brought
to the attention of a speech therapist; more commonly it is simply not
noticed except by strangers. This is because we learn to discount superficial divergences in others, even the drastically altered speech of
young children, through processes we have ourselves suppressed; we
may even be able to apply them in mimicking others, or spontaneously,
in baby-talk to an infant or sweet-talk with a lover.

This is a *natural* theory, in the sense established by Plato in the
Cratylus, in that it presents language (specifically the phonological aspect
of language) as a natural reflection of the needs, capacities, and world
of its users, rather than as a merely *conventional* institution. It is a
natural theory also in the sense that it is intended to *explain* its subject
matter, to show that it follows naturally from the nature of things;
it is not a conventional theory, in the sense of the positivist scientific
philosophy which has dominated modern linguistics, in that it is not
intended to *describe* its subject matter exhaustively and exclusively, i.e.,
to generate the set of phonologically possible languages.

The subject matter of the theory is also appropriately designated
natural phonology in that, as Kruszewski first pointed out in his 1881
treatise on phonological alternations, the phonetically natural aspect of
phonology (as in the [s]:[z] alternation of German *Haus:Häuser* 'house:
houses')[2] is distinct in its nature, evolution, psychological status, and
causality from the phonetically conventional aspects, whether the latter
have taken on morphological motivation (as in the [aṵ]:[ɔy̰], [ɑ:]:
[ɛ:], [ɔ]:[œ], [u:]:[y:] alternations of *Haus:Häuser, Rad:Räder* 'wheel:
wheels', *Loch:Löcher* 'hole:holes', *Buch:Bücher* 'book:books') or not
(as in the [z]:[r] alternation of *gewesen:war* 'been:was'). The same distinctions were drawn by Sapir, particularly in his explanation (1921:
chapter 8) of the evolution of umlaut in Germanic nouns from a phonetic
process to grammatical process. Natural phonology properly excludes
the topic of unmotivated and morphologically motivated alternations.
Although these have often been lumped together with natural alternations in generative phonology, they *should* be excluded from phonology

if it can, in principle, furnish no understanding of them. Of course, such alternations typically stem historically from phonetically motivated alternations, and these *are* in the province of phonological theory, as are the factors whereby the phonetic motivations were lost. The natural subject matter of an explanatory theory includes all and only what the theory can, in principle, explain. In the case of natural phonology this means everything that language owes to the fact that it is *spoken*. This includes far more than it excludes. Most topics which in conventional phonology have been viewed as sources of 'external evidence' (Zwicky 1972b) are in the province of natural phonology as surely as the familiar matter of phonological descriptions.

The study of natural phonology was abandoned early in this century, not because of any serious inadequacies, but because the questions about language that had inspired it were set aside in favor of questions about linguistics—its methodology and its models of description. The goal of explanation which had directed natural phonology, as well as parallel studies of other aspects of language, was rejected as unscientific by Bloomfield and his generation, which concentrated its efforts on analytic methodology. For the generation of Chomsky, which has concentrated instead on formal constraints on linguistic descriptions (grammars), the goal of explanation was simply redefined: an explanatory theory is one which provides, in addition to a description of the set of possible grammars (universal grammar), a procedure for selecting the correct grammar for given data (Chomsky 1965:34). Chomsky's model is adopted in some detail from that of the conventionalist philosophers Goodman (1951) and Quine, according to whom reality is "what is, plus the simplicity of the laws whereby we describe and extrapolate what is" (1953, quoted by Halle 1961:94).

Although Chomsky's program is widely accepted, we doubt whether it can achieve even its descriptive goal, universal grammar. The problem, as Chomsky and Halle admit in *Sound Pattern of English* (1968:4), is distinguishing essential from accidental universals. They illustrate by imagining that after a future war only people of Tasmania survive: any accidental property of their language would then be a linguistic universal.[3] The answer to Chomsky and Halle's question of how to tell what universals are essential is that an *essential* universal is one which we can show to follow necessarily from the *essence* of things—one we can explain. To paraphrase Quine, reality is what is, and what naturally follows from what is. Ultimately we cannot know *what* can be without understanding *why* it can be.

It may be objected that if universal grammar is innate, as Chomsky has proposed (1965), then we would have an explanation of language universals. We do not think, though, that linguists find this satisfying, any more than someone asking why man walks erect would be satisfied by the answer that erect stance is an innate trait of man. We might as well be told that it is God-given. The issue of innateness, despite all the debate it has aroused, is entirely beside the point. What we want to know, whether the trait is innate or whether it is universally acquired, is *why*: the question, like the questions that guided Darwin, is a question of *value*.

Distinctive value was the foundation of the structuralists' functional definitions of the phoneme as an oppositive element (Saussure 1949), definable in terms of its distinctive features (Jakobson 1932a, Bloomfield 1933). This relativistic conception of phonemes, which provided a rationale for concentrating just on the differences capable of distinguishing words, is understandably appealing to the linguist confronted by a growing but somehow irrelevant mass of instrumental phonetic detail. But words are not only distinguished by sounds, they are made up of them. It is no less important that the sounds that constitute words be distinguishable than that they be pronounceable, combinable, and perceivable (articulate, audible). Jakobson (1942) and Martinet (1955) attempted to explain the various centrifugal (polarizing, dissimilative) tendencies in phonology in terms of this distinctiveness principle. But we have shown in our studies of vowel shifts that these tendencies apply to the nondistinctive as well as the distinctive features of sounds, and that they very often end in the merger of phonemic oppositions (Stampe 1972a, Donegan 1973a, 1976). There are perfectly good *phonetic* explanations of centrifugal tendencies, as diachronic phoneticians such as Sievers (1901:282), Fouché (1927:21–24 et passim), and Grammont (1933: 229, 238, 269ff.) had already pointed out. More important, the distinctiveness principle obviously cannot explain the opposite, centripetal tendencies behind assimilation and reduction, which, as Saussure (1949) had emphasized, are destructive of phonological (and secondarily, grammatical) structure.

Thus, for example, in opposition to the polarizing tendency whereby all spirants become stops, there is an assimilative tendency whereby stops become spirants adjacent to open sounds like vowels. We might account for the first tendency as follows: stops are in themselves easier to produce than spirants, which require a more controlled approximation of the articulators; perceptually, stops present a sharper contrast with adjacent vowels. As for the second, the articulation of spirants requires shorter

travel of the articulators between adjacent vowels than that of stops.[4]
Both tendencies are real, both are functional, and both are necessary
parts of an understanding of phonology. We have to understand not
only why a Tamil speaker, for example, hears a spirant as a stop, but also
why, between vowels, he pronounces a stop as a spirant. The discrepancy between the sound perceived and intended, and the sound pronounced, is simply phonology.

This tension between clarity and ease is one of the most obvious, and
oldest, explanatory principles in phonology. Modern theories, however,
to the extent that they incorporate analogous principles, tend to make
them monolithic, like the principle of distinctiveness in structuralism or
simplicity in generative phonology. This is because they are conceived
in modern theories as conventional rather than explanatory principles:
they are intended to furnish a choice between alternative descriptions, in
accordance with the conventionalist framework we have described. In
that framework, positing conflicting criteria would be like pitting Ock-
ham's razor against an anti-Ockham who multiplies entities as fast as
the razor can shave them off: it would defeat their purpose of evaluating alternative analyses. But an evaluation criterion, necessarily monolithic, cannot replicate conflicting explanatory principles. The structuralist criterion of distinctiveness predicts that the optimal language should
lack contextual neutralizations altogether, and the generative criterion
of simplicity predicts that it should lack 'rules' altogether. This is the
impasse that confronted Halle (1962) and Kiparsky (1965) in their
attempts to furnish a generative explanation of the nature of sound
change: the simplicity measure predicts that change would involve the
loss of old phonetic substitutions, rather than the accretion of new ones.
Postal, who proposed (1968) that rules are added to a grammar for
the same reason that manufacturers add fins to cars (presumably for
no reason at all) seems at least to have grasped the hopelessness of explaining sound change in terms of the simplicity of grammars.

The basic difficulty is that descriptive models like structural and generative phonology, by the very fact that they provide models for the
empirical analysis of languages, provide explanations for what is *learned*.
But there is no evidence that the processes which govern phonetically motivated alternation and variation, children's regular sound-
substitutions, and phonetic change are learned. On the contrary, there
is massive evidence that they are natural responses to phonetic forces,
centripetal and centrifugal, implicit in the human capacity for speech
production and perception. As Passy (1890), Baudouin (1895), and

many others have observed, the child has many phonetically motivated substitutions, but few, if any, morphologically motivated or unmotivated ('traditional') substitutions; in learning language, he suppresses the inappropriate natural substitutions and acquires the appropriate conventional ones. From this observation it is a small step to the conclusion that phonetic changes must arise from the failure of children to constrain certain natural substitutions, and that variation in adults, another likely source of change, must result from natural substitutions which the individual has suppressed in certain speech styles but which apply inadvertently in other styles.

This account of the correspondences of phonological development, variation, and change explains much that was inexplicable in the structuralist and generative frameworks. For example, according to Jakobson's model of phonological development (1942), the child's phoneme system grows by the step-by-step mastery of oppositions. But there is much evidence not only that the child's mental representations cannot be deduced from his utterances, according to the structuralist definition of the phoneme, but also that they correspond rather closely to adult phonemic representations (Stampe 1969 and forthcoming, Edwards 1973). This means that the child's mapping of phonemes onto phonetic representation, with its massive neutralization of oppositions, is far more complex than the adult mapping. In terms of generative phonology, the child has many more 'rules' than the adult. This paradox disappears when we recognize that the mappings are not rules at all, but simply natural processes motivated by the innate restrictions of the child's phonetic faculty.

An analogous paradox exists in the fact that inattentive (i.e., ordinary) speech presents far more substitutions than attentive speech (Dressler 1972, Stampe 1973a). Variants like [kɛpt ~ kɛp] *kept,* [prɑbɨbli ~ prɑbbli ~ prɑbli ~ prɑli ~ prɑi] *probably,* [aẹdõʔnɔu̯ ~ m̩m̩m̩] *I don't know* pose obvious problems for the structuralist conception of the phoneme, and also for the generative conception of 'rules', since it is when attention is relaxed that 'rules' are multiplied. To avoid these embarrassments, both theories have restricted themselves to artificial phonetic representations (the 'clarity norm' of Hockett 1955, the Kenyon and Knott citations of Chomsky and Halle 1968), dismissing actual speech as 'ellipsis' (Jakobson) or 'performance' (Chomsky and Halle), and thereby failing to account for the main characteristics of the unique 'accents' of the languages under description. The view that speech processing is mediated by systems of natural processes, on the other hand, predicts that actual speech should normally be quite elliptical and variable. The extent of stylistic and dialectal variability has been brought out quite clearly by the studies of Labov, Bailey, and other 'variationists'.

When loanwords are adapted to the native system, they undergo systematic substitutions, many of which cannot be explained by a system of rules based on native alternations. For example, speakers of many languages which lack final obstruents devoice these when they are pronounced in foreign loanwords. Obviously, neither structuralist phonotactics or generative morpheme-structure constraints would posit, in a vowel-final language, a rule devoicing final obstruents. But devoicing of final obstruents is a natural process, and since it is one which would not be suppressed in the acquisition of a language lacking final obstruents altogether, this devoicing in foreign words is precisely what we should expect. (See further Ohso 1972, Lovins 1973, 1974.)

The summary paradox confronted by the view that all phonological alternations are rule-governed is that the vast majority of such 'rules' are harder to disobey than to obey. The phonetically motivated devoicing of final obstruents as in *Hau*[s]:*Häu*[z]*er,* to recall Kruszewski's examples cited earlier, is a 'rule' that is difficult if not impossible for a German speaker to disobey—even, for example, in pronouncing English *cows.* Only phonetically unmotivated rules, like the vowel umlaut of *Haus:* *Häuser,* which is conditioned by the *-er* plural (contrast the singular noun *Mauser* 'molt'), can be disobeyed without phonetic effort. Or consider an English example, the difficulty of suspending the phonetically motivated devoicing of the [z] of *is* to [s] in [ðætsɒl] *that's all,* versus the ease of suspending the phonetically unmotivated voicing of the [s] of *house* to the [z] of the plural *houses.* Like umlaut, this voicing of plurals must be learned: we have all heard children say *hou*[s]*es,* and perhaps occasional adults. But we have not heard anyone, least of all a child, say [ðætz], and no one has reported a child who failed to devoice final obstruents in acquiring German, or Russian, or any other language which devoices final obstruents. In fact, every child we are aware of whose earliest pronunciation of English has been recorded has regularly devoiced final obstruents, e.g. Joan Velten's [nɑp] *knob,* [bɑt] *bad,* [ut] *egg,* [duf] *stove,* [wus] *rose* (Velten 1943). And those who continue in adulthood to devoice final obstruents, e.g. [bæ:t], for *bad,* require some effort not to devoice, particularly in situations where the voiced obstruent cannot be released, e.g. in [bæ:tnu:z] *bad news.* There is nothing to indicate that phonetically motivated alternations are governed by rules which are acquired.

The basic forms as well as the alternants of words conform to natural phonetic restrictions. Just as English [z] becomes [s] after a tautosyllabic voiceless segment as in [ðæts] *that's,* likewise there are no simple English words or syllables ending in voiceless segment plus [z]; there are [frɪts] *Fritz* and [fɑks] *fox,* but not *[frɪtz] or *[fɑkz]. There are no languages in which all final obstruents are voiced,[5] but many in which they are all voiceless, e.g., Vietnamese. Such restrictions, although they do not result from substitution, can be explained, like alternations, as process-governed. This explanation is strongly suggested because, as is well known, speakers of Vietnamese and other such languages devoice final voiced obstruents in foreign words. For speakers who never encounter such words, the devoicing process remains merely a tacit restriction, but one which limits the universe of words which they might coin. Incidentally, Vietnamese, a near-perfect example of an isolating language, is the sort of language which is sometimes said to have no phonological rules; but one need only listen to the 'accent' a Vietnamese imposes on French or English to see that, rules aside, there are as many processes governing the phonology of speakers of Vietnamese as of other languages.

It was with respect to restrictions like these on basic forms (called phonotactics in structural phonology and morpheme structure in generative phonology) that generative phonological theory, according to Chomsky (1964, 1965), first achieved the level of 'explanatory adequacy'. He argued that the admissibility in English of the nonoccurring word *blick* and the inadmissibility of *bnick* is explained by the theory's evaluation procedure, which rejects any rule that predicts fewer features than are required to state it (viz. 'Liquids are nonlateral after initial voiced labial stops before high front lax vowels before voiceless velar stops') and accepts any rule which predicts more ('Consonants after initial stops are non-nasal'). The first rule is true only of *brick* while the second is true of *beautiful, bwana, brick,* and for that matter, *blick;* hence, *bnick* is ruled out, but *blick,* should it turn up, is ruled in. Now, most people accept something as an explanation only if there is some reason to believe that this something does in fact obtain. Chomsky gave no reason whatever to believe that such a feature-counting criterion obtains in the language acquisition of children. Nor did he explain how it would follow from this explanation that *blick* is easy to pronounce and *bnick* is not.[6]

The reason, we believe, is that syllable margins are phonetically optimal, ceteris paribus, when their constituents present the greatest mutual contrast of sonority. The contrast of stop is greatest with vowels (stop-vowel syllables are universal), then glides, liquids, nasals, fricatives, and finally, other stops. This is of course the hierarchy of prominence/aperture of Sievers, Jespersen, Saussure, Grammont, et al. After syllable-initial stops English admits everything from vowel through liquid: [ki] *key,* [kju] *cue,* [kwɪt] *quit,* [kru] *crew,* [klu] *clue,* *[kn . . .] (except in Scots *knife,* etc.), *[ks . . .], *[kt . . .] (inadmissible in all dialects). *Blick* falls on the near side of the cutoff point and *bnick* on the far side.[7]

2. NATURAL PROCESSES

2.1 *Ontology and teleology.* "Children's speech has far more neophonetic alternations . . . than the normal language. As children's language comes to resemble that of adults, the child . . . loses the most innovative variants." (Baudouin 1895:210). Writing for an age which had not grasped the concept of synchronic process, Baudouin spoke of neophonetic alternations where we would speak of phonetically motivated processes. Such processes explain not only alternations (e.g., our daughter Elizabeth's [hʌgɨ ~ hʌk] *hug,* with the word-final obstruent devoiced unless an epenthetic vowel protected it), but also children's *non-*alternating substitutions as compared with adult speech (e.g., Joan Velten's invariably devoiced [z] in [wus] *rose* (Velten 1943:287)).[8] Baudouin recognized that such alternations in adult languages, as in German [tɑːgə]:[tɑːk] 'days:day' were not simply imitated but were developed independently by the child (1895:209); again we would add that this is true of the corresponding restrictions in languages whose final obstruents are invariably voiceless, as in the suffixless Vietnamese above, whose speakers' devoicing of voiced final obstruents in foreign words we have alluded to already. The total system of processes, then, governs both superficial alternations and underlying restrictions.

This dual function can even be performed by a single process, for example the process deleting [h] as in [(h)ɪstɔrɪkl̩] *historical* and [(h)wɛil] *whale.* The deletability of [h] is an inverse function of stress and an inverse function of the sonority of the following segment. We will consider only the latter here. In Old English [h] did not precede obstruents. In Middle English it was deleted before other consonants, e.g., from OE [hnutu] *nut,* [hlæxxan] *laugh,* [hrɪŋg] *ring.* Some Modern English speakers (e.g., DS) hold the line here, but others (PJD) delete

[h] before [w] as in *whale,* and still others (HJ) delete it also before [j] as in *hue.* In all these dialects optional deletion can occur in relaxed speech, especially under lighter stress. So we have the following distribution:

	whale	*hue*	*high*
DS	[hwɛi̯l ~ wɛi̯l]	[hju ~ ju]	[hɑ̥e̥ ~ ɑe̥]
PJD	[wɛi̯l]	[hju ~ ju]	[hɑ̥e̥ ~ ɑe̥]
HJ	[wɛi̯l]	[ju]	[hɑ̥e̥ ~ ɑe̥]

For DS, *whale*:*wail, hue*:*you,* and *high*:*eye* are phonologically distinct, though they may merge phonetically. For PJD, *whale* and *wail* are homophones, and for HJ likewise *hue* and *you.* The [h]-deletion process governs the variation [hɑ̥e̥ ~ ɑe̥] and at the same time governs the restriction against basic forms like [hwɛi̯l]. PJD and HJ delete [h] from new *wh*-words learned by ear from speakers like DS, and in fact often seem not to perceive the [h] in the first place. We can predict from these facts an English of the future, in which [h]-deletion will apply absolutely, and even *high* and *eye* will be homophonous. This has occurred in the Romance languages, some Indic languages, Greek, and so on, always with the children leading the way. This is not to say that the Italian speaker, for example, is still deleting the [h] of Romulus and Remus; he does not even confront an [h], except in foreign words. But in these words he deletes it just as we delete the [h] of *high* in relaxed styles of speech. The process applies without premeditation in our ongoing speech, and the hierarchies, within phrases, are perfectly observed: we hear *huge white house* pronounced [hju̯ǰ hwɑe̯t hɑo̥s], [hju̯ǰ wɑe̯t hɑo̥s], [ju̯ǰ wɑe̯t hɑo̥s] or even [ju̯ǰ wɑe̯t ɑo̥s], but not *[hju̯ǰ hwɑe̯t ɑo̥s], etc.

The fact that processes operate in ongoing speech production is most clearly evidenced by their application to here-and-now, 'non-lexical' outputs of secret-language rules and slips of the tongue (Bond 1969, Fromkin 1971, Stampe 1973a). For example, when the intended words *mostly* [mou̥stli] or *mainly* [mɛ̃i̥nli] are unexpectedly replaced by the blend [mõu̥nli] or [mɛistli], the nasalization of the exchanged stressed vowel depends not on its ordinary phonetic quality ([ou̥] vs. [ɛ̃i̯] but on whether or not its novel, slipped context includes a nasal. This suggests that lexical /mɛi̯nli/ or /mou̥stli/ become by tongue-slip (specifically, by vowel exchange) /mou̯nli/ and /mɛistli/ and that then nasalization applies—or fails to—producing [mõu̥nli] or [mɛistli]. Tongue-twisters—sequences which force tongue-slips—show the same

thing: *sane lad slain* [sḛ̃ĩn læd slḛ̃ĩn], when repeated rapidly, often comes
out [sɛ̰id ĩǽn . . .]; when the final consonants are switched, the preceding
vowels agree with them with respect to nasality even though the vowels
themselves keep their original positions. That is, /sɛ̰in læd/ becomes
/sɛ̰id læn/ by the slip, and then nasalization produces [sɛ̰id lǽn]; the
inadmissible *[sḛ̃ĩd læn] never occurs. With our students we have observed hundreds of slips, obtained from tongue-twisters designed to
produce sequences phonetically inadmissible in English. In not one case
was such a sequence observed to be articulated.

It should not be supposed from this that processes are peripheral,
physical events—merely the results of articulatory mistimings or of
over- or under-shootings of articulatory targets. We have no reason
to suppose that the articulatory musculature or its peripheral innerva-
tion can make the kinds of adjustments processes involve (Lashley
1951). Anticipatory substitutions, in particular, suggest that the substitutions occur in the central nervous system—i.e., that they are mental
substitutions. The very suppressibility of processes argues for their mental
nature—the English-speaking child (Velten 1943) learns not to devoice final stops after all. And note that processes apply even in silent
mental speech, in which purely physical inaccuracies of articulation would
play no part (Stampe 1973a).

But although processes are mental substitutions, they are substitutions
which respond to physical phonetic difficulties. To illustrate this, it is
well to look at variants, like the ordered pairs [tɪn kæn] ~ [tɪŋ kæn] *tin
can, rai*[n,m]*bow, se*[t,p]*back, re*[d,b]*man,* etc., which provide direct
access to the inputs as well as the outputs of processes, and thus reveal
the teleology of substitutions more directly than categorical alternations
do. The phonetic motivation of a variable process is usually introspec-
tively quite perceptible: the (more) basic representations (the left-
hand members of the paired variants above) seem more difficult to produce than the derivative (right-hand) ones.

2.2 *Natural application of processes.* Processes apply in ways that follow from their nature and teleologies. First, since processes represent
responses to phonetic difficulties, it follows that if a certain difficult representation undergoes a substitution, all other representations with the
same difficulty will, ceteris paribus, undergo the same substitution. This
explains why processes operate on 'natural classes' of segments. To this
observation, which dates from the Neogrammarians (Sievers 1901:7),
we should add that they operate over natural prosodic constituents—

syllables, accent-groups, words, etc. (Donegan and Stampe, forth-coming).

For example, our English reflects the following process:

(1) Sonorants become nasalized before nasalized segments within a stress-group, but only optionally across syllable boundaries.

Thus we pronounce *rallying* [rǽl.i.ĩŋ] or [rǽl.ĩ.ĩŋ] or [r̃ǽl.ĩ.ĩŋ], *relying* [ri.láe̯.ĩŋ] or [ri.ĩãe̯.ĩŋ] but not *[r̃ĩ.ĩãe̯.ĩŋ] (*re-* being outside the stress-group containing nasality), *rollicking* [rá.lɪk.ĩŋ] but not *[rá.ĩɪk.ĩŋ] (*k* being a non-sonorant). Natural classes are not a matter of descriptive simplicity, as suggested by Halle (1962), but a matter of fact: nasalization applies to novel sonorants and before novel nasals, as in our pronuncia-tions of [y] in French *lune* and the vowel before [ɲ] in Spanish *cañon*.

And natural classes cannot be explained as a matter of cognitive simplicity (what structuralists called pattern congruity and generativists call generality) in the acquisition of a 'rule'. The natural classes a process operates on have a natural connection. Nasalization never applies just before non-nasals, or before aspirates, or in alternate syllables. The natural connection is the phonetic teleology of the process.

Each natural process, then, applies to a natural class of representa-tions (namely, all representations which share a common articulatory, perceptual, or prosodic difficulty to a common degree), and each process makes substitutions by altering a single phonetic property to remedy the difficulty. Since the substituted sound should, in each case, be as perceptually similar to the original target as possible, it follows that the changes processes make will be minimal: a process normally changes only one feature. This means that apparent two-feature changes take place in two steps—for example, a change in which [ʊ] → [ʌ] is in fact [ʊ] → [ɨ] → [ʌ] or [ʊ] → [ɔ] → [ʌ].

It has been suggested that such series of simple changes are changed into single substitutions by an operation called 'rule telescoping' (Hyman 1975), so that (consecutive) processes A → B and B → C are collapsed to A → C. This may be true of learned rules, which lack phonetic motiva-tion and which may therefore substitute one phoneme for another re-gardless of the number of feature changes involved. But processes do not telescope, because distinct processes have distinct phonetic causali-ties. To establish the telescoping of two processes A →B and B → C would require examples of languages in which A → C while B does not become C.

Stampe (1973a) has cited the opposite case of an American speaker who pronounced syllable-final /l/ always as [u̯], but who, in attempting to actually pronounce the light [l] of German, frequently said [ɫ]; this is precisely what we should expect if, comparing other speakers whose final /l/'s vary between careful [ɫ] and careless [u̯], we assumed that this speaker had the same processes, [l] → [ɫ] and [ɫ] → [u̯], as the others, but that in his case the [ɫ] → [u̯] process was obligatory except when overcome in aiming at the totally foreign pronunciation [l].

The principle that each process has its own phonetic motivation (and different motivations mean different processes) explains the mutual dependencies or independencies we find in certain sets of substitutions. Inputs to distinct processes are independently difficult and vary independently: in *what kind,* [hw, w], [t, k], and [d, Ø] are independent variables because each of the substitutions involved (hw → w, t → k/ __k, and d → Ø/n __#) represents a response to a different phonetic difficulty.

But, on the other hand, inputs to a single process with a single motivation, if not equally difficult (as *ti*[n]*can, rai*[n]*bow,* etc. seem to be), are unilaterally hierarchic in difficulty and vary dependently: the [h, Ø] variation discussed above in *huge white house* illustrates this dependency, as does its dependence on relative stresslessness; in *hĕr hénhòuse,* pronouncing [h] in *hĕr* entails pronouncing it in *hòuse,* which in turn entails pronouncing it in *hén,* so that [ø]*ĕr*[h]*én*[ø]*òuse* is admissible but *[h]*ĕr*[ø]*én*[h]*òuse* is not. Similar (in this case identical) substitutions in a dependent relationship like this are single responses to a single phonetic difficulty present in different degrees. Only in such cases do we say the substitutions result from a single process. We should expect that substitutions which respond to a given difficulty apply to the more-difficult segments if they affect the less-difficult ones, though such substitutions may affect *only* the more-difficult segments in the class. That is, processes are subject to *implicational hierarchies of applicability.* For example, we have argued (Stampe 1972a, Donegan 1973a) that the vocalic features of palatality ("frontness") and sonority ("openness") are articulatorily and acoustically incompatible features, and that there is a process which resolves this difficulty in favor of sonority by substituting non-palatal vowels for palatal ones (a → ɑ, ɛ → ʌ, ɪ → ɨ). Of [a, ɛ, and ɪ], it is most difficult to maintain a palatal character for the open [a], less difficult for mid [ɛ], and quite easy for close [ɪ]; and correspondingly, any language in which depalatalization changes [ɛ] to [ʌ] will also change [a] to [ɑ] and any language in which the process changes [ɪ] to [ɨ] will also change [ɛ] to [ʌ] and [a] to [ɑ]. The depalatalization of a lower vowel, however, implies nothing about the depalatalization of any higher vowel; i.e., the implications are unilateral—and this follows from the fact that the scale of difficulty is unidirectional. Implicational conditions on process applicability are also discussed by Chen (1974b), Donegan (1976), Neeld (1973), Schourup (1973b), Zwicky (1972a) and others.

Each process is sensitive to a number of *different* hierarchical constraints on its application. For example, not only are lower vowels more susceptible to depalatalization than higher ones, but lax vowels are more susceptible than the corresponding tense ones, and labiopalatals are more susceptible than 'pure' palatals. In each case the more susceptible is the less palatal.

But it should be noted here that even though their categorizations are based on physical realities, the phonological features in terms of which processes are specified are mental categories—not just physical scales. For example, labiality in vowels is a feature which corresponds to an articulatory gesture of constricting the lips. Different labial vowels differ in degree of constriction, and there are phonological processes which are sensitive to this difference: less labial vowels are more susceptible to delabialization, less likely to cause assimilative labialization or dissimilative delabialization of adjacent segments, etc. But these processes are not applied as if labiality were a simple physical scale corresponding directly to degree of lip constriction. Instead, processes which depend on degree of labiality depend on height (higher labial vowels are more constricted than the corresponding lower ones), *or* on tenseness (tense labial vowels are more constricted than the corresponding lax ones), or both. To cite just one example: mid (and presumably tense) [ō] unrounded in one language (IE *ō > Sanskrit ā) where no high vowels unrounded, but high lax [ʊ] unrounded in another (English [ʊ] → [ʌ]) where no tense vowels unrounded. One might be tempted to hypothesize that IE *[ō] was less rounded than *[ʊ], but that English [ʊ] was less rounded than [ō]. But categorical differentiations of this sort in the application of processes occur so often that we are drawn to the conclusion that processes are not dependent on purely physical characteristics, but rather on our mental categorizations of these physical characteristics. If it were otherwise, processes would apply regardless either of their perceptual or of their articulatory consequences, since it is in the mental categorizations of sounds that their double nature is unified.

Speech styles vary, and speech is used with different degrees of attention and emotion. Consequently, different degrees of difficulty—and different *kinds* of difficulty—are tolerated in different situations or settings. Processes may be optional—they may apply or not depending on the setting, and if they apply, their input classes may expand or contract (within the patterns set up by the implicational restrictions) depending on the setting (cf. Zwicky 1972a, Dressler 1972).

2.3 *Constraints on process application.* The varying applications of a natural process from language to language, from child to child, from time to time, or style to style, reveal, when compared, the implicational hierarchies along which a natural process may be limited. Although processes are universal, they do not, of course, apply identically in all situations.

It is the constraints his language imposes on processes, rather than the processes themselves, that a child must learn. The mysterious perfection of this childhood learning remains a mystery, but we can hope to make the task seem slightly less awesome by pointing out that most phonological alternations and restrictions are motivated by the nature of the learner rather than the language and do not involve the cognitive burden implied by the distributional analyses and evaluation criteria of modern phonological theory. The German child does not have to learn to devoice all and only the class of word-final obstruents, nor does the Vietnamese child have to learn to avoid coining words that end in voiced obstruents: these are natural restrictions. For a minority of languages, including English, children must learn to pronounce words with voiced final obstruents. This is obviously not easy, but it is something which obviously can be accomplished by children.

The mechanism of learning in natural phonology is simply described: the learner must master certain inputs of natural processes, as required by the words of his language. The child who learns to say the [g] of *hug* instead of devoicing it, even if only conditionally, also can say the [g] of *bug* under the same conditions. Elizabeth, for a while, could pronounce these only with release; unreleased varieties remained voiceless. At the same time she continued to devoice the palatal affricate [ǰ] as in *orange*. We would say that she had *limited* devoicing to unreleased or palatal obstruents. To use the current notation:

$$\begin{bmatrix} + \text{obs} \\ \left\{ \begin{matrix} - \text{rel} \\ + \text{pal} \end{matrix} \right\} \end{bmatrix} \longrightarrow [- \text{voice}] / \underline{\quad\quad} \#$$

Had she now stopped devoicing *any* obstruents, we would say she had suppressed the process. However, so far she has overcome invariable devoicing only in anterior unreleased stops, as in *tub, bed;* unreleased [g] is still devoiced, and so is [j]:

$$
\left[\begin{array}{c} + \text{obs} \\ \left\{ \begin{array}{l} \left[\begin{array}{l} - \text{rel} \\ (- \text{ant}) \end{array} \right] \\ [+ \text{pal}] \end{array} \right\} \end{array} \right] \longrightarrow \text{id.}
$$

That is, she has *variably* limited the devoicing of unreleased stops to posterior ones as in *hug.*

Obstruents are difficult to voice because they impede the airflow required to vibrate the vocal folds. The more impedance, the more difficulty, along several parameters: nonrelease and palatality offer greater impedance due to intrinsically greater duration; posteriority due to the smaller air-chamber between articulator and glottis; there are others, but this should suffice to illustrate the phonetic basis of the various hierarchies of applicability of a process like devoicing.

Because 'degree of difficulty' may depend on several different factors and each process may consequently be subject to several applicability hierarchies, the gradual suppression or limitation of a process may require considerable complexity in the statement of consecutive stages. But naturalness is a matter of phonetic motivation, not formal simplicity. Thus we find that the complex process statements of variationist literature (Labov 1972, Bailey 1974, etc.), are due, in fact, to the complexity of natural processes. Clearly, the view that phonetic change by 'generalization' (Halle 1962, Kiparsky 1965, 1968b, Chomsky and Halle 1968: chapter 6, King 1969b) consists in the simplification of the feature specifications of processes is easily falsified. In English, vowels which are [+tense, −low] are diphthongized (*see, say, sue, sow*); in the southern U.S. this is generalized to all [+tense] vowels (including the low vowels of *sad* [saɛd] and *saw* [sɒɔ]). So far, so good. The problem is that there are many southern speakers who diphthongize only one of the low tense vowels, saying for example [sæd] and [sɒɔ]. This is clearly an intermediate dialect, but the process input here is formally more complex than either the southern or the northern process: [+tense, {−low, +round}]. Failure to limit a process in precisely the same fashion as an earlier generation may yield a simpler process—or it may yield a more complex or variable one. It is not the form of the process, but its function, that matters.

2.4 *Types of processes.* According to a traditional but well-evidenced typology, there are *three* main types of processes, each with distinct functions:

(a) *Prosodic processes* map words, phrases, and sentences onto prosodic structures, rudimentary patterns of rhythm and intonation. Insofar as syllabicity, stress, length, tone, and phrasing are not given in the linguistic matter, they are determined by the prosodic mapping, which may most easily be described as an operation in real-time speech processing of which setting sentences to verse or music are special cases. (Stampe 1973b, and compare Goldsmith's paper and references, in this volume.) The application of prosodic processes is the most important factor in the living phonological pattern of a language and its long-range phonological 'drift'; the selection of segmental processes is largely determined, even in childhood, by the way segmental representations are mapped onto prosodic structure in speech (Major 1977, Stampe and Donegan forthcoming). However, since the remainder of our discussion is mostly concerned with segmental issues, we must turn to the processes which govern segments.

(b) *Fortition processes* (also called centrifugal, strengthening, paradigmatic) intensify the salient features of individual segments and/or their contrast with adjacent segments. They invariably have a perceptual teleology, but often incidentally make the segments they affect more pronounceable as well as more perceptible. Dissimilations, diphthongizations, syllabifications, and epentheses are fortition processes. Some fortition processes may apply regardless of context, but they are particularly favored in 'strong' positions, applying especially to vowels in syllable peaks and consonants in syllable onsets, and to segments in positions of prosodic prominence and duration. Similarly, they apply in situations and styles where perceptibility is highly valued: attentive, formal, expressive, and lento speech.

(c) *Lenition processes* (also called centripetal, weakening, syntagmatic) have an exclusively articulatory teleology, making segments and sequences of segments easier to pronounce by decreasing the articulatory "distance" between features of the segment itself or its adjacent segments. Assimilations, monophthongizations, desyllabifications, reductions, and deletions are lenition processes. Lenition processes tend to be context-sensitive and/or prosody-sensitive, applying especially in 'weak' positions, e.g., to consonants in 'blocked' and syllable-final positions, to short segments, unstressed vowels, etc. They apply most widely in styles and situations which do not demand clarity (inattentive, intimate, and 'inner' speech) or which make unusual demands on articulation (e.g. rapid tempos).

The fortition/lenition distinction, under various names, is a traditional one in diachronic phonetics. Due to its teleological character it has played no systematic role in modern phonology. But it is indispensable in any attempt at explanation, because almost every phonological process has a corresponding process with exactly opposite effects. For example:

(2) (f) After nasals, before spirants, a stop is inserted homorganic to the nasal and of the same voicing as the spirant, e.g., [sɛn(t)s] *sense,* [bæn(d)z] *bans.*

(l) Stops after homorganic nasals before spirants (etc.) are deleted, e.g. [sɛn(t)s] *cents,* [bæn(d)z] *bands.*

(3) (f) Pretonic resonants are syllabified, e.g. [prɛi̯d] *prayed* → [pr̩ɛi̯d] (emphatic).

(l) Pretonic syllables are desyllabified, e.g., [pr̩ɛi̯d] *parade* → [prɛi̯d] (casual).

(4) (f) Achromatic syllabics assume a color (palatal/labial) opposite that of their off-glides, e.g., [ɑe̯] *I* → [ɒe̯] (Cockney), [ʌu̯] *oh* → [ɛu̯] (affected RP British, occasional U.S.).

(l) Achromatic syllabics assume the same color as their off-glides, e.g., [ɑe̯] *I* → [ae̯], [ʌu̯] *oh* → [o].

Here we have (2) insertion/deletion, (3) syllabification/desyllabication, (4) dissimilation/assimilation in identical contexts, but in each case the fortition (f) typically accompanies strong articulation and the lenition (l) weak. The vowel substitutions in (4) typically accompany longer (f) versus shorter (l) pronunciations, as in [gɛ:u̯] *go,* [gʌ·u̯z] *goes,* [gɑɪŋ] *going.* The causalities of the (f) and (l) processes are opposite, reflecting respectively the clarity versus ease principles of traditional phonology.

2.5 *Processes and rules.* It is not the case that all phonological alternations are governed by natural phonological processes. The principles which underlie alternations which are not process-governed—like 'Velar Softening,' 'Tri-syllabic Laxing,' etc.—we refer to as phonological rules. The real nature of such rules is not entirely clear to us, but it *is* clear that they differ from natural processes in many important respects.

First, and most importantly, processes have synchronic phonetic motivation and represent real limitations on speakers' productions. Rules lack current phonetic motivation; they are sometimes the historical result of 'fossilized' or conventionalized processes which have lost such motivation (cf. Baudouin's paleophonetic alternations [1895])—German umlaut is an example. On the other hand, processes *lack* positive semantic or grammatical functions, which some rules (like umlaut) do have. (Processes may of course have the negative effect of neutralizing semantically relevant phonological distinctions (*latter/ladder*).)

Processes are 'innate' in the sense that they are natural responses to innate limitations or difficulties; we pronounce *profound* [profãǫ̃nd] rather than *[profaǫnd] because we *can't* say the latter without acquiring greater velar precision. But since there is no phonetic reason for saying [profʌndɪti] instead of *[profãǫ̃ndɪti], we must say the former simply by convention—because that's what other speakers say: rules are learned.

Processes apply involuntarily and unconsciously, and are brought to one's consciousness only negatively, by confrontation with pronunciations which do not conform to the process, as in second language acquisition. Even the causes of a process may be quite unavailable to consciousness; they may consist in allophonic differences the speaker is quite unaware of. Rules, although they may become habitual and therefore involuntary and unconscious in their application, are formed through the observation of linguistic differences of which the speaker is or was necessarily conscious.

Processes not only govern alternations—they represent constraints on our pronunciations and can be violated only if the speaker makes a special effort (and sometimes not even then). Rules only govern alternations; they often tolerate phonetic exceptions: pronunciations like [æftn̩] *Afton* and [bɒstn̩] *Boston* violate the rule which deletes the /t/'s of *soften, fasten,* etc., but the alternation is nevertheless quite regular for the morphological construction to which it does apply.

Processes apply to tongue-slips, as noted above (2.1), to Pig Latins, to foreign words, etc. (Stampe 1973a). Rules do not ordinarily apply in these cases. This leaves open the question of whether rules in fact *apply* in speech production.

Processes can't be borrowed, any more than speech impediments can be borrowed. If a process in the loaning language produces frequent alternations in vocabulary which is borrowed into another language, and if certain morphological conditions are satisfied, the borrowers may formulate a rule corresponding roughly to the process in the loaning language. But it is merely a rule, and has none of the properties of a process except those of superficial resemblance (cf. Lovins 1974).

Processes may be optional (variable) or obligatory. Rules, on the other hand, seem always to be obligatory. Apparently, the entirely conventional nature of rules exempts them from the phonetic pressures (toward ease or clarity) of style and tempo variation. Since a rule's application has no phonetic value, rules are no more or less likely to apply in any given style, no matter what its phonetic demands.

Constraints on admissible forms in a language are either phonetically motivated or not. Forms which violate phonetic constraints, e.g., [bnɪk], [bax] *Bach*, [vɛ̃] *vin*, [dhobi], [sphoṭa] etc., are typically adjusted to correspond to these constraints by the phonological processes of the language. Forms which are inadmissible for other reasons—typically accidental or historical—although they are rarely chosen when speakers coin new terms, are adopted without change: e.g., [bwɪk], *Houck, Cowper, Sharnk,* etc. This is because there are no processes active in the language to provide substitute pronunciations in the latter case; other forms the speaker has learned have taught him to pronounce these. (As is suggested by our explanation of [bnɪk] versus [blɪk], being able to say [brɪk] entails being able to say [bwɪk], [r] being less sonorous than [w].)

3. DERIVATIONS[9]

In this section we turn to the interactions of processes with each other and with rules. (We have nothing to say here about interactions of rules with each other.) For purposes of discussion we use the taxonomy of interactions of Kiparsky (1968b) of *feeding/counterfeeding* and *bleeding/counterbleeding,* which is presented in many other works.[10]

3.1 *Feeding and counterfeeding.* Because of their specificity, when processes repair one sort of unpronounceability, they sometimes create another. In such cases other processes in turn repair these secondary unpronounceabilities, until a pronounceable representation is obtained. For example, we have the processes

(5) Elision of nasals before homorganic (tautosyllabic) (voiceless) consonants, e.g. [mɛnt] *meant* → [mɛ̃t]—also with regressive nasalization.[11]

(6) Flapping of intervocalic syllable-final apical stops, e.g. [ðætæpl] *that apple* → [ðæɾæpl], [bætɨd] *batted* → [bæɾɨd].

(7) Progressive nasalization of (tautosyllabic) sonorants in unstressed syllables after nasalized segments, e.g., [sɪgnɨl] *signal* → [sɪgnɨ̃l].

Each of these processes 'feeds' the next, in turn, in the processing of a phrase like [plæntɪt] *plant it* → [plæ̃tɪt] → [plæ̃ɾɪt] → [plæ̃ɾɪ̃t]. If it were otherwise, the functions of flapping and nasalization would be realized only on basic representations and not on derivative ones.

The hypothetical intermediate steps, which are necessary to explain the pronunciation given,[12] also occur as variant pronunciations in their own right: Zwicky (1972a) cites [plæ̃ntɪt ∼ plæ̃ɾɪ̃t], Stampe (1973a) [plæ̃ɾɪt] ∼ [plæ̃ɾɪ̃t]. Even in speakers who invariably say [plæ̃ɾɪ̃t], intermediate representations can be brought to light in speech situations which block any of the processes; e.g., in secret languages like Ob or Alfalfa which infix [áb] or [ǽlf] before each syllabic, *plant it* is [plɑbɪntàbɪt]; in singing, it is often [plæ̃.ɾɪt]. The sequentiality of substitutions like this is confirmed by the fact that no process affects derivative representations unless the process which would create them actually applies; when nasal elision is not applied, or is blocked as in Ob, flapping never applies: (*[plæ̃nɾɪt]).

But there exist speakers who, though they regularly flap basically intervocalic [t] as in *pat it,* do not flap the derivatively intervocalic [t] of [plæ̃tɪt] *plant it.* They apply flapping but constrain it not to apply in sequence after nasal elision. (This is called 'counter-feeding' application: flapping is counterfed by nasal elision.) Such non-universal constraints are relatively common, though Koutsoudas et al. (1971), Vennemann (1974c), Hooper (1976) and others, on various *a prioristic* grounds, have denied their existence.[13] Although no doubt some examples in the literature actually can be predicted on universal principles (as in 3.2), and others are of dubious synchronic status, many examples, like the present one, seem unavoidable. This seems all the clearer from the existence of single speakers, like ourselves, with sequenced application ([plæ̃ɾɪ̃t]) in informal styles varying with nonsequenced ([plæ̃tɪt]) in formal styles, while basically intervocalic [t]'s are almost invariably flapped: *pat it* is [pærɪt], not *[pætɪt]. Additional examples (cf. also Bailey 1974) will appear below.

We speak of counterfeeding as a *constraint* because, even for speakers with stylistic variation, representations derived from counterfeeding application, like [plǽtɪt], are more difficult to say than those from feeding, like [plǽɾ̃ɪt]. The difference is not so marked as between [pætɪt] and [pærɪt] *pat it,* but it is a difference of the same sort—a difference in phonetic difficulty. If flapping of intervocalic [t] has a phonetic motivation (and this can scarcely be doubted), then so does its extension to derivatively intervocalic [t]'s.

Kiparsky (1971) also noted the exceptional character of pronounciations derived by counterfeeding and hypothesized that this makes counterfed processes more difficult to discover (more 'opaque') than fed processes, and so explains the diachronic tendency for counterfeeding to be replaced by feeding. This hypothesis makes sense only if, as is assumed in conventional theories, processes in fact must be discovered. But even if there were any evidence to support that view, we cannot see how the difficulty one might have encountered, as a child, in learning (for example) when to flap could explain *synchronic* variation between counterfeeding in formal speech and feeding in informal, or how it could explain why representations derived by counterfeeding are invariably harder to *pronounce* than those derived by feeding.

As Stampe had already argued (1968b, 1969, cf. 1973a), all these facts, synchronic as well as developmental and diachronic, are accommodated by the theory that the unconstrained application of processes, singly or in concert, is *phonetically* motivated. It is not the processes, but constraints on the processes, which must be acquired. The constraints, however, are equally well motivated, in that they all bring speech closer to its phonological intention. Suppressing the application of a process to the output of another, e.g., not applying flapping to the output of nasal-elision (saying [plǽtɪt] instead of [plǽɾ̃ɪt] for *plant it*), like suppressing its application altogether, e.g., not applying flapping at all (saying [pætɪt] instead of [pærɪt] for *pat it*), lets this much of the phonological intention (the [t], in these examples) manifest itself in actual speech. Constraints of either sort typically prevent the merger of phonologically distinct representations (e.g. of *plant it* with *plan it* [plǽɾ̃ɪt], *pat it* with *pad it* [pærɪt]). Of course, this clarity that phonological constraints afford is achieved only by an expenditure of phonetic effort, and it may be sacri-

ficed in less formal styles and less conservative dialects. In formal situations, and for conservative speakers, however, the unconstrained productions may be perceived as careless, inarticulate, or uneducated.

The recognition that constrained as well as unconstrained application
of processes is motivated (cf. Donegan 1973b, Kaye 1974, Chen 1972,
Kisseberth 1976) was slow to come because it was assumed that constrained applications are due to historical accident, and that only the
relaxations of constraints (generalization, change to feeding application)
are motivated. In particular, it was assumed that processes (or rules) are
applied in an order which, unless 'restructuring' occurred, reflected the
historical chronology of the processes as sound changes (Halle 1962,
Kiparsky 1968b, King 1969). As Bloomfield, who also experimented with
ordered-process descriptions (1939), noted, this assumption has been
implicit in the methodology of internal reconstruction since the Neo-
Grammarians developed it. If changes of the synchronic order of processes are in the direction counterfeeding to feeding, then, by the ordering
theory, any counterfeeding application must reflect the original chronology, i.e., an older process counterfed by a younger feeding process.

However, there are counterfeeding derivations in which the counterfed process is the younger, where (to continue using the terms of the
ordering theory) rather than going to the end of the line of processes, the
newcomer has slipped into line ahead of an older feeding process. In
her LSA paper "Southern Discomfort" (1974), Donegan cited record-
ings of several generations of speakers of the Great Smoky Mountains.
Younger speakers have processes, usually variable (and thus unquestionably synchronic), assimilating a mid glide to its syllabic, so that [aǫ]
→ [aː], as in *house* [haǫs ∼ haːs], *plow,* etc., and diphthongizing [ɒː] to
[aǫ] (via [ɒǫ]), as in *saw* [sɒː ∼ sɒǫ ∼ saǫ], *dog,* etc. These are always
applied in counterfeeding order: even in six-year-olds the diphthongized
[aǫ] is never re-monophthongized by glide-assimilation to [aː]: *saw* is
never *[saː], *dog* never *[daːg], etc. In the ordering theory, this situation
could only arise if the counterfed process ([ɒː] → [aǫ]) had entered the
language before the feeding process ([aǫ] → [aː]). But records of older
speakers indicate that the chronological order was the opposite: most
older speakers diphthongized [ɒː], but monophthongization of [aǫ] is
rare in older speech.

Let us cite a more accessible example. English speakers from an
ancient date have had the process:

(8) Apical stops become homorganic to following (tautosyllabic)

stops, e.g. [hændpɪkt] *hand-picked* → *[hænbpɪkt] → [hæmbpɪkt],
and note the inadmissibility of words like *[hænb].

The following younger process also applies in many dialects:

(9) Palatal syllabics [æ, ɛ, ɪ] become resp. [æe̩, ɛi̩, ɪi̩] before tautosyllabic [š, ŋ, g], e.g. [bæŋ] *bang* → [bæe̩ŋ], [fɪš] *fish* → [fɪi̩š],
[lɛg] *leg* → [lɛi̩g]. (The generality of the input and context varies
by dialect.)

Now, given their chronology, (8) should feed (9), so that, e.g.,
[mænkɑend] *mankind,* if pronounced with stop assimilation ([mæŋ-
kɑend]), should also undergo vowel assimilation to [mæe̩ŋkɑend]. Some
speakers *do* use such feeding-derived pronunciations, at least in informal
styles; but most speakers, even those who find it difficult to pronounce
bang without the transitional glide, feel that [mæe̩ŋkɑend] sounds careless and say [mæŋkɑend] instead. Examples like these show that phonological conservatism can motivate counterfeeding constraints. Since we
have argued that phonetic limitations motivate feeding, we must conclude
that the synchronic interactions of processes have nothing whatever to do
with their history.

Furthermore, we know of no evidence supporting the related assumption of a phonology as a linearly ordered list of processes (or rules) such
that a given phonological phrase undergoes each applicable process in
turn, and no process applies more than once (Halle 1962, Chomsky
and Halle 1968). Sequenced substitutions can be explained simply as
the effect of processes applied wherever they are phonetically motivated,
without recourse to ordering (Stampe 1969, 1973a, S. Anderson 1969,
1974, Koutsoudas et al. 1971). Chomsky and Halle themselves (1968)
cited examples—though they did not grasp their significance—which
demonstrate clearly that processes apply more than once, namely processes which feed themselves. Some examples have appeared in our
discussion, e.g. sonorant nasalization, both progressive (7) and regressive (1), and apical stop assimilation (8). The device Chomsky and
Halle proposed to account for such examples (applying the process to
strings of susceptible segments simultaneously) disregards the standard
arguments for recognizing sequenced substitutions, and it cannot cope
with the contingencies of optional application. For example, regressive
sonorant nasalization is obligatory only within syllables, and we there-

fore have such complex patterns of pronounceability (unstarred) in derivatives as *[kær.ɨ.lɨ̃n] *Carolyn* → *[kær.ɨ.lɨ̃n] → [kær.ɨ.ĺɨn] → [kær.ɨ̃.lɨ̃n] → *[kær.ɨ̃.lɨ̃n] → [kæ̃ɾ.ɨ̃.lɨ̃n]. On the iterative interpretation of processes, such examples are precisely accounted for by the simple statement 'nasalize sonorants before (tautosyllabic) nasals.' (For detailed discussion cf. Stampe op. cit., S. Anderson 1969, 1974, Dell 1970, Morin and Friedman 1971, Kenstowicz and Kisseberth 1973, among others.) Furthermore, Stampe (1969, 1973a), S. Anderson (1969, 1974), and Newton (1971) have presented examples of processes applying nonconsecutively more than once in a single phrase (AXA) and applying in different sequences in different phrases (AB/BA).

Most of those who take feeding to be unordered application seem to take counterfeeding (if they accept its existence) to be an ordering constraint on *pairs* of processes, of the form 'B may not succeed A', where B is the (counter)fed and A the feeding process. This presupposes that processes must apply in sequence. But this is not the only possible explanation of feeding. *If processes can apply and re-apply iteratively, then feeding must result even if all processes apply simultaneously.* This would mean that distinct processes apply in the same way as subprocesses of a single process, which are generally accepted to apply simultaneously.

Counterfeeding, on this view, might be a constraint against iterating the counterfed process. Such a constraint on flapping (6), for example, would allow it to apply to basic representations like [pætɪt] *pat it,* but not to derivative representations like [plæ̃tɪt] from [plæntɪt] *plant it.* Interpreting counterfeeding as a constraint on iteration differs empirically from interpreting it as a constraint on order, whether linear or 'local' (pairwise), in that it predicts that if a process is counterfed with regard to one feeding process it will be counterfed with regard to all others. For example, if one uses the pronunciation [plæ̃tɪt], with flapping inapplicable to intervocalic [t] derived by nasal-elision, then one should also use the pronunciation [fɛu̯tɪt] for [fɛltɪt] *felt it,* with intervocalic [t] derived by lateral-vocalization, rather than the pronunciation [fɛu̯ɾɪt]; if [t] and [ɾ] vary in *plant it,* they should vary in *felt it;* and if only [ɾ] occurs in *plant it,* only [ɾ] should occur in *felt it.* Likewise, the vowel assimilation process (9), if it is counterfed by stop assimilation (8), giving [mæŋkɑe̯nd] rather than [mæe̯ŋkɑe̯nd] for *mankind,* is also counterfed by the palatalization process in [pæsju] *pass you* → [pæsju] (not *[pæe̯šju]); but speakers who do use the 'fed' pronunciation [pæe̯šju] also say [mæe̯ŋkɑe̯nd]. Stampe (1973a:ch. 2) cited some cases of this sort; for example, speakers (like Stampe) who unexceptionally raise basically prenasal [ɛ]

to [ɪ], as in [pɪn] *pen* (homophonous with *pin*), [ǰɪm] *gem* (homophonous with *gym*), but do not raise [ɛ] in e.g., [lɛmi] *lemme* (from
[lɛtmi] *let me* via [lɛʔmi]), where it is derivatively pre-nasal vio glottal-
deletion, also never raise [ɛ] which is derivatively pre-nasal via regressive
nasalization (e.g. [sɛmn̩ti], from [sɛvn̩ti] *seventy*) or via vowel and flap
elision ([lɛmaọt], from [lɛɨmaọt], from [lɛɾɨmaọt], from [lɛtɨmaọt] *let 'em
out*).

Ordering theories, whether linear (e.g. Kiparsky op. cit.) or local
(Anderson op. cit.), not only do not explain such cases, they do not even
envision them. Consequently the question of whether a process can be
simultaneously fed by one process and counterfed by another has not,
to our knowledge, previously been raised.[14] We have been unable to find
a single such example. Instead, we find many examples, of which the
above are a small sample, where, whether a process is fed, or counterfed,
or variably fed ∼ counterfed, it has this relation to all other relevant
processes.

The most straightforward explanation seems to be that feeding, counterfeeding, and variable feeding represent iterative, noniterative, and variably iterative application of single processes, under the hypothesis that
all processes apply simultaneously with all others. A noniteration constraint on a process would prevent it from applying to the output of any
other process. Such a constraint would pertain to a particular process,
without specific reference to other processes, just like any other kind of
constraint.

3.2 *Precedence.* We turn now to further relations of processes, the first
of which is the 'bleeding'/'counterbleeding' contrast. Process B is 'bled'
by process A if there are representations to which both A and B are applicable but A's application changes these so that B is not applicable.
This can occur only if the application of A precedes that of B. If B
precedes A, or if A and B apply simultaneously, then B is not bled (is
'counterbled') by A, and both apply. Kiparsky (1968b) argued that
counterbleeding is natural, historically replacing bleeding. So also Anderson (1974), who follows Kiparsky's generalization (abandoned by
Kiparsky since 1971) that maximal application (hence feeding and
counterbleeding) is natural. Stampe (1973a) pointed out, however, that
maximal application is not self-explanatory, and that if it is understood
as phonetically motivated, it would only explain feeding, not counterbleeding: whereas counterfeeding fails to eliminate derivative unpro-

nounceabilities (3.1), neither bleeding nor counterbleeding fails in this regard.

Koutsoudas et al. (1971) had argued, in fact, that bleeding applications do not occur at all, and had proposed that processes apply simultaneously, where possible. Their proposals are made in the framework of a theory that the 'order of application' of processes is universally determined (cf. Koutsoudas 1976 and references). Vennemann (1974c) and Hooper (1976) and some others have assumed variants of this position. We have argued that this is clearly wrong in the case of feeding/counterfeeding examples like those in 3.1. Koutsoudas et al. presented convincing reanalyses of most of the putative bleeding applications in Kiparsky's examples of bleeding-to-counterbleeding changes. To account for other cases they proposed various universal precedence principles, such as Proper Inclusion Precedence (a process whose input is properly included in the input of another precedes the other), Obligatory Precedence (an obligatory process precedes an optional one, cf. Ringen 1972), etc., with various seniorities. We lack space for examples, and will instead give a counterexample:

(10) (a) Pretonic sonorants are optionally syllabified, e.g., [prɛi] *pray* → [pr̥ɛi̯] or [pɨrɛi̯] *pr-ay!* (3f).

   (b) [r] obligatorily becomes a flap [ɾ] after tautosyllabic [θ], e.g. [θri] *three* → [θɾi].

Here (b) should precede (a) on grounds both of Proper Inclusion and Obligatory precedence, but in fact (a) bleeds (b): [θri] *three* → [θɨri] *thr-ee!*, not *[θɨɾi]. It is probably impossible to refute any precedence hypothesis: when we propose an alternative to account for (10), as we will do in (3.2.1), all we have done is to 'bump' the others into positions of lesser seniority. It is the explanatory value of the hypotheses, not merely their empirical, predictive value, which matters. But Koutsoudas et al. have argued exclusively from empirical grounds.[15]

Kenstowicz and Kisseberth (1971) presented many examples of bleeding interactions, most of them resembling (10), and on the strength of these Kiparsky (1971) revised his original position that counterbleeding is the natural interaction, proposing instead that counterbleeding is opaque: for example, in the counterbled pronunciation of *three*, *[θɨɾi], the conditions under which [r] is flapped are obscured by the intrusive [ɨ]. As argued in 3.1, this is no explanation if the counterbled process is not learned, and [r]-flapping after [θ] is certainly not a rule.

If processes apply simultaneously, the result is counterbleeding. Examples are legion:

(11) Regressive nasalization (1) is not bled by nasal-elision (5): [kænt] *can't* → [kæ̃t], not *[kæt].

(12) [t]-flapping (6) is not bled by desyllabification of a following syllabic: [šætɾɪŋ] *shattering* → [šæɾrɪŋ], not *[šætrɪŋ]; contrast [pætrɪk] *Patrick*.

(13) Nor is flapping bled by syncope of a following syllabic: [pʊtɨtɨwεi̯] *put it away* → [pʊɾtɨwεi̯] (→ [pʊdtɨwεi̯]), not *[pʊttɨwεi̯].

(14) Pre-nasal [ε]-raising (3.1) is not bled by nasal-elision (5), e.g. [sɪ̃t] *sent* (cf. [sɪnd] *send*), not *[sε̃t].

It is significant that the bleeding pronunciations do not seem even remotely possible (learnable) as variants—[šætrɪŋ] for *shattering,* for example, seems pronounceable only in a style or dialect in which flapping does not apply at all. This is in striking contrast to the feeding relations of 3.1, where counterfeeding variants do seem possible even to those who do not use them. And whereas feeding/counterfeeding variation is commonplace in synchronic, diachronic, and developmental phonology, we are not aware of a single good example of counterbleeding/bleeding variation. (Lee [1975–76] has independently observed the non-occurrence of bleeding/counterbleeding variation.) In this respect, therefore, we agree with Koutsoudas et al. (1971) that there is no possibility of extrinsic constraints on processes which are counterbled or bled. Bleeding occurs, we think, only as an incidental result of universal precedence principles.[16] We turn to two of these which are independently evidenced by other relations besides bleeding.

3.2.1 *Fortitions first, lenitions last.* The application of all fortition processes precedes that of all lenition processes. In discussing the fortition/lenition distinction (2.4), we noted that these processes tend to apply in complementary styles. However, many derivations conjoin fortitions and lenitions.

(15) Nasal-elision (5) occurs only before homorganic consonants, e.g., [læmp] → [læ̃p] *lamp,* [tεnθ] → [tε̃θ] *tenth,* but [wɔrmθ] *warmth* does not become [wɔ̃r̃θ]. However, when a stop is inserted (2f), the elision then occurs: [wɔ̃r̃mθ] → [wɔ̃r̃mpθ] → [wɔ̃r̃pθ].

(16) Various dialects have variable fortitions [ʊu̞] → [ɨu̞] → [ɪu̞] → [iu̞], e.g. [tʊu̞] ~ [tiu̞] *two,* and/or the variable lenitions [iu̞] → [iy] (or [yu̞]) → [yy̞], e.g. [viu̞] ~ [vyy̞] *view.* Where these co-occur, the processes link to give [tyy̞] *two,* rhyming with [vyy̞] *view* (Donegan 1978).

(17) The fortitions of (16), or their counterparts in [nɔu̞] ~ [nɛu̞] *no,* [nɑo̞] ~ [nao̞] *now,* feed the assimilative palatalization of velars, as in [kʊu̞l] ~ [ciu̞l] *cool,* [gɔu̞] ~ [ɟɛu̞] *go,* [kɑo̞] ~ [cao̞] *cow.*

In these examples fortitions feed lenitions. We have observed no styles or dialects, however, in which the lenitions are counterfed, so that, for example, [læp] *lamp* co-occurs with [wɔ̃ɾmpθ] *warmth* (15), [tʊu̞] ~ [tiu̞] *two* with [viu̞] ~ [vyy̞] *view* (16), or [ciu̞] *cue* with [kiu̞] *coo* (17), and, unlike the counterfeeding pronunciations cited in 3.1, these strike us as not just difficult but impossible to master.

There are many instances of fortitions counterfed by lenitions, for example:

(18) Casual-speech syncope, e.g., [sɪnɨstɾ̩] ~ [sɪnstɾ̩] *sinister,* [tɪmɨθi] ~ [tɪmθi] *Timothy,* never feeds the stop-insertion of (2f): *[sɪntstɾ̩], contrast [spɪn(t)stɾ̩] *spinster;* *[tɪmpθi], contrast [ɟɪm(p)sn̩] *Jimson.*

(19) Tensing of palatal or labial vowels in hiatus, e.g., [i] (not [ɪ]) in *various, reality, idea,* [u] (not [ʊ]) in *graduate, duet, suet,* etc., does not apply to vowels put into hiatus by a lenition process, e.g., the allegro deletion of flaps: [dɪɾɨt] *did it* ~ [dɪit] not *[diɨt], [wʊɾɨt] *would it* ~ [wʊit] not *[wuɨt].

Normally, feeding application would be more natural than counterfeeding, but pronunciations like *[tɪmpθi] *Timothy* and *[wuɨt] *would it,* with lenitions feeding fortitions, seem absolutely unnatural.

The following examples, contrasting fortitions and lenitions with identical inputs (20) or outputs (21), are particularly instructive:

(20) In most dialects chromatic vowels before tautosyllabic [r] are laxed, but in some Middle Atlantic dialects (like PJD's native Baltimore) they are tensed: *beer* [bɪr] vs. [bir], *bare* [bɛr] vs. [ber], *bore* [bɔr] vs. [bor], etc. Various lenitions feed the laxing, e.g. [sir] ~ [sɪr] *seer,* [lerɾ] ~ [lɛr] *later,* [lɒnmoɾ] ~ [lɒnmɔr] *lawn mower,* but lenitions never feed the tensing: [bɪrɾ] ~ [bɪr] *bitter,* not *[bir]; [bɛrɾ] ~ [bɛr] *better,* not *[ber].

(21) The essentially context-free diphthongization of [æ] to [æẹ] in the South (referred to in 2.3) for many speakers feeds a dissimilation to [aẹ] and even [ɑẹ], e.g. [baẹd] *bad,* [grɑẹs] *grass.* But assimilative diphthongization of [æ] to [æẹ] (9) never feeds such dissimilations: [bæẹŋ] *bang,* not *[bɑẹŋ]; [hæẹš] *hash,* not *[hɑẹš].*[17]

The principle that fortitions precede lenitions explains all these otherwise aberrant examples.

Many examples of bleeding, which the simultaneous application hypothesis cannot explain, involve a fortition bleeding a lenition. Example (10) falls under the fortition-first principle, since the optional syllabication of sonorants is a fortition and [r]-flapping is a lenition (assimilation to [θ]).

(22) In dialects with palatalization of [t,d] by tautosyllabic [r], e.g. [tru] ∼ [čru] *true,* [drʌŋk] ∼ [jrʌŋk] *drunk,* this process is bled by sonorant syllabification: [tṛu] *tr-ue!,* not *[čṛu]; [dṛʌŋk] *dr-unk!,* not *[jrʌŋk].*[18]

(23) The English [z] and [d] suffixes, as in [hʌgz] *hugs,* [hʌgd] *hugged,* are devoiced after voiceless segments, e.g. [dʌks] *ducks,* [dʌkt] *ducked.* This assimilation is bled by vowel epenthesis after sibilants, e.g., [kɪsɨz] *kisses* (not *[kɪsɨs]), and dentals [nɪtɨd] *knitted* (not *[nɪtɨt]), respectively.[19]

In fact, most of the bleeding examples cited by Kenstowicz and Kisseberth (1971) are of this sort, epentheses bleeding assimilations. They consider the hypothesis that processes altering syllable structure precede processes dependent on syllable structure, but reject it because, for example, the deletion of a vowel or glide normally fails to bleed the assimilation of a consonant to that vowel or glide, as in Japanese [mats(ɯ)] 'wait (for)', [matš(i)kɑmɑerɯ] 'be on the watch (for)', from [mat-] 'to wait (for)'. Since insertions are fortitions, our hypothesis predicts that the former must apply before assimilations.

Deletions are lenitions, however, and under the simultaneity hypothesis (3.1) would not apply before other lenitions (including assimilations) but rather simultaneously. This seems to be borne out in many examples; the following is typical.

(24) The assimilation of vowels to [ŋ] (9), as in [bæẹŋ] *bang* (which does not apply before [k], e.g. [bæk] *back*), is not bled by nasal elision, e.g. [bæ̃ẹ̃k] *bank,* not *[bæ̃k].

Perhaps this is the reason for the different behavior of insertions and deletions that Kenstowicz and Kisseberth observed.[20]

3.2.2 *Rules first, processes last.* Phonological rules (2.5), or, for that matter, all rules of language (syntactic, morphological, secret language, etc.) which are not phonetically motivated, apply before phonological processes. This is a traditional hypothesis, except in the standard generative literature. It is abundantly evidenced, and its phonetic teleology is self-evident. The principle resolves a number of otherwise problematic cases. For example, the rules deriving *obscenity* and *dreamt* from *obscene* and *dream,* apparently lenitions, bleed the fortition processes diphthongizing tense vowels, e.g. [i] → [ɪi̯]. But they are *not* lenitions, because they lack any contemporary phonetic motivation. The same rules feed the dialectal [ɛ]-raising before nasals which we described as counterfed by all other processes, e.g., *obsc*[ɪ]*nity, dr*[ɪ]*mt.*

To take a less obvious example, the contraction of *it is* [ɪtɪz] to [ɪts] *it's* (presumably via [ɪtz]) bleeds flapping ([ɪɾɪz]), rather than applying simultaneously to give *[ɪɾz]. If the rules-first principle is correct, it is probably the case that contraction is not a phonological process. We don't really know *why* it isn't, though we could cite a number of excuses. The question, which is at least in part a question of morphosyntactic principles, transcends our subject matter, and our knowledge.

3.2.3 *Remarks.* Most of the examples in the literature conform to these two principles. The exceptions occur mostly in languages for which we have not had access to speakers. In the past, speaker judgments have rarely been elicited on these issues, but without judgments of negative possibilities (like *[tɪmpθi] for *Timothy*) it is impossible to obtain direct evidence that nonoccurring interactions (like syncope feeding epenthesis) *could* not occur.

The strength of these judgments, and of the independent evidence (2.4–5) on which the rule/process and fortition/lenition distinctions are based, provide strong support for the two precedence principles proposed here. Both principles—that nonphonetic operations yield the last word to phonetically motivated operations and that perceptually motivated operations yield to articulatorily motivated ones—have straightforward phonetic teleologies, and therefore might ultimately provide something more than a description of the facts.

3.3 *On constraints.* In 3.1 counterfeeding was treated as a counter-iteration constraint. Whenever its expository value, counter-iteration is *not* an independently evidenced constraint. Self-feeding processes never are constrained to apply to just one of a string of susceptible segments, e.g. *[hænbpɪkt] *hand-picked,* *[meɪ̃nli] *mainly.* Rather, like all processes, their scope is limited by *phonetic,* including prosodic, conditions.[21] For example, sonorant nasalization (1, 7) is halted only by a nonsonorant segment, or by a syllable or accent-group boundary (2.2).

Counterfeeding is a constraint on the derivational status of susceptible representations. Whereas in feeding (unconstrained application) a process applies to *all* susceptible representations, and in suppression it applies to *none,* in counterfeeding the process applies to all susceptible basic representations but to no derivative ones. If we consider what this implies about a speaker's phonetic capacity, it is easy to see why, as we have argued in 3.1, a process which is counterfed by one process should be counterfed by others. Having learned not to flap an intervocalic [t] in [plæ̃tɪt] *plant it,* one has acquired the capacity to pronounce it in [feutɪt] *felt it* as well.

The question which remains conspicuously unanswered, however, and which is surely behind the lingering skepticism about counterfeeding even in the face of numerous examples, is why, if one can pronounce derivatively intervocalic [t] in *plant it* and *felt it,* should one find it difficult to pronounce basically intervocalic [t] in *hit it?* In fact, mastering a derivative representation ordinarily *does* enable one to pronounce the corresponding basic representation. Speakers who pronounce intervocalic [t] in *plant it* and *felt it* ordinarily can also pronounce it in *hit it,* for example to distinguish this from *hid it.* But such pronunciations are occasional at best, and require special effort which the counterfed representations do not.[22]

The reason, we think, is that at the margins of competence, it is easier to achieve a specific objective by aiming at an objective whose difficulty transcends that of the original. This principle is well known to anyone who has done anything difficult, from playing piano scales rapidly to removing a stuck jar-lid. Consider the example of flapping. If the average American speaker *aims* to say an intervocalic flap, e.g., in imitating the British pronounciation of *hear it,* he usually fails. If he aims at an intervocalic /t/, on the other hand, he normally achieves the flap [ɾ], although even here he occasionally deletes it altogether. If he aims at a long intervocalic /t:/, as in Italian or Japanese, he may achieve a simple [t], though, as teachers of these languages can attest, he occasionally only achieves a flap; a total deletion of this target, however, is not so likely.

Translating this last example into occurring English representations, if the target is /VntV/ or /VltV/, an intervocalic [t] is more likely to result than if the target actually is /VtV/.

This 'Excelsior!' principle is clearly what is, in part, behind such recurrent fortitions as (a) [aǫ] → [aǫ] (e.g. *cow,* general US) → [æǫ] → [eǫ] (recent Baltimore); (b) [aer] → [air] (eg. *ire,* general US) → [ajə] (southern US lowlands) → [aja] (Faroese); (c) [nd] → [nt] (e.g. Yiddish *hint* 'dogs') → [nts] (Bantu), etc. The likelihood of the lenitions (a) [aǫ] → [ɒ] (e.g. *law,* early English), (b) [aer] → [ɑr] (southern US highlands), or (c) [nd] → [nn] (occasional US *candy*) → [n] (*and*) is lessened by increasing, through fortition, the distance between the actual target and the shortfall lenition product. This 'prophylactic' strategy, which students of sound change from Grammont through Martinet have recognized, is another reason why, as we argued in 3.2.1, even synchronic fortitions precede lenitions. To keep *bands* /bændz/ distinct from *bans* /bænz/, we bleed the deletion of [d] by prior fortition of [z]: [bændz̧]; to keep [aǫr] *our* distinct from *are* /ɑr/, we bleed the applicable reductions by prior fortition of [o] and [r]:[auŗ]; and so forth.

It is time to summarize. The model of the natural phonological system presented in 3 can be diagrammed thus:

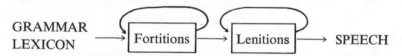

GRAMMAR
LEXICON   →   Fortitions → Lenitions → SPEECH

There are, broadly, three degrees of extrinsic nonphonetic constraint on processes: application to *any* susceptible representation, application to *none* (suppression), and application just to basic representation (counterfeeding).[23] The diagram reflects our conclusion (from examples like (15–17) in 3.2.1) that lenitions cannot be prevented from applying to the output of fortitions.

4. REPRESENTATION.[24]

We now consider, very briefly, the phonological representations which underlie our speech, which we perceive as underlying the speech of others, and which we commit to memory as the phonological forms of the words of our language. We have argued that the phonological processing of what we say is governed by phonetic teleologies. It can be reasoned that the processing of what we hear is a (subconscious) form of teleological analysis, projecting from what is heard to the phonological intentions of the speaker. This analysis is carried out (with some adaptations to the speaker in question) through the same system of processes that governs our own speaking. This is evident from the fact that, when we listen to our own speech, what we perceive is not what we actually say, but precisely what we *intend* to say.[25]

Although Sapir (1921, 1933) pointed out that this intended representation is far more readily brought to consciousness than the 'actual rumble' of speech, it is remarkable that half a century later there is little agreement about the character of phonological representations even in the language of the majority of the world's linguists.

One reason is that the search for phonological unity underlying the superficial phonetic variety of speech started, from the beginning, from two distinct points of departure—phonetics and grammar—and arrived at two distinct (although, before the thirties, not clearly distinguished) conclusions—phonemic and morphophonemic representation. The structuralists approached language 'inductively', from the hearer's (or even the learner's) vantage, and neglected (or even rejected) morphophonemics. The generativists have approached language 'deductively', from the speaker's vantage, and have rejected phonemics.

The other reason for the current disagreement is that in both structural and generative phonology, phonological representation has been treated more as a device for simplifying and generalizing phonological descriptions than as an empirical hypothesis. Until the past decade (Stampe 1968a, Kiparsky 1968a, b, etc.—see Zwicky 1972b for references), evidence independent of the facts under description was virtually never cited. Sapir's psychological reality paper (1933) was ignored by structuralists who rejected morphophonemics, and Twaddell's Old High German umlaut paper (1938), for example, was ignored when the generativists rejected phonemics.[26] From the hearer's vantage, [rẽ́ĩ́rĩ̃ŋ] is unambiguously analyzable as [reɪ̯nɪŋ] *raining*,[27] whereas [reɪ̯rɪ̃ŋ] is ambiguous between [reɪ̯dɪŋ] *raiding* and [reɪ̯tɪŋ] *rating*, in the absence of further, nonphonological information. A purely phonological, or *phonemic,* underlying representation of [rẽ́ĩ́rɪ̃ŋ] and [reɪ̯rɪ̃ŋ] would be /reɪnɪŋ/ and /reɪdɪŋ/, respectively, since all English intervocalic flaps derive unambiguously from stops. But whereas the nasal flap can only derive from a voiced nasal stop (since English lacks voiceless nasal stops), the non-nasal flap might derive from either a voiced or voiceless stop, both of which occur in English and both of which become voiced flaps between vowels (process (6)). Phonological representations distinguishing

|rɛi̯dɪŋ| and |rɛi̯tɪŋ| are called *morphophonemic* because they incor-
porate information derived from other pronunciations of the respective
morphemes, e.g. [rɛi̯dz] *raids* versus [rɛi̯ts] *rates*. Thus *rating* has different representations at three 'levels': phonetic [rɛi̯ɾĩŋ], phonemic
/rɛi̯dɪŋ/, and morphophonemic |rɛi̯tɪŋ|. Structuralist grammars typically
treated phonemic and morphophonemic representations separately.

This English example 'translates' a Russian one from which Halle
(1959) argued that incorporating the phonemic level merely complicates
a phonological description, in that it may require a single process (flapping) to be separated into phonemic ([n] → [ɾ̃]) and morphophonemic
([t] → [ɾ]) parts. Actually the English example is even more complicat-
ing than Halle's Russian one. The immediate output of flapping applied to
[t] is not actually [ɾ] but the voiceless [ɾ̥], which surfaces occasionally
in word-final contexts (e.g. [rɛi̯ɾ̥] *rate*), but which is obligatorily voiced
between voiced segments. Flapping [t] → [ɾ̥] is therefore a phonemic
process, while flap-voicing [ɾ̥] → [ɾ] is morphophonemic (it merges
[rɛi̯ɾ̥ĩŋ] with [rɛi̯ɾĩŋ]). But the phonemic process applies *before* the
morphophonemic process,[28] and therefore the phonemic representation
of *rating*, /rɛi̯dɪŋ/, does not arise at *any* step in its processing.

But Halle attacked a straw man. Phonemic descriptions were never
process descriptions, and they made no attempt to describe the relations
between levels, even *within* the phonemic component of the description,
in terms of processes. Typically the realizations of one phoneme were
listed with their respective contexts (e.g., /n/ = [ɾ̃] between vowels, [˜]
before voiceless homorganic stop, etc.) without systematic cross-reference
to the realizations of other phonemes (e.g. /d/ = [ɾ] between vowels,
[d̪] before /θ/, etc.), regardless of parallels. This is not to say that
phonemicists were unaware of processes. Allophones arising from the
same processes were usually described in the same order and the same
wording under their respective phonemes. But there is nothing in phonemic theory or practice to suggest that a single process might not govern
alternations of allophones in one case and phonemes in another. For
example, the whole point of Twaddell's highly regarded phonemic
analysis of Old High German umlaut (1938), was that this process was
phonemic in some applications but morphophonemic in others. Halle's
argument is totally irrelevant to the status of phonemic representation.

In fact, it is only in the generative theory of 'systematic phonemics'
(Halle op. cit., 1962, Chomsky 1964, Chomsky and Halle 1968) that
phonological representations are supposed to correspond to a specific
point in a list of ordered processes. According to this theory, phonological

representations arise after the application of 'morpheme structure' (or 'phonological redundancy') rules, which govern basic representations, and before the application of proper 'phonological rules', which govern alternations. We have already mentioned examples which falsify this. The constraint against intrasyllabic clusters of stop plus nasal (*|bnɪk|) is due to the obligatory syllabification of the nasal, by the same process that accounts for optional syllabic alternants of liquids or glides, e.g. [blʌɾi] ~ [bl̩ʌɾi] *bloody!*. The constraint against |h| before consonants (cf. OE *hnutu*) is due to the obligatory deletion of the aspirate by the same process that accounts for optional alternants like [hjuj] ~ [juj] *huge*.[29] Further, the constraint against intrasyllabic clusters of voiced and voiceless obstruents (*|sgɪpd|) is due to the same processes that assimilate voicelessness in alternations like [ɪts gɒn] ~ [skɒn] (*It*)'*s gone,* [rɪbd] *ribbed* but [rɪpt] *ripped,* etc. What these examples show is that some processes that govern phonological representation also govern phonetic representation.

There is other evidence against the systematic phonemic theory. Note that according to the conception of levels as corresponding to a point in an ordered list of rules, all morphemes would have phonological representations at the same point in the list of processes. For example, in German, since [ve:k : ve:gə] *Weg : Wege* 'road : roads' and [vɛk : vɛkə] *Weck : Wecke* '(breakfast) roll : rolls' require their phonological representations to be 'prior' to the process devoicing final obstruents, [vɛk] *weg* 'away' also requires a representation prior to devoicing. Since the latter is uninflected, there is no way to determine whether its final obstruent is phonologically voiced, with devoicing by the devoicing process, as in *Weg,* or whether it is phonologically voiceless, as in *Weck.* Therefore the obstruent of *weg* is supposed to be represented as an 'archisegment' phonologically unspecified for voice. W. S–Y. Wang and Stampe (1967, oral interventions on Kiparsky 1968a) pointed out that the development of Eastern Yiddish (Sapir 1915), wherein the devoicing process ceased to apply, argues against this. Medieval German *wec* (*Weg*) and *onwec* (*weg*) became Yiddish *veg* and *avek* and, in general, forms with invariably final obstruents were treated exactly like forms where these alternate with nonfinal voiceless obstruents. The archisegment hypothesis suggests, incorrectly, that they should have become randomly voiced or voiceless.

The idea of incompletely specified phonological segments is a persistent recurrence in descriptive phonology, from Twaddell's 'macrophoneme' (1935), Trubetzkoy's 'archiphoneme' (1969), through Jakobson, Fant, and Halle's blanks in feature matrices (1951), down to generative archisegments (Chomsky and Halle op. cit., Hooper 1976). It began with the structuralist definition of phonemes, according to Saussure (1949), as opposite elements, the sum of their *distinctive* features (Jakobson 1932, Bloomfield 1933), and the observation that in positions of 'neutralization' by this definition there are segments of dilemma, neither distinctively *x* or non-*x*. For example, beside the distinctively voiceless and distinctively voiced stops of *pin* and *bin,* there is the stop of *spin,* which is not *distinctively* voiceless because **sbin* is not admissible. In generative phonology, this problem was simply transferred from phonemic to morphophonemic representations. Only Twaddell seems to have grasped that neutralization is a refutation of the idea that phonemes are oppositive elements.

The single argument that is offered for archisegments—uncertainty—has about as much force as a blindfolded man arguing that it is neither night nor day (or that it is both) because he can't see which it is.[30] In fact there are many ways to ascertain how speakers evaluate such segments. It might be noted that no alphabet provides special symbols for archiphonemes distinct from phonemes. Or that archiphonemes rhyme better with one phoneme than the other: for example, *spin* alliterates perfectly with *s'pose* but not with *s'bbatical* even if they are pronounced alike with [sp]. Or that when the cluster is split up by epenthesis or prothesis in children (e.g. [sɨkul] *school*) or in historical change (e.g. Spanish *escuela*), the stop, removed from the devoicing influence of the [s], shows up as voiceless.[31] Of course, this is precisely what is predicted from the fact that English has a process obligatorily devoicing stops after tautosyllabic voiceless segments, as in the example [skɒn] *(It)'s gone* cited above.

From this example and the example of Yiddish *avek* one might conclude that all processes governing phonetic representation also, in the absence of motivating alternations, govern phonological representation. This would amount to claiming that the basic level of phonological representation is the phonetic level.[32] But there is much evidence against this. For example, the arguments against the archisegmental evaluation of stops after tautosyllabic /s/ show that speakers do not perceive these as a third phonological value distinct from both initial voiceless and voiced stops. But they also show that invariant phonetic values are not necessarily phonological, because stops after /s/ do have, in English, a third phonetic value distinct from those of initial stops. Speakers are, however, totally unconscious of the difference between e.g. initial [kʰ] and non-initial [k], even in alternations like *crunch : scrunch, it's cold : 's cold,* etc. Sapir (1933) provided a similar argument when he pointed out that his Nootka guide wrote *ḥi, ḥu* for the invariant syllables [ḥɛ], [ḥɔ], disregarding the lowering of the vowels by [ḥ]. Therefore, if Sapir's characterization of phonological representation as that which is most readily 'brought to consciousness' is accepted, as we think it must be if the notion is to have any psychological significance, we must conclude that many phonetic features of speech, even though invariant, find no place in our phonological consciousness or memory.

But *which* invariant features are nonphonological? We have already seen that the conventional answer to this question in both structural and generative phonology, that it is the redundant features which are absent from phonological representations, is incorrect: stops after tautosyllabic /s/ are perceived as voiceless despite the fact that this voicelessness is predictable and nondistinctive. Conversely, the vowel of e.g. [kæ̃t] *can't* is perceived as nonnasal even though it is distinctively nasal (contrast [kæt] *cat*). The distinctiveness principle fails left and right. What alternatives are there?

With Sapir, we could understand phonological representation to be the phonological intention (and perceived phonological intention) of speech. We have characterized the natural phonological system as the system of limitations which stand between the intention and the actualization of speech—i.e., between phonological and phonetic representation. The principle of phonological perception must be *naturalness: if a given utterance is naturally pronounceable as the result of a certain intention, then that intention is a natural perception of the utterance* (i.e., a possible phonological representation).

The utterance [spɛ̃t] will illustrate this naturalness principle. We can perceive this as |spɛnt| because if we pronounce |spɛnt|, what we actually say is precisely [spɛ̃t]—nothing in our acquisition of English has taught us *not* to nasalize vowels before nasals (1), or *not* to delete nasals before homorganic voiceless consonants (5). We cannot simply perceive the utterance as |spɛ̃t| because, if we tried to pronounce |spɛ̃t|, what we would actually say is [spɛt]—nothing in our acquisition of English has taught us to pronounce vowels as nasalized on purpose. Our English phonological capacity is dominated by a fortition process which denasalizes all nonstopped segments, including, as in the present instance, vowels. This tendency to denasalize is well known to those who teach French or Hindi to English students, and its natural character is attested by its occurrence in children (e.g., Joan's [ɑts] *ants* [Velten 1943]) and in historical change (e.g., the loss, in Icelandic, of the nasalization of vowels recorded by the First Grammarian in words like *i* 'in'). We do not de-nasalize the [ɛ̃] of *spent,* of course, because fortitions do not follow lenitions (3.2.1).[33]

But why don't we perceive [spɛ̃t] as |sbɛnt|? After all, there is a process which devoices stops after tautosyllabic voiceless segments, and in fact if we try to pronounce |sbɛnt| what we naturally say is [spɛ̃t]. But while we cannot intentionally pronounce |ɛ̃|, English has taught us to pro-nounce |p|, and therefore we have no reason not to take the [p] of [spɛ̃t] at face value.

Or consider the example [bæ̃ɾ̃]. Its face value representation |bæ̃ɾ̃| would be pronounced [bædɾ], since nonstops (including flaps) are de-nasalized, as noted above, while flaps are (simultaneously) stopped. (This fortition is heard in American attempts at the initial [ɾ] of Japanese; it is also heard in children [Edwards 1973: appendix] and in historical change, in fact in some Japanese dialects.) To obtain [bæ̃ɾ̃], therefore, we must aim at |bænɾ|, which regressive and progressive nasalization (1,7) and flapping (6) convert to [bæ̃ɾ̃].

These examples minimally illustrate how, in the analysis of utterances, the naturalness principle establishes a basic level of phonological per-ception, distinguishing features which are phonological from those which are merely phonetic. This level corresponds closely to the phonemic level the structuralists sought to capture.[34] It is an instructive exercise to seek out, in the intrinsic restrictions imposed by the natural phono-logical system, the natural analogues of structuralist analytic criteria, concepts of markedness, implicational laws, and so forth. It is also in-structive to compare natural phonemic analyses, which are typically unique, with the alternative analyses the structuralists debated for English diphthongs, Spanish glides, or more recently, Kabardian vowels. But this must await other times and perhaps other authors.

Here we must be content to point out that, as our examples show, only sounds which pass the muster of the obligatory fortition processes of a language are phonemes. The remainder, optional or lenition-created variants ('allophones') of the phonemes, play a role only in the subcon-scious aspects of perception, and therefore find no direct representation in our morphophonological memories, our formulations of phonological or grammatical rules, our spelling systems, our verbal play, or even our lapses of speech or hearing.

Some of these results are implicit in evidence discussed, to other ends, above; and some are illustrated in Stampe (1973a). Here we will cite just the example of rhyme (Stampe 1968a), which (like alliteration,

Icelandic *hendingar,* Welsh *cynghanedd,* etc.) requires phonemic identity. If pronounced with phonemic identity, *fitter : bidder : hit 'er, scan it :*
plant it, fans : hands, expense : rents, hen : tend, stole : old, mix : sticks :
sixth(s), mess : pest : tests : desks are rhymes, despite their morphophonemic differences. (Of course, rhymes due to casual neutralizations, as
in *hen : tend,* naturally sound correspondingly casual, or even silly, beside those due to obligatory neutralizations, e.g. *hens : tends.*) And unless
morphophonemically identical words are pronounced with phonemic
identity, they do not rhyme: *rolled : ol(d), twined : rin(d), plot them :*
got (th)em, etc. Phonetic identity, moreover, is entirely irrelevant: in
There was a gnat/ upon a cat/ upon a pad/ upon a mat, gnat and *pad* do
not rhyme even if pronounced as [nær] and [pær],[35] whereas *gnat* and *cat*
rhyme perfectly even if pronounced distinctly as [nær] and [kæt] or
[kæʔ]. Only the phonemic identities matter.[36]

Morphophonemic representations certainly exist, of course. [spẽt] can
be perceived, without violations of the naturalness principle, as |sbɛnt|
(It)'s bent as well as |spɛnt|, and [bæ̃r̃] can be perceived as |bæn hr̩|
ban her or |bæntr̩| *banter.* Such perceptions are motivated when a form's
various pronunciations are not *collectively* derivable, through the natural
processes of the language, from their phonemic representations. The
utterances [télɨgræf] *telegraph* and [tɨlégrɨfi] *telegraphy,* phonemically
/tɛlʌgræf/ and /tʌlɛgrʌfi/, require the morphophonemic |tɛlɛgræf| to
derive both from a single representation through the natural process of
vowel reduction. The 'depth' of such representations is an idiosyncratic
matter, as we have argued earlier, varying from form to form.

Phonological representation is best understood not as a level but as
a *kind* of representation, namely the representation of forms in perma-
nent memory. With this conception it is easier to understand why phonological representations do not incorporate sounds beneath the level of
phonological perceptibility, the phonemic level as defined by the naturalness principle.

The importance of the phonemic level is reflected in a variety of sub-
tle ways: in the fact that we say that *banter* or *ban her* are pronounced
like *banner,* not vice versa; that eye dialect spells *for*—[fɔr] ~ [fr̩], the
latter phonemically /fʌr/—like *fur* [fʌr], not vice versa; and of course, by
the gradual historical replacement of morphophonemic representations
(|tɛst| for [tɛs] *test,* due to plural [tɛs] *tests*) by phonemic ones (dialectal
|tɛs|, compare the plural [tɛsɨz]).

These conclusions flatly contradict Chomsky's claim (1964) that
phonemic representation is without linguistic significance, and cast doubt

on his claims for a level of systematic phonemics. There is one further claim to examine: that phonetic and phonological representations are mediated not only by natural processes, but also by rules in the strict sense of 2.5. We do not hope to *settle* this issue, because generative phonologists have provided no explicit empirical characterization of systematic phonemics. However, since Halle (1959) and Chomsky (1964) claim that it is close to Sapir's phonological representation, we believe it is reasonable to expect that systematic phonemics too should be more readily available to consciousness than other representations. This expectation seems particularly reasonable since systematic phonemic representations like |de = kīd + iVn| *decision* and |ærtifik + i + æl + i + ty| *artificiality,* and the rules which relate them to phonetic representation, obviously presuppose operations which are more *cognitive* than the phonemic and morphophonemic representations we have been discussing. However, we doubt whether Sapir's empirical criterion would be accepted, because when independent evidence like Pig Latin (Halle 1962) or metrical scansion (Kiparsky 1972) has been examined, it has been concluded that these interact with phonological derivations at 'natural breaks' somewhere midway in the list of ordered rules. No general characterization of such 'breaks' has been offered, and no explanation of why such 'breaks' should occur at midpoints rather than at the systematic phonemic level.

The fact is that no independent evidence of *any* kind (a list of kinds and references is provided by Zwicky 1972b) requires a systematic phonemic explanation.[37] Secret language rules, for example, provide one kind of independent evidence for phonological representations—as when infixing secret languages like Alfalfa or Ob allow recovery of neutralized natural phonological representations by blocking the neutralizing process: [plælfɨntælfṛ] *planter* versus [plælfɨnælfṛ] *planner* (infixes italicized). But systematic phonemic representations, e.g., the |d| posited for [ž] in *decision,* or the |k| posited for [š] in *electrician,* fail to turn up: [dabɨsabɨžabɨn], [abɨlabɨktrabɨšabɨn]. We have seen that rhymes, although basically phonemic, are much better with (morpho-)phonological identity. We would expect this also to be true of systematic phonemic identity. But it is not: *decision* (*decide*) rhymes perfectly with *revision* (*revise*) and *precision* (*precise*); and so it goes for *extension* (*extend*), *retention* (*retain*), *convention* (*convene*), and *tension* (*tense*); for *resign* (*resignation*) and *incline* (*inclination*); for *meant* (*mean*), *bent* (*bend*), and *tent*. Finally, the enormous difficulty phonologists have discovering systematic phonemic representations and the kind of phonological rules they require, *even in their native language,* hardly squares with Sapir's criterion of accessibility. In short, we see no reason whatever to believe that phonological representations are motivated by phonetically unmotivated rules.

5. FINAL REMARKS

In the previous section of our paper, we invoked an empirical criterion of Sapir's on the issue of representation. It is remarkable that we should have to reach back into traditional phonology for an empirical criterion after half a century of empiricist theories. But the fact is that although structural and generative phonology are empiricist they are not empirical. Chomsky based his critique of structuralist phonology on the fact that structuralist theory did not define the particular sorts of representation which were generally agreed to be phonemic. If there had not been this fortunate agreement that, e.g., *can't* is phonemically /kænt/ rather than /kǽt/, Chomsky's critique would have been impossible. The structuralists had provided no independent empirical characterization of phonemic representation: they did not say what it is supposed to explain. They did, however, say what it is supposed to be explained by, namely the distinctiveness principle. In generative phonology we have no characterization of either what is supposed to follow from the theory, or what it is supposed to follow from. It is neither falsifiable, on the one hand, nor explanatory, on the other.

This is apparent from the fact that when any particular aspect of either structural or generative phonology has been falsified by data, either the data have been declared irrelevant, or the hypothesis has simply been revised, and the respective theories have gone on their way unruffled. When the distinctiveness principle in structural phonemics confronted the problem of neutralization, some structuralists declared the problem of identifying the phoneme in the position of neutralization irrelevant, and others simply changed to alternative principles. Generative phonologists, confronted by difficulties with the feature-counting principle originally proposed as an 'explanatory theory' of phonological representation, either abandoned the problems it had been proposed to explain (Chomsky and Halle 1968: chapter 8), or turned to alternative principles like markedness (op. cit.: chapter 9) or other equally unrelated criteria (Zwicky 1972b provides twenty-six criteria from the literature). In other sciences, the abandonment of such basic goals or principles would be revolutionary.

In structural and generative linguistics, they have occurred with less notice than is accorded a change of notation. For all their rigor and explicitness, neither structural nor generative phonology has *essential* empirical content. They are, to put it simply, not theories.

Natural phonology, although it lacks any a priori methodology or formalization, is both testable and explanatory. By its nature, it is ultimately accountable for, as we put it earlier, everything language owes to the fact that it is spoken. And by its nature, it must follow from the character of the human capacity for speech.

It has been objected that too little is known about phonological universals and about phonetic capacity (especially in its neurological aspect) to falsify the theory. Even if we accepted this assessment of the phonological and phonetic literature, it would not follow that the theory is unfalsifiable *in principle*. (In fact, however, we think that the literature has already proven adequate to support systematic investigations of many aspects of the relations between phonology and phonetics.)

Others have objected that the theory is too obviously true to be falsified. We can only conclude that this objection is based on an unawareness of the intricate, complex, paradoxical, and nonpatent nature of the facts to be accounted for. In any event, if it is obviously true, it is certainly not obvious why the theory has lain dormant for a half-century.

In the meantime, the goals of explanation which were set by the pioneers of phonology and phonetics referred to at the beginning of our paper have largely been forgotten, along with the considerable progress they made in achieving these goals. In their place we have, as the late Paul Goodman wrote of modern linguistics in general, 'an enormous amount of machinery, but few edible potatoes.' We hope we have been able to show in this paper that a return to the traditional goals may increase our yield.

NOTES

This paper is dedicated to the memory of Harry V. Velten of Indiana University, whose studies have lighted our way.

1. There are by now other more or less independent varieties of the theory current, and most recent revisions of generative phonology have converged with natural phonology. There are also divergent views within the various schools, even between the co-authors of this paper. The common

ground is the basic thesis that phonological systems are phonetically motivated.

2. That is, obstruents ([z]) become voiceless ([s]) in final position. The reverse is not true, e.g. *weiss* : *wissen* '(I) know : (they) know' retain [s] throughout. Although Kruszewski and Baudouin recognized that alternations are unidirectional, and that one alternant is basic and the other derivative, they avoided interpreting them as processes because of the diachronic overtones this notion had in their time.

3. The hypothetical example is superfluous: with a whole world of languages at hand, one issue after another in the book is 'left open', because of 'a scarcity of data for choosing between the many alternatives that readily come to mind' (379 and passim). This suggests that the issues are really pseudo-issues. A theory for which one can find no evidence is, in effect, a theory with nothing to explain.

4. For this informal explanation to hold water, of course, it needs caulking with perceptual and articulatory substance. The objective measure of perceptual and articulatory difficulty is necessarily one of the main goals of natural phonology. However, it is a goal presenting enormous obstacles, not the least of which is that even articulatory difficulty seems usually to be as much mental as physical. Therefore, at the risk of some misunderstanding (e.g., Ohala 1974), we employ the notions of perceptual and articulatory difficulty as interim hypothetical constructs, deduced from the rich evidence furnished by the nature and frequency of substitutions in phonological variation, acquisition, and change. This is not circular, because of the coincidence of conclusions drawn from quite different kinds of evidence, e.g., the greater difficulty of perceptibly rounding low as against high vowels is independently attested by their consistently different behavior in a wide variety of substitutions (e.g., Donegan 1973a, 1976, 1978). In fact, it seems to us that natural phonology furnishes systematic data on the nature of features, sounds, and sound-structures which are otherwise unavailable, though indispensable, to linguistic phonetics.

5. Except for some Munda languages, with both voiceless and voiced obstruents, which permit only the latter finally in morphemes; they are pronounced as voiced when syllable-initial (e.g. before a vocalic suffix) but are checked and usually devoiced when syllable-final (Stampe 1965: 333 f. on Sora).

6. Chomsky and Halle (1968) present two revisions of the theory, the first (ch. 8) viciously circular, the second (ch. 9) failing to distinguish admissible from inadmissible *segments* (Stampe 1973c). No explanatory theories of admissibility were proposed by the structuralists, perhaps because (as Chomsky 1964 proposed) they never aspired to this level of "adequacy."

7. Donegan and Stampe (forthcoming). The main process governing this restriction seems to be one which syllabifies the second segment, as in [bṇɪk] or [bɨnɪk]; the expressive [bḷu] *bl-lue!*, [kuɪt] *qu-it!* seem to derive from optional applications of the same process—(3f) of section 2.4.

8. There is of course rich evidence that the child's mental target resembles adult speech rather than her own (e.g., Stampe 1969, 1972b, Smith 1973,

etc.). In Joan's case this came in the spontaneous and across-the-board appearance of vowel length and, shortly afterwards, voicing in precisely the words which end in voiced obstruents in adult speech.

9. In this section we sketch a theory differing from our oral paper in two respects, (1) the assumption of simultaneous application (Donegan 1974) rather than freely sequential application (Stampe 1973a), (2) the extension of the 'fortition first, lenition last' hypothesis from pairs of processes with opposite effects (Stampe 1973a) to all processes. These minor revisions have far-reaching consequences, not all of which we can evaluate here.

10. E.g., Koutsoudas et al. (1971), Kiparsky (1971), Anderson (1974), Hooper (1976), etc.

11. Parenthesized conditions are variable. On regressive nasalization cf. 2.2.

12. We have skipped over some steps in the 'spread' of nasalization and have presented nasalization and nasal-elision as simultaneous.

13. In the case of Vennemann and Hooper, the grounds seem to be 'concreteness' for its own sake. They identify processes with empirical statements, expecting them to express true generalizations about phonetic representation. This criterion can be met only at the expense of reducing phonology—which after all has a perceptual side—to articulatory phonetics. To hug the phonetic ground closely is not necessarily to embrace the truth.

14. However, in a non-ordering framework, Lee (1976) has anticipated the observation which follows.

15. The same is true of the arguments of Kiparsky (1972) and Anderson (1969, 1974) for an 'elsewhere' or 'disjunctive ordering' principle which deals mainly with cases where the effects of a specific rule would not be manifest unless it is appropriately ordered with respect to a contradictory and more general rule. Stampe (1973a: ch. 2) has given counter-analyses to Anderson's examples, which, despite Anderson (p. 103, note 8) are abundantly documented—in fact in the handbooks Anderson cites (note 5 of p. 102), to which may now be added Jordan (1974: §25)—and need not be rehearsed here. Kiparsky gives the self-evident logical argument for the principle, citing ancient Indian authority, including Pāṇini's similar convention, but it is obvious that such an argument is completely inapplicable if we are dealing with phonetically motivated processes rather than rules formulated by the learner.

As to Pāṇini, it is surely anachronistic to interpret the descriptive conventions of the Aṣṭādhyāyī (as also in Kiparsky's paper in this volume) as if its author had been a conventionalist, i.e., as if the conventions were intended as hypotheses in a theory of language; even Patañjali's exhaustive commentary gives no hint of theoretic rather than descriptive intent. As Stampe remarked at the conference, rules in feeding, bleeding, disjunctive, and cyclic application can be found in any complicated set of instructions, like *The Joy of Cooking*, but one does not interpret these as part of a universal human *faculté de cuisine*.

16. Jensen and Stong-Jensen (1976) point out that many prosodic processes, e.g. alternating stress or length, bleed themselves: application on the

*n*th syllable will bleed application on the *n*th ± 1. These examples disappear in a prosodic theory which treats the alternating prominences as part of a prosodic pattern, and maps the segmental material onto this pattern (2.4).

17. In a narrow description of non-southern English, it might be overlooked that these dissimilations of [æe̯] to [ɑe̯] exist, since there is nothing for them to apply to. On our view, this only suggests that there is no reason for them to have been suppressed. And in fact they regularly show themselves in northern imitations of the southern pronunciations [bæed], [græes] as [bɑed], [grɑes]. One 'dictionary' of southern speech for northerners glosses *died* as 'father'.

18. Lest it be doubted that the lenitions in (10) or (22) are living processes, speakers with these processes often apply them to the outputs of the lenition desyllabifying pretonic sonorants (31), e.g. [θro̯u̯] *Thoreau* → [θro̯u̯] → [θro̯u̯] or [tr̯ɪfɪk] *terrific* → [trɪfɪk] → [črɪfɪk], though many also use the counterfed pronunciations [θro̯u̯] and [trɪfɪk] as variants.

19. There can be little doubt that the much-debated alternants of these affixes have synchronic phonetic motivation in English, because they are adjusted to fit tongue-slips (Fromkin 1971). The distinction in the spelling of the [z]-suffix between *cats, dogs* versus *matches* reflects, we suspect, the phonemic (not morphophonemic) status of the inserted vowel, according to the perceptual hypothesis sketched in 4 (cf. also Read 1975).

20. Strictly speaking, there seem to be no natural insertions or deletions; the former involve 'splitting' segments by dissimilation or assimilation, e.g. [æ] → [æe̯], and the latter are simply complete assimilations, e.g. [[ænt] → [æ̃æ̃t] = [æ̃t] (Stampe 1972a, Donegan forthcoming). Note that if [æ] → [æe̯] were really an insertion, its simultaneous application with regressive nasalization would make [bæŋ] into *[bæ̃e̯ŋ], with non-nasal [e̯]!

21. Kisseberth (1973) cites Lardil examples of Hale (1973) to argue that two processes, vowel apocope and grave consonant apocope, may evidence a counter-iterative constraint on their application, to prevent [ŋawuŋawu] *termite* (cf. the inflected form [ŋawuŋawu-n]) → [ŋawuŋaw] → [ŋawuŋa] (the correct pronunciation) → *[ŋawuŋ] → *[ŋawu]. We have no data on this language, but we suspect, both from the usual pattern of Australian languages and from reduplicative structure of this word, that there is some accent (whether primary or secondary) on the basically penultimate vowel, and that apocope, as is normally the case, does not apply to accented vowels.

22. DS, who pronounces *bad guy* [bæggɑe̯] and *let me* [lɛmi], finds it quite difficult to pronounce *bag* as [bæg] rather than [bæe̯g], or *lemming* as [lɛmɪŋ] rather than [lɪmɪŋ].

23. We do not have space here, unfortunately, to discuss nonphonetic constraints involving grammatical, semantic, or lexical categories, and frequency, etc. (Stampe, forthcoming).

Our model bears a strong resemblance to traditional practice, e.g., in Sapir and his contemporaries (Kenstowicz 1976), where one finds globally expressed interactional constraints like "inorganic [i.e. derivative] increments and losses have no effect" [on the application of the constrained process]. For a modern discussion from this point of view see also Kisseberth (1973). We are much indebted to Greg Lee and Don Churma for discussion of various topics in section 3.

24. Based chiefly on Stampe (1968a), unpublished.

25. 'Tongue-slips' are the exceptions that prove the rule: they are perceived as slips because they constitute jumblings of the intention of speech. They arise in the input to the phonological processes, and since the processes operate perfectly, as usual, both in synthesis and (allowing for noise and ambiguity) in analysis, we correctly perceive our resultant utterance (spoken or not) as not corresponding to our original intention.

26. It should be pointed out that Twaddell's paper presented phonemics as an explanation of the spelling of OHG umlaut, rather than presenting the spellings as evidence for phonemics. This is a good example of the way phonemics was taken for granted. Similarly, more has been written on how generative representations of English explain English orthography than on how the orthography supports the representations.

27. For purposes of exposition, we ignore for now the analysis [rɛi̯ntɪŋ] *rainting, which is also possible.

28. Against the morphophonemic precedence principle of Dinnsen and Koutsoudas (1975). There are many similar examples: Kabardian [əw] varies allophonically with [o:] but [q'] merges with the distinct phoneme [q'ʷ] before round vowels, including [o:] (Kuipers 1960:24 n.10); Yana women devoiced final vowels and merged voiced consonant phonemes with voiceless ones before the devoiced vowels (Sapir 1929:207); English /1/ is labiovelarized in syllable codas, and many speakers delateralize the resultant segment in certain contexts, merging it with [o̯] as in [hao̯] *how, howl;* etc.

29. Actually, this example is strictly speaking not a phonological redundancy rule, because such rules are supposed to supply redundant feature values, not delete, insert, or change segments. However, any such formulation of the constraint against [hn] would imply, incorrectly, that if confronted with a word like *hnutu,* an English speaker who could not pronounce it would change it to something other than [nutu] or [hn̩utu]. Halle (oral comment, 1971, on Stampe 1973c) argues that these are considerations of loan phonology and are not relevant to the description of English. But the observable constraints and alternations of English, or any other language, are a subset of the regular substitutions its speakers would impose on unpronounceable words from other languages (cf. Ohso 1972, Lovins 1973).

30. Moreover, the idea is never applied even-handedly: if *sixth* and *sixths* were obligatorily pronounced to rhyme with *six,* no one would represent all [ks] sequences as an 'archisequence' |ks(θ(s))|. The duck/rabbit perceptual phenomenon, incidentally, argues against the archisegment idea; in the ambiguous drawing we see a duck *or* we see a rabbit—not both at once.

31. Stampe (1973a) cites numerous further arguments (cf. Velten 1943). Hooper (1976) cites interesting counterarguments of Blair Rudes' showing that Gaelic takes stops after |s| to be voiced. We do not know why this

should be. But our point is that no language takes such segments to be indeterminate. Gaelic is not exceptional.

It has been argued that *spin* has |b| from the fact that when the [s] of *spin* is removed by electronic mutilation the residue is heard as *bin* rather than *pin*. The reasoning here is on a par with claiming that lizards are snakes because if you cut off their legs people will think that they're snakes.

32. This is the simplest hypothesis, given the evidence cited. Stampe presented it, with the counterevidence that follows, in several papers (e.g. 1968a, 1973a), although no one had actually espoused the hypothesis. But now Vennemann (1974) appears to have done so.

33. Joan Velten's denasalization in *ants,* which is regular, might have several explanations: (1) she failed to perceive the vowel nasalization at all (|æts|); (2) she perceived it as phonemic (|æ̃ts|) and applied denasalization; (3) she perceived it as allophonic (|ænts|), but applied denasalization after nasalization and nasal-elision, against 3.2.1. We are not very happy with any of these alternatives. Worse, many children write *ants* as ATS (Read, 1975, with important discussion).

34. This claim was anticipated in a remarkable 1954 article by Bazell, in which he argued that phonological identifications are governed not by the principle of (non)distinctiveness but by a principle of *motivation* (essentially our principle of naturalness). We do not identify [h] and [ŋ] in English, Bazell says, even though they are not distinctive, because pronouncing /ŋ/ initially as [h], or /h/ finally as [ŋ], is not motivated.

35. A fluent reading eliminates the quantity difference.

36. The omnipotence of the word asserts itself in the perfect rhymes of *fitter* : *bidder* : *hit 'er* (with clitic *her*) versus *a gnat upon* : *a pad upon.* The former are invariably pronounced alike and thus are phonemically identical; the latter, even in this context, are only facultatively alike (contrast [ənæt'] : [əpæ:d]) and thus are phonemically distinct.

37. Aspects of English orthography which purportedly require a systematic phonemic explanation are better explained historically.

CHAPTER SEVEN

The Phonological Component as a Parsing Device

William R. Leben

1. THE APPROACH

This paper will deal mainly with the problem of accounting for idiosyncratic morphophonological properties of words. Past approaches have ranged from ignoring these properties altogether to describing them as if they were on a par with the more productive alternations and phonetic processes of the language. I will argue that the phonological rules of a language apply in two blocks. One block, containing the productive phonological rules, converts underlying phonological representations into their phonetic realizations. The rules of this block will be termed phonetic rules. The other block, containing the phonetic rules plus rules of a more idiosyncratic type that are often termed morphophonological, performs a different function and operates in a different way. The rules of this block operate in reverse, taking the underlying phonological representations back to more remote representations for the purpose of satisfying the description of morphological rules. This procedure provides a way of capturing systematic morphological relationships among words by parsing morphologically complex words. The rules of this latter block will be termed parsing rules, and the model that captures the phonological and morphological relationships among words in the way to be described will be termed a parsing model, since it aims to model the ways in which speakers deal with parsing morphologically complex words that are systematically related to simpler words. I will argue, on the one hand, that this model makes for a more adequate treatment of morphophonemic alternations than the system of Chomsky and Halle (1968: SPE) and, on the other hand, that it provides an appropriate complement to the treatment of phonetic rules in frameworks with relatively concrete phonological representations, such as natural phonology and natural generative phonology.

The approach to phonology proposed here mirrors to some extent the approach to morphology outlined in Aronoff (1976). Morphological rules apply in two blocks. Rules of word formation generate words that are not in the lexicon, and rules of word analysis parse existing words. The functions of word formation and word analysis are separate, even though the rules involved may be the same. The lexicon contains "all and only those words which are exceptional, i.e. arbitrary in at least one of their features" (Aronoff, p. 43). The claim I make for phonology parallels this, except for the fact that I will maintain that the phonological rules for word analysis contain as a proper subset the phonological rules that apply productively; in addition to these there is a set of rules with a purely morphophonological or interpretive function. In addition, whereas Aronoff provides for the morphological structuring of the lexicon by means of rules of word analysis, I will assume that the application of phonological rules in word analysis has no direct effect on the phonological structuring of the lexicon; e.g., if we undo a rule changing k to s in a given form, we do not change s back to k in the lexical entry. Instead, the undoing of phonological rules is simply part of the procedure for establishing the morphological relatedness of words.

A consequence of the proposal to exclude from the lexicon information about the purely morphophonological behavior of words is that special diacritic features, or suppletive representations of the type proposed by Hudson (1974), are superfluous. For instance, the fact that the final vowel of *cello* is truncated in *cellist* while the final vowel of *solo* remains in *soloist* is captured not by distinguishing the bases *cello* and *solo* in any way but rather by listing *cellist* and *soloist* directly in the lexicon. Similarly for the application vs. nonapplication of Trisyllabic Shortening in *profanity* vs. *obesity*. How the grammar deals with such differences is described and motivated in some detail below. But there is some initial plausibility to the idea that the locus of exceptionality of *obesity* is in the word *obesity* itself rather than in its base *obese*. Consider the word *highness,* which among its meanings has the idiosyncratic property of being a title of honor. It would be needlessly roundabout to capture this fact by marking the adjective *high* to undergo a special semantic rule when *-ness* is attached. I can see no objection to handling *highness* in the more direct way of listing it lexically with its special meaning.

Furthermore, as Aronoff (1976: 18–19, 32–33, 38–39) points out, the word *transmission* can refer to a car's transmission in addition to referring to the act of transmitting, and the word *monstrosity,* unlike *porosity, curiosity,* etc., is difficult to interpret as referring to a quality. Such idiosyncrasies are captured by listing *transmission* and *monstrosity* in the lexicon with their meanings. As Aronoff proposes, the morphological rules for *-ion* and *-ity* specify a semantic function defining the meaning of the derived word in relation to the base word. By comparing the divergence between the actual meanings and predicted meanings, the grammar captures the extent to which the semantic correspondences are regular.

Such an approach provides the beginnings of a model of how we come to associate the meanings of a morphologically complex form with the meanings of its parts. For someone who considers *severance* to refer only to the compensation received when one is separated from one's job, there is still a relation to the verb *sever,* even though we cannot predict this meaning from *sever.* Similarly, the term *cubist* bears an obvious, though indirect, relation to *cube.* We do not redefine *sever* and *cube* on the basis of *severance* and *cubist.* Rather we analyze the meanings of the derived words in terms of the meanings of their parts. The approach to idiosyncratic morphophonological properties outlined in this paper is similar in that it does not seek to redefine the phonological and morphological features of *solo* and *cello* on the basis of their behavior before the ending *-ist.* Instead it takes the derived words as given and defines the rules that work to relate these derived words, despite their differences, to the appropriate bases.

2. A NOTE ON PHONOLOGICAL REPRESENTATIONS

In generative phonology, different sorts of considerations have led to conflicting positions on the degree to which underlying phonological representations may differ from surface forms. SPE avoids placing any generally specifiable restrictions on the correspondence between underlying phonemes and their systematic phonetic realizations, apart from the requirement that both be represented by distinctive features drawn from a fixed inventory and that the rules of correspondence satisfy certain formal requirements. Each specific phonemicization is decided on its own merits, as determined by a general evaluation measure. This constitutes an interesting way of abandoning the strictures of classical phonemic theory that, as Halle (1959) and Chomsky (1964) demonstrate, lead to lost generalizations and are difficult to define consistently—interesting in that it leaves phonology with a theory, yet one that differs markedly in some respects from its predecessors. Still, there are signs that the theory is wrong, judging from evidence, principally from linguistic change, suggesting that additional restrictions can and should be placed on the construction of underlying representations. The pioneering work of Kiparsky in this area has been pushed further by many other researchers, leading, among other things, to the formulation of competing theories, such as natural phonology (Stampe 1973b) and natural generative phonology (Vennemann 1971, Hooper 1976). Unfortunately, the frameworks that propose the strongest restrictions on phonological representations represent a weaker theoretical position, a paradox that has yet to be fully appreciated. Consider, for example, the position summarized by Hooper (1977): "The major claim of natural generative phonology is that speakers construct only generalizations that are surface-true and transparent." This severely restricts underlying representations by limiting the types of rules that express their correspondence to phonetic manifestations. But the theory, in order to provide for phenomena that do not lend themselves to treatment by rules meeting the conditions just cited, contains an escape clause. There are "via rules," unconstrained by the theory, to express lexical correspondences that cannot be captured by surface-true, transparent rules (Vennemann 1972a, Hooper 1976). Similarly, the approach to natural phonology outlined by Donegan and Stampe (1977a) makes no allowance for phonological relationships that fall outside the domain of natural processes:

> The phonetically natural aspect of phonology (as in the [s] : [z] alternation of German *Haus* : *Häuser*) is distinct in its nature, evolution, psychological status, and causality from the phonetically conventional aspects, whether the latter have taken on morphological motivation (as in the *au* : *äu, a* : *ä, o* : *ö, u* : *ü* alternations of *Haus* : *Häuser, Rad* : *Räder, Loch* : *Löcher, Buch*: *Bücher*) or not (as in the *s* : *r* alternation of *gewesen* : *war*) . . . Natural phonology properly excludes the topic of unmotivated and morphologically motivated alternations. [Donegan and Stampe, p. 127]

Their examples point up the problem encountered if we seek to embed natural phonology in a theory capturing morphophonemic alternations as well. Devoicing, a phonetically natural process, and umlaut, a conventional rule, both function morphophonemically in German. Thus, if we are to consider whether morphophonemic alternations figure in phonology, it is of little value to suggest that they do if natural phonology can handle them and that they do not if natural phonology cannot handle them. Below I show that though the two types of rule may be different, they are not totally different.

There is, in any event, a growing consensus that SPE's level of underlying representation is too abstract. Though there is hardly a consensus on the question of how abstract this level really is, or on what sorts of rules relate underlying to surface forms, how these rules are ordered, and so on, efforts at answering these questions have proceeded sufficiently far to warrant discussion of the subject to be treated in the present paper. Granting that underlying representations are closer to the surface than may have been thought in 1968, how does one now deal with the abstract phonological relationships captured in the SPE system? For example, granting that the vowel of *sane* is underlyingly distinct from the corresponding vowel of *sanity,* how can we capture the fact that knowledge of the language permits speakers to relate these two words without having to be explicitly taught that they are related?

Faced with a choice between the abstract underlying level of SPE and the more shallow representations of, say, Stampe (1973b), I think there is good reason to adopt the latter—but only if we can find an alternative way of securing the results that at first seemed to favor the more abstract level. The reason behind this choice is simply that the sorts of evidence (largely external) martialed by Stampe (1973b) are more compelling than the sorts of evidence (largely internal) presented by SPE, especially when we can show that there are adequate ways of dealing with the internal evidence that depart from the assumptions of SPE. As argued by Stampe (1973b), as well as by Donegan and Stampe (1977a), if we hypothesize that words are encoded lexically in ways that abstract from redundancies resulting from phonetically natural processes, we can explain why these words undergo the changes they do in speech errors and in other novel situations. Whether or not one agrees with the particular characterizations of natural processes offered by Donegan and Stampe, this argument has some appeal, since it (i) provides a theoretically straightforword, nonarbitrary way of pinpointing the level of lexical representation and (ii) suggests a division between phonological rules that is hardly apparent from SPE: one block of rules is, in effect, ordered before the other. The first, containing the more idiosyncratic type of rule, functions (backward) only in the lexicon. The second block (which may also apply in the lexicon) contains only the rules that generate surface forms from lexical representations.

Since in this paper I am primarily concerned with the first type of rule, I will sidestep the open questions surrounding the second type by giving them the purely operational definition of being those whose effects show up in the tests devised by Stampe (1973b), involving transfer of rules to novel situations. I will assume that the level of phonological representation is the level that abstracts from the sorts of regularity that respond to these tests. This level, in order to avoid the famous problems for taxonomic phonemics discussed in Halle (1959) and Chomsky (1964), must not be so strongly restricted as to prevent Russian [dad,bi] or English [rajɾər] from being interpreted phonemically as /dat,#bi/ and /rajd#ər/. That is, for reasons presented in Chomsky (1964), we may not impose the requirements of linearity, invariance, biuniqueness, and local determinacy on phonological descriptions. Yet suppose that, in accord with the operational definition of "phoneme" suggested above, we wish to bar the representation /rixt/ for English *right,* which SPE proposes in order to capture the behavior of the related form *righteous.* While it is conceivable that this might be done adequately by placing conditions on the actual rules that relate phonological to phonetic representations, an equally attractive possibility is to posit that any phoneme /P/, with the realizations $[p_1, p_2, \ldots, p_n]$, must be nondistinct from at least one of its realizations, in the sense of nondistinct as defined by Chomsky and Halle (1968: 336). Though the assignment of other phones to /P/ is not limited by this definition, we can eliminate many obviously incorrect correspondences, such as the assignment of $[t^h]$ to /k/ in English, by the evaluation metric. Despite recent attacks on the evaluation procedure, I believe that it is an entirely suitable device for handling tasks of this sort.

The condition that a phoneme be nondistinct from at least one of its realizations, while permitting phonemicizations /dat,#bi/ and /rajd#ər/, suffices to rule out /rixt/ as a phonemicization of *right,* since English has no realization of putative /x/ that it is nondistinct from. Of course, there are numerous additional restrictions that one can imagine placing on underlying representations. But my purpose here is just to illustrate how a level intermediate between the systematic phonemic and systematic phonetic levels of SPE could be developed to accommodate the arguments that formed part of the foundation of early work in generative phonology.

3. A PARSING APPROACH TO MORPHOPHONOLOGY

Suppose that we have a set of phonetic rules specifying the relationships between lexical representations of words and their phonetic realizations in context, pictured here:

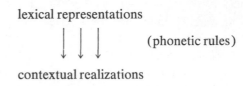

lexical representations

(phonetic rules)

contextual realizations

Another set of rules, sometimes of a quite different sort, governs relations between lexical items. These rules frequently admit exceptions, are often less plausible phonetically, and are much less susceptible to transfer in novel situations. The distinction between the two types of rule is a fundamental one, and just as it is important not to confuse one with the other, it is important not to neglect one in pursuit of the other. Contrary to the unfounded assumption witnessed in some current work, the proper domain of phonology is the study of all types of regularities in language that make use of phonological terms. Below I discuss evi- for this assertion. Let me first illustrate how the more idiosyncratic morphophonological rules operate in the parsing model.

Briefly stated, the model takes arbitrary pairs of lexical representations, compares them with respect to a morphological rule, and attempts to make them satisfy the environment of the morphological rule by successively undoing layers of phonological changes. In derivations that are successful—where a match between a morphologically complex word and some other word is found—we say that the grammar has parsed the morphologically complex form. Now the picture given above can be completed:

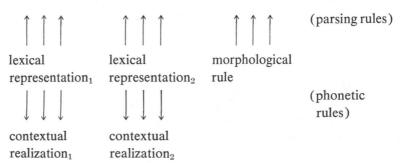

(parsing rules)

lexical   lexical   morphological
representation₁   representation₂   rule

(phonetic rules)

contextual   contextual
realization₁   realization₂

In this model only as many parsing rules are undone as is required to establish that a pair of lexical representations jointly satisfy the environment of an appropriate morphological rule. For example, as will be illustrated in greater detail below, *soloist* is identified as a derivative of *solo* and *obesity* is identified as the nominalization of *obese* directly at the lexical level, without undoing any morphophonemic rules. But to identify *cellist* as a derivative of *cello* and *profanity* as the nominalization of *profane,* certain phonological differences must be compensated for before they will fit the environment of the appropriate morphological rule.

This brings up one of the ways in which the present proposal differs from past approaches to morphophonemics, including the systematic phonetic representations of SPE. In the parsing model there is no morphophonemic level as such. Instead each parsing rule, or each permissible combination of parsing rules, defines a "level" of sorts, but such a level is reached only in case the morphology warrants it. As J. L. Malone (personal communication) has pointed out, this provides a nice way of dealing with the morphophonemic indeterminacy that has previously confounded researchers. For example, Malone (1970) notes that in Classical Mandaic a contrastively long consonant may have any of a number of morphophonemic interpretations. Three of these are /CC/, /?C/, and /C?/. But, Malone observes, for many nouns there is no principled way of determining what the morphophonemic source of their long consonant is, since in these nouns the long consonant does not alternate in ways that would reveal a morphophonemic source. Furthermore, Malone argues, Schane's (1968b) proposal that in such cases the ambiguity is resolved by choosing the least marked underlying representation would sometimes give the wrong results.

In the parsing model, this is not a problem. In fact, morphophonemic indeterminacy is a totally unsurprising phenomenon. Morphophonemes are not the source of anything. They are rather abstractions from phonemes and appear only when prompted by the morphology. Morphophonemic indeterminacy thus provides one sign that the phonological component is split up into two sections, whose rules have a quite different status.

For a simple example of a parse, consider the facts of (1), noted by Ross (1972) as puzzling cases.

(1) a. violin   violinist
     b. solo   soloist
         oboe   oboist

      c. cello   cellist
         piano   pianist

Comparison of (1b) with (1c) shows that it is arbitrary whether a word loses its final vowel before -*ist*. We can encode this arbitrariness simply by listing -*ist* words in the lexicon. But the grammar must parse the morphologically complex forms, relating *soloist* to *solo* and *cellist* to *cello*. To do this, let us adopt the conventions in (2):[1]

(2) a. Rules that would apply in the order A, B, C in a conventional generative treatment are undone in the order C, B, A, except as provided by (2c).

      b. A rule of the form $X \rightarrow [-F] / Y\_\_\_\_Z$ is undone by replacing $[-F]$ with $[+F]$ on segment X in the environment $Y\_\_\_\_Z$. Analogously, a rule of the form $X \rightarrow \emptyset / Y\_\_\_\_Z$ is undone by replacing $\emptyset$ with X in the context $Y\_\_\_\_Z$.

      c. A rule blocks if undoing it would not increase the compatibility of forms A and B with respect to morphological rule R.

The meaning of "compatibility" in (2c) will become clearer in the discussion of derivations (5) and (6) below. The rules needed to relate the pairs in (1) are expressed in (3) and (4).

(3) Word Formation Rule
     $[X]_N \longrightarrow [X\text{-}ist]_N$

(4) Truncation
     $V \longrightarrow \emptyset / \_\_\_\_ - V$

Note that rule (4) is widespread, though not totally productive, in English. Along with applying in *cello/cellist, piano/pianist*, it applies in *Mexico/ Mexican, orchestra/orchestral*, etc.

By the conventions in (2), representative pairs from (1) are related as in (5):

(5)		Word A	Word B	Morphology
	a. LEXICAL FORMS:	/vājəlin/$_N$	/vājəlinist/$_N$	$[X]_N \rightarrow [X\text{-}ist]_N$
	b. LEXICAL FORMS:	/sōlō/$_N$	/sōlōist/$_N$	$[X]_N \rightarrow [X\text{-}ist]_N$

    c. LEXICAL

FORMS:	/čelō/$_N$	/čelist/$_N$	$[X]_N \to [X\text{-}ist]_N$
i. Rule(4)	—	čelVist$_N$	—

For cases (5a,b), no phonological rules need be undone in matching words A and B with the left and right member of the morphological rule; therefore, by condition (2c), no rules may be undone. In (5c), the lexical representations do not yield an immediate match: if /čelō/ is substituted for X in the left member of the morphological rule, X cannot be *čel* in the right member. Accordingly, we must undo the rule of truncation causing a vowel to be inserted before *ist* in /čelist/. By stipulating that X in the left member of a rule matches Y in the right member as long as X and Y are nondistinct, we guarantee that *čelō* and the derived representation *čelV* will qualify as matching each other in this rule.

The procedure just illustrated extends naturally to more complex cases, like *Christ/Christian,* using the SPE account of the alternations in this pair as a basis for constructing the derivation:

(6)	Word A	Word B	Morphology
LEXICAL			
FORMS:	/krājst/$_N$	/krisčən/$_A$	$[X]_N \to [X\text{-}\bar{\imath}j\partial n]_A$
i. Glide deletion e.g. j → Ø / č __	—	krisčjən$_A$	—
ii. Palatalization e.g. t → č / __ j	—	kristjən$_A$	—
iii. ī → Ø / C __ j	—	kristījən$_A$	—
iv. Vowel Shift	krīst$_N$	—	—
v. Trisyllabic shortening	—	krīstījən$_A$	—

As one can judge from the phrasing of condition (2c), it is intended to apply purely locally. It is not permitted to look ahead in order to see whether a derivation will ultimately succeed or not. It does not presuppose a relationship between words A and B but rather is part of the procedure for determining whether the words can be related. Thus, for example, each step in derivation (6) satisfies (2c) without referring to future steps. Step (6.i) is well formed because insertion of *j* increases the compatibility of word B with the morphological rule. Step (6.ii) increases the resemblance between words A and B. Step (6.iii) completes the reconstruction of the suffix of word B, so that it matches the suffix in the morphological rule. Step (6.iv) brings the stressed vowels of words A and B closer together, and step (6.v) makes the vowels identical.

The function of condition (2c), as it has been illustrated here, is to make derivations as brief as possible. In contrast to the approach taken in conventional generative phonology, in which derivations initiate with a systematic phonemic representation and terminate with a systematic phonetic one, derivations illustrated here often do not involve the reconstruction of a representation corresponding to the systematic phonemic level. Derivations are only as long as they need to be in order to make words A and B match the environment of a morphological rule, as is illustrated by (5) and (6). As a result, the present theory differs sharply in several respects from others that have been proposed. For one thing, as has been noted above, what was previously regarded as the systematic phonemic level is really not a level at all, since not all words receive an interpretation at this level, due to condition (2c). Therefore, one would expect that redundancies of the sort expressed by SPE in terms of systematic phonemes should be either devoid of psychological significance or expressible at some other level, using the terms appropriate to that level The work of Greenberg and Jenkins (1964) and of Hooper (1975) gives some indication of how generalizations previously thought to belong in the domain of systematic phonemics can be expressed without presupposing the existence of this level.

In further contrast to SPE, condition (2c) provides a *principle* governing the length of derivations. To the extent that the complexity of derivations, as defined, say, by the number of steps in a parse, has a psychological correlate (for instance, in the time it takes a speaker to recover a morphological relationship or in the direction that a morphological class takes in changing), this model will make predictions, while the SPE model will make none. Below, in sections 6 and 7, I note some examples in which condition (2c) in fact plays a crucial role in explaining diachronic changes.

The procedure illustrated in (5) and (6) cannot, of course, be construed as guaranteeing that a genuine relationship exists wherever a derivation manages to make two words fit into the environment of a morphological rule. Indeed the process can run awry even in cases where no phonological rules are undone. We relate *cubic* to *cube* and *Chadic* to *Chad* but not *caustic* to *cost* or *comic* to *calm*. In view of this, we must stipulate that the parser specifies word relationships that are linguistically possible. It cannot certify that they are attested: this is the province of the lexicon. This is something that all theories of morphology have in common. In any theory, the phonological resemblance of *caustic* to *cost* is parallel to that of *cubic* to *cube,* and both pairs are, by virtue of their form, susceptible to being interpreted as related by the morphological rule forming adjectives from nouns by means of the suffix *-ic.* For the linguistic model to explain why some of these pairs are judged related by speakers while others are not, it will have to equip its morphological rules with semantic characterizations that must be satisfied by words related by such rules. In addition, the model must either abstract from speaker differences or attune its predictions to individual variations resulting from a complex of factors, including education, alertness, and pure chance. The parsing procedure, then, provides a necessary but not a sufficient condition for establishing morphological relationships.

4. ALTERNATIVE TREATMENTS OF EXCEPTIONS

The derivations in (5) illustrate how, equipped with condition (2c), the parser deals with the truncation of the final vowel of *cello* in *cellist* despite the retention of the corresponding vowel of *solo* in *soloist,* while expressing the obvious relationships. If we accept this account, there is no temptation to manufacture abstract ways of encoding the difference in the deletability of the final vowels of *cello* and *solo.* There would be no point, for example, in representing *solo* as $solo^{1\ 3}$ and *cello* as $cello^{1\ 0}$ and limiting truncation to deleting only unstressed vowels before *-ist.* Such a proposal would constitute what Kiparsky (1973b) has termed the diacritic use of a phonological feature and, for the reasons Kiparsky has given, deserves to be disallowed. Further, it suffers from a flaw shared by certain more direct attempts at capturing the difference in deletability. For example, one might mark the final vowel of *cello* but not the final vowel of *solo* with a special diacritic triggering a rule which truncates this vowel before *-ist.* Or, extending Hudson's (1974) and Hooper's (1976) proposal for inflectional morphology to derivational morphology, one might give *cello* the suppletive representation $cell \left\{ {\emptyset \atop o} \right\}$, with a special rule selecting the first version, with $\emptyset$, before *-ist* and a general convention selecting the other version elsewhere.

Both alternatives resemble the approach I am advocating in that the difference between the two classes of words is captured, in effect, by a list. If we choose the diacritic solution, the lexicon must say for each relevant entry whether or not it is marked with the diacritic. If we choose suppletive representations, the lexicon must say for each relevant entry whether or not it has this suppletive representation. Despite this similarity, however, the two alternatives just mentioned do differ empirically from the parsing approach, and I believe that the facts show that these alternatives are inferior. For one thing, the position that we capture the deletability of the vowel before -*ist* by a difference in the marking of the base forms *solo* and *cello* implies that if *cello* is marked to undergo deletion before a vowel-initial suffix, it should be realized as *cell-* not only before -*ist* but also before any vowel-initial suffix. By contrast, in the parsing model, any word not formed productively is listed in the lexicon, leaving open the possibility that even though *cell-* precedes -*ist,* the full form *cello* might precede some other vowel-initial suffix. I have found no crucial examples for words in -*ist,* but I suspect that, given that the relevant words could come into the language centuries apart, with no necessary regard for the morphology of words that have already come into the language, the disappearance of a vowel before one suffix need not have anything to do with what happens before another suffix. This suspicion is strengthened by pairs like *verb/verbal* vs. *adverb/adverbial.* Here, though we are not dealing with truncation of a vowel, the behavior of a morpheme in one word is quite independent of its behavior in another, assuming that the morpheme *verb* is common to both pairs.

Similarly, consider the morpheme *vert,* in *subvert, introvert, revert, divert.* This morpheme is discussed in Aronoff (1976: 105). Evidence that we are dealing with the same morpheme *vert* in all of these cases is that they share an idiosyncrasy in their nominalizations in -*ion.* Before -*ion* we get [ž]: *subver*[ž]*ion, introver*[ž]*ion, rever*[ž]*ion, diver*[ž]*ion.* Compare the regular reflex of -*t* in *assert/assertion, exert/exertion, contort/contortion;* here we always get [š], not [ž]. But now note that the morpheme *vert* does not always exhibit the same allomorphy. Before -*ive,* we get either ver[s]-, as in *subversive, introversive,* or ver[t]-, as in *revertive, divertive.* This sort of idiosyncrasy presents difficulties for a theory embracing diacritic features or suppletive representations. We cannot say that the morpheme *vert* contains a diacritic [+ D] to trigger a rule converting *vert* to *vers* before -*ive,* because this would incorrectly yield **rever*[s]*ive, *diver*[s]*ive.* On the other hand, we cannot say that *vert* has the feature [+ D] in *subvert* and *introvert* but [− D] in *revert* and *divert,* since this would mean that the morphemes are not identical. Analogously, the words *subvert* and *introvert* cannot be given suppletive representations *subver* $\left\{\begin{smallmatrix} s \\ t \end{smallmatrix}\right\}$ and *introver* $\left\{\begin{smallmatrix} s \\ t \end{smallmatrix}\right\}$, with a special rule selecting the variant in *-s* before *-ive*. Since this suppletive representation could not be posited for *revert* and *divert,* this would again obscure the fact that all of these words contain the same morpheme, *vert.*

In fact, the suppletive analysis encounters a more serious problem in these cases. The appearance of [s] before *-ive* is related to the appearance of [ž] before *-ion.* The voicing difference is a result of the automatic devoicing of a consonant before *-ive,* as Aronoff (1976:106) notes. (See section 7 below for an account that differs somewhat from Aronoff's.) Thus a truly general suppletive account would represent the alternants as *subver* $\left\{\begin{smallmatrix} z \\ t \end{smallmatrix}\right\}$ and *introver* $\left\{\begin{smallmatrix} z \\ t \end{smallmatrix}\right\}$. [z] would then predictably be realized as [ž] before *-ion* but as [s] before *-ive.* But in the light of *revert/rever*[ž]*ion, divert/diver*[ž]*ion,* the suppletive analysis would also posit *rever* $\left\{\begin{smallmatrix} z \\ t \end{smallmatrix}\right\}$, *diver* $\left\{\begin{smallmatrix} z \\ t \end{smallmatrix}\right\}$. Yet now we must somehow state that the first alternant, in -[z], is selected before *-ive* for *subvert* and *introvert* but that the second alternant is selected before *-ive* for *revert* and *divert.* I see no way of doing this without sacrificing the claim that we are dealing with the same morpheme *vert* in all of these cases.

The point of this discussion has been to compare different ways of listing idiosyncratic features. What has been shown thus far is that diacritic features or suppletive representations do not adequately capture cases in which a given morpheme behaves differently for morphologically arbitrary reasons. The parsing model does not suffer from this defect. Because the words *subvert, subversive, subversion, divert, divertive, diversion,* etc., cannot be generated by productive rules, all are listed in the lexicon. The grammar captures the relationship of *subvert/subversive* and *divert/divertive* in the same way, by comparing these pairs in relation to a morphological rule of *-ive* suffixation and undoing phonological changes as required. By condition (2c), none are undone in *divert/divertive;* for the pair *subvert/subversive,* a rule changing *t* to *s* is undone. At the same time, the parsing of *subvert/subversion* is totally parallel to that of *divert/diversion.* Alternations before *-ive* and before *-ion* are discussed somewhat further in section 7, along with another argument showing that the parsing model distinguishes two types of exception, while the alternatives just considered do not.

A final position to consider is that the words *cello* and *cellist* are related by a "via" rule (Vennemann 1972a, Hooper 1976), which says that the vowel ō sometimes alternates with Ø. But this is not a real alternative, since it says nothing. We have seen examples of possible via rules but never an example of an impossible one. Thus at present the claim that there are via rules is empty: nothing hinges on the existence of such rules. The via rule solution would be as consistent with the putative pair *cell/ celloist* as with the real pair *cello/cellist*. Furthermore, the prospects for restricting these rules in a nonarbitrary way do not look very bright, if we continue to maintain that the function of via rules is merely to record that a speaker had an intuition of relatedness between two forms or between two sets of forms. The problem with this stems from the fact that our goal as theorists is, by definition, to find a way of predicting how languages will behave, and by extension how speakers will deal with a language they acquire. Our goal cannot simply be to find a way of recording an observed intuition. Via rules, as presently construed, satisfy the latter goal but not the former one.

There is a more positive way of stating this argument: the only type of via rule that it makes theoretical sense to posit is the parsing rule. If we find a use for a given rule in one reverse derivation, it will be available for use in others as well. Although there is no guarantee that a given rule will produce a successful match in all cases, we will see below, in the discussion of recoverability, that repeated failures will lead to change. This permits us to test the accuracy of a rule. If application of the rule to novel forms consistently predicts relationships where they are in fact impossible, then we know either that the rule is wrong or that it will soon be lost.

5. RULES THAT SERVE A DOUBLE FUNCTION

The distinction between phonetic processes and more idiosyncratic morphophonological operations is not always clear-cut, for phonetic processes can perform a parsing function as well. This is one reason for thinking that it is wrong—or at least hasty—to divorce phonetic influences from morphophonology, as advocated by Hooper (1977) and by Donegan and Stampe (1977a). An example is C Drop in Polish, formulated by Gussman (1976) as (7):[2]

(7) C Drop

$$[+ \text{cor}] \rightarrow \emptyset \ / \ \begin{bmatrix} + \text{cor} \\ + \text{ant} \end{bmatrix} \ \underline{\quad\quad} \ \begin{bmatrix} + \text{cor} \\ + \text{nas} \end{bmatrix}$$

Among other things, this rule deletes *t* from between *s* and *n,* and *d* from between *z* and *n.* It is responsible for the forms on the right in (8), which

are the ordinary unguarded discourse variants of the careful speech forms
on the left. Examples are in Polish orthography except for the bracketed
phonetic segments.

(8) *Careful speech*   *Ordinary speech*

    u[stn]y   u[sn]y   'oral'

    po[stn]y   po[sn]y   'lenten'

    zawi[stn]y   zawi[sn]y   'begrudging'

    gwie[zdn]y   gwie[zn]y   'stellar'

(7) is in many respects a prototypical phonetic process. It applies generally in fast speech, does not admit lexical exceptions (though it need not
apply), and involves a modification of the timing of articulatory gestures
in that blockage of the air stream for *t* and *d* is delayed until the velum
is lowered for the following segment, thereby obliterating the stop. In
the last respect it resembles the sort of timing change described by
Hooper (1976: 114–115). This is just the type of rule whose effects
should not be reflected in lexical representations. The lexical forms are
taken to contain the *t* and *d* of the deliberate speech variants in the left
column of (8).

But in addition to being a fast speech process, (7) also performs a
morphophonological function. To see this, consider first the morphological structure of the adjectives from (8). As expressed by (9), they are
formed by adding an adjectival affix *-n* and an inflectional ending to a
noun stem. Examples appear in (10).

(9) Word Formation Rule[3]
    [Stem − Ending]$_N$ → [Stem − *n* − Ending]$_A$

(10) *Noun*   *Adjective*

    u[st]a   'mouth'   u[stn]y   'oral'

    po[st]   'fast'   po[stn]y   'lenten'

    zawi[śċ]   'grudge'   zawi[stn]y   'begrudging'

    gwia[zd]a   'star'   gwie[zdn]y   'stellar'

The noun stems for (10) are arrived at by omitting the final vowel, if
there is one. The stem of a noun ending in a prepalatal segment or cluster
is arrived at by ignoring its palatality; [śċ], which corresponds to IPA
[ɕ tɕ], is the prepalatal alternant of *st*.[4] Thus the stem of zawi[śċ] is
zawist-.

Now, as Gussman notes, Polish has a fair number of adjectives similar
to those in (8) in that they contain the sequences [sn] and [zn], but different in that they lack a careful speech variant [stn] and [zdn]:

(11) *Noun*   *Adjective*

rado[śĉ]	'joy'	rado[sn]y	'joyful'
nieszczę[śĉ]e	'woe'	nieszczę[sn]y	'woeful'
bole[śĉ]	'pain'	bole[sn]y	'painful'

We can account for the lack of an adjectival careful speech variant in [stn] here by positing lexical /sn/, as opposed to the /stn/ posited for the adjectives in (8).[5] But the fast speech rule (7) still serves a function in words like these: it fills in the missing *t* when we try to recover the adjective's correspondence to a related noun. For example, we employ this rule in parsing the form rado[sn]y, in derivation (12):

(12)	Word A	Word B	Morphology
LEXICAL FORMS:	rado/śĉ/$_N$	rado/sn/-y$_A$	[Stem − Ending]$_N$ → [Stem − n − Ending]$_A$
i. stĭ → śĉ (cf. fn.4)	rado/st-ĭ/$_N$	—	—
ii. (7) C Drop	—	rado/stn/-y$_A$	—

Now the morphology can analyze *rado[sn]-y* as the stem *radost-* plus the adjectival affix *-n* plus its inflectional ending. This is a case in which a phonetic rule that any grammar posits also relates pairs of lexical representations.

Next consider the question, can the rules that parse lexical items be restricted to productive phonetic rules? Or, failing this, could we say that lexical structure not phonetically determined is purely haphazard? The facts at hand, I believe, show that either position would be arbitrary and incorrect.

For example, Isačenko (1972), cited in Aronoff (1976), shows that the Russian adjectival affix *-sk* (which appears in *leningradskij*, from *Leningrad*) occasions the deletion of preceding *sk* if this preceding *sk* is a morpheme. *Bask* 'Basque' does not lose its *sk* in *baskskij*, because this *sk* is not a separate morpheme. But *Tomsk* 'city of Tomsk' loses its *sk* in the corresponding environment, *tomskij*, because the base word is analyzed as /tom-sk/, derived from the name of the river Tom. The fact that the morphological structure of *Tomsk* continues to be perceived explains why the form **tomskskij* has never developed.

A good indication of the extent to which lexical structure need not be phonetically determined comes from considering the role of recoverability of lexical relationships, which is the subject of the next section.

6. RECOVERABILITY AS A FACTOR IN LINGUISTIC CHANGE

A number of recent studies, including Kaye (1974, 1975), Eliasson (1975, 1977), and Gussman (1976), present evidence of a tendency in language to make phonological relationships recoverable. Although the relationship most often discussed in this context is between a given surface form and its underlying representation, we can restate the recoverability principle in light of the assumptions of the parsing model: morphologically complex words change to make their relationship to a base word more easily recoverable.

Increased recoverability provides the most direct explanation of the fact, discussed by Schuh (1972), that Hausa singular/plural pairs like *ɓawnaa/ɓakaanee* 'bush cow' and *buuzuu/bugaajee* 'Tuareg' are gradually losing their old plural in favor of a more transparently derived one, *ɓawnaayee* and *buuzaayee*. The rules for forming the plurals of this class, as described by Newman (1972), are these. Heavy roots add infix *-aa-* after the initial CVC, where V can be a long or short vowel or a diphthong. If we analyze the roots of the above forms as /ɓakn-/ and /bugz-/, this gives *ɓak-aa-n-* and *bug-aa-z-*. To this result, the ending *-ee* is affixed, giving *ɓak-aa-n-ee* and *bug-aa-z-ee*. The latter form becomes *bugaajee* by a general rule. The absence of *k* and *g* from the corresponding singulars *ɓawnaa* and *buuzuu* is a result of a historical process weakening syllable-final labials and velars to *w*, which gave **baknaa* > *ɓawnaa* and **bugzuu* > *buwzuu*. In the latter form *uw* is interpreted as *uu,* an exceptionless fact in Hausa. (The generality of Newman's account of plural formation is evidenced by singular/plural pairs *kaskoo/kasaakee* 'bowl' and *birnii/biraanee* 'city', which lack the morphophonemic alternations that complicate the first set of examples.) The innovative forms *ɓawnaayee* and *buuzaayee* follow the pattern of heavy roots containing a long vowel or diphthong, like *kiifii/kiifaayee* 'fish', *gawlaa/gawlaayee* 'idiot'. For the latter, the above rules first add *-aa-* after the root CVC, giving, for example, *gawl-aa,* and then they add *-ee,* giving *gawl-aa-ee*. (Note that the diphthong *aw* counts as V in CVC.) *y* is inserted between *aa* and *ee* by a general rule of epenthesis.

Schuh attributes the replacement of the older plural forms to the fact that the historical process weakening syllable-final labials and velars to *w* left Hausa with words in which *w* in the singular corresponded to a variety of consonants in the plural, including *f, b, ɓ, m, k, ƙ,* and *g*. Rather than analyzing the *w* in the singular as underlying the appropriate labial or velar consonant, Schuh proposes that their underlying forms are essentially the surface forms in these cases, that the singular is the base from which the plural is derived, and that accordingly each *w* in the singular is marked for one of a set of inverse rules selecting the appropriate consonant in the plural. (See Vennemann 1972a for a discussion of inverted rules. The rules in the case at hand are inverted in the sense that the historical rule changed consonants to *w* while Schuh's synchronic analysis contains a set of rules taking *w* back to its etymological sources.) Schuh comments that this situation is difficult for speakers to deal with and thereby explains why speakers have gradually been changing their plurals. They eliminate the special markings on *w* in the singulars, causing them to be realized as [w] in the plural as well.

But, as noted in Leben (1974), this analysis forces one to posit a stage in which a previous condition on plural formation was lost, followed by a stage in which the same condition mysteriously reappears. Prior to the alleged rule inversion, the underlying sequence CVwC is interpreted as C-diphthong-C, and so *-aa-* is placed to the right of CVwC in plurals. In the proposed stage of inversion, when etymological syllable-final labials and velars are rephonemicized as *w*, this interpretation must be relaxed, so that /ɓawn-/, for example, can become *ɓaw-aa-n-ee,* which goes to *ɓakaanee* by an inverse rule. Finally, as the older plurals are lost, the earlier interpretation of CVwC re-emerges, so that /ɓawn-/ gives /ɓawn-aa-ee/ > *ɓawnaayee* in the plural. This is hardly a satisfying scenario.

With the parsing model, it is possible to capture Schuh's basic insight while avoiding the anomaly raised by the putative rule inversion. The morphologically complex forms are changing so as to increase the ease of recovering the relationship between singular and plural. In the light of the unpredictability of the plural from the singular, we list plurals in the lexicon along with singulars, and we measure the recoverability of the singular/plural relationship in terms of the number of rules that apply in a reverse derivation. For older singular/plural pairs, such as *ɓawnaa/ ɓakaanee* and *buuzuu/bugaaǰee,* several rules must be undone before *-awn-* and *-uuz-* in the singular can be identified with the corresponding sequences *-ak . . . n-* and *-ug . . . ǰ-* in the plural. For the innovative forms, no phonological rules need be undone at all: *ɓawnaa/ɓawnaayee* and *buuzuu/buuzaayee* are transparently related, especially since, as shown in Leben (1977b), the parsing approach permits one to formulate the Hausa plural formation rule as attaching *-aayee* to a singular stem.

There is another type of morphologically motivated change in which recoverability is a factor. This is where at one stage any one of a number of phonological characteristics of a base form may correspond to a single characteristic in derived forms. What makes this situation difficult, from the point of view of the parsing model, is roughly that there are a number of conflicting strategies leading to possibly appropriate base forms, making the one correct base form relatively hard to locate. An example is the development of Polish adjectival forms like those in (8) and (11) above, as discussed by Gussmann (1976). Consider first a simple example. Gussmann cites evidence that the adjective *postny* 'lenten' goes back to an older form *pośny,* which was less transparently related to the noun *post* 'fast' than the new form. From Gussmann's point of view, this development at first seems puzzling, since it increased the opacity of C Drop (7) by creating a new exception to it. But Gussman explains the example by suggesting that forms change to increase the recoverability of the underlying form from the surface form. We can adjust this statement to say that the adjectives changed to facilitate recovery of their relationship to corresponding nouns. Prior to the change, Polish not only had adjectives in -*śn*- related to nouns in -*st;* it also had adjectives in -*śn*- related to nouns in -*s* (e.g. *gło*[*s*] 'voice' / *gło*[*śn*]*y* 'loud'; *sko*[*s*] 'obliqueness' / *sko*[*śn*]*y* 'oblique') and some in -*śn*- related to nouns in -*ść* (see below). What made this situation difficult for speakers is roughly that from looking at a given surface form in -*śn*- one could not immediately tell whether the noun it was related to would end in *st, s,* or *ść.* The change of *pośny* to *postny* helped to rectify the recovery problem by removing one class of bases that previously had adjective forms in -*sn*-.

One might resist such an explanation, citing a simpler one which would say that the fossilized *pośny* was simply lost, having been supplanted by the productively derived *postny.* (A parallel development in English would be the gradual replacement of *ferocity* by the productively derived *ferociousness.*) But this interpretation will not work in general. Consider the development of a form like *rado*[*sn*]*y,* which is morphologically related to *radość* (cf. (11)). In Old Polish, according to Gussman, this form was *rado*[*śn*]*y.* We cannot explain this development as a replacement of the old form by a productively derived new one. Adding -*n* and an inflectional ending to the noun *radość* would give *radośćny.* The *ć* would convert to *t* by anterior depalatalization, which Gussman formulates as (13):

(13)

$$\begin{bmatrix} C \\ -\text{cont} \end{bmatrix} \longrightarrow [-\text{high}] / \underline{\hspace{1cm}} [+\text{cor}]$$

and preceding *ś* would follow suit, becoming *s* by a rule making a coronal spirant agree with a following nonpalatal cluster in palatality. Thus we would expect *radostny* instead of the attested *radosny*. This case is also difficult to explain as a haphazard analogical development. The obvious analogical pattern for the adjectival form of *radość* to fit is exemplified by *zawiść*$_N$/*zawistny*$_A$. This, too, would incorrectly predict *radostny*.

As Gussman observes, this case looks problematic from many angles. It increases the opacity of the rule palatalizing spirants before adjectival morpheme *-n*, since where we used to have [*śn*], we now have [*sn*]. By the same token, the rules of Palatal Assimilation and C Drop, which formerly in a non-bleeding order (giving *radost'-n-y* → *radośt'-n-y* by Palatalization and then *radoś-n-y* by C Drop) now apply, in Gussman's analysis, in bleeding order: first *radost'-n-y* changes to *rados-n-y* by C Drop, and then the environment for Palatal Assimilation is no longer met. Furthermore, the change has increased allomorphy. Previously the noun stem within the adjective invariably appeared as *radoś-*, regardless of case endings. Now the noun stem within the adjective is either *rados-* (as in *radosny*) or *radoś-* (as in *radośni,* nom. pl. personal, where *s* has assimilated in palatality to *ɲ*), depending on the case ending.

This development provides particularly strong evidence for the recoverability principle, simply because other commonly used explanations fail. As was mentioned earlier, along with adjectives in *-śn-* related to nouns in *-ść*, Polish had adjectives in *-śn-* related to nouns in *-s* (e.g., *gło*[*s*] 'voice' / *gło*[*śn*]*y* 'loud'). Thus, even though Old Polish *radośny* was perfectly parsable as the adjectival form of *radość*—the rule of C Drop is simply undone, restoring the coronal segment (in this case *ć*) between *ś* and *n*—the situation was relatively difficult for speakers because from looking at a given surface form in *-śn-* one could not immediately tell whether the related noun would end in *s* or *ść*. By changing the adjectival forms of nouns in *-ść,* Polish rectified the recovery problem. I will return to this example below. Note for now that the changes *pośny* > *postny* and *radośny* > *radosny* show that the older derived forms were not simply treated as frozen relics of the past. It is only because their structure was perceived and because the recovery of this structure was nonetheless found difficult that such forms changed as they did.

7. RECOVERABILITY: A REFINEMENT

The notion of recoverability introduced in the preceding section can be interpreted as influencing a language to change so as to facilitate the process of finding an appropriate base word A to compare against a given derived word B with respect to some morphological rule R. Recoverability is enhanced to the extent that the grammar minimizes the number of paths that lead back from a lexical representation to more abstract representations.

In this section I will address one problem that arises out of the recoverability principle when it is phrased as vaguely as I have put it here. We must distinguish the Polish situation from others which, though parallel in certain respects, do not exhibit the pressure for change that the Polish forms have undergone. A good example comes from a few classes of English adjectival forms in -*ive* and nominalizations in -*ion*. If an adjectival form ends in -[s]*ive,* the [s] can be related to one of the following segments:[6]

(14) [s] express/expressive; obsess/obsessive
       [z] abuse/abusive; effuse/effusive
       [t] permit/permissive; subvert/subversive
       [d] explode/explosive; evade/evasive

For nominals in -[s]*ion* we have related verbs that end in the following segments:[7]

(15) [š] abolish/abolition; admonish/admonition
       [s] confess/confession; impress/impression
       [t] assert/assertion; assimilate/assimilation
       [d] apprehend/apprehension; suspend/suspension

These alternations look parallel to the ones in Polish, in that a single phoneme in derived forms—[s] in (14) and [š] in (15)—corresponds to any one of a number of phonemes in a related base word. The recoverability principle, as stated for Polish, would pressure English to eliminate some of these possible sources of [s] in -[s]*ive* and of [š] in -[š]*ion.* In the absence of any sign that this pressure is being felt, we must somehow distinguish the English alternations from the Polish ones. Interestingly, for the English alternations but not for the Polish ones it is possible to construct an orderly chain of segments that are successively tried in searching for an appropriate base word. For the examples in (15), the case in which [š] comes from a verb in -[š] is the simplest: to relate *abolition to abolish* no rules need be undone, except possibly for the stress rule.[8] For the cases in which this does not lead to a correct base word, the next segment to try is [s], which involves the smallest number of changes from [š] of the group listed in (15); from here the closest segment is [t], and from [t] we go back to [d]. Thus we can posit a sequence of rules which gradually take the segment [s] back to [d], through stages with attested alternants of [š]:

(16) š ← s
    s ← t
    t ← d

I have omitted environments from these rules, but a full account must express them, to preclude application in environments where no alternation is possible while permitting them to apply in environments other than *-ion,* as illustrated by *space/spacious* and *pirate/piracy.*

    The forms in (14) can be related in similar fashion. Before the adjectival ending *-ive* a preceding consonant is always voiceless. This regularity can be built into the morphological rule, so that it specifies not only that the suffix *-ive* is attached but also that the preceding consonant is devoiced. As a result base words in [s] and [z] are recovered without undoing any rules of segmental phonology. For the remaining forms we need a phonological operation taking *s* and *z* back to *t* and *d.* The second rule in (16), which need not refer to voicing since it does not adjust this feature, will perform this function nicely.

    By contrast, in Old Polish recovery of *głos* from *głośny* and of *radość* from *radosny* cannot be undone in a uniform chain of steps, as can be seen by comparing the two derivations below:

(17)	Word A	Word B	Morphology
LEXICAL FORMS:	głos$_N$	głosśn-y$_A$	[Stem - Ending]$_N$
			$\longrightarrow$ [Stem - *n* - Ending]$_A$
i. Palatalization before *-n*	—	głosn-y$_A$	—

(18)

LEXICAL FORMS   radość$_N$ radośn-y$_A$ [Stem-Ending]$_N$

$\longrightarrow$ [Stem - n - Ending]$_A$

i. C Drop   —   radoś$\left[\begin{array}{c} C \\ + \text{ cor} \end{array}\right]$n-y$_A$ —

For *głośny* we undo the rule palatalizing a consonant before adjectival affix *-n*. Having recovered [s], we see that the environment for the morphological rule is now satisfied by this adjective and the noun *gło[s]*. But for *rado[ś]ny,* there is no possibility of undoing the palatalization rule. By condition (2c), rules are undone only when they increase the compatibility of two forms with respect to a morphological rule. Palatalization would not qualify in this case since the noun *rado[śĆ]* has [ś] exactly where the adjective has it. Similarly, condition (2c) prohibits us from rewriting *radość* as *rado/st-ĭ/,* since this would make this form less similar to *radośn-y.* Conversely, note that it is impossible to employ C Drop, which is the first rule successfully undone in (18), as the first rule in (17). By condition (2c), this step is impossible, since inserting a consonant after [ś] in *głośny* would make it less similar to *głos.*

The absence of a chain of successfully applied steps does not make recovery impossible, but it does make it more difficult. When the forms described above changed, the result aided recovery of the segments in question. In modern Polish, [ś] is simply taken back to [s]; [s] is simply taken back to [st].

The principle suggested here, that recovery is hindered when there is more than one path that can be followed in taking a segment in a derived word back to a representation compatible with the corresponding segment in a base word, successfully differentiates the Old Polish situation from the English one. But it remains to show that the difference cited is a relevant one. One thing that suggests that it is is that some English forms breaking an established chain of rules have been changing in a way that we would predict. As noted by Leben and Robinson (1977), forms like *caprice/capr[i]cious* and *prestige/prest[i]gious* do not exhibit the normal vowel alternations.[9] Where [ī] alternates with a lax vowel, that vowel is usually [e], as in *serene/serenity,* and where [i] alternates with a tense vowel, that vowel is normally [āj], as in *vice/vicious.* Now, despite this fact, forms like *capricious* can still be successfully parsed by the rules that undo the vowel alternations in *serene/serenity, vice/vicious,* etc., as shown here:

(19)	Word A	Word B	Morphology
LEXICAL FORMS:	kəprījs$_N$	kəprišəs$_A$	$[X]_N \rightarrow [X - ījəs]_A$
i. Glide deletion e.g. j → Ø / s____	—	kprišjəs$_A$	—
ii. Palatalization e.g. s → š / ____ j	—	kəprisjəs$_A$	—
iii. ī → Ø / C____ y	—	kəprisījəs$_A$	—
iv. (Vowel Shift)	—	—	—
v. Diphthongization	kəprīs$_N$	—	
vi. Trisyllabic shortening	—	kəprīsījəs$_A$	—

But in order to recover /ī/ from /i/, we have bypassed the rule of Vowel Shift, by condition (2c). This breaks the established chain of rules, pointing to a recovery problem under the principle proposed above. Innovative forms *capr[īj]cious* and *prest[īj]gious* solve the recovery problem by eliminating the vowel alternation altogether.

The case just examined, I think, points up a very interesting consequence of the parsing approach. Where previous approaches to morphophonemics dealt with one type of exception feature, the present model in effect says there are two. One kind, involving lexically governed differences in rule application as in *obese/obesity* vs. *serene/serenity, solo/soloist* vs. *cello/cellist, zawiść/zawistny* vs. *radość/radosny,* have resisted change, at least partly because they have posed no recovery problem under the definition given here. The other kind, again involving a lexically governed difference in rule application, exemplified by *caprice/capricious* vs. *vice/vicious,* has been noticeably more susceptible to change. If this result is at all general, it will indicate that the parsing model brings us closer to an explanatory theory of morphophonology than previous approaches. Note that the suggested difference between the two sorts of exception is here a principled one, in that the difference follows automatically from the interaction of the recoverability principle with the conditions on well-formed derivations, including the rules and the conventions on rule application.

This account makes crucial use of the characteristic, inherited through the evaluation metric of standard generative phonology, of sometimes factoring complex alternations into a sequence of simple ones, as illustrated by the rules in (16) and the derivations (6) and (19). To reject this possibility at present would, as far as I know, require sheer dogmatism. If the account proposed here is correct, it provides new empirical support for maximizing the simplicity and range of applicability of rules.

The recoverability principle serves one more important function, that of helping to explain why it is that the rules of the parsing model are not more general than they might otherwise be. To see this, recall that parsing rules are not redundancy rules. Trisyllabic Shortening, for example, cannot be interpreted as a redundancy rule, since it is violated by *obesity, notify,* etc. But since parsing rules only specify what *can* be done in some derivations rather than what *must* be done in all derivations, this leaves open the possibility of making these rules absurdly general. For example, Trisyllabic Shortening could be stated without any environment, though it would only happen to apply fruitfully in a few environments, most of them trisyllabic. Or the Truncation rule for *cellist* could be re-expressed as V → Ø, with no environment, and this rule could now be collapsed with rules deleting consonants and glides. The recoverability principle provides a sensible way of avoiding these absurdities. To the extent that a rule is overly general, it will potentially define steps in derivations that must never be taken, leading to a large-scale recovery problem. Hence the recoverability principle limits the generality of the rules.

I conclude that even with a substantial set of limitations on the phonological content of lexical representations, it is possible to construct a systematic and theoretically interesting account of alternations which, though not productive in the usual sense, exert an influence on linguistic change.

NOTES

This paper is a revision of a paper presented at the Conference. The revision was prepared while I was on sabbatical leave in the Department of Linguistics and Philosophy at M.I.T. I wish to thank the Department for making its resources available to me. I am particularly grateful to Joan Bresnan, Edmund Gussman, James Harris, and Paul Kiparsky for thoughtful challenges and suggestions based on an earlier version of this paper and to Noam Chomsky and Morris Halle for comments which, while not always sympathetic, have been most helpful.

1. To simplify the exposition I state these conventions in a way that makes parsing rules easier to relate to rules familiar from conventional generative

phonology. The appearance that the actual rules in a parsing model are arrived at by first doing a standard generative analysis should be ignored. In particular, Robinson (to appear) shows that the procedures outlined here permit one to simplify ordering statements. Furthermore, as rule (4) in fact illustrates, phonological rules in the parsing model are sometimes formulated more generally than in a conventional generative account. For discussion of a principle constraining the generality of rules, see section 7.

2. Rubach (1977:130–135) observes that the rule, taken as a fast speech rule, is more general. He gives it the following formulation:

$$\begin{bmatrix} -\text{cont} \\ -\text{del. rel.} \\ +\text{cor} \\ +\text{ant} \end{bmatrix} \longrightarrow \emptyset \;/\; <\!\text{C}\!> \begin{bmatrix} +\text{obstr} \\ +\text{cor} \end{bmatrix} - \begin{bmatrix} +\text{cons} \\ <\!+\text{cont}\!> \end{bmatrix}$$

But this creates no problem for employing it as a parsing rule, as in derivation (12) in the text, since this more general formulation will, by virtue of including (7) as a sub-part, still be able to restore *t* in all of the places in which it is called for.

3. Gussmann (to appear) proposes that the adjectival suffix is not *n* but rather *Vn,* where V is some vowel that has a raising effect on the vowel of the preceding syllable. The existence of this effect is demonstrated by the last pair in (10), *gwiazda/gwiezdny,* in which the vowel *a* of the noun corresponds to the vowel *e* of the adjective. I accept this proposal but, to simplify matters, will ignore it in the text.

4. Gussmann (1976 and to appear) handles this fact by regarding [śč] as a reflex of /stĭ/. Under this proposal we arrive at the stem of nouns in -*śč* in the same way as for other nouns, by deleting the final vowel. I will accept this proposal for expository purposes but must note that, despite the abundant morphophonological evidence for it in Gussmann (to appear), it involves manufacturing a tense/lax contrast that, as far as I know, is never manifested as such on the surface in Polish. Furthermore, tests that one might apply in order to verify the presence of the vowel of /stĭ/ as an actual vowel seem unlikely to support this proposal. For example, the putative final /ĭ/ does not make the preceding syllable count as penultimate for the purposes of the penultimate stress rule.

5. The proposal that these adjectives are listed lexically rather than all being productively derived is corroborated by the fact, noted by Gussmann, that some of them differ unpredictably in meaning from their corresponding nouns. For instance, the adjective corresponding to 'fear' is glossed as 'terrible', and the one corresponding to 'foetus' is glossed as 'fertile'.

6. In addition to these, words in -[s]*ive* can contain allomorphs that are peculiar to one morpheme. In instances like *cohere/cohesive,* we are not really dealing with an alternation between [r] and [s], and in *compel/ compulsive* we are not dealing with a relation between Ø and [s]. Rather, as Aronoff (1976: 109) has proposed, in *cohere/cohesive* we have relations between allomorphs /hīr/ and /hīz/ (/z/ becomes [s] before -*ive,* as noted later in the text); similarly for /pel/ and /pʌls/. A sign of this is that other

instances of the same morpheme will tend to exhibit the same alternation (as with *adhere; impel, repel*), but other morphemes ending in the same segment will tend not to exhibit this alternation. The situation is quite different with the examples in (14).

7. In addition, there are cases that involve allomorphy either of the root or of the suffix—it is not clear which: cf. Aronoff (1976: 104), who cites as examples *define/ definition, repeat/ repetition*. Morphemes like *-here* and *-pel*, mentioned in fn. 6, also change before *-ion*.

8. It may not even be necessary to undo the stress rule for the forms in (15), since the stress difference can be built into the morphological rule: stress is invariably on the syllable preceding the ending *-ion*. This seems a good way to say that stress is morphologized in such cases, as many have claimed.

9. The original observation, I have found, stems from J. D. McCawley, cited in an obscure footnote in Ross (1972).

CHAPTER EIGHT

The Aims of
Autosegmental Phonology

John Goldsmith

In this paper, I shall discuss several aspects of an approach to generative phonology known as "autosegmental phonology." Autosegmental phonology shares with more traditional generative phonology a commitment to a formal account of phonological processes, and also a commitment to developing a formalism in which the common, expected, or "natural" developments in a language are represented in a formally simple way. What distinguishes autosegmental phonology from the *Sound Pattern of English* type of generative phonology is, first, the development of a multi-linear phonological analysis in which different features may be placed on separate tiers, and in which the various tiers are organized by "association lines" and a Well-Formedness Condition; and, second, analysis of phonological phenomena less in terms of feature-changing rules as such, and more in terms of rules that delete and *reorganize* the various autosegments, through the readjustment of the association lines.

The general program for research has gone in a number of directions, and I shall emphasize in this paper a few of these areas. In the first part (§1), an informal account of the original motivations for the autosegmental treatment of suprasegmentals is presented. It deals with issues discussed in more detail in Goldsmith (1976b). In the second part (§2), I shall illustrate the power of an autosegmental approach in dealing with an intricate corner of the tonal system of Igbo. In the third part (§3), some of the interesting and exciting suggestions made by Clements, McCarthy, Haraguchi, and others regarding the treatment of other suprasegmental phenomena in an autosegmental way are discussed, and in the fourth section, (§4), I sketch some of the ways the general approach can deal with typically segmental assimilation phenomena. I try,

202

furthermore, to motivate the existence of autosegmental levels in languages classically considered to contain suprasegmentals, and even those which appear more traditional. Finally, in §5, I remark upon the view of phonology I see lying behind the autosegmental approach, and how this view may be seen to differ from that lying behind various others of the theories presented at this conference.

1. American phonology has shown—not always, but at times—a peculiar rigidity in its conception of the "shape" of phonological representations. One of the aims of autosegmental phonology is to investigate the consequences of having structures in phonology more complex, or more articulated, than a simply linear string of segments. I shall discuss some of the tools offered, and some of the problems they can deal with.

The aim, then, of autosegmental phonology is to deal with the consequences for generative phonology of multi-linear phonological analysis and representation. That is, we let go of the assumption that phonological and phonetic representations consist of a single string, or concatenation, of segments. Instead, we set up underlying and surface forms consisting of parallel strings of segments arranged in two or more tiers. Features are distributed over the various tiers in the sense that no feature may appear on more than one tier. This somewhat richer phonological representation then serves as the basis for a more enlightening, and ultimately simpler, formal phonological analysis.

Part of this idea, certainly, is not new to linguistics. The Firthians are quite serious in their attention to prosodies, those units in the phonological analysis above and beyond the sequential "phonematic units," or segments, as we might call them.

It seems to me that in their attention to such processes as vowel harmony and the complexity of tonal systems, and in their rejection of a strictly linear view of phonological representations, the Firthians are right on the mark. So too were Bernard Bloch (1948) and Zellig Harris (1944) in their discussions of the more complex possibilities of segmentation in their articles in *Language*. Apart from this major point of agreement with Firthian or prosodic analysis, the autosegmental approach differs on at least two other important points. The first is the centrality of the distinction maintained in the autosegmental approach among the notions of *segment, feature, rule* and *association*. This four-way distinction does not correspond in any natural way to the concepts and constructs found in Firthian phonology. The notion of *feature* in the generative framework corresponds in the Firthian framework to the notion *prosody*—an element which furthermore plays the role corresponding to phonological rule and to "true suprasegmentals" (in our terms, autosegmentalized features).

But the only types of prosodies that correspond to autosegmental analyses are those in which the prosodies are phonetically homogeneous—which, as a review of the literature will show, is a small percentage of the extant prosodies. (For further discussion, see Goldsmith [in preparation a].)

The second major difference between Firthian and autosegmental analysis lies in the emphasis, in the latter, placed upon rules and their interaction with the Well-Formedness Condition. We shall see an example of this in section 2 below.

If there were several precedents for breaking away from a strictly linear representation, how this was to be done within the framework of generative grammar has been problematic.[1] The clearest generative position on this is found in Chomsky (1955:29):

> (T)hough the representations that we construct on any linguistic level are unidimensional, we have not required that left-to-right order of representation correspond directly to temporal order in the represented utterance. . . . By accepting a linear system of representation, we rule out the possibility of certain kinds of discontinuity. If more general kinds of discontinuity than we can handle occur in language, a more general theory of representation will be necessary.
>
> FN: In this study, suprasegmental features (pitch, stress, juncture) have not been seriously considered. Ultimately, of course, these phenomena must be incorporated into any full syntactic theory, and it may be that this extension still requires a more elaborate system of representation.[2]

A significant step was taken by William Leben (1973) and Edwin Williams (1976). Leben's and Williams' suggestion did not change the picture of phonetic representation as a linear sequence of segments—thus *not* reverting to the Bloch-Harris position—but they did suggest that the representation underlying some particular sequence of "phonetic" segments could consist of two separate and quite independent sequences of phoneme-type segments, one sequence providing the tonal information, the other sequence containing everything else. Naturally, to have a surface or phonetic representation that was entirely one-dimensional—that is, a simple sequence of segments—they each provided for "feature mapping," which joined two separate sequences of segments into one single linear sequence.

The autosegmental approach arose out of certain inadequacies that were brought to light explicitly and implicitly by Williams' and Leben's work. The most glaring problem was the nature of "contour-toned" vowels—that is, vowels whose surface tone is rising or falling, a situation that can often be shown to be the result of a concatenation of Low and High level tones. How can a single segment bear or carry two tonal specifications in sequence? This was the first problem to resolve.

Intimately related to this was the necessity of explaining the relationship of the left-to-right ordering *inside* the segment (it seemed) and the left-to-right order of segments themselves. A tonal assimilation occasioned by a Low tone that affects a High tone to its right, for example, will turn that High tone into a Rising tone—never a Falling tone. (1) represents this as a strictly linear system would; but, strictly speaking, this way of representing a contour tone makes no sense. We may look at the solution to this problem as a "boundary condition" on the solution to the first question, the representation of contour tones.

$$(1) \quad \begin{bmatrix} V \\ -\text{high} \end{bmatrix} Co \begin{bmatrix} V \\ +\text{high} \end{bmatrix} \longrightarrow \begin{bmatrix} V \\ -\text{high} \end{bmatrix} Co \begin{bmatrix} V \\ -\text{high}/+\text{high} \end{bmatrix}$$

Yet another problem in the theory of tonal representations (cf. Goldsmith 1975b) is what I have called "stability," and, rather interestingly, its import is apparent only within a generative framework. "Stability" refers to the resistance of the tonal features of a vowel to deletion, even when the vowel that bore the tonal features is deleted or desyllabified.

The resolution of these problems was the introduction of several parallel strings of segments in the phonological *and* phonetic representations, enriched in a significant way by "association lines"—lines which, at the phonetic level, indicate the "co-registration" of the different tiers of segments. A language in which tonal features are autosegmentalized will represent a bisyllabic word with a tone pattern High - Low as in (2); a rule that would cause the second syllable to assimilate in tone would modify (2), change the relative domains of the tonal and non-tonal segments, and produce, in turn, (3).

(2) C V C V
   | |
   H L

(3) C V C V
   H L

(3) represents, it should be clear, a bisyllabic word whose tone pattern is High-Falling.

This autosegmental representation automatically solves our first three problems. The contour-toned vowels are, as (3) suggests, those in which the association is not purely one-to-one; tone-spreading rules that give rise to certain kinds of contour tones are the effect of a rule that adds an association line. We see such a change occurring between (2) and (3). We might note, furthermore, that the only rules which have the simple geometric property of adding an association line do, in fact, produce "natural"—that is, occurring—types of assimilation. Thus simplicity in the formalism does seem to match naturalness in the phonological system. Thirdly, stability of tonal features is the natural consequence of a rule deleting a segment on the tier consisting of non-tonal features (the upper tier, that is, in (2) or (3)). Now, in a language in which such an autosegmental representation is appropriate at the underlying level, two possibilities are open. Either the lexical entry for a word consists of a pair of strings of segments—much as in (2), but without the association lines—or else each tier might constitute a separate lexical entry. Thus two "morphemes" may in fact constitute the single underlying phonological level—one on the tonological tier, one on the non-tonological tier.

This kind of independent-minded behavior is familiar to linguists under the guise of "floating tones"—morphologically identifiable elements (a High tone, for example) whose position with respect to the syllables in the sentence is determined by the syntactic structure. That is to say, it can frequently be shown in tone languages that the tone pattern of a sentence is composed of the tonal patterns of the individual words in the sentence plus an additional tone, a morpheme which contributes only to the tonal pattern and not to the number or make-up of the syllables.

Conversely, it is often found in such tone languages that certain syllables are underlyingly devoid of tone, and receive a tone only through the influence of their neighboring tone-lending syllables. In general, then, a language with N level tones has the potential of N + 1 types of morphemes, tonally speaking. In a language with N level tones, a syllable may underlyingly be any of the N tones (or some concatenation of these) *or* it may be not marked for any tone. An interesting example of just such a situation is described in Wilkinson (1976).

Both of the cases described in the last two paragraphs, it should be clear, are examples of an underlying "mismatch" between the number of tonal segments and the number of syllabic segments—a difficult concept to deal with within a more familiar generative approach.

A crucial problem that arises now for any generative approach of the sort we have been considering is this: what is the technical device that relates the two tiers of segments? So far we have made allusion to association lines and their function; but at this point, we should make clear their origin. We may assume that all association lines (on segments other than boundaries) are introduced at some point in the derivation after the underlying representation. This amounts to, in effect, saying that there are no association lines in the stored or underlying representation. And this, in turn, implies that all underlying representations are linear.[3]

If underlying representations, then, contain no association lines, these association lines are first introduced by rule. The range of possible association rules is still undetermined, but in African tone languages, for instance, it is clear that a major rule in this respect is mapping one tone per syllable, starting from the left (see Edmundson and Bendor-Samuel (1976), Williams (1976), Leben (1973, 1977a), Goldsmith (1976b); for a far-reaching study of the interaction of accent and association rules, see Haraguchi (1976); on Sanskrit, May and Goldsmith (1975); on the interaction with the cycle, Elimelach (1976)).

A rather powerful convention—perhaps too powerful, actually—on derived forms was suggested in Goldsmith (1976a, b) and elsewhere, a convention called "the Well-Formedness Condition" (WFC). This convention has the effect of adding or deleting association lines at any point throughout the derivation. Stated informally (see Goldsmith [1976b] for a more unified statement), it reads:

Well-Formedness Condition
1. Each vowel must be associated with (at least) one toneme.
2. Each toneme must be associated with (at least) one vowel.
3. No association lines may cross.

One consequence of the WFC can be seen in (4). When a toneless suffix appears on a stem, the tone associated with the stem automatically has its domain extended to the suffixes as well (cf. (5)).

(4) C V + C V + C V   (5) C V + C V + C V
        | |
        L   L

Such a Condition, it can be seen, would have the effect of placing floating tones on some vowel or other—of "docking" the floating tone, we might say. Certain additional principles—some language-specific, some universal—may be necessary to effect the results required by the WFC.

In general, however, the autosegmental approach is not meant to deal only with tone; other languages (for example, Guarani) approach nasalization in an autosegmental way, and other features (other than the major class features)[4] could be dealt with autosegmentally.[5]

2. Let us look at a typical autosegmental analysis, based on data from Igbo. A crucial fact about tone in Igbo is that there are three contrasting tones: High, Low, and Drop (or Mid). High, Low, and Drop contrast after a High or Drop, but the three-way contrast is reduced to a two-way contrast after a Low tone; in particular, High and Drop are indistinguishable phonetically when they follow a Low tone. Furthermore, a Drop tone is distinguished from a High tone in that the Drop tone is produced a pitch-step lower than a preceding Drop or High tone. A High tone (N.B.) will be produced at the *same* pitch as a preceding Drop or High. Schematically we can summarize this as follows:

(6)

High High   High Drop Drop   High Drop High

Williams (1976) argued a certain tonal mutation in nouns (which we shall call "Object Mutation") in Igbo can be used as a diagnostic for the presence of a (sometimes floating) H tone preceding these mutated nouns. In Goldsmith (1976b) the analysis is deepened, and the floating tone is shown to account for an interesting set of alternations. Two aspects are crucially "autosegmental": first, positing a tonal deletion rule feeding the Well-Formedness Condition, and second, derived structures as in (7). Crucially, in one case ((14) below), the domain of a Drop tone is spread over two syllables, yielding a configuration as in (7).

(7) CV   CV

D

In a context after a High or Drop tone, it has the same phonetic rendering as a sequence of Drop+High syllables but it does *not* have the same phonetic realization as a sequence of Drop + Drop syllables (cf. (6)). Thus in (14), the spread of the domain of the Drop tone *must* be viewed autosegmentally, rather than as a segmental assimilation of tonal features.

The relevant facts are these. (i) Each verb stem is lexically marked as being underlyingly Low-toned or non-Low. In the II Root pattern, the pattern we shall consider, there appears a prefix /a/ (or its harmonic alternant). The tone of the prefix is underlyingly the opposite of the tone of the stem; thus, with Low-toned verbs, the prefix is High-toned, the stem is Low-toned, and the suffixes to the verb are all High-toned—this last being the effect of the "floating" (affixal) H that Williams argues for. Consider thus (8).

(8) ézè   á   zà   á
    │ │   │   │   │   "Eze swept . . ."
    H L   H   +   L   +   H
    ‿‿‿   ‿‿   ‿‿   ‿‿
NP Subject   Prefix   stem   suffix

If no suffixes on the verb occur, the Stem L-tone and the suffixal H-tone converge on a single syllable, as in (9). A rule of Low-High simplification is an easily motivated rule in Igbo, given transparent alternations elsewhere in the language.

(9) únù   á   fǔ   èzí
    │ │   │   +   /\   │ │
    H L   H   L   ⁄   H   L H
                     prefix stem suffix
                     ‿‿‿‿‿‿‿‿‿‿‿
                          Verb

(10) Low-High Simplification

         V   V
        /\   ⟶   │
      L   H   D

(The tone on the object *ezi* in (9) actually changes to D due to the role of Object Mutation mentioned above, but that is not directly relevant here.) Thus the surface form of (9) is (11).

(11) únù áfù èzí

(ii) When the subject NP ends in a High tone, the tone on the verb and prefix is altered. In particular, the tone of the prefix is deleted; thus the vowel of the prefix associates with the tone of the stem, through the Well-Formedness Condition. Thus we find—totally exceptionlessly—contrasts like those in (12) and (13), where the relevant independent variable is the final tone of the subject NP.

(12) úcè   á   +   zà   +   á   ámá   N.B.: *za* is
    | | | | | V   Low-toned verb.
   H L   H   L   H   D
  Subject   Prefix   stem   suffix
   NP   ‿‿‿‿‿‿‿‿‿
                    Verb

(13) À d h á   à + z à + á   à m á
    | | | V | V
    L   H   L   H   D

(14) Prefix Tone Deletion: Main Clauses only

   H ⎡   ⎡T   ("T" stands for any toneme)
     ⎢   ⎢
     ⎣verb ⎣prefix
   1   2   →

   1   ∅

(iii) The evidence that this schematic way—i.e., an autosegmental deletion—is the correct way to view the alternation is quite strong. First, we may observe that the shift of the tone of the prefix from High to *Low* (as in (12)–(13)), triggered by the High tone on the subject NP, is matched by a shift of the prefix tone from High to *Drop* when there are no suffixes (and concurrently the stem *appears* to shift from Drop to High). This is illustrated in (15); compare it with (9) and (11), where the prefix tone does not delete. This shows clearly that although the final H of the subject NP *triggers* the tonal change in the verb prefix, it does not determine what the new tone will be. In fact, the tone of the prefix will be simply the tone of the stem, as determined by the Well-Formedness Condition.

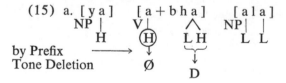

(15) a. [y a]   [a + b h a]   [a l a]
     NP | V| ∧   NP| |
      H   Ⓗ   L H   L   L
by Prefix   ⟶   ↓   ‿‿
Tone Deletion   ∅   ↓
                   D

yields:
   b. y á   à + b h á   à l à
     | V | |
    H   D   L   L

(The tonal accent marks over the syllables are the transcriptions given by Green and Igwe (1963), i.e., the best segmental interpretation of the tones.)

(iv) Actually, the case for viewing the domain of the tone of the verb stem as being the prefix as well as the stem in certain cases is even stronger. There are two further arguments. The first is based on the fact that the Low-High combination on a single vowel (as in (9) and (15)) simplifies to *Low* if the following tone is High (otherwise it simplifies to Drop, of course). Again, this rule—let us call it "Floating H Deletion" (cf. Goldsmith [1976b])—is clearly motivated as well by the tonal properties of the nominal compound system; I will not review that material here. The process is illustrated in (16)–(17). However, the effect of this rule is to create a rather striking contrast between forms like those in (15) where the object NP begins with a Low tone, and those in (18), where the object NP begins with a High tone; observe the effect on the prefix tone in (18), precisely as expected.

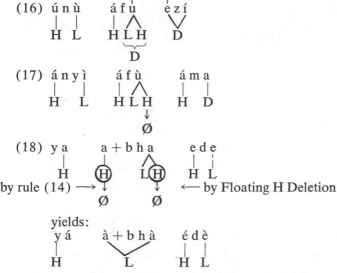

(v) We can find a second, rather different, reason to support this analysis of the tonal alternations of the verb-prefix as expressed in (14). All the examples we have viewed so far have involved inherently Low-toned verbs. In this same construction, High-toned verb stems may appear, and, as (14) Prefix Tone Deletion predicts, the tone of the prefix again depends on the final tone of the Subject NP. The relevant facts are summarized in (19).

(19) a. Subject ends in Low tone:
          é z è   à c í á   á n ú
          subject verb   object
      b. à d h á   á c í á   á k w á
          subject   verb   object

(We have the same verb in both (19 a and b.)

Our analysis so far has led us to the conclusion that the tone pattern on the prefix is closer to its underlying form when the subject NP ends with a Low tone, and that the underlying tone on the prefix is deleted when the subject ends in a High tone; in this latter case, the prefix vowel reassociates with the vowel of a verb-stem by the Well-Formedness Condition. All that is left to observe is that this is precisely what we do in fact observe in (19) as well, on the assumption that the underlying tone pattern for High-toned verbs in this construction is as in (19a)— that is, Low tone on the prefix, Drop tone on the stem. (20) illustrates how (19b) derives from a structure like (19a) through the operation of (14) Prefix Tone Deletion.

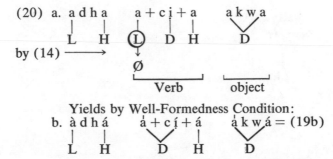

(20) a.

by (14) ⟶

Verb   object

Yields by Well-Formedness Condition:

b.

3. The study of other systems traditionally called "suprasegmental" has proceeded in the autosegmental framework. Haraguchi (1976) (and similarly Goldsmith [1975a] though not based on a comparably broad base of detail), show how the Japanese system of pitch and accent can be assimilated to a system of analysis originally suited to fit the intricacies of African tone languages. Ostler (in press) has recently proposed some simplifications of Haraguchi's survey in an elegant fashion. G. N. Clements has developed in several papers an autosegmental approach to traditional vowel harmony systems (Clements [1976a, b, c]). Such a treatment analyzes the harmonic feature—tongue-body position, tongue-root position, and so forth—as a feature on a separate autosegmental tier. The autosegment associates across the entire domain of the word by the Well-Formedness Condition, as in (21) (an example from Akan, from Clements [(1976a)]).

(21)

ofitii =

$$\# \begin{bmatrix} + \text{back} \\ + \text{round} \\ - \text{high} \end{bmatrix} + \int \begin{bmatrix} + \text{high} \\ - \text{back} \\ - \text{round} \end{bmatrix} t \begin{bmatrix} + \text{high} \\ - \text{back} \\ - \text{round} \end{bmatrix} + \begin{bmatrix} + \text{high} \\ - \text{back} \\ - \text{round} \end{bmatrix}$$

\# [− adv. tongue root] \#

The vowel harmony process in Akan, as (21) suggests, is harmony for the feature "advanced tongue root." This approach permits, and requires, a unified statement of harmony within the stem as well as across morpheme boundaries. We thus avoid an arbitrary separation of vowel harmony into intra- and extra-stem processes. By the same token, we do not have what Kiparsky (1968a) called "a phonological use of morphological features"; the harmony autosegment is indeed a purely phonological item. More appealing yet, we can provide a natural account for words with more than one harmony domain, a capability not even available, as Clements notes, to advocates of "phonological use of morphological features," that is, to those advocating assigning a stem *as a whole* to one harmony class or the other. Clements (1976b) discusses an example from Akan, where /a/ is quite generally an "opaque" element, that is to say, it blocks vowel harmony from spreading across it. A word like *bisa* 'to ask' produces tense vowel harmony among its prefixes, and lax harmony in its suffixes. This is illustrated in (22).

$$(22) \quad \# \; \underset{\#}{\text{Q}} + \text{b} \; \text{I} \; \text{s} \; \text{a} + \text{I} \; \#$$

$$\# \; [+\text{ATR}] \; [-\text{ATR}] \; \#$$

The /a/ is assigned to the [−Advanced Tongue Root] segment either underlyingly (cf. note 3) or as the first association rule, and the Well-Formedness Condition adds the other association lines in (22) (cf. Goldsmith [1976b], Clements [1976b], e.g., for discussion of the principle giving precedence in association to unassociated segments).

The approach sketched here has been developed in a series of papers by Clements. The results described there, as well as the discussion of nasalization in Guarani in Goldsmith (1976b), suggest strongly that the formal properties of tonal suprasegmentals are matched in many respects by vowel harmony, though many of the details remain to be worked out.

One aspect of vowel harmony which I made a passing reference to above seemed unusual when the attempt was first made to apply autosegmental principles to vowel harmony. That is, in the vowel harmony system most discussed in the literature of generative phonology (including Akan, Hungarian, Turkish, Igbo, Nez Percé), a single harmonic domain was the rule and multiple domains the exception. This did not parallel the case in tone languages, where tone *melodies* consisting of several segments in sequence often provide crucial information about tense, mood, and other grammatical factors. Could a principled reason be found for this difference, or were the two systems in fact more similar than appeared at first?

John McCarthy, in a very interesting paper (1977) on Arabic vocalism, has argued, in effect, for the latter position. He reviews the well-known facts of Classical Arabic verbal morphology, and capitalizes on the qualitative difference found between, on the one hand, the *kind* of alternation occasioned by inflection—limited to varying the vowel patterns in a rigidly fixed syllable pattern—and, on the other hand, the derivational processes that form the often idiosyncratic conjugation or "measures," processes that drastically alter the syllable structure as well as the *number* of consonants involved. Despite the vagaries of the derivational morphological process, however, the inflectional morphology remains constant across different forms ("measures").

Thus, in Classical Arabic the vowel pattern for the Perfect Active is /a/—but in this case, there may be two or three syllables in the root, depending on the measure (i.e., depending on the effects of the derivational morphology). The vowel in *each* syllable will be /a/, however, in the Perfect Active. In the Perfect Passive, the final vowel will be /i/, preceded by one or two occurrences of /u/, depending on the syllable structure determined, again, by the derivational morphology. In this latter case, then, we find a vocalic melody pattern of /u i/, where /u/ has precedence in spreading. See (23), for example.

(23) t V k V tt V b   Form determined by derivational morphology
    u   i   =   tukuttib

McCarthy considers a range of similar examples, and points out the close parallel in both the form *and* the function found in the Arabic vowel system and the Tiv tonal system described in Goldsmith (1976a, b). Although the data is complex, the parallel he draws is quite convincing, as in his analysis in general, pointing to vocalic systems like that of Arabic as being precisely the logical link between harmony systems of the sort analyzed by Clements and the tonal systems described earlier.

4. The last subject I would like to touch on is double in nature. First, can we extend the autosegmental approach to processes of a mere "local" nature—not prosodic in the usual reckoning—and if so, how? Second, what kind of answer can be provided to the deeper question, why are some features, in some languages, autosegmental?

In Goldsmith (1976b) I offered some speculations on the second question. The general thrust of the approach was to suggest that the first stage in a child's acquisition of the phonology of a language was a stage in which the phonological features were independent, or in our terms, autosegmental. This would suggest one ought to find rampant harmony processes in early speech, which is, as is well known, quite true. The point of the hypothesis, however, was not to analyze children's speech, although the recent work of Lise Menn (1977) provides some striking support for this approach. The point, rather, was:

(1) those features or feature-complexes which are in fact independent in child-speech should be precisely those which may be autosegmental in the adult grammar;

(2) the process of language acquisition includes a task of "de-autosegmentalization" or, to use a less awkward term, restructuring of the phonetics into linear segments. Suppose that this is one of the tasks performed by the child: decreasing the number of independent features in the phonetics, and realizing, for example, that there is in the English phonological system an entity that we call an "n" that has both nasality and stophood as characteristics. If this is one of the child's tasks, then there is no reason that the de-autosegmentalization should bring the number of independent tiers down to the singular number one. Thus the very same language acquisition procedures may be employed by a child learning English, Igbo, or Guarani, but the child learning Igbo, for example, will never be presented with a reason to unlearn its initial assumption that tone is an independent property (the traces of natural phonology become noticeably distinct here).

The general line of thought, then, is that the autosegmental status of tone in Igbo, or nasality in Guarani, or tongue position in Hungarian, is not a complex phonological process learned late in the process of language acquisition, but is rather the *systematization* (lending of significance of imposition of symmetries, rules, and so on) to a stage through which all learners of all languages pass. Thus the learner of English passes through a vowel harmony stage; such a learner would "have it wrong" for English, and later de-autosegmentalize English vowels. If that child had been learning a different language, though, the child would have maintained that "hypothesis," and gone ahead to elaborate the independence of the tongue position features from those represented in the other segments.

This general line of thought has a further consequence for research. There is no reason to believe that the part of language acquisition I have called "de-autosegmentalization"—that is, the child developing a more or less single, linear model or representation for a language like English—should occur entirely before the child acquires more familiar sorts of phonological rules. That is, the child could begin to adopt rules of phonology for English, or whatever language, even at the point when the child's model for the underlying structure of the language is autosegmental.

If we assume, moreover, that these intermediate autosegmental levels of representation are present even in the adult grammar, then this hypothesis about language acquisition will give us a new tool for approaching the description of the adult grammar, and likewise if this new description is supported by the facts, we will be more secure in pursuing our hypothesis about language acquisition.

Now, what sort of evidence would we look for in the adult phonological grammar? Much of the evidence for autosegmental analyses of tone languages, for example, derived from "morphological" arguments— that is, a "morpheme" could be argued to be present on one autosegmental tier but not another. Such arguments will not be possible here, because we are attempting to fathom, now, an autosegmental representation which is derived from an underlyingly linear system. What evidence could we look for?

Just as much of the clear evidence for underlying autosegmental phonology comes from the existence of (underlying) morphemes which are present on only one autosegmental tier, so here the evidence we would look for would be *derived* segments present on only one *derived* autosegmental tier. One common phonological process that typifies this sort of process is the s → h change, two instances of which we consider shortly. As in the Igbo analysis, we try to show the naturalness of a large variety of phenomena when viewed as deletions.

To summarize, we are considering a model in which the number of autosegmental tiers (or "index") at the phonetic level is greater than the number of tiers underlyingly. Schematically, this presents a picture like this:

(24) $\begin{bmatrix} \alpha_1\,F_1 \\ \alpha_2\,F_2 \\ \cdot \\ \cdot \\ \cdot \end{bmatrix}$ $\begin{bmatrix} \beta_1\,F_1 \\ \beta_2\,F_2 \\ \cdot \\ \cdot \\ \cdot \end{bmatrix}$ Underlying Representation

$\downarrow$ Phonological rules

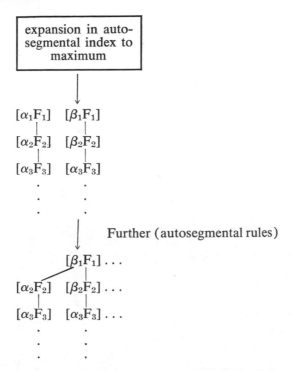

One example of this sort of process is found in many dialects of Spanish. Here I will restrict my attention to a preliminary analysis of one specific dialect, one spoken in Buenos Aires. In this dialect, all s's between a vowel and a consonant, roughly, are converted into [h].

(25) s → h / [+ syl] — [− syl]

This happens both inside a word ([asta] → [ahta] "until") and across word boundaries. Thus [dos] before a vowel, but [dohpapas] "two potatoes".

A restatement of (25) in terms of features fails to express the linguistic naturalness of this process. The fact that the /s/ becomes [h] rather than [r], [p], or [z] is left unexplained.

If we say, on the other hand, that the [h] derived from the /s/ does not have the same segmental status as the h in English, but is rather derived only after the autosegmentalization of the various features occurs, then a different picture emerges. The segmental process in (25) becomes a deletion of the supra-glottal features instead, and the laryngeal features of the /s/ are all that remain. Reassociation of the now-floating h-autosegment follows. In the derivations that follow, we consider reassociation to the left.

(26) a.

$$
\begin{bmatrix} - \text{high} \\ + \text{back} \\ + \text{cont} \\ + \text{syl} \\ - \text{spr gl} \end{bmatrix}
\begin{bmatrix} + \text{anterior} \\ + \text{coronal} \\ + \text{spr gl} \\ + \text{strident} \end{bmatrix}
\begin{bmatrix} - \text{syl} \\ . \\ . \\ . \\ - \text{spr gl} \end{bmatrix}
$$

Underlying:

Autosegmentalization   ⇓

b.

oral

$$
\begin{bmatrix} - \text{high} \\ + \text{back} \\ - \text{cont} \\ + \text{syl} \end{bmatrix}
\begin{bmatrix} + \text{anterior} \\ + \text{coronal} \\ + \text{strident} \end{bmatrix}
\begin{bmatrix} - \text{syl} \\ . \\ . \\ . \end{bmatrix}
$$

laryngeal [spread glottis] [+ spread glottis] [− spread glottis]

"s-deletion"   ⇓

c.

$$
\begin{bmatrix} + \text{syllabic} \\ + \text{high} \\ - \text{back} \end{bmatrix}
\qquad\qquad
\begin{bmatrix} - \text{syllabic} \end{bmatrix}
$$

[− spread glottis] [+ spread glottis] [− spread glottis]

I am assuming at the moment that the rule deleting the oral "s" segment also explicitly specifies the reassociation of the laryngeal segment. There is much variation between dialects as to whether that segment reassociates leftward or rightward, and some even with this dialect. Even under these limited conditions, however, we do find some significant advantages to this view of the process.

If the vowel preceding the underlying /s/ is an /i/, there are two possible allophones of the /i/, the normal highly tense, high front vowel found in the other occurrences of /i/, and a slightly laxer version I shall represent as /I/. Now, although i and I vary freely before s-plus-consonant, h is not the surface form of /s/ after the tense /i/. In fact, we get the surface variants as follows:

(27) /asta/   /mismo/
        ↓
      [ahta]   [miçmo]   [mIhmo]

After /i/, not surprisingly, the tongue maintains its position throughout the period, just as (26c) asserts it should. Consequently, the unvoiced flow of air causes turbulence at the tongue blade when it is in the /i/ position.

The point of all this is simply that representation (26c) says all that need *be* said. In particular, there is no need to add an additional rule turning [h] into [ç] after [i]—in reality, once the deletion of the oral autosegment was effected, the phonetic realization of a structure like (26c) was a *fait accompli*. Only one last point should be emphasized: the fact that the turbulence occurs at the tongue blade after [i] and not [I] is not a fact expressed formally in the phonological grammar at all; it is a consequence of the articulatory phonetics. This presents a good illustration of how some facts of phonetics may best be excluded from phonology, whereas others—like *which* articulatory organs are relatively independent and thus may be autosegmentalized—are of great significance to phonology.

A very similar analysis has been proposed by Hoskuldur Thrainsson (1978) for Icelandic. He reviews the facts concerning the well-known "preaspiration" of stops in certain contexts, and argues persuasively that the pre-aspirated stops are synchronically, as well as diachronically, derived from geminate tense stops. The first of the two stops, however, is weakened to an [h]—giving the impression of preaspiration.

> In the case of Icelandic preaspiration, we could . . . say that the laryngeal articulatory gesture for the phonologically long or geminate stop is made at the "correct" point in time—i.e., when the first half of the stop is to begin—whereas the supralaryngeal articulatory gesture, namely the oral closure, is not made until the second half of the phonologically long or geminate stop begins. In other words, we have to get from a phonological sequence of two fully specified stops, as it were, to a sequence where the first member is only specified for the appropriate laryngeal features. What this means, then, is that the phonological rule of preaspiration has to wipe out or delete the set of supralaryngeal features for the first half of the stop and leave only the laryngeal feature specifications. . . . But is there any way of adequately formulating a rule of this kind within a generative framework? The answer is yes. The theory of autosegmental phonology offers a rather neat way of doing this . . . Thus it seems that in some cases a certain subset of the phonological features composing a phoneme can behave as a unit. I want to argue that preaspiration in Icelandic is just such a case [Thrainsson, p. 35].

At this point, just how these kind of analyses would be integrated into a more general view remains to be determined, but the convergence of these last two proposals seems to me to indicate a very promising direction.

5. CONCLUSIONS

In distinguishing autosegmental analysis from more traditional types of generative phonology, the emphasis here has been on the more articulated types of phonological structure proposed by autosegmental theory, disallowed by *Sound Pattern of English* postulates. On the other hand, this should not be taken as an attempt to refute the SPE tradition; *Sound Pattern* itself is clearly a working paper, a summary of results and hypotheses offered by some working phonologists at a certain point of time. Suggestions that there is a "congealed . . . [and] classically dogmatic" consensus in post-*Sound Pattern* phonology (to use Roger Lass' [1976] phrases) I find quite unrealistic. Generative phonology, quite to the contrary, has been quite supple; and I submit autosegmental theory as a proposal, which, if correct in all the ways I have suggested here, will revise in some radical ways the generative view of phonology, while remaining essentially within the general view of the goals of phonology spelled out in *Sound Pattern*.

On the other hand, I do disagree with a number of the papers presented at this conference on some basic points, even holding aside questions of immediate empirical adequacy (but cf. Goldsmith (in preparation c)).

There is a view that has been repeatedly voiced at this conference to the effect that falsifiability is, or should be taken as, a measure of a theory's adequacy and success. As such, this seems to me to be a mistaken view, possibly arising as a misinterpretation of the by-now conventional wisdom of Karl Popper. Popper was only defending the view that falsifiability is one criterion to be used in separating science from non-science, not in choosing between approaches to a subject. If occasionally it is said that even the falsifiability measure chooses between two theories "all other things being equal," it can be said only in irony since other things never are.

In any event, "falsifiability" is a sophisticated notion itself, for it surely cannot be taken in the obvious sense of producing counter-examples. Falsification at best can only be done by alternative theories, and just what the "logic" of competition between theories is is still open to considerable controversy (for some skeptical views, see Lakatos [1970] and especially Feyerabend [1975]). At all events, it is by no means obvious that the ease with which a theory can be destroyed—what we might call its "moribundity index"—is simultaneously a measure of its strength. Slightly altering Feyerabend's (1970) apt phrase, the strength of a theory might well be measured by the degree to which "the principle of tenacity" (retaining a theory despite confounding evidence) is successfully appealed to; but this raises difficulties concerning the notion "success" which we cannot go into here.

So much for the notions of falsifiability and vulnerability. I would mention a second viewpoint, one which contends that the plausibility, attractiveness, and in the end the *value* of any theory of phonology depends on its ability to deal with a language comprehensively and in depth. That is, a theory—as opposed to a specific analysis—should lend itself to, and indeed provoke, a full-scale investigation of the details of language systems, not just considerations of a few scattered facts in various languages. When is the investigation "full-scale"? When it reveals something unexpected, surprising, and remarkable about the nature of the language being looked at, I would say. In sum, I think that the criteria for choosing a theory have little to do with falsification directly. Rather, we must adopt a theoretical viewpoint which allows for the elegant interaction of hypothesis and data that has typified science. Of course, to the extent that the hypothesis and the data must mesh to be elegant, falsification plays a role—but very much a secondary one.

Returning to phonology, we have seen that autosegmental representation provides to generative phonology one way to incorporate some more traditional and phonetically-based notions. On the other hand, as the example in section 2 has shown, it allows for revealing analyses of "suprasegmental" elements using basic techniques of generative phonology.

Whatever gains have been achieved result from the enriched descriptive power of the formalism, we should note. I have no doubt that the potentials of the formalism are not yet exhausted, and that where even a multi-tiered approach is too weak to approach the facts, a further enrichment of the formal devices can and must be developed—as, for example, that proposed by Sigurd (1972), Liberman (1975), and Liberman and Prince (1977). In short, one important way to advance phonology is to open the formal floodgates as wide as possible. I think we need not worry about drowning in any consequent torrent of formal gadgetries; as ever, the idle and useless formalisms will eventually drown themselves. The good ideas can take care of themselves.

NOTES

I am grateful to a number of people for comments on an earlier version of this paper, most especially Nick Clements, William Leben, and Carmen

Lozano, and those at the Conference in Bloomington, who, by disagreeing, helped polarize my position.

1. Curiously, no such attempt was ever made in Terence Langandoen's unsympathetic review of Firthian phonology from a generative point of view. Stephen Anderson's suggestions have been rather more serious (cf. Anderson [1974, ch. 14], [1976]). Anderson's representations are in essence identical to Bloch's, but his analysis of the advantages of a relaxation of the assumption of linearity are in close agreement with a number of the arguments in the autosegmental literature, and it seems to me we are dealing with much the same issue.

2. As I have noted in Goldsmith (1976a, b), the multi-dimensional representation is not a "discontinuous" one, in the familiar or the technical sense of the word; a careful reading shows Chomsky is not suggesting it is either, of course.

3. As stated, this assumption is possibly too strong. Leben (1977a) and Clements (1976 a, c) present quite attractive analyses in which exceptional tonal and harmonic behavior, respectively, are treated in terms of anomalous underlying association lines.

4. One criticism of autosegmental theory that has been raised (for example, in unpublished work by A. R. Walton) is that explicit criteria have not been given for determining which features are autosegmentalized within a specific language. Within the rather static picture discussed in this paper in the first three sections, and in the first three chapters of Goldsmith (1976a), in which the number of autosegmental tiers is fixed throughout the derivation, the segmental status of a particular feature is determined by its behavior with respect to such criteria as (1) whether the change in value of that feature coincides or not with the change in value of the other features; (2) whether "melodies" consisting of values for that feature must be listed in the lexicon; and several other criteria. The issue is discussed at some length in the first chapter of Goldsmith (1976b) and in Goldsmith (1976a).

Within an extended or dynamic autosegmental theory, as sketched in section 4 below, the segmental status of the various features is approached in an interesting way for the first time, I believe. There I suggest that, superficially, essentially all segments are represented on separate tiers; the more "abstract"—or, better, psychologically-oriented—levels of the derivation, however, have progressively fewer and fewer tiers, to the extent that the data of the language permit this "de-autosegmentalization". Cf. §4 below.

5. In Goldsmith (in preparation b) I try to deal with the elimination of one of the three major class features—"syllabic." It seems clear that an articulated theory of syllable structure (as discussed in the preface to Goldsmith (1976b) or Kahn (1976)), the feature *syllabic* is redundant, and many if not all of the traditional rules adjusting the value of the feature *syllabic* or inserting glides homorganic with neighboring vowels (cf. Anderson (1974), Harris (1969)) should rather be dealt with in terms of the autosegmental notions of adjustment of association lines at the syllabic level.

CHAPTER NINE

Siddha and Asiddha
in Pāṇinian Phonology

S. D. Joshi and *Paul Kiparsky*

What is a grammar of Sanskrit written around 500 B.C. doing on the agenda of a conference on current phonological theories? We shall try to demonstrate that Pāṇini's grammar possesses both a theoretical content and a contemporary relevance which make it more than just a chapter in the history of linguistics. The grammar includes a generative phonology of a depth and exhaustiveness to which no modern generative phonology has even come close, which is moreover integrated with a fully worked out generative syntax and morphology, in a system of 4000 formalized rules based on very specific and elaborate principles of linguistic description. True, only a relatively small part of these underlying principles themselves are stated among the rules of the grammar. The rest must be deduced from the structure of the system and the way in which the facts of Sanskrit are analyzed there, a task which was begun by the traditional commentators and continued by modern scholars, but still remains to be carried out to the end. Thus, while the text itself is long on analysis and short on theory—just the opposite of a typical modern contribution to linguistics—it nevertheless presupposes and reflects what can be construed as a theory of grammar (though naturally differing from generative phonology in being arrived at on the basis of one language only, and in having no psychological pretensions). As for its contemporary relevance, this springs from the fact that very little in its phonological analysis of Sanskrit has to our knowledge yet been superseded, the various partial efforts at synchronic reanalysis[1] having evidently so far not led to any major revision. (Of course, Pāṇini's grammar continues to be the basic analysis of Sanskrit accepted by traditional scholars in India to this day.)

Therefore certain aspects of Pāṇini studies can be counted on to make contributions to linguistics proper: elucidating the principles underlying Pāṇini's grammar, comparing them with current theories, and investigating their empirical linguistic validity. This necessarily involves confronting Pāṇinian analyses with modern ones, not only in Sanskrit but even in other languages, e.g., English. Such comparisons can be carried out in a provisional way even now, though in the present state of our knowledge they run the risk of being unfair to both sides. They are unfair to Pāṇini because the prerequisite of reconstructing his linguistic theory and of reconstructing the motivation of his particular analyses of Sanskrit has not yet been fully satisfied. They are unfair to modern generative theory, partly because there isn't any generative grammar or even any generative phonology available for *any* language which remotely compares in richness with Pāṇini's analysis of Sanskrit,[2] and partly because there isn't any complete theory of generative phonology yet, but rather a collection of partial theories of varying scope and varying degrees of mutual compatibility, as is evident even from the proceedings of the present conference.

As long as these limitations of the enterprise are kept in mind, a comparison between Pāṇini and more recent theories can be helpful, both in giving a perspective on the interpretation of Pāṇini's grammar and in bringing out ideas which may deserve to be incorporated into present-day theories as well.

As we cannot present or even summarize all of Pāṇinian phonology within the space available to us, we have chosen to restrict ourselves to a particular topic: the problem of how rules interact with each other and with themselves in derivations, in short, the *ordering* of rules. Even here we must limit ourselves to some of the main points. Our account is abstracted from a fuller presentation which will appear elsewhere. It is based on joint work done at Cambridge in 1971–72 and at Poona in 1976–77, which has led us to an interpretation of the system which differs from the traditionally accepted one on several points.

1. SIDDHA AND ASIDDHA

Pāṇini's theory of ordering rests on the fundamental ordering relations between rules which Sanskrit grammar calls *siddha,* literally 'effected', and *asiddha* 'not effected'. As the traditional explication puts it, "rule A is *(a)siddha* with respect to rule B" means "rule A is to be regarded as (not) having taken effect when rule B is to take effect".

There are several equivalent ways to define *siddha* and *asiddha* precisely. We will here choose the one which may be most congenial to the linguist's way of thinking about ordering. Let $B(A(\varphi))$ denote the result of applying, to a given input φ, rule A and rule B *in that order;* and let $B,A(\varphi)$ denote the result of applying, to a given input φ, rules A and B *simultaneously*. Then:

(1a)   A is *siddha* w.r.t. B = For all φ such that $B(A(\varphi)) \neq B,A(\varphi)$, A is applied before B to φ.

(1b)   A is *asiddha* w.r.t. B = For all φ such that $B(A(\varphi)) \neq B,A(\varphi)$, A is not applied before B to φ.

The definitions are deliberately framed so as to allow the relations to be specified vacuously even for rules which never actually interact (i.e., where there is no φ s.t. $B(A(\varphi)) \neq B,A(\varphi)$), as is done in Pāṇini's grammar.

Siddha and *asiddha* can be used to specify the ordinary sequential ordering relations in the obvious way, as will be clear from the following example.

Ex. 1: Consider the contraction rule which replaces vowel sequences of the form *a+i* by the single vowel *e*.[3] Vowel sequences of this type arise by the operation of several rules. The contraction rule must apply to the *a+i* sequences produced by some of these rules, but not to the *a+i* sequences produced by others. For example, the operation of a vocalization rule (*saṃprasāraṇa*) changing *y* to *i* in the reduplication of certain verbs[4] produces such sequences, e.g. *atra yāj+yāj+a* → *atra iāj+yāj+a* (→ *atra iyāja*) 'he sacrificed here', to which contraction must apply: *atra iyāja* → *atreyāja*. Vocalization, therefore, is *siddha* w.r.t. contraction. Another rule deletes word-final glides (*y* and *v*) after *a* and certain other vowels,[5] turning e.g., *ayajay indram* 'I sacrificed to Indra' into *ayaja indram*. Vowel sequences resulting from glide-deletion must on no account undergo contraction: *ayaja indram* ↛ **ayajendram*. Glide-deletion is therefore *asiddha* w.r.t. contraction. This corresponds to the ordering:

1. vocalization   (...a y... → ...a i...)
2. contraction   (...a i... → ...e...)
3. glide deletion   (...ay i...→ ...a i...)

This ordering, however, is specified not directly but in terms of how the rules interact. Thus, when A *feeds* B, as vocalization does contraction here, A is *siddha* w.r.t. B, and when A *counterfeeds* (is blocked from feeding) B, as glide deletion does contraction here, A is *asiddha* w.r.t. B.[6] Similarly, when A *bleeds* B, A is *siddha* w.r.t. B, and when A is *blocked from bleeding* B, A is *asiddha* w.r.t. B. When A changes the way B applies to a form, A is *siddha* w.r.t. B (e.g. let A be a rule deleting final syllables and B a rule assigning penultimate stress), and when A is blocked from doing so, A is *asiddha* w.r.t. B. When A could have no effect on the application of B, it can equally well be considered *siddha* or *asiddha* w.r.t. B.

The interest of the (a)*siddha* relation lies in the fact that it provides comparable definitions of various other types of ordering relations which figure both in Pāṇini's grammar and in modern linguistics. In the tradition of generative grammar these have been characterized in quite heterogeneous, unrelated ways, so that no unified framework for talking about rule interaction has been able to emerge. By taking (a)*siddha* as the basic relation, all ordering can be located on a point between the two extremes of *simultaneous* ordering (no rule interaction) and *transparent* ordering (maximal rule interaction), definable as follows:

(a) *Simultaneous* ordering: all rules are *asiddha* w.r.t. all other rules.

(b) *Transparent* ordering: all rules are *siddha* w.r.t. all other rules. (Note that *intrinsic* ordering is a term used for transparent ordering in rule systems with the special property that only the feeding relation *can* hold between rules.)

The other types of ordering can be defined by imposing various restrictions on transparent ordering. Thus, (b) can be restricted in one or both of the following ways:

(c) *Linear* ordering: any rule is *asiddha* w.r.t. any rule that precedes it in a listing.

(d) *Strict cyclical* ordering: any rule A is *asiddha* w.r.t. any rule B in cases where A applies in an outer cycle (viz. where A and B are applicable minimally within constituents P and Q, respectively, and P dominates Q).

The interaction of a rule with itself can be characterized in the same terms as the interaction of rules with each other, e.g.

(e) *Simultaneous* application: a rule is *asiddha* w.r.t. itself.

(f) *Iterative* application: a rule is *siddha* w.r.t. itself.

There are several points worth emphasizing here:

(1) In modern treatments (e.g. Kiparsky 1973a) transparent rule

ordering comes across as a principle of a rather different sort from linear or simultaneous ordering. It is sometimes even said to be a "functional" principle as opposed to the other, "formal" principles (whatever that distinction may exactly mean, in this case). It becomes clear from the Sanskrit grammarians' treatment that transparent ordering is entirely on the same footing as the other familiar kinds of ordering.

(2) In modern treatments (e.g. Kean 1974, Mascaro 1976) the condition of strict cyclicity, though empirically preferable to the older non-strict version of cyclicity, is in no way more natural from a formal point of view. On the contrary, it appears as an added complication, a special restrictive clause put on top of the condition that rules apply cyclically. If (*a*)*siddha* is taken as the basic ordering relation, cyclic application will automatically be defined as *strict* cyclicity (see section 3 below), and it is rather any other (non-strict) version of cyclicity which requires additional restrictions. It is fair to conclude that if modern linguists had thought about the interaction of rules in terms of the (*a*)*siddha* relation, the correct interpretation of cyclic rule application would have been found from the beginning.

(3) The modern treatment of ordering provides no a priori reason to expect that rules should relate to themselves either in the simultaneous manner or in the iterative manner, viz. (e) or (f) above. In terms of a Pāṇinian framework, however, (e) would be naturally associated with (a) and (f) would be naturally associated with (b). In fact, the most general formulations of (a) and (b) (obtained by dropping *other* in them) would subsume (e) and (f) as special cases.

2. TRANSPARENCY AS THE BASIC ORDERING PRINCIPLE

We shall now proceed to outline how the sequencing of rules in derivations is determined in Pāṇini's grammar. Most of the operative principles are not formulated in the grammar itself. Not all of them are formulated even in the traditional commentaries, and some of the principles which the commentaries do put forward must be eliminated or amended, in our opinion.

A preliminary remark on the character of Pāṇini's grammar is necessary. Pāṇini's basic procedure is to abstract everywhere as general statements as possible (*sāmānya*) and to restrict them appropriately by special statements (*viśeṣa*), each of which may in turn be restricted by even more special statements, and so forth. Moreover, the most general principles do not have to be specially stated if they are implicit in the special principles which restrict them. Patañjali explains this with an analogy from the religious laws. "Five five-clawed animals may be eaten" implies: "the others may not be eaten." The latter, general case does not have to be specially stated, but can be inferred from the statement of the special case, which can be thought of as having an implicit "only," viz. "*only* five five-clawed animals may be eaten."

The most general principle governing the order in which rules are to be applied is that of transparent ordering:

(2) All rules are *siddha* w.r.t. all rules   (*sarvatra siddham*).

Most rules are correctly sequenced by (2). But (2) must be curbed for cases where it gives the wrong ordering (e.g., for cases of counterfeeding or counterbleeding order), and supplemented for cases where the potential interaction of rules is symmetrical (e.g., mutual bleeding). We shall be concerned with the former kinds of cases here. A number of special conditions, of varying generality, serve to restrict the validity of (2) by implementing non-transparent ordering in certain cases. These special conditions accordingly state that (contrary to [2]) such-and-such rules are *asiddha* with respect to such-and-such other rules of the grammar. Where not overridden by one of these conditions, (2) fixes the sequencing of rules as transparent.

Like the law cited by Patañjali, (2) does not have to be specially stated in Pāṇini's grammar. It is implicit in the various special restrictions which have been stated in the grammar, which say that certain rules are *asiddha* w.r.t. certain other rules. By them we know: the others are *siddha*.

In order to appy the rules of the grammar to a form φ, we must find a derivation which satisfies the ordering principles. In practice we might proceed as follows:

1. Find all which are applicable to φ.
2. Determine the partial ordering imposed on the rules by such special ordering principles as are applicable, and otherwise by the general ordering principle (2).
3. Apply rule R to φ, where R is any rule not preceded by another rule in the partial ordering established by step 2.
4. Taking the result of step 3 as the new φ, repeat the procedure beginning with step 1.

Pāṇini's system of rules seems intended to enable a unique output (up to free variation) to be derived from any given input. An ordering which yields a wrong form should violate (2) or one of the special principles.

It is evident that a procedure of this sort could, in principle, lead to enormously complicated operations at stage 2. Given *n* applicable rules, it is necessary to check nx(n − 1) ordered pairs of rules for whether the *siddha* or *asiddha* relation holds between their members. But the actual forms which arise in derivations normally involve a choice between at most a few rules. Indeed, perhaps the most frequent situation is that only one rule is even applicable. It is a remarkable fact about Pāṇini's grammar (and perhaps about language) that so few rules tend to compete for a form. It makes the practical application of the grammar rather straightforward in most cases.

Ex. 2: As a typical illustration, we choose the whole derivation of the expression *atreyāja* whose last stage was already discussed in Ex.1. The first word, *atra* 'here', is derived from the pronominal stem *etad* 'this'. A semantically conditioned rule designates a "locus" of an action as being an *adhikaraṇa,* a "deep structure" locative (*kāraka*).[7] This feeds a rule which inserts suffixes of the seventh (locative) case (in this case *i*) after stems which are *adhikaraṇas*.[8] No other rules are applicable:

etad + i

This in turn feeds a rule which adds the ending *tra* after pronominal stems which end in a locative case suffix.[9] No other rules are applicable. (We disregard here accent rules, whose effect will be wiped out by the last rule in this derivation anyway. The rule adding *tra* does not reapply a second time, cf. section 6 below.)

etad + i + tra

This feeds deletion of the case suffix *i* by a rule which deletes case suffixes inside nominal stems.[10]

etad + tra

Since *etad* thereby comes to stand directly before *tra,* this rule feeds a rule replacing *etad,* when anaphoric, by unaccented *a* before *tra* (and *tas*), and making the suffixes unaccented at the same time.[11] It also potentially could feed a rule which devoices obstruents before voiceless obstruents (8.4.55 *khari ca*). Which rule must apply? Both devoicing and *etad → a* potentially bleed each other, so that (2) cannot decide the preference between them. But devoicing (8.4.55) is designated by Pāṇini as *asiddha* w.r.t. all rules that precede it, including in particular the *etad* → *a* rule (2.4.33), so that devoicing cannot bleed *etad* → *a*. (The *etad* → *a* rule would as it happens win over devoicing anyway by another basic principle of the grammar, which we will not discuss here.) We therefore derive the final form:

   a + tra

The second word *iyāja* 'he sacrificed' (perfect tense) is derived from the root *yaj*. The abstract tense marker *liṭ* is added to the root when past time anterior to the present day and not witnessed by the speaker is to be denoted:[12]

   yaj + liṭ

This *liṭ* is replaced by the basic active endings, in this case *ti*:[13]

   yaj + ti

In the active perfect, these suffixes are replaced by another set of suffixes:[14]

   yaj + a

The suffix *a* which thereby comes to stand after the root triggers the substitution of *ā* for *a* in it:[15]

   yāj + a

The root is reduplicated in the perfect:[16]

   yāj + yāj + a

The *y* of the reduplicating syllable is vocalized (fn.4):

   iāj + yāj + a

The vowel after the vocalized *i* is deleted:[17]

   ij + yāj + a

Non-initial consonants in reduplicating syllables are deleted:[18]

   i + yāj +a

The syllable preceding the suffix -*a* is accented:[19]

   i + yā́j + a

It will be seen that *all* crucial ordering relations in the derivation of both words involve feeding. The interaction of rules here is in its entirety predicted by (2).

There are other types of ordering, not involving feeding, which also fall under (2), if the *siddha* relation is defined in the general manner of (1), as we have suggested. Numerically the next most important set of cases involve the *bleeding* relation. Here principle (2) says that rules are to be applied in bleeding order. Examples 3–5 will illustrate how this is the case.

Ex. 3: śiṣṭāt (imper. of *śās* 'instruct'). The underlying *śās + hi* is subject to a rule which replaces *śās* by *śā* before the suffix *hi*.[20] This process is bled by the optional replacement of *hi* by *tāt*.[21] The other, non-transparent ordering would give the incorrect output (*śās + hi* → *śā + hi* → **sā + tāt*).

Ex. 4: rudihi (2 sg. imper. of *roditi* 'cries'). In underlying *rud + hi,* there is a chance of changing the suffix *hi* to *dhi* by a rule whose context specifies a root ending in a consonant.[22] But this is bled by a rule which adds the augment *i* (*iṬ*) to a consonantal suffix, changing it to *ihi,* which is no longer subject to the former rule.[23] Thus we derive *rud +hi* → *rudihi* and not the incorrect *rud + hi* → *rud + dhi* → **rud + idhi.*

Since affixation rules (as opposed to augment rules) are rarely phonologically conditioned, but themselves feed and bleed the operation of morphophonemic rules, it follows that affixation rules will normally apply before morphophonemic rules. This does not have to be stated as a separate principle, but follows from the condition that rules apply in transparent order:

Ex. 5: tudati 'hits'. In *tud + ti,* the root vowel might be replaced by *guṇa* (*o*) because it is the penultimate segment of a stem followed by a *sārvadhātuka* suffix.[24] But this rule is bled, and therefore preceded, by the morphological rule inserting the *vikaraṇa* (*Śa*) between the root and the suffix. We thus get *tud + ti* → *tud + a + ti,* a form to which *guṇa* is no longer applicable. The other, non-transparent ordering would have given us *tud + ti* → *tod + ti* → *tod + a + ti.*

Cases like Examples 3–5 are common. But the later tradition, interestingly enough, does not account for them by (2). It instead supposes a separate principle to the effect that a *nitya* 'constant' rule takes precedence over a non-*nitya* rule. Given two rules A and B which are applicable to a given form, rule A is *nitya* (and rule B non-*nitya*) when A is still applicable if B applies first, but B is no longer applicable if A applies first. Saying that *nitya* rules precede is equivalent to saying that rules are applied in bleeding order.

In Kātyāyana's *vārttikas,* the *nitya* relation is very rarely utilized (e.g., on 6.4.88). It may be a later development necessitated by the illegitimate expansion of the *antaraṅga/bahiraṅga* relation to the word-internal domain (see below).

Aside from ordinary bleeding and feeding, (2) covers rule interactions of the following sort.

Ex. 6: We take the derivation of *susyūṣati* 'wants to sew' from the stage *siv + sa + ti.* The desiderative suffix *sa* triggers two rules here: reduplication of the root (*siv → sivsiv*)[25] and replacement of the root-final *v* by *ū*.[26] Which wins? According to (2), *v → ū* is applied first, since that makes it *siddha* with respect to reduplication. The *siddha* order, then, is *siv → siū → sisyū,* whereas the *asiddha* order would be *siv → sivsiv → sivsiū,* equivalent to simultaneous application. After applying the first rule, reduplication is still applicable, but *v → ū* has fed a new rule, which replaces *i* by the glide *y* before a vowel.[27] The *siddha* order is again obtained if this glide formation rule is applied *before* reduplication (*siu → syū → syūsyū,* not *siū → sisiū → sisyū,* which would be the *asiddha* order, equivalent to simultaneous application). We thus derive ultimately *susyūṣati* (by deleting the second consonant in the reduplication and shortening its vowel) rather than **sisyūṣati.* Whatever processes are applicable to the root must be applied before the root itself is copied: a root-changing rule precedes reduplication in the *siddha* order.

The relationship between the root-changing rules and reduplication in this example is not feeding or bleeding in the ordinary sense, since reduplication will apply regardless of whether the root-changing rules are applied or not. The root-changing rules affect the *way* reduplication will apply. This kind of relationship can arise when the second rule contains any sort of variable expression. From a formal point of view it may be convenient to extend the notions of feeding and bleeding so that they will apply here too. This can be done by regarding variables as abbreviations for all specific cases they cover. Thus reduplication would be an abbreviation for a large set of specific copying rules, one for each specific root shape. Then glide-formation, for example, can be regarded as bleeding one of these specific subcases (namely the rule

$si\bar{u} \rightarrow sisi\bar{u}$) and as feeding another (namely the rule $sy\bar{u} \rightarrow sy\bar{u}sy\bar{u}$).

The common principle which underlies all cases we have dealt with up to now can be simply put as follows: a rule which potentially affects the environment of another rule takes priority over it. In other words, *environment-changing rules apply first*.

3. ANTARANGA AND BAHIRANGA

The first restriction on (2) which we shall discuss involves the relation *antaranga/bahiranga* '(applying to) an internal/external constituent.' Some questions about the precise characterization of this relation are controversial (and we shall add to the controversy below), but the general idea is clear. Suppose we have two constituents as indicated by the brackets, and three rules A_1, A_2, B with domains of application as marked off underneath:

Here both A_1 and A_2 are *antaranga* in relation to B, the corresponding *bahiranga* rule. In particular, any rule applicable *within* a word is *antaranga* in relation to a rule which applies *across* word boundaries. The restriction is then stated as follows:

(3) *Bahiranga* rules are *asiddha* w.r.t. *antaranga* rules.

Principle (3) is not stated in Pāṇini's grammar, but it is formulated by the earliest commentator (Kātyāyana) and shown by Pāṇini's formulations of rules to have been assumed in the construction of his grammar. As the tradition correctly notes, (3) means in particular that:

(3a) *Bahiranga* rules cannot bleed *antaranga* rules.
(3b) *Bahiranga* rules cannot feed *antaranga* rules.

Here (3a) corresponds to the *cycle,* and (3b) corresponds to the *strict cycle.*

Ex. 7: In $a + yaj + a + i\ indram$ (cf. Ex. 1), two rules are applicable: A rule which contracts cognate vowels, e.g. $i + i \rightarrow \bar{\imath}$,[28] and the rule which we have seen must actually apply there, the contraction $a + i \rightarrow e$

(fn. 3). The precedence of the latter contraction follows from the fact that it is *antaranga:*

$$[a + yaj + a + i] \text{ [indram]}$$

A

B

(3) says that B is *asiddha* w.r.t. A, i.e. that A must not be applied to the output of B. Hence A must be applied before B, after which B is no longer applicable. The effect is that of cyclic application.

The relation between the rules is reversed in the following example.

Ex. 8: atra i + ij + us 'they sacrificed here.' Here we have $i + i \rightarrow \bar{\imath}$ applying first because it is *antaranga:*[29]

$$[atra] \text{ } [i + ij + us]$$

A

B

Thus we have the derivation:
    atra i + ij + us
    atra īj + us   6.1.101
    atrejus   6.1.87

The following examples show how (3) induces an analog to the strict cycle, in cases where the *antaranga* and *bahiranga* rules are not applicable at the same time, but only the *bahiranga* rule is initially applicable, in such a way as to feed the *antaranga* rule. The effect of (3) is to block this feeding.

Ex. 9: pacāvedam 'let us two cook this.' The representation *pacāva idam* undergoes contraction of the sequence $a + i$ to a single vowel *e.*[30] The single substitute *e* counts as the final segment of the imperative ending.[31] Therefore it becomes subject to the substitution of *ai* for *e* in first person imperative endings.[32] This unwanted consequence is prevented by (3). According to (3), the *bahiranga* operation $a + i \rightarrow e$ (involving two words) is *asiddha* w.r.t. the *antaranga* operation of replacing *e* by *ai* in imperative endings.

Ex. 10: dadhy atra 'yoghurt here.' In *dadhi atra*, *i* is replaced by *y* in the context of the following vowel.[33] As a result of this process, the rule deleting the last consonant of a word-final cluster becomes applicable.[34] This is prevented by (3), which directs that the operation $i \rightarrow y$, *bahiranga* by virtue of being conditioned by the initial vowel of the next word, is *asiddha* with respect to the cluster simplification rule, which takes place within the first word and is thereby *antaranga*.[35]

4. THE NON-EXISTENCE OF WORD-INTERNAL BAHIRANGA RULES

It is an open question in generative phonology whether rules must cycle on *word-internal* constituent structure. It is therefore especially interesting to inquire how Pāṇini's grammar deals with this question. According to tradition, the *antaranga/bahiranga* relation also holds word-internally, and (3) is valid in such cases too. In our opinion this is certainly false. While operations across word boundaries are reliably *asiddha* w.r.t. word-internal operations in practically all the numerous cases which arise, the situation is altogether different when both rules are word-internal. As often as not, it is the *"bahiranga"* rule which then must apply first, contrary to what (3) would predict. The following two examples are representative of the two main types of cases which arise. The first example shows how a word-internal, supposedly *"bahiranga"* rule can bleed an *"antaranga"* rule.

Ex. 11: In *prati + ac + as* 'turned toward (gen. sg.),' the rule deleting the vowel of the derivational suffix *ac* before certain case suffixes, such as gen. sg. *as* (6.4.138 *acaḥ*) bleeds the replacement of *i* by *y* before vowels (6.1.77 *iko yaṇ aci*). Thus: *prati + ac + as* → (6.4.138) *prati + c + as*, and then → (6.3.138) *pratīcas*. Otherwise we would derive **pratycas*. But 6.4.138 is supposedly *bahiranga* w.r.t. 6.1.77.

In the next example, a word-internal *"bahiranga"* rule must be allowed to feed an *"antaranga"* rule (contrast Ex. 9–10, illustrating that a *bahiranga* rule operating across word boundaries must *not* be allowed to feed an *antaranga* rule).

Ex. 12: In *akṣa + div + sU*[36] 'gambler', *v* is replaced by *ū*[37] in the context of the deleted suffix *v* (KvIP), and this *ū* must then be allowed to trigger the replacement of *i* by *y* before vowels (6.1.77 *iko yaṇ aci*): *akṣa + div + (KvIP +) sU* → (6.4.19) *akṣa + diū + s* → (6.1.77) *akṣa + dyū + s*.

By tradition, the process $v \rightarrow ū$ is *bahiraṅga* relative to the process $i \rightarrow y$, and nevertheless supplies the environment for the latter, in violation of (3):

$$\ldots \text{div} + \text{KvIP} + \text{sU}$$

(3) would prevent glide formation from applying when, as in this case, it is fed by a *bahiranga* rule, with the result that the wrong form *akṣadiūs* would be derived.

A systematic review of the counterexamples to the *antaranga*-principle within words, and of the examples which supposedly require it, suggests the following conclusion:

(4) The *antaranga/bahiranga* relation does not hold between word-internal processes.

The ordering among word-internal processes is, rather, strictly determined by the general ordering principle (2), i.e. by transparency. It will be seen that this gives the correct ordering in Examples 11 and 12. In *prati + ac + as* (Ex. 11), the deletion of *a* in the suffix *ac* bleeds glide-formation and therefore applies before it. In *akṣa + div + sU* (Ex. 12) *v → ū* feeds glide-formation and therefore applies before it. This is consistency the Pāṇinian order of application within the domain of word phonology, regardless of which rule might be considered "*antaranga*" or "*bahiranga*" according to tradition.

We will review here some additional examples which differentiate between (3) and (2) in favor of the latter, in the domain of word-internal processes. First, some cases showing that word-internal supposed "*bahiranga*" rules must be allowed to bleed the corresponding "*antaranga*" rules.

Ex. 13: seduṣas (acc. pl. of pp. *sedivas* 'having sat'). In *sed + vas + as,* two rules are applicable: the insertion of the augment *i* (*iṬ*) before consonantal *ārdhadhātuka* suffixes (*vas*),[38] and the *samprasāraṇa* replacement of *v* by *u* conditioned by the ending *as*.[39] The insertion of *i* is *antaranga*, on the traditional theory, but if it is applied first, we get after *samprasāraṇa* and glide formation the wrong form **sedyuṣas*. Principle (2), that rules are applied in transparent order (in this case, bleeding order), correctly predicts that *samprasāraṇa* is applied first. Then the suffix, now *uas* (> *us*), is no longer consonantal, so that *i* cannot afterward be inserted. The result is the correct form *seduṣas*.

Ex. 14: praśna 'question.' To the base form *prach + na,* two rules are applicable: insertion of the augment *t* (*tUK*) on a short vowel before *ch*,[40] and replacement of *ch* by *ś* before a nasal suffix.[41] The insertion of

t, being root-internal, is *antaranga,* on the traditional theory. But applying it first gives the wrong form (*pratśna). If the replacement of *ch* by
ś is applied first, *t* can then no longer be inserted, and the correct form
praśna is derived. The desired order (bleeding, i.e. the environment-
changing rule applied first) is predicted by (2).

Ex. 15: *prasthāya* 'having departed.' The base form *pra* + *sthā* + *Ktvā*
can undergo either replacement of root-final *ā* by *i* before the following *K-it* suffix in *t,*[42] or replacement of the suffix *Ktvā* by *LyaP* in compounds, as here after the prefix *pra.* If the supposedly *"antaranga"* process *ā* → *i* is applied first, the wrong form is derived (*pra* + *sthā* + *tvā*
→ *pra* + *sthi* + *tvā* → *pra* + *sthi* + *ya* → *prasthitya).[43] Transparency
predicts that *Ktvā* → *LyaP* should apply first, since it bleeds *ā* → *i.* This
yields the desired form *prasthāya.*

The tradition introduces a special ad hoc condition to take care of the
above cases with *Ktvā* → *LyaP,* to the effect that a replacement by *LyaP*
takes precedence even over *antaranga* rules.[44] This condition is not necessary now, as its effect follows directly from (2).

We now give some additional examples of the feeding type, i.e., cases
like Ex. 12, where a word-internal supposedly *"bahiranga"* rule must
feed a supposedly *"antaranga"* rule.

Ex. 16: *papuṣas* (act. pp. of *pā* 'protect', acc. pl.).
     pa + *pā* + *vas* + *as*[45]
     pa + *pā* + *uas* + *as* (*v* is replaced by the *samprāsaraṇa*
       vowel *u*)[46]
     pa + *pā* + *us* + *as* (*u* and *a* replaced by *u*)[47]
     pa + *p* + *us* + *as* (*ā* is dropped before the following *K-it*
       ārdhadhātuka u).[48]

The *"bahiranga"* process of *samprasāraṇa* must feed the *"antaranga"*
process of *a*-deletion. We cannot justify this derivation if we assume that
(3) is applicable. But principle (2), that rules are to be applied in transparent order, predicts the correct form.

Ex. 17: *yūnas* (acc. pl. of *yuvan* 'young').
     yuvan + *as* (4.1.2, see fn. 45)
     yuuan + *as* (replacement of *v* by *samprāsaraṇa u* conditioned
       by the following *bha*-forming suffix *as*)[49]
     yuun + *as* (see fn. 47)
     yūn + *as* (replacement of *uu* by a long vowel)[50]

Here the process of *saṃprasāraṇa*, which is supposedly *bahiraṅga* relative to contraction because it is conditioned by the case suffix, must nevertheless feed it. Principle (3) cannot justify this derivation. The correct result is obtained by the principle of transparency (2).

> *Ex. 18: maghonas* (acc. pl. of *maghavan* 'bountiful').
> *maghavan + as*
> *maghauan + as*
> *maghaun + as*
> *maghon + as* (the vowel sequence *au* is replaced by the single *guṇa* vowel *o*)[51]

Except for the last rule, this example is parallel to the previous one. The derivation again requires the transparent (feeding) order (2), against the *antaraṅga*-principle (3).

> *Ex. 19: dvau* 'two' (nom. du.).
> *dvi + au*
> *dva + au* (the final segment is replaced by *a*)[52]
> *dva + ṬāP + au* (the feminine suffix *ṬāP* is added because the nominal stem ends in short *a*)[53]

The replacement by *a*, which is conditioned by the case termination, would traditionally be considered *bahiraṅga* relative to the addition of the suffix *ṬāP*, which depends on the stem only. But the replacement by *a* feeds the addition of *ṬāP* and therefore applies before it, in violation of the *antaraṅga* principle. The correct result is predicted by (2).

Similar examples are provided by other pronominal stems, e.g., *etad* 'this': nom. sg. fem. *etad + sU* → (7.2.102) *etaa + sU* → (4.1.4) *etaa + ā + sU* (→ *eṣā*).

> *Ex. 20: rājñas* (acc. pl. of *rājan* 'king').
> *rājan + as*
> *rājn + as* (the vowel in the ending *an* is replaced by zero before the suffix *as*)[54]
> *rājñ + as* (assimilation of palatality)[55]

The deletion of the vowel *a*, being conditioned by the case suffix, is according to the traditional view *bahiraṅga* relative to the replacement of *n* by *ñ*, and yet must feed it, contrary to the *antaraṅga*-principle (3) but in accord with transparency.

> *Ex. 21: pratidīvnas* (acc. pl. of *pratidivan*).
> *pratidivan + as*

> *pratidivn + as* (see fn. 54).
>
> *pratidīvn + as* (*i* of the root *div* is lengthened due to the following consonant)[56]

The deletion of *a* (the *"bahiranga"* rule) must feed the lengthening of *i* (the *"antaranga"* rule) against the *antaranga*-principle, but in accord with transparency.

> *Ex. 22: jakṣatus* (3. du. perf. of *ad* 'eat').
>
> *ad + atus*[57]
>
> *ghas + atus* (optional suppletion of *ad* by *ghas* in the perfect)[58]
>
> *ghas + ghas + atus* (reduplication in the perfect)[59]
>
> *ja + ghas + atus* (phonological changes in the reduplicating syllable)[60]
>
> *ja + ghs + atus* (*a* is dropped before the following vocalic *K-it* suffix)[61]
>
> *ja + ghṣ + atus* (*s* becomes *ṣ* after a velar)[62]
>
> *ja + kṣ +atus* (*gh* → *k* before a voiceless sound)[63]

If we extend the *antaranga/bahiranga* relation to word-internal processes, then the deletion of *a*, which requires the person ending *atus,* has to be *bahiranga* relative to the root-internally conditioned process *gh* → *k* but it nevertheless feeds it, against (3). Once again, the correct order is in accord with (2).

Why then does the tradition maintain the validity of the *antaranga*-principle in word phonology? The case appears to rest mainly on a single family of examples, including such forms as *dhiyati, asusruvat, adīdipat.* They are all of the same type, so that it will be enough for us to look at one.

> *Ex. 23: dhiyati* (3 sg.pres. of *dhi* 'think'). At the stage *dhi + tiP* (2) requires us to insert the *vikaraṇa Śa* (*dhi + a + ti*)[64] rather than changing the root vowel to *guṇa*[65] (cf. the discussion of *tudati,* Ex. 5). At that stage there are again two rules to consider: *guṇa* might still apply (by a different rule)[66] and the *i* of the root, being prevocalic, could be replaced by *iy.*[67] It is *i* → *iy* which actually applies, viz. *dhi + a + ti* → *dhiy + a + ti.* The tradition attributes this to the fact that *i* → *iy* is *antaranga* relative to *guṇa*:

$$\text{dhi} + \text{a} + \text{ti}$$
$$\text{A} \ \llcorner\!\_\!\_\!\_\!\_\!\_\!\lrcorner$$
$$\text{B} \ \llcorner\!\_\!\_\!\_\!\_\!\_\!\_\!\_\!\lrcorner$$

But in point of fact, $i \to iy$ is the *only* rule which can apply to *dhi* + *a* + *ti*. *Guṇa* is blocked there by the prohibition formulated explicitly by Pāṇini that there is no *guṇa* before *K-it* and *Ṅ-it* suffixes.[68] And *Śa* is a *Ṅ-it* suffix in Pāṇini's system by virtue of the rule that any *sārvadhātuka* suffix is *Ṅ-it* unless it is *P-it*.[69] Thus, the situation is as follows: in *dhi* + *ti*, *Śa* bleeds *guṇa* and is therefore inserted (transparency). Then in *dhi* + *a* + *ti*, *guṇa* can no longer apply and $i \to iy$ gives *dhiyati*. There is no question here of invoking the *antaraṅga*-principle at all.[70]

5. SPECIAL RESTRICTIONS NECESSITATED BY (2)

The case for our interpretation can be made still stronger. In certain cases Pāṇini complicates his description in ways which would have been pointless if (2) were not the basic principle which determines the sequencing of rules in derivations, but which are necessary when that principle is assumed, because they serve to block its unwanted consequences. From such cases, then, we can be certain that we are not merely reading (2) into the system in order to make the rules work, but that Pāṇini, as shown by his own formulations of rules, wittingly based his grammar on (2).

The restrictions required by (2) are in some cases completely ad hoc, and in other cases rather general in nature. We will proceed from the former to the latter. The general point which we wish to illustrate is that *all special conditions or rules for determining rule interaction which are found in the Aṣṭādhyāyī are limitations of transparent ordering,* i.e., cases in which the implicit principle (2) would be insufficient.

Ex. 24: Recall the rule 7.1.37 replacing the gerund suffix *Ktvā* by *LyaP* in compounds. In example 15 above we saw how Pāṇini tacitly lets this rule bleed processes which are conditioned by *Ktvā*. Now let us see how he deals with a contrary example where the *Ktvā* → *LyaP* replacement *fails* to bleed a rule. The root *ad* 'eat' is replaced suppletively by *jagdh* before suffixes beginning with *t* and carrying diacritic *K*, e.g. *ad* + *Ktvā* → *jagdh* + *Ktvā* (→ *jagdhvā*). We also happen to get *jagdh* before *Ktvā* in the cases where *Ktvā* is replaced by *LyaP*, viz. *pra* + *jagdh* + *Ktvā* → *prajagdhya*. This form could be derived by applying *Ktvā* → *LyaP* (7.1.37) after *ad* → *jagdh*. But that would be the non-bleeding, opaque order of application. For this reason, Pāṇini has to complicate

the environment of the *ad* → *jagdh* rule by specially mentioning in it
the context *LyaP* in addition to the general case: 2.4.36 *ado jagdhir
lyap ti kiti.* This complements our earlier argument based on Pāṇini's
derivation of *prasthāya* (Ex. 15). Together, these two examples provide a clear contrast illustrating the role of transparency in the
Aṣṭādhyāyī.

Ex. 25: In the derivation of *adhītya* 'having learned,' the representation *adhi + i + LyaP*[71] is subject to both vowel contraction ($i + i → ī$)[72]
and the addition of the augment *t* (*tUK*) to the *P-it kṛt* suffix *LyaP,* because it is preceded by a short vowel.[73] Contraction will of course bleed
t-augmentation, for it creates a long vowel, after which *t*-augmentation
is no longer applicable. Transparency predicts, then, that contraction
should apply first. But this yields the wrong form **adhīya.* To get the
correct *adhītya,* Pāṇini introduces a special ordering statement[74] to the
effect that contraction is *asiddha* 'not effected' for purposes of *tuk*-
augmentation.

Ex. 26: In nom. sg. *asau* 'that', underlying *adas + sU* fits the structural analysis of a rule deleting suffixal consonants after a consonantal
stem. But this is bled by the change of the stem-final *-s* to *au.*[75] Transparency therefore would predict *adau+sU,* whence **asauḥ* by other
rules, whereas the correct form is *asau.* Since transparency forbids Pāṇini
from making use of the underlying consonant stem to trigger the deletion of the suffix *-sU,* that deletion (*sulopa*) had to be specially mentioned for this pronoun in connection with the *s* → *au* change: 7.2.107
adasa au sulopaś ca.

Where transparency does not conflict with the *antaraṅga*-principle,
the tradition itself cites such examples in the case of the bleeding
(*nitya*) relation. Pāṇini cites the perfect participle *upeyivān* as a ready-
made (*nipātana*) word.[76] Why was it necessary to cite the whole form?
At the stage

$$upa + i + vas$$

two rules are applicable: reduplication[77] and the addition of the augment *i* (*iṬ*)[78] to the suffix *vas.* The augment rule requires a mono-
syllabic (*ekāc*) root. Hence it is applicable before reduplication but
not after reduplication, while reduplication is applicable whether or not *i*
has been added. Transparency (and its special case, the *nitya* relation)
would require reduplication to be applied first, so as to bleed *i*-insertion.
But the correct form *has* the augment *i.* Since the general ordering con-

vention in this case gives the wrong result, Pāṇini is compelled to make a special provision to secure the augment *i*. He does this by citing the entire form *upeyivān* in 3.2.109. This citation would be pointless if Pāṇini did not suppose that the augment would otherwise fail to be inserted because of transparent ordering.

In two cases Pāṇini has designated the rules in a certain section of the grammar as being *asiddha* with respect to other rules in a more general way. The first case is the section headed by 6.4.22 *asiddhavad atrā bhāt,* which states that any rule in this section is to be considered *asiddha* w.r.t. any other rule in this section. That is, rules of this section do not interact at all, but apply in simultaneous fashion. The placement of rules under 6.4.22 is always motivated by the need to avoid undesirable feeding and bleeding order which would be imposed by (2).

Ex. 27: In the derivation of 3.pl. impf. *āyan* 'went', the representation *i+an* is subject to glide formation,[79] and the verb is also liable to receive a tense augment. This augment is *ā* before vowels and *a* before consonants.[80] Transparency would dictate that we first apply glide formation (the environment-changing rule) and then add the short augment, as the verb now begins with a consonant. But the actual form is *āyan,* not **ayan*. Noticing the problem, Pāṇini has put both 6.4.81 and 6.4.71–2 into the special subsection headed by 6.4.22 in which every rule is *asiddha* with respect to every other rule (i.e. where all rules are to be applied simultaneously). Thus, as far as the augment rule is concerned *y+an* is still treated as beginning with a vowel (*i+an*) so that the desired *āyan* is obtained. There is no other reason for including 6.4.81 in the special subsection of simultaneous rules.

A parallel argument is furnished by *āsan* 'were', from *as+an*. The root *as* loses its vowel here[81] but must be treated as vocalic to get the long augment. As this again goes against transparency, 6.4.111 also had to be put into the section of unordered rules.

Ex. 28: In the derivation of 3.pl.mid.perf. *dadhre* 'gave', *da+dhā+ire* is subject to a Vedic rule replacing the suffix *ire* by *re,*[82] which would bleed, and therefore by transparency have to precede, the deletion of the root-final *ā* before a vocalic *ārdhadhātuka* suffix.[83] This would yield the form **dadhā+re* (→ **dadhire* by 6.4.66 *ghumāsthāgāpājahātisāṃ hali*). In order to derive *dadhre,* Pāṇini has put these rules into the simultaneously ordered section (6.4.22 ff.).[84]

The second general section of *asiddha* rules, which constitutes the most important restriction on transparent ordering in the whole grammar, works in a somewhat different way. According to 8.2.1 *pūrvatrāsid-dham,* any rule from 8.2.1 on to the end of the grammar is *asiddha* w.r.t. any preceding rule, regardless of whether this preceding rule is before or after 8.2.1 in the grammar. In other words, beginning with 8.2.1 Pāṇini's grammar shifts into the familiar mode of linear ordering. The section 8.2.1 ff. is known as the Tripādī, "the Three Chapters."[85]

Ex. 30: Recall that glide deletion[86] (*ayajay indram* → *ayaja indram,* see Ex. 1) must be prevented from feeding contraction[87] (*ayaja indram* → **ayajendram*). This is done in Pāṇini's grammar by putting glide deletion into the Tripādī section. By virtue of 8.2.1, then, it is *asiddha* w.r.t. contraction, which precedes it in the listing of the grammar.

Ex. 31: An *n* which is stem-final and also word-final is deleted.[88] This deletion rule is put into the Tripādī section in order to stop it from feeding a rule replacing the instr. pl. ending *bhis* by *ais* after stems end-ing in short *a*:[89] *vṛkṣa+bhis* → *vṛkṣa+ais,* but *rājan+bhis* → *rāja+bhis* ↛ **raja+ais.*[90] It is also put into the Tripādī section in order to stop it from bleeding a rule lengthening a vowel before stem-final *n* in the strong cases:[91] *rājan* → *rājān* → *rājā.* Thus the *(a)siddha* concept enables Pāṇini to block both feeding and bleeding by means of a single restriction.

When a rule A must be fed or bled by a rule B which is for some other reason in the Tripādī, A must also be put in the Tripādī, and it must follow B there. In such cases, A is assigned to the Tripādī not in order to be *asiddha* w.r.t. some rule preceding A, but in order that an-other Tripādī rule (viz. B) should be *siddha* w.r.t. A.[92]

We have discussed some of the numerous devices by which the basic ordering principle (2) is kept in check where it overapplies. As might be expected, principle (3), being of more limited import to begin with, requires less such policing. Nevertheless, there are cases where Pāṇini was forced to complicate his rules in order to overcome an undesirable consequence of (3).

Ex. 32: The standard example is *śivehi* 'come, Śiva,' from *śiva ā+ihi.* The connection between the preverb *ā* and the root being closer than the connection between the vocative *śiva* and the preverb *ā,* by (3) we should first apply the *antaraṅga* contraction *ā+i* → *e* (fn. 30) in the second word and then contract the resulting *e* with the *a* of *śiva,*[93] yielding the wrong form **śivaihi.* It is simply a fact about the preverb *ā* that we get the exceptional treatment *śivehi,* and similarly in any such three-vowel sequence. The right form could of course be derived by contract-ing the first two vowels first: *śiva ā+ihi* → (fn. 28) *śivā+ihi* → *śivehi.* But this is impossible in Pāṇini's system because it goes against (3). In order to account for this case, Pāṇini therefore specially states that *a* + *V* contracts to *V* when *V* contains the preverb *ā*,[94] not by the usual rule (fn. 93) to *ai, au*. The particular way in which Pāṇini handles the exception shows quite clearly that he thought of underlying *śiva ā+ihi* as *first* undergoing contraction of the second pair of vowels. The exceptional nature of these cases is then seen as consisting of a special treatment of *a* followed by an *e* or *o* which morphologically contains the preverb *ā*.

Internal analysis of the system shows, then, that Pāṇini wrote his grammar on the basis of the unstated principles (2) and (3). They are not only necessary in order to derive the right output (sections 3 and 4), but also presupposed by Pāṇini's formulations of rules (this section). We find that a number of special complications of rules are motivated by the existence of (2) and (3), and that the assignment of rules to the *asiddha* sections headed by 6.4.22 and 8.2.1 is apparently *wholly* explicable as a consequence of these principles.

6. THE APPLICATION OF RULES TO THEIR OWN OUTPUT

From (2) it follows, as we already remarked, that a rule is not *asiddha* w.r.t. itself. This means that a rule will feed itself (and, in principle, also bleed itself, although there appear to be no examples of this case).

Ex. 33: 3.sg. prec. *bhū* + *yās* + *st*[95] is subject to a rule deleting *s* as the first member of word-final or pre-obstruent clusters.[96] The output *bhū* + *yā* + *st* again undergoes the same rule, becoming *bhū yāt*.

Ex. 34: In *madhuliḍ sīdati*,[97] 'the bee is sitting', an augment *dh* is placed before the *s*: *madhuliḍ dhsīdati*.[98] A devoicing and deaspiration rule, conditioned by a following voiceless sound,[99] then applies twice in a row: *ḍ dhs* → *ḍ ts* → *ṭ ts* (*madhuliṭ tsīdati*).[100]

The reapplication of a rule to its own output is, however, limited by another unstated constraint, which appears to be best formulated as follows:[101]

   (4) A rule cannot be conditioned twice in a derivation by the same context.

The way in which (4) restricts self-feeding is illustrated by the following case:

Ex. 35: In *atra* 'here' (Ex. 2), the *t* may optionally be geminated by a rule which applies in the context between a vowel and a non-vowel.[102] But the output *attra* may not again be subjected to this gemination (**attra, *attttra* etc.), since the left-hand environment "after a vowel" would again be satisfied by the *same* vowel *a*.

Constraint (4) is not introduced merely for this purpose. It applies equally when other rules intervene in the derivation.

Ex. 36: In the perfect of *āp* 'obtain', the vowel of the reduplicated syllable is shortened,[103] and after losing its consonant[104] contracts with the root vowel:[105] *āp + āp + a → ap + āp + a → a + āp + a → āpa*. The contracted *ā* counts as the reduplication (as well as the stem),[106] but it must nevertheless *not* undergo shortening once more by the reapplication of 7.4.59 (**apa*). This is prevented by (4).

The same principle (4) holds even when the first application is vacuous. In general, vacuous application must count as application in Pāṇini's grammar, just as it must in generative phonology. The tradition expresses this by saying that the rules of grammar are like the rain, in that they fall equally on the empty and on the full.[107] Thus, precisely the same situation as in Ex. 36 holds in *aṭ + aṭ + a → āṭa*. Here too, shortening applies to the reduplication, albeit vacuously, so that it cannot then reapply after contraction.

That Pāṇini must have wittingly operated with (4) or something close to it can also be concluded from the fact that he formulates explicit restrictions designed to stop the application of rules to their own output *only* when (4) proves insufficient to do the job.

Ex. 37: Consider the derivation of *vivyādha* 'pierced' (perfect).

vyadh + vyādh + a
viadh + vyādh +a   (*saṃprasāraṇa* by 6.1.17, fn. 4)
vidh + vyādh + a   (fn. 7)
vi + vyādh + a   (fn. 18)

What is crucial here is that the *saṃprasāraṇa* rule 6.1.17, which vocalizes a glide in the reduplication, must be prevented from reapplying once more to *vivyādha,* where it would give **uivyādha → *uvyādha*. Since this reapplication is *not* blocked by (4), Pāṇini needed an *ad hoc* restriction to block it. This is 6.1.37 *na saṃprasāraṇe saṃprasāraṇam*, which simply states that a glide is not to be vocalized before a vocalized glide. Here again the existence of an implicit general principle is revealed through the explicit special measures adopted to deal with its undesirable effects.

7. CONCLUDING REMARKS

There is much more to determining the right interaction of rules in Pāṇini's grammar than what we have brought up here. Most importantly, we have not touched at all on the interesting problem of how the *vipratiṣedha* ('mutual contradiction,' roughly 'mutual bleeding') situation is resolved. The disjunctive ordering of special (*apavāda*) and general (*utsarga*) rules,[108] and the precedence of rules which otherwise would have no chance to apply at all (*anavakāśatva*) require careful analysis, as does the establishing of the equivalent to opaque order by the devices of assigning the outputs of rules the contextual value of their inputs in certain specific types of cases (*sthānivadbhāva* and *pratyayalakṣaṇatva*). There are in addition a number of rules in which *ad hoc* cross-referencing is used. It could be shown that these devices, too, all serve to countermand the general transparent order imposed by (2), in the specific cases where it gives the wrong result. Some of them we hope to analyze elsewhere.

The purpose of this sketch has been to show how the main types of ordering relations between rules which have been envisaged in generative grammar also figure in Pāṇini's grammar, but were thought of there in terms of a single, unified framework. The fundamental relation *siddha* and its contrary *asiddha* together serve to define the various types of ordering in a way which makes their formal kinship evident. As in many traditional grammars (Kenstowicz 1976), transparent ordering has a privileged status in Pāṇini, being the order in which rules apply unless some provision to the contrary is made in the grammar. Indeed, with the understandable exception of Bloomfield (1939), which is modeled on the Tripādī, the theory of Chomsky and Halle (1968) is the only phonological theory countenancing rule ordering at all which does *not* recognize the distinction between transparent and opaque ordering. It appears that this distinction, far from being an abstruse afterthought, actually lies at the very heart of the way we mentally organize the interaction of rules.

NOTES

This paper is supported in part by the National Institute of Mental Health MH 13390–11. Our thanks to Nicholas Oster for catching some slips.

1. For a vivid vindication of Pāṇini against some attempted re-analyses, see Sag (1974, 1976). Cf. also Bedell (1974), Allen (1962).

2. This is not to deny that fragments of linguistic description concentrating on selected phenomena in English and some other languages have achieved a greater depth than Pāṇini's grammar. The comparison we are making concerns fully worked out grammars or phonological components of grammars.

3. Itself a special case of a more general rule which replaces *a* followed by *i, u, ṛ, ḷ* (long or short) by *e, o, ar, al*, respectively (6.1.87 *ād guṇaḥ*, to be taken with 1.1.51 *ur aṇ raparaḥ*, and delimited by other rules).

4. 6.1.17 *liṭy abhyāsasyobhayeṣām.*

5. 8.3.19 *lopaḥ śākalyasya.*

6. The terms *feeding* and *bleeding* are explained, e.g., in Kiparsky (1968b), Anderson (1974:145), Hyman (1975:129). Schane (1973) has them wrong.

7. 1.4.45 *ādhāro 'dhikaraṇam.*

8. 2.3.36 *saptamy adhikaraṇe ca.*

9. 5.3.10 *saptamyās tral.*

10. 2.4.71 *supo dhātuprātipadikayoḥ.*

11. 2.4.33 *etadas tratasos tratasau cānudāttau.*

12. 3.2.115 *paro'kṣe liṭ.*

13. 3.4.78 *tiptasjhi* . . . The number is determined by the "reference" of the verb (1.4.21–22) and the person by the (present or deleted) "coreferent" (i.e. subject) of the verb (1.4.105–108).

14. 3.4.82 *parasmaipadānām ṇalatususthalatusaṇalvamāḥ.*

15. 7.2.116 *ata upadhāyāḥ.*

16. 6.1.8 *liṭi dhātor anabhyāsasya.*

17. 6.1.108 *samprasāraṇāc ca.*

18. 7.4.60 *halādiḥ śeṣaḥ.*

19. 6.1.193 *liti.*

20. 6.4.35 *śā hau.*

21. 7.1.35 *tuhyos tātaṅ āśiṣy anyatarasyām.*

22. 6.4.101 *hujhalbhyo her dhiḥ.*

23. 7.2.76 *rudādibhyaḥ sārvadhātuke.*

24. 7.3.86 *pugantalaghūpadhasya ca.*

25. 6.1.9 *sanyaṅoḥ.*

26. *ūṬH*, by 6.4.19 *chvoḥ śūḍ anunāsike ca.*

27. 6.1.77 *iko yaṇ aci.*

28. 6.1.101 *akaḥ savarṇe dīrghaḥ.*

29. Actually, this rule would apply here first anyway for another reason.

30. 6.1.87 *ād guṇaḥ.*

31. 6.1.85 *antādivac ca.*

32. 3.4.93 *eta ai.*

33. 6.1.77 *iko yaṇ aci.*

34. 8.2.23 *samyogāntasya lopaḥ.*

35. The interesting feature of Ex. 10 is that it shows how apparently quite "low-level" rules can become opaque through the effects of principle (3). Another striking example is *nārpatya*, where the final *r* of the first member of the compound does not become *ḥ* (contrast e.g. *punaḥprasaṅga*)

because it is derived by the operation of *vṛddhi* triggered by the suffix *ya* in the outer cycle. However, there are also several exceptions to (3) which involve *antaraṅga* rules in the last two sections of the grammar (8.3 and 8.4). It is sometimes held that (3) is not valid when the *antaraṅga* rule is in the Tripādī section (8.2.1 ff., see below). On that proposal Ex. 10 and similar cases would be the exceptions.

36. From *akṣa + Śas + div + KvIP + sU* (3.2.76 *kvip ca*), with the internal case suffix *as* deleted by 2.4.71 *supo dhātuprātipadikayoḥ*, and the derivational suffix *v* (*KvIP*) deleted by 6.1.67 *ver apṛktasya*.

   37. *ūṬH*, by 6.4.19 *chvoḥ śūḍ anunāsike ca*.

   38. 7.2.35 *ārdhadhātukasyeḍ vāladeḥ*.

   39. 6.4.131 *vasoḥ saṃprasāraṇam*.

   40. 6.1.73 *che ca*.

   41. 6.4.19 *chvoḥ śūḍ anunāsike ca*.

   42. 7.4.40 *dyatisyatimāsthām it ti kiti*.

   43. With *t* inserted by 6.1.71 *hrasvasya piti kṛti tuk*.

   44. Pbh. 55 *antaraṅgān api vidhīn bahiraṅgo lyab bādhate*.

   45. 3.2.115 *paro'kṣe liṭ*, 3.2.107 *kvasuś ca*, 6.1.8 *liṭi dhātor anabhyāsasya*, 7.4.59 *hrasvaḥ*, 1.2.46 *kṛttaddhitasāmāsāś ca*, 4.1.2 *sv au jas am auṭ chaṣ ṭā bhyām bhis ṅe bhyām bhyas ṅasi bhyām bhyas ṅas os ām ṅy os sup*.

   46. 6.4.131 *vasoḥ saṃprasāraṇam*.

   47. 6.1.108 *saṃprasāraṇāc ca*.

   48. 6.4.64 *āto lopa iṭi ca*.

   49. 6.4.133 *śvayuvamaghonām ataddhite*.

   50. 6.1.101 *akaḥ savarṇe dīrghaḥ*.

   51. 6.1.87 *ād guṇaḥ*.

   52. 7.2.102 *tyadādīnām aḥ*.

   53. 4.1.4 *ajādyataṣ ṭāp*.

   54. 6.4.134 *allopo 'naḥ*.

   55. 8.4.40 *stoḥ ścunā ścuḥ*.

   56. 8.2.77 *hali ca*.

   57. 3.4.82 *parasmaipadānām ṇalatususthalathusanalvamāḥ*.

   58. 2.4.40 *liṭy anyatarasyām*.

   59. 6.1.8 *liṭi dhātor anabhyāsasya*.

   60. 7.4.60 *halādiḥ śeṣaḥ*, 7.4.62 *kuhoś cuḥ*, 8.4.54 *abhyāse car ca*.

   61. 6.4.98 *gamahanajanakhanaghasāṃ lopaḥ kṅity anaṅi*.

   62. 8.3.60 *śāsivasighasīnāṃ ca*.

   63. 8.4.55 *khari ca*.

   64. 3.1.77 *tudādibhyaḥ śaḥ*.

   65. 7.3.84 *sārvadhātukārdhadhātukayoḥ*.

   66. 7.3.86 *pugantalaghūpadhasya ca*.

   67. 6.4.77 *aci śnudhātubhruvāṃ yvor iyaṅuvaṅau*.

   68. That is, before suffixes with diacritic *K* or *Ṅ* (1.2.5 *kṅiti ca*).

   69. 1.2.4 *sārvadhātukam apit*.

   70. Of course the tradition has seen the possibility that 1.1.5 *kṅiti ca* blocks *guṇa* here. It rejects it on insufficient grounds (Mbh. on 1.1.5).

   71. From *adhi + i + Ktvā* by 7.1.37, cf. above.

72. 6.1.101 *akaḥ savarṇe dīrghaḥ*.

73. 6.1.71 *hrasvasya piti kṛti tuk*.

74. 6.1.86 *ṣatvatukor asiddhaḥ*. Were it not for this type of example, the mention of *tuk* in 6.1.86 would be unnecessary.

75. 7.2.107 *adasa au sulopaś ca*.

76. 3.2.109 *upeyivān anāśvān anūcānaś ca*.

77. 6.1.8 *liṭi dhātor anabhyāsasya*.

78. 7.2.67 *vasv ekājādghasām*.

79. A special rule for this root, 6.4.81 *iṇo yaṇ*. The general rule 6.1.77 *iko yaṇ aci* (Ex. 6, fn. 27) would not be applicable.

80. 6.4.71 *luṅlaṅlṛṅkṣv aḍ udāttaḥ*, 6.4.72 *āḍ ajādīnām*.

81. 6.4.111 *śnasor allopaḥ*.

82. 6.4.76 *irayo re*.

83. 6.4.64 *āto lopa iṭi ca*.

84. In principle, 6.4.22 allows Pāṇini to have simultaneous ordering of rules in cases which could not be fit into a framework making exclusive use of linear ordering. Though Pāṇini does employ this capability a few times, it is interesting that the phonology of Sanskrit never clearly requires it. The standard case is the derivation *śās+hi → śā+dhi* 'instruct!' by rules replacing the root *śās* by *śā* before the suffix *hi* (6.4.35 *śā hau,* cf. fn. 20) and a rule replacing the suffix *hi* by *dhi* after a root ending a consonant (6.4.101 *hujhalbhyo her dhiḥ*). Either of the possible ordered applications would give the wrong result: **śāhi* if the *śās → śā* rule is applied first, and **śāsdhi* if the *hi → dhi* rule is applied first. But in a framework of linear ordering the problem can be gotten around easily by simply changing the environment of *śās → śā* from *hi* to *dhi*.

85. This section is studied closely in Buiskool (1939).

86. 8.3.19 *lopaḥ śākalyasya*.

87. 6.1.87 *ād guṇaḥ*.

88. 8.2.7 *nalopaḥ prātipadikāntasya*.

89. 7.1.9 *ato bhisa ais*.

90. The reason why *n*-deletion applies here is that the stem is technically also a word (*pada*) before *bhis* (and other consonantal endings) by virtue of a special rule.

91. 6.4.8 *sarvanāmasthāne cāsambuddhau*.

92. See Buiskool (1939:65), who refers to this type of situation as "secondary *asiddhatva*."

93. 6.1.88 *vṛddhir eci*.

94. 6.1.95 *omāṅoś ca*. This rule also gives another case in which such exceptional contraction takes place, viz. the word *om*, e.g., *śivāya om → śivāyom* '*om* to Śiva'.

95. From *bhū + yās + t* by 3.4.107 *suṭ tithoḥ*.

96. 8.2.29 *skoḥ saṃyogādyor ante ca*.

97. From *madhu+lih sad+a+ti* (and ultimately *madhu+am+lih+KvIP+ sU+sU sad+Laṭ*).

98. 8.3.29 *ḍaḥ si dhuṭ*.

99. 8.4.55 *khari ca*.

100. Note that this is one of the exceptions to (3) which are found in the Tripādī section, as mentioned above in fn.35.

101. Cf. *lakṣye lakṣaṇaṃ sakṛd eva pravartate* (see on Pbh. 111).

102. 8.4.47 *anaci ca*.

103. 7.4.59 *hrasvaḥ*. Cf. *jagāha* 'plunged', from *gāh*.

104. Note 18.

105. Note 28.

106. 6.1.85 *antādivacca*.

107. Pbh.111: *parjanyaval lakṣaṇapravṛttiḥ*.

108. Cf. Kiparsky (1973b) on the need for adopting this principle in generative grammar too.

PART TWO

REVIEW ARTICLE

CHAPTER TEN

How Different Are They?

Fred W. Householder

With the exception of the paper on Pāṇini, all the participants in this conference are implicitly criticizing or, at least, expanding on the phonological theory presented in *Sound Pattern of English* (Chomsky and Halle 1968). It behooves us, therefore, to start by specifying as explicitly as we can the principal tenets of this theory, which cannot be found on any one page of SPE (or anywhere else, to the best of my knowledge). We can then note where and in what ways each of the conferees has chosen to differ from SPE (and it must be said that few of them differ on any really fundamental issue), and we may also point out choice axioms for future "phonologies" to reject. It must be noted that few of the "phonologies" of this volume differ substantially on fundamentals from the SPE theory, though perhaps Sanders' Equational Phonology comes closest (except for Pāṇini, of course) to an appreciable difference; indeed for some, such as Dinnsen and Houlihan-Iverson, it is hard to say that they differ at all on essentials. If we had had a representative of Pikean or Firthian or stratificational phonology, or of New Wave or Labovian phonology, the differences would be more conspicuous.

I will try to subsume the principle axioms of SPE phonology under five main heads, listing relevant page numbers after each paragraph.

(1) The task of the linguist (as grammar writer for a particular natural language) is to duplicate in explicit notation the grammar which is implicitly present in the idealized speaker-hearer's brain, a grammar which he acquired as a child by the use of a number of specialized innate language learning devices. The explicit notation must somehow correspond functionally to some of the innate devices. The idealization involves, among other things, (a) the selection in most cases (of words,

inflections, syntactic patterns, etc.) of a single one of the known optional or dialectal or stylistic variants as the correct word, form, etc., (b) the inclusion of all grammatical competence and etymological information possessed by any speaker of the language—not excepting grammarians and etymologists, and (c) the assumption that language acquisition is instantaneous. (3, 4, 25, 322, 331, etc.)

(2) In dealing with the phonological part of his task, the linguist (i.e., phonologist) must provide the correct lexical representations, distinctive features, and phonological rules to map terminal strings of the syntax onto systematic phonetic strings. The answers to questions about the systematic phonetic structure of any language are intuitively given (i.e., segmentalization, choice of features, inventory of segments, etc.); for English in SPE, these answers closely resemble those belonging to the Smith-Trager autonomous phonemic analysis of English. The same set of features must be used throughout, though the kind of values (binary, m − u, +−, n-valued, etc.) may change. The rules must be ordered in a single sequence, with no back-tracking except perhaps for cyclical application. (5, 9, 11, 12, 14, 23, 25, 75, 296–98, etc.)

(3) The innate universals include a set of universal features, a set of rules and restrictions for combining them into segments, a set of permissible phonological rule types, the cyclic principle, a natural drive to eliminate allomorphy by means of rules, and an evaluation metric to rate alternative rules or rule sets. The phonologist must use all and only these devices used by the language-learning child. (ix, 18, 19, 43, 249, 251, 295, 296, 297, 333, 335, 356, 364, etc.)

(4) The primary function of the rules is to account in a phonetically plausible way for all the surface forms (i.e., inflexions or contextual variants) of a given lexical item and all derivatives from a given etymological root (or whatever you may wish to call it) with a single minimally specified base form. Suppletion or listing is to be resorted to only in rare and special cases. (ix, 381, 388, and passim)

(5) The linguist, whether as phonologist or syntactician or semanticist, need not concern himself with the uses or functions of language. (No mention at all in SPE; the notion "natural" appears on 335, 400, etc., and "plausible" on 401, 419, etc., but neither term is linked to function.)

As we remarked above, Pāṇini's phonology is perhaps the most strikingly divergent from these principles; there is no reason to suppose that he would have subscribed to any of section (1) or (3) or (5), and while he certainly does use the single base (at least for grammatical morphemes, and in large part also for ordinary words, as represented in the list of roots—Dhātupāṭha—associated with the Aṣṭādhyāyī), it is considerably more abstract than SPE theory allows, and the rules that operate on it form a kind of Unrestricted Rewrite System; nor does he appear to view correctness as an empirical matter in the sense of SPE: 331. Rather he writes what we would describe as a linguist's grammar, aiming at maximum economy with at most a kind of weak equivalence to a speaker's internalized grammar. A good deal of structural phonology in the forties and fifties was written from the same (not necessarily hocus-pocus) point of view. Pāṇini's methods of ordering the application of rules as here presented by Joshi-Kiparsky do not, in the main, coincide with those of SPE, though the principle of "proper inclusion" or "elsewhere" discussed here by Anderson is certainly important. It, too, was commonly used by the structuralists.

Since Anderson's paper constitutes, in part, a history of the developments within generative phonology during the last ten years, I shall deal with it first. Much of it deals with the earlier activity of contributors to this volume and of others who could have been, but much also deals with his own activities, which seem to involve four matters which go beyond the relatively minor issue of mechanical principles of rule application (including a rejection of the cycle): (1) arguments for the necessity of a set of morphological rules distinct from the phonological rules as well as phonetic rules and "quasi-systematic relations" among lexical items; (2) arguments against the strict linear ordering of rules and in favor of principles to determine relative ordering in particular cases (both of these are minor details of paragraph (2) above); (3) the proposal of a principle of exegetic adequacy (i.e., adequacy for retrospective explanation rather than prediction); (4) a rejection of the notion of complete universal naturalness (as implemented by the marking schemes of SPE: chapter 9). All these, though touching none of the major points of the theory, seem to me to be distinct improvements on SPE.

Goldsmith's Autosegmental Phonology has two layers: at the first level it merely accepts the SPE invitation to consider matters of tone which were completely avoided by Chomsky and Halle, but at the second it offers a potentially radical revision in the nature of both the lexical representation and the systematic phonetic one, which are conceived in SPE as single-stranded concatenations of segments each of which consists of a cluster of simultaneous features. Goldsmith at least envisages the possibility of several parallel concatenations with variable linkages ("association lines") between segments in one and segments in another.

Again no fundamental axioms of SPE are altered. The proposal suggests various testable speculations about language acquisition by children and eases the formalization of various changes, particularly assimilations, some of them also improvable by theories such as R. Cheng's (1977), which make the sequence single but the units in it syllables, each syllable being a bundle of simultaneous features which may be arranged in various ways on the surface. Many of the same goals may be attained either by multiplying the strings vertically or by broadening the beads horizontally.

Atomic Phonology (Dinnsen) and Functionally Constrained Phonology (Houlihan-Iverson) make virtually no changes in the basic theory of SPE, nor do they expand it in the manner of Autosegmental Phonology. Instead they each attempt to provide some restriction on the nature and content of phonological rules. These are proposals for universals, in some sense. Dinnsen's proposal has to do with the notion of complement rule-pairs: these are two rules which (essentially, though redundant features may alter things slightly) differ only in regard to the value (+ or −) of a single feature in the input (left side of environment). For all such pairs it is claimed that only one will be attested—i.e., if there are languages which drop final labials after rounded vowels, there will be none which drop labials only after unrounded vowels. The member of the pair which exists is called an atomic rule, the other member a non-atomic rule. The only test for atomicity appears to be heuristic; look through the languages of the world. (Incidentally, Charles A. Ferguson sent all the participants in the conference an invitation to use the Stanford Phonology Archive to search through 200 languages for data of this sort; so far as I know, none of them has done so yet.) Though non-atomic rules (without their mates) are said to be non-existent, all rule generalization or simplification is said to take place by the merger of an atomic rule with its mate, i.e., in the example mentioned above, a change to a rule dropping final labials after all vowels. Though Dinnsen says this applies also to generalization by Greek letter variables, it would seem that pairs which could be so generalized would involve opposite values in two places, often on both sides of the arrow; e.g., a rule that drops only labials after rounded vowels would merge with one that drops only non-labials after unrounded vowels. This seems to require a redefinition of the term "complement rule." Another claim made in the Dinnsen article, though it does not seem to be connected with atomic or complement rules, is that all intervocalic voicing rules are allophonic, i.e., do not merge phonemes which are elsewhere distinct. But in the passage from Latin to French somewhere, intervocalic p and b, which remain distinct initially, merge, ending up as v (and f and v are also distinct initially). Of course, once they have merged, there will be no contrasting segments in the input any more.

The Houlihan-Iverson paper makes proposals very similar to Dinnsen's, and comes no closer to being a new or distinct phonological theory. Their main principles seem to depend on a notion of markedness which is quite different from that in SPE (where the marked value of a feature may vary according to context), and which they define solely in terms of implicational universals: if there are languages with value α and without $-\alpha$, but none with only the $-\alpha$ value, then the α value is marked (presumably in all positions as well as all languages). There has always been a hedge available to phonologists when new data appear to upset an implicational universal—they can simply say that a different feature is involved. "It's not voicing here, it's tenseness."

Their second main point has to do with the difference between neutralization effects and allophonic ones where they choose the rather specialized Kiparskyan definition of neutralization. In these terms certain rules are claimed to be always neutralizing (e.g., final devoicing), others always allophonic (e.g., intervocalic voicing, as in Dinnsen). It is interesting that final devoicing is said to be always neutralizing, in view of the original Halle-Lees argument against taxonomic phonemes (that a taxonomic system could not capture in one rule the universality of assimilative voicing in Russian, since for some phonemes—including [x], [ɣ]—it was only allophonic, while for others it was phonemic). Houlihan-Iverson however claim that final devoicing—including [ɣ] → [x]—is always neutralizing in Russian, citing a good taxonomic phonemicist, George Trager. Azerbaijani, however, has a final devoicing rule which affects not only stops and ordinary fricatives (for all of which a good case for phonemic voicing exists) but also the phoneme /r/, which certainly does not have contrastive voice. So here Houlihan-Iverson would require two rules, one for the other obstruents and one for /r/ (whose voiceless final allophone is, in fact, a fricative). In their Corsican example, however, where word-initial voiceless stops become voiced after preceding vowels while word-initial voiced stops become fricatives (presumably by a rule which is extrinsically ordered earlier, in the SPE manner), they have apparently altered their definition of "in the input" in Kiparsky's definition of neutralization so that it no longer means "existing *at some level of derivation* before the rule applies," since, if they stick to that, the Corsican rule must be neutralizing.

Among their implicational universals (which refer, as they say, to inventories of *phonetic* segments), one, at least, seems to be questionable, (7)f "The presence of mid vowels implies the presence of high vowels," since several Amerindian languages (e.g., Apache, Mazateco, Potawatomi; see Hockett 1955:81–5; Ferguson's computer program could surely supply more) have [o] as their highest back vowel. Perhaps the universal could be interpreted to mean "some high vowel," not "a corresponding high vowel," and indeed Apache, etc. do have an [i]. This definition of markedness in terms of implicational universals forces them to maintain that voicing (of obstruents) is equally marked in all positions, but it has long been accepted that voiced obstruents are very frequent in intervocalic position, while voiceless ones are especially common initially and finally, and this distribution of allophones is actually found in some languages which lack a voicing contrast. (I discussed this matter a little in Householder 1971.)

Although they do not quite claim that neutralization to a marked member never occurs, they certainly suggest that; and if fricatives are always marked relative to stops, it is interesting that final velar and palatal stops in Azerbaijani are always neutralized to the corresponding fricatives, and this cannot be allophonic for the velar fricative. Examples contrary to other Houlihan-Iverson predictions were provided at the meetings by Jonathan Kaye—one from Quechua, others from Algonquin and Montagnais.

The one paper which presents the maximum of notational innovation, but also resembles in various ways the Dinnsen and Houlihan-Iverson papers, is Sanders' Equational Phonology. This one does differ from SPE principles on the matter of ordering (paragraph 2) and on the relevance of language use (paragraph 5), as well as on notational details coming under paragraphs (2) and (3). His position on the ideal speaker's grammar (1) and on innateness (3) is not clear from this paper. Aside from the metatheoretical material in the earlier pages, Sanders' most explicit claims have to do with unary features (i.e., features may be added or deleted, but absence of a feature—i.e., minus value—cannot be specified in the input), the use of general principles for settling conflicting rule application possibilities (similar to those mentioned by Anderson), and a claim much like the Houlihan-Iverson and Dinnsen ones (but broader) that all changes in final position (i.e., before juncture or silence) must be deletions, e.g., devoicing rather than voicing, segment loss rather than segment insertion. The same examples which violate their principles also violate Sanders'. (To make Dinnsen's position resemble Sanders' more closely, it is only necessary to insure that all atomic rules applying to final segments mention only + values in the input.)

In all three of these papers (Atomic, Functionally Constrained and Equational) it is either stated or implied that there cannot be rules of opposite sense (i.e. A → + B/C___ and A → − B/C___) either in different languages, different stages of one language, or simultaneously in the same language. Leben and Robinson (1977) cite an example from Schane attributed to Rumanian (where the environments are slightly different, but one is included within the other) and Sanders cites a Spanish example from Saporta, both of which are rejected. Pullum (1976) calls this (when the rules apply within the same language) the Duke of York gambit, and after a long discussion comes to the conclusion that there is no "basis for a general constraint that would prohibit" it: "The child is *NOT* equipped with a subconscious instruction" to avoid constructing grammars allowing Duke of York derivations.

From the counterexamples to all three of these papers, it is clear that the "universals" in question (regardless of how best to state them) are not true universals, comparable, e.g., to the claim that all natural languages have, on the phonetic surface, both consonants and vowels, or that no language lacks obstruents, or even the Chomsky-type universal that no language requires every word to be a phonetic palindrome. They are what we called "statistical universals" at Dobbs Ferry; propositions that are usually true of human languages, but whose failure to apply does not make a language incredible. They cannot, therefore, be part of the genetically transmitted LAD (unless we can assume mutations in some tribes), nor can they be logical necessities for any language implicit in its defining characteristics. They may, however, be accounted for in at least two different ways: either they make a language more efficient at whatever it is for (the factor considered irrelevant in SPE), or else they are due to primarily physiological causes but still do not make a language conspicuously *less* efficient.

If we turn now to Hooper's Natural Generative Phonology, we find, again, differences that hardly warrant considering it a whole new phonology, but which are of some importance. It shares more than the name with Stampe and Donegan's Natural Phonology: both make a sharp distinction between natural phonetic processes or P-rules and learned phonological or morphophonemic rules (MP-rules), the main difference being that Hooper goes further in claiming exceptionless unsuppressability for processes, while Stampe allows some of them to be overridden by rules acquired later. For Hooper a process is always surface-true, but she does allow a certain range of strength; it may be applied relatively more weakly or more strongly, resembling in this respect (at least) the low-level phonetic rules of SPE. Some P-rules are productive; others are unproductive, and this can be tested by their application to new loans or innovative creations. She does not, however, seem to make the distinction set up by Anderson between purely morphological rules (where, e.g., a change of one feature in itself signals a morpheme) and MP-rules. Much of her argumentation is based on speculations about how language-learners construct generalizations (including MP-rules), a kind of evidence nowhere evident in SPE, where the convention of paragraph (1) that language-learning is pretended to be instantaneous effectively cuts it out. Such arguments are also used by Stampe, Goldsmith, Leben and Anderson, and seem to me to be properly used in many cases. Hooper explicitly rejects the principle of paragraphs (3) and (4) that all forms of a derivational or inflexional paradigm must be phonologically derived from a single base form (root or stem), and allows for allomorphs in the lexicon. However, speculations about variants should pay more attention to the known facts, as when she couples the variant plurals *hoofs* and *roofs, hooves* and *rooves* (actually this conceals additional variants: the *oo* in all four forms may represent /uw/, but only in the first three /ʊ/, at least in American dialects known to me). The status of the variants is quite different: both *hoofs* and *hooves* have been in spoken and written use for centuries, and for some of that time *hooves* has had a slight preference in most areas, but the form *rooves* has only become common in relatively recent years, and only in a few areas (and is almost unknown in printed usage), whereas *roofs* has been virtually standard everywhere for centuries.

Much of the presentation of Vennemann's theory of rule inversion and semantic transparency should certainly have been linked up with Kuryłowicz (1949) on Analogical Change, but even Vennemann (1972a) does not so link it; many of the details are similar. Also, one form of the semantic transparency hypothesis may be amenable to testing by psycholinguistic experiments. Essentially the argument is that speakers will make use of every available phonological clue to decide an ambiguity; I have heard this doubted, however, and would very much appreciate an objective demonstration of some kind. Particularly the claims that "morphologically conditioned rules are never deletion rules" seems a bit strong. Even in English we have forms like *has, had* for [hævz], [hævd], which surely looks like a morphologically conditioned rule. Hooper's discussion assumes an equal pairing of one against one, but if, as here, it is one or two forms with zero against many without, the reasoning of the language-acquiring speaker might conceivably be different. The celebrated case of the Russian genitive plural in zero must also be relevant here. Finally, I don't think it can be considered to be self-evident to a language-learner (or a linguist) which semantic category in a paradigm is basic. Why did the Greeks opt for first-person singular present-tense as basic? Phonologically it won't work, as they realized themselves.

Turning now to Donegan and Stampe, we find a great deal more concern with what SPE regards (in part rightly, I think) as low-level irrelevant surface phonetic variation. They apparently reject the whole enterprise of generative phonology (as one questioner complained, this is not a phonology at all) as set out above in paragraphs (2) and (4), and even conclude their paper by reinstating the autonomous or taxonomic phoneme, using very much the same argument as one I used myself in Householder (1965), the argument from native speakers' awareness. However, as was shown in Saporta and Contreras (1960), for instance, native speakers are perfectly aware of *some* sub-phonemic matters. In the main the paper tries to make a contribution to the theory of language acquisition and of phonological performance, in both of which we have a natural emphasis on "processes" or P-rules. SPE is specifically contradicted as to point (5), much of point (1), almost all of (2), most of (3) (where a different set of devices are put in the brain of the language-learning child), and all of (4). But, in spite of this wholesale rejection, nothing much is put in the place of what is rejected. We are not told what exactly the function of the phonologist *is,* what the nature of the lexicon is or the shape of lexical entries, and very little about any early steps leading from the lexicon to performance, and what we get about the later steps is heavily anecdotal. There is a weak negative specification: "it is not intended to *describe* its subject matter exhaustively, i.e., to generate the set of phonologically possible languages," but that doesn't help much, since SPE nowhere, even in the famous chapter nine, claims to do that, though it may be somehow suggested that such a goal is desirable. Donegan and Stampe, unlike Hooper, deal more in tendencies than in exceptionless P-rules, and, since two tendencies may have opposite effects, the natural result is something like Anderson's exegetic adequacy. The main novelty of Donegan and Stampe's theory is the doctrine of language acquisition as suppression of natural substitutions (P-rules), selectively governed, I guess, by the child's observation of the speech of older children and adults. They pay a great deal of attention (properly, I think) to phenomena of relaxed or allegro speech, but then grossly exaggerate the frequency of these phenomena ("the ordinary pronunciation of languages"). Anyone who takes the pains to listen carefully (play at half-speed or in reverse, if you like; make sound spectrograms of dubious items) to large quantities of spontaneous, natural speech will be surprised not by the "complex mappings of intended sounds and actual sounds" but rather by the relative rarity of these reductions and slurrings. Donegan and Stampe cite other bits of unsupported evidence, e.g., "speakers of many languages which lack final obstruents devoice these . . . in foreign loanwords" (I don't know of one such language and Donegan and Stampe do not name one); the American speaker who cannot pronounce final /l/ in English, but can in German because he is trying for a light /l/; the southern idiolects which interchange the vowels of *bad* and *bite* (reminding me of the Hoosier speaker who interchanges the vowels of *barn* and *born* or the German immigrant who interchanges /w/ and /v/); "most English speakers" who substitute [oʔm] for [opm] (not me, at any rate; my glottal closure is simultaneous with the labial closure, not prior to it, and my velic release is well after the labial closure); the non-statistics on palatalization (or dipthongization) in *bash* as opposed to *passed you*. I am not alleging that any of these statements is false, merely that we have no way of checking and are offered no reason to believe that they have been checked. I also admire the Ob language in which all stressed vowels are merged, making *painting, panting, punting* and *pointing* identical; I am more familiar with Ug, in which the inserted syllable is unstressed. In Ug, however, *betted* and *bedded* might still be identical. The Middle Welsh change of /y/ to /ɨ/ looks very similar to the possible confusion of Azerbaijani /Ø/ with /ɯ/; it is quite easy to get the same acoustic effect with centralization as with rounding (and this is presumably what is meant by the expression "internal rounding" which occurs in the literature); see Householder (1972). Such a "two-step" change is like the familiar morphosemantic change of perfect to past which has occurred in so many languages of Europe, and is probably a legitimate exception to Austin's law (1957).

Like Donegan-Stampe, Leben offers as "Upside-down" phonology something that can be called a phonology at all only by straining the meaning of the term. Everyone else at this conference seemed to agree with SPE that a phonology is a device for mapping lexical representations onto phonetic actualizations. Leben's theory does not purport to do this. Instead, it attempts to satisfy the SPE concern over etymology in a different way, and answers this question: "If a native speaker ever happened to wonder if lexical item A was related to lexical item B, how could he go about testing?" Remember that for SPE phonology we have an idealized native speaker who intuitively knows all such relationships and has machinery to derive one of these items from the other if the relationship is real; he could never even pose Leben's question. (Like Hooper and Donegan-Stampe, Leben is clearly rejecting this idealized speaker-hearer.) The method chosen is essentially a parsing algorithm: the speaker compares pairs of lexical entries with respect to one or more "morphological" rules (by this Leben means the phonological rules of SPE, at least in large part; and also the phonological rules of Anderson —perhaps with the addition of some of Anderson's morphological rules —and surely Anderson's "quasi-systematic relations") and then reaches a decision as to relatedness. But two questions are left unanswered: (1) how can this algorithm be considered, in any sense, a part of the grammar of speaker's competence? (2) who is going to ask such questions? Does a speaker who never asks them have a defective competence? Leben realizes that there will be some false positives, among which he mentions *caustic-cost* and *comic-calm* (apparently for him these contain the same surface vowel), and I have also thought of *Cuba-cubic, fill-filth, terrible-tear, oar-oral* and many more. To solve this problem, he stipulates that the parser must specify "word relationships that are linguistically possible." But how on earth are we going to do that? This is the traditional bugbear of the historical etymologist: how much semantic similarity is sufficient for plausibility? And what native speaker-hearer, no matter how unidealized, is going to have access to appropriate criteria? There are really only two solutions to this problem: either (1) concede that any similarity which satisfies the native speaker is O.K.— which may well entail allowing mutually inconsistent pairings (and different for different speakers) simultaneously in the manner of Varro and other pre-Indo-Europeanist etymologists, e.g., relating *filth* independently to *foul, fool, fill* and perhaps *feel,* or (2) reject the criterion of semantic similarity entirely, which would unquestionably allow all the mutually inconsistent pairings just mentioned. Perhaps the most realistic is a third: accept the word of a big dictionary. This is certainly what real speaker-hearers often do. But however it is done, it clearly does not *have* to be done at all; a real speaker-hearer could have perfect command of his language without ever wondering about any such pairs, at least as far as Leben has shown.

So much for the papers in this volume. What might a stranger have expected of this conference? Several of the audience, in fact, told us about their disappointments. A glance at the SPE tenets (1–5) listed above shows very many opportunities for divergence and disagreement, phonological theories which would really be different theories. For instance, one could reject the notion of paragraph (1), striving instead for simple weak equivalence (the grammar produces the same output), using any conveniently intelligible notation and nomenclature without attempting to justify them by proofs from psycholinguistic experiments or otherwise. Automatically the rest of paragraph (1) would also be rejected. Even without that, one could follow Labov and others in rejecting (1a), and trying to account for variation correctly. If you reject all or part of paragraph (2), you could then look upon it as part of the phonologists' task (as it is the taxonomists') to justify a particular surface segmentation (Is /ay/ in *like* one segment or two? Is long /ō/ in any language with a length contrast one segment or two? etc. Does the boundary between initial /p/ and a following stressed vowel in English begin at the moment of release, at the onset of voicing, or after the formant transition is complete?), or a particular surface "phonemicization." Or else you could reject the notion of very long sequences of rules between lexicon and surface, requiring lexical entries to be less abstract (as, in part, Leben does, and possibly Donegan and Stampe or Hooper, though it is difficult to tell). Rejecting the innateness hypothesis might not, as Donegan and Stampe suggest, make any difference, but it might encourage people to look harder for functional or survival-value explanations of universals. Many of the details here have, as Anderson points out, already been rejected by most or many phonologists.

Paragraph (4) has already been rejected by several of the conferees; but if paragraph (1) is rejected, this sort of deep lexical structure could be reinstated in the manner of Pāṇini, allowing the convenience of many bits of abstractness which cannot be justified by a brain-correspondence theory. A linguist's grammar (as for Pāṇini, Saussure and Bloomfield) could again become a worthy and respectable enterprise. SPE is, in many respects, such a linguist's phonology, as is shown particularly by the idealized speaker-hearer and the instantaneous acquisition elements. Surely also we could modify the lexical entry (as I suggested in Householder 1971) by including orthography; this greatly simplifies many of Leben's problems: you would not link *caustic* to *cost* because orthographic *au* and *o* rarely if ever correspond, but *admission, adhesion, adhesive* and the rest (not to mention *telegraph* and *telegraphy*) become less problematic. It is not that orthography corresponds so well to systematic phonemics (as Chomsky and Halle say), but that systematic phonemics has been created out of orthography; and many of the rules of SPE are modified rules of spelling-to-sound conversion. Several of the conferees have already rejected point (5), but more use can still be made of the functional aspect of native-speaker reactions. For instance, consider neutralization rules, which concerned several of the theoreticians. I cannot affirm what happens in all languages which have a rule of final devoicing when another speaker fails to apply it, but I can report the responses of speakers of two such languages (Turkish and German). (1) Failure to devoice goes quite unnoticed or else (if the speaker is a foreigner) receives praise. Many speakers flatly deny that they do devoice. (2) If an inherently voiceless final, however, is voiced, that is noticed; it either elicits criticism or blocks communication. (3) If an inherently neutral final (i.e., one which has non-distinctive voicing in some positions) is voiced, this also may go unnoticed. Neutralization does not seem to be wholly neutral.

One last possible reform that used to be much in the news involves restricting the "power of the theory," i.e., making it impossible to do certain things. This was one of the motivations for chapter nine of SPE, which, as Anderson remarks, appears to be a really dead issue. Sanders offers some details to restrict the power slightly, but even in his scheme many impossible rules can be written. Dinnsen's atomic rule proposal, likewise, involves only a slight restriction, and nobody else seems to have any proposals of this sort, though most of them would entail at least a reduction in the number of rules. Is this line of innovation really dead? Or would we not rather keep the powerful devices and concede that they are, after all, linguists' devices that correspond to nothing particular in the speaker's brain?

PART THREE

REMARKS AND REPLIES

CHAPTER ELEVEN

On Arguing about Phonological Theories

Fred R. Eckman

1.0 During the general discussion session for this conference, there appeared to be some disagreement as to whether or not the proponents of the theories represented at the conference had provided any empirical basis for judging their theories to be superior to other current theories. The purpose of this paper is to sketch how it is that linguistic theories can be empirically differentiated, and to point out that, in fact, some of the papers did attempt to provide such a differentiation.

2.0 One of the principal goals of a theory of language is to provide a characterization of the notion "human language." Most generative theories of language have gone about this by specifying a framework within which grammars of individual languages can be constructed. Such a framework has been referred to as a general linguistic theory, or linguistic metatheory. A grammar of some language constructed within any given metatheory constitutes a theory of that language. A metatheory, on the other hand, constitutes a theory about grammars, or equivalently, a theory about language. A metatheory attempts to characterize the notion "human language" by specifying what can and cannot be a grammar of a language.

In view of this it is clear that metatheories and grammars are theories about different types of objects, and therefore are supported or falsified by different types of evidence. A grammar can be falsified by showing that it is incapable of generating certain well-formed utterances in the language, or that it generates certain ill-formed utterances. A metatheory is falsified by showing that there is some language for which that metatheory fails to provide an adequate grammar, or that the metatheory provides grammars for objects which are not human languages. Consequently, metatheories are not shown to be false by falsifying a particular grammar, or a particular analysis, since the falsification of a particular grammar does not show that some other grammar, which is adequate, cannot be constructed within that same metatheory. What must be shown in order to falsify a metatheory is that the type of grammars that are constructed within that metatheory are inadequate, or alternatively, that although some adequate grammars can be constructed, the metatheory provides for the construction of grammars which are not grammars of human languages.

Conversely, a particular metatheory is not shown to be correct by showing that it provides adequate grammars for some language or some set of languages, since the possibility is left open that the metatheory provides grammars for objects which are not human languages. What must be shown, if the metatheory is to make any claim at all about the nature of human language, is not only that the metatheory correctly provides for adequate grammars of objects which are human languages, but also that it correctly excludes other objects as being impossible human languages. In other words, there must be some set of objects which the metatheory correctly excludes from the class of possible human languages by making it impossible to construct grammars for these objects within that metatheory.

Within this context, then, it is not sufficient for proponents of the individual metatheories represented at this conference to show that they can provide a simpler, more general or more elegant analysis of some set of facts. Rather, if these theories are to have any empirical import at all, they must show what it is that they correctly allow and what it is that they correctly disallow in terms of types of languages. In what follows, I will attempt to point out where some of the papers in this volume followed this reasoning explicitly and, therefore, provided an empirical basis for differentiating their particular theories.

It should be pointed out that the general conclusion that can be drawn from this is not altered significantly if it is the case, as was suggested in the general discussion session, that the theories represented at the conference are not really different metatheories, but only extensions or revisions of the Standard Theory presented in Chomsky and Halle (1968). Even if these theories do constitute merely revisions to the Standard Theory, they constitute revisions to a metatheory. That is, they represent changes in the form of grammars that can be constructed within this metatheory. In arguing for the revised form of a metatheory, one is arguing for the characterization of the notion human language that this revised metatheory provides. Thus, again, one must show what it is that this revised metatheory allows and disallows in the way of human languages.

3.0 The paper by Dinnsen (this volume) argues for the superiority of the theory of atomic phonology by showing that this theory explicitly excludes some types of rules from occurring in the phonologies of human languages. The central thesis of this theory is that the phonological component of human languages can contain only rules drawn from a set of atomic rules, or rules derived from these atomic rules by a principle of complementation. Thus, according to this theory, if the rule in (1) is an atomic rule, then the rule in (2) may not occur independently in the phonology of any language.

(1)

$$\begin{bmatrix} - \text{sonorant} \\ - \text{continuant} \end{bmatrix} \longrightarrow [- \text{voice}] \ / \ \_\_\_ \ \#$$

$$\begin{bmatrix} - \text{sonorant} \\ + \text{continuant} \end{bmatrix} \longrightarrow [- \text{voice}] \ / \ \_\_\_ \ \#$$

Consequently, the theory of atomic phonology excludes from the class of possible languages any language which has a rule which devoices only word-final fricatives. This theory makes the empirical claim that there will be no language which has a voice contrast in stops, a voice contrast in word-medial fricatives, but no voice contrast in word-final fricatives.

Similarly, the paper by Houlihan and Iverson (this volume) is an attempt to explicitly exclude language types from the set of human languages. Given their Markedness Constraint, it is claimed that it is impossible for the grammar of any language to contain a phonologically conditioned rule which is a neutralization rule and which converts only relatively unmarked segments into only relatively marked ones. Within this framework, it is claimed that there will be no language whose grammar contains an intervocalic voicing rule which is neutralizing. That is, there will be no language which exhibits a superficial voice contrast in some positions, say, word-initial and word-final positions, but exhibits only voiced obstruents in word-medial position.

Another example of a theory which shows how it can be empirically falsified by showing what it excludes as a possible language is the theory of equational grammar as put forth by Sanders (this volume). Within this framework, all grammatical rules must be expressed in the form of equivalence statements, and all principles governing the directionality, optionality and interaction of these rules must be universal. The universality of these principles, as Sanders explicitly states, excludes the possibility that the grammar of one language will have a phonological rule which is the converse of a phonological rule in the grammar of some other language. Thus, for example, if one language has a rule of terminal devoicing, there can be no language which has a rule of terminal voicing. This metatheory therefore predicts that there can be no language with only word-final voiced obstruents, some of which alternate with word-medial voiceless obstruents.

Having considered some examples of phonological theories which have shown how they can be empirically falsified by showing what it is that they explicitly exclude from the class of possible human languages, I would now like to briefly comment on some theories which did not take this approach.

The paper by Goldsmith (this volume) is an exposition of the theory of autosegmental phonology, which differs from standard generative phonology in that autosegmental phonology views phonological and phonetic representations as multilinear rather than as a single string of segments. Goldsmith argues for the superiority of autosegmental phonology by demonstrating the adequacy of this theory in characterizing the facts of a number of tone languages. However, Goldsmith does not try to show how it is that in characterizing these facts, the theory of autosegmental phonology also correctly excludes certain objects as being possible human languages. In fact, he takes the opposite approach, as shown by the following statement:

> . . . one important way, it seems to me, to advance phonology is to open the formal floodgates as wide as possible.

The reasoning behind this seems to lie in the assumption that increasing the conceptual framework of a metatheory enables one to gain certain insights which would otherwise be missed. What is not clear to me is how one gains more insight into the notion human language by increasing the class of possible grammars rather than by limiting this class. Hypotheses which pursue the latter approach are more easily falsifiable, and the metascientific value of the falsifiability of any hypothesis has been established, it seems to me, beyond question.

Another example of a theory which does not explicitly show what it excludes in terms of language types is the theory of natural generative phonology, as put forth by Hooper (this volume). In this paper, Hooper gives an extensive discussion of morpho-phonemic rules (MP-rules).

Among the properties attributed to these rules are that they are morphologically conditioned, and the structural changes that they make are
phonologically arbitrary. Thus, according to this theory, the phonologies
of human languages can contain a set of surface-true, phonetically-
motivated phonological rules (P-rules), and a set of MP-rules which are
governed not by principles of phonology but by the Semantic Transparency Hypothesis. The consequence of this is that morphologically-
conditioned phonological rules are excluded as possible rules in the
phonologies of human languages.

So far Hooper seems to be proceeding in the direction of showing
what it is that the theory of natural generative phonology excludes from
the class of possible human languages, thereby making an empirical claim
concerning what this metatheory characterizes as a possible language.
Thus, she states near the beginning of her paper,

> There must be general principles that control the speaker's analysis
> of the morpho-syntactically motivated alternations of the language.

One such principle is the Semantic Transparency Hypothesis, about
which she says,

> This principle is not, then, just a way of explaining a few cases of
> analogical change, but rather a general principle that should guide syn-
> chronic analyses of morphologically motivated alternations. . . .

Therefore, given that P-rules are governed by phonetic constraints, and
that MP-rules are governed by the Semantic Transparency Hypothesis,
it should be possible to determine what can and cannot be a rule in
the phonological component of a language, and thereby make some
claim about what can and cannot be a human language.

The problem with this is that it is not clear that anything is excluded
from being a MP rule by the Semantic Transparency Hypothesis. Not
only are the alternations governed by MP rules phonologically arbitrary, but the rules themselves are considered to be part of the arbitrary
sound-meaning correspondence, similar to the principle which relates
the semantic concept of a table to the phonetic string [mesa] in Spanish.
Since we have no constraints (other then phonotactics) which govern
what can and cannot be a possible sound-meaning correspondence, it
would appear that nothing is excluded from the class of MP rules. This
being the case, it is not clear what natural generative phonology excludes
from the class of possible grammars, and therefore it is not clear what

characterization natural generative phonology gives to the notion of human language.

4.0 The purpose of this discussion has not been to argue for or against any of the theories presented in this volume, since, as was pointed out in the discussion sessions, there are many unsolved problems. The fact that some of the papers pointed out how it is that the metatheory which they were espousing could be falsified obviously does not attest to that metatheory's correctness; nor does the fact that other papers may not have shown what it is that the metatheory they were presenting explicitly excludes confirm the ultimate incorrectness of that metatheory. Rather, the purpose of this discussion has been to attempt to illustrate how it is that a proponent for any given metatheory should go about arguing for that metatheory.

CHAPTER TWELVE

On the Alleged Correlation
of Markedness and Rule-function

Jonathan Derek Kaye

In their contribution to this volume Houlihan and Iverson (H & I) claim that "phonologically-conditioned neutralization rules convert relatively marked segments into relatively unmarked segments" (page 61). As a corollary to this principle they further claim that "phonologically-conditioned rules which produce exclusively marked segments from relatively unmarked ones are allophonic" (page 61). Sanders in his paper (also found in this volume), states, "except for a few minor differences, mostly non-substantive, Houlihan and Iverson's constraints seem *essentially related as the segmental counterparts of the representational constraints on derivational function* determined by Maximalization of Terminality and the Law of Unmarked Terminality" (emphasis mine/JDK, page 88).

In this paper I will show that the above claims of H & I are false. It should be noted that to the extent that these claims fall out as automatic consequences of Sanders' equational phonology, that theory is also in peril. I would also like to suggest that the view of language which prompted the line of research undertaken by Houlihan, Iverson and Sanders is equally unfruitful and leads inevitably to the mistaken claims to be found in the current discussion.

A discussion of the counterexamples which I am about to present would be pointless in the absence of a competing theory which could handle them as well as the evidence cited by the authors to support their position. In the absence of such a theory one would merely relegate these examples to the ample class of linguistic facts which remain mysterious, with the expectation that some eventual modification to the theory will render them comprehensible. In fact, most of the positive evidence cited in H & I follows from the theory of markedness developed in Chomsky and Halle (1968). The principles proposed by H & I in no way follow from this competing theory. I maintain that these data which I am about to present constitute genuine counter-examples rather than mysterious unexplained cases compatible with no known theory and should, accordingly, result in the abandonment of all theories in which they play an essential role.

To resume briefly the claims involved here, H & I state that rules which convert marked segments into unmarked segments must be neutralization rules. They follow the definition of a neutralization rule similar to that of Kiparsky (1976). According to this definition, a rule A → B /C____D is neutralizing if the string CBD is found in the class of inputs to this rule. CBD may exist as a part of an underlying form or may be created by a rule which must apply prior to the application of the rule in question. All rules which are not neutralizing are allophonic.

The fact that neutralization rules generally result in less-marked segments is hardly surprising given the notion of markedness (Chomsky and Halle 1968, chapter 9; see also Waugh's comments on this subject in this volume) and the above definition of a neutralization rule. Since the presence of marked segments in a language typically implies the presence of their unmarked counterparts, it is to be expected that rules that result in unmarked segments will do so in the context of a phonological inventory that already contains these segments. Similarly the claim that rules resulting in relatively marked segments are allophonic rules follows from the fact that marked segments are found less frequently and are thus less likely to be found among the underlying phonemes of a language or as the output of another phonological rule applying before the rule in question. It follows, then, that the fact that H & I's principles are *generally* true is in no way an argument in their favour. The one original point of their analysis is that the correlation between markedness and neutralization rules plays some constraining role in the set of possible phonologies. It is precisely this point that I will show to be false.

I will first discuss a case in which a rule converting marked segments to unmarked ones is an allophonic rule. This example involves a rule from Algonquin which creates segments that already exist in the inventory of underlying segments. It is not a neutralization rule since these underlying segments are not present in the context of this rule. If one assumes, as do H & I for similar examples, that even non-alternating forms undergo this rule, then the rule is allophonic. I agree with H & I's analysis of these cases (i.e., the fact that such cases do not involve neutralization rules). Since such cases remain problematic for a number of phonologists, I will first present a structurally identical case from Quechua which involves a rule changing unmarked segments into marked ones. H & I's principle will handle the Quechua case only if the rule is considered allophonic; but then they cannot handle the Algonquin case. If, however, one should treat this rule as neutralizing, the Algonquin case is no problem but the Quechua one no longer works. I remain convinced that both rules are allophonic and that it is the Algonquin one that poses the problem for H & I. In any event there is no way out.

The Quechua data are taken from Solá and Parker (1964) and from discussions with my colleague Claire Lefebvre. Originally Quechua had a three-vowel system given in (1).

(1) Original Quechua vowel system included:

i   u

a

and a rule which lowered high vowels to mid in the environment of a post-velar:

(2) Lowering $[+ \text{voc}] \longrightarrow [- \text{high}]$ % $[+ \text{cons}, - \text{high}, + \text{back}]$
(% = mirror image)

This is exactly as H & I would have it. Rule (2) converts unmarked segments (i,u) into marked ones (e,o). It is clearly allophonic since e and o arise only as the result of this rule.

In the post-contact era Quechua has acquired an enormous number of loan words primarily from Spanish. Many of these words contain the mid-vowels e and o in non-post-velar contexts. It is generally assumed that these two vowels have been incorporated into Quechua's inventory of underlying phonemes, and accordingly Quechua now has the system shown in (3).

(3) Present Quechua vowel system

i   u

e   o

a

Forms such as those in (4) show that e and o are no longer predictable variants of their corresponding high vowels. Further, the word for 'gourd' shows that these vowels may also appear in words of Quechua origin.

(4) puru 'feather' pero 'but'
    poro 'gourd' piruru 'whorl'

The lowering rule (2) must still be assumed to be present in Quechua because of alternations such as those in (5).

(5) taki-y 'to sing' take-q 'singer'
    tusu-y 'to dance' tuso-q 'dancer'

Assuming that all morpheme-internal instances of *e* and *o* in the context of *q* as in *moqo* 'knee', *qena* 'quena,' *toqa-* 'spit (v)', *meqoř* 'better', are derived from /i,u/ (this is the position of Solá and Parker (1964:10) as well as that assumed implicitly in H & I), one may maintain rule (2) as an allophonic rule since *e* and *o* would not show up in the context of *q* in underlying forms. A problem may arise in morpheme-final position (Quechua has no prefixes). There appear to be no Quechua verb stems in *-o*. Thus an alternation such as *takiy - takeq* would not contrast with hypothetical *takey - takeq* and the allophonic status of the rule may be preserved. This precisely parallels the Algonquin case to be discussed below. Nouns, however, may end in *-e* or *-o* although they appear to be relatively rare: *poro* 'gourd', *koso* 'large corral', *klase* 'type'. There is an enclitic that contains an initial *-q,* viz. the topic marker *-qa*. If this enclitic triggers lowering, i.e., *masu-qa* [masoqa], then we may have to alter the status of lowering to that of a neutralization rule because of the contrastive situation shown by such forms as *koso - kosoqa* vs. *masu - masoqa*. If such were the case, this would violate H & I's principle from the other direction—a rule converting unmarked segments to marked ones would be a neutralization rule. Let us assume that we can maintain (2) as an allophonic rule and that Quechua does not provide a counter-example to H & I's principle. We have now prepared the groundwork for considering the Algonquin case.

Algonquin consists of a series of dialects spoken near the Ontario-Québec border. These dialects belong to the Ojibwa complex of the *Algonquian* (note the spelling difference) family. Many of these dialects have a rule which devoices initial obstruents (I will deal with data from Lac Simon; David Jones has reported a similar phenomenon at Maniwaki). This initial devoicing rule turns relatively marked segments (voiced) into relatively unmarked ones (voiceless) and ought to be a neutralization rule following H & I's principle. In fact, it is an allophonic rule. Although both voiced and voiceless obstruents exist in Algonquin, only voiced obstruents occur in word-initial position—the context in which initial devoicing applies. The lack of (underlying) word-initial voiceless obstruents is due to a word structure constraint which excludes them in this context. Now it may seem perverse to claim that a language has both a word structure constraint excluding word-initial voiceless obstruents and a phonological rule that devoices all word-initial obstruents. Once the historical processes that led to this state of affairs are understood, the situation seems much less bizarre.

Proto-Algonquian is assumed to have the following obstruent system:

(6) Proto-Algonquian Obstruents
simple p t k θ s š
cluster Xp Xt Xk Xθ Xs Xš (where X = ?, h, θ, n, s, š)

Proto-Algonquian also contained the word structure constraint (7).

(7) Proto-Algonquian WSC
No word may begin with a consonant cluster.

At some point early in the history of Ojibwa-Algonquin a number of clusters were simplified. Specifically, obstruent clusters with initial ?, *h,* θ became "fortis" consonants (traditionally written as geminates by Algonquianists), that is, voiceless (pre or post) aspirated consonants. These changes resulted in the early Ojibwa-Algonquin obstruent system shown in (8) and a modified version of the WSC shown in (9).

(8) Early Ojibwa-Algonquin Obstruents
simple p t č k s š
fortis pp tt čč kk ss šš

(9) Early Ojibwa-Algonquin WSC
No word may begin with a cluster or fortis consonant.

Doubtless at the early stage it was possible to derive fortis consonants from underlying clusters and hence retain the original formulation (7) of the WSC. In the course of history the source of these fortis consonants has become more and more opaque from a synchronic point of view and the modified WSC (9) became necessary at some point. The situation described here still holds for some conservative Northern and Western Ojibwa dialects.

In Eastern Ojibwa dialects, including Algonquin, the former fortis-simple (lenis) distinction has been replaced by a voicing distinction. The former simple consonants which were unaspirated and redundantly voiced in at least some contexts are now voiced consonants. The former clusters which developed into the fortis consonants (aspirated and voiceless) are now the voiceless consonants. This situation is illustrated in (10) with the required modification to the WSC shown in (11).

(10) Eastern Ojibwa-Algonquin Obstruents
    voiced (former simple) b d ǰ g z ž
    voiceless (former aspirated) p t č k s š

(11) Eastern Ojibwa-Algonquin WSC
    No word may begin with a cluster or a voiceless consonant.

It is worth noting here that the historical developments described here are neither unnatural nor, in themselves, uncommon. Constraints against initial clusters, simplifications of consonant clusters, and changes from an aspirated-unaspirated distinction to a voiceless-voiced distinction are each well attested in diachronic studies. What is crucial here is that the *confluence* of these events results in a synchronic system where a voiced-voiceless distinction which is contrastive elsewhere does not exist in word-initial position. Only voiced obstruents are found there. (This is a case of "static neutralization" in H & I's terminology.) This contrast is not neutralized in this position; it is simply absent.

This brings us to the Algonquin situation. The picture here is as described for Eastern Ojibwa-Algonquin. The one difference is that several Algonquin dialects have added a rule of initial devoicing. Data illustrating this rule are given in (12) below (these data are my own from the Lac Simon dialect).

(12) a. tɨgošɨn   'he arrives'   kɨdɨgošɨn   'you arrive'
       či:ma:n   'canoe'   kɨǰi:ma:n   'your canoe'
       ki:nɨba: 'he slept'   kɨgi:nɨba: 'you slept'
   b. kɨtɨga:n   'cultivated field'   kɨka:t   'your leg'

The data of (12a) show the alternation between an initial voiceless and a non-initial voiced consonant. In (12b) we see the direction of the rule: it must be an initial devoicing rule and not a non-initial voicing rule. Non-initial voiceless consonants abound morpheme-internally: *kitiga:n,* and morpheme-initially: *kɨka:t* (-ka:t 'leg' is a dependent noun and is obligatorily preceded by a prefix. It does not constitute a violation to the WSC). The initial devoicing rule is completely transparent. There are no word-initial *phonetic* voiced obstruents. Initial devoicing, while not as common as final devoicing, seems a reasonably natural process. It is reported in Tübatulabal, Mordve Erza and Kirghiz. And so it has come to pass that Algonquin has both a WSC excluding word-initial voiceless obstruents and a phonological rule that devoices all word-initial consonants. This phonological rule is an allophonic rule since a contrast is not neutralized by this rule. The difference between this allophonic rule of initial devoicing and a neutralization rule such as German final devoicing is shown in (13).

(13) Algonquian Initial Devoicing   German Final Devoicing
      tigošin - kidigošin   rat - räder   /vcd/ vcl ~ vcd
      absent because of WSC   tat - täter   /vcl/ vcl ~ vcl
      ki- 2nd person prefix   unt   non-alternating

Given the allophonic status of the initial devoicing rule non-alternating initial obstruents are derived from initial voiced ones (cf. H & I's treatment of English schwa). Algonquin thus provides us with a clear case of a rule converting marked to unmarked segments which is an allophonic rule.

It can also be shown that the corollary to the markedness constraint is incorrect. These are cases of rules converting unmarked segments into marked ones that are neutralization rules.

An interesting example having this property is the dialect of French spoken by the Algonquins of Lac Simon (and perhaps other villages as well). The French spoken there is similar in most respects to Quebec French. One of the hallmarks of Quebec French is a rule of affrication given in (14).

(14) Quebec French Affrication

$$\begin{bmatrix} t \\ d \end{bmatrix} \longrightarrow \begin{bmatrix} t^s \\ d^z \end{bmatrix} / \underline{\quad} [- \text{cons}, + \text{high}, - \text{back}]$$

Following this rule *tu* is pronounced [t^{s}y]; *dire* [d^{z}ɪ^{j}r]; *tiens,* [t^{s}jẽ], and so on. This rule presents no problem for H & I since the only source of these affricates is rule (14). Quebec French possesses the affricates č and ǰ which are found primarily in English loanwords. These latter affricates are nonetheless completely integrated into the Quebec French consonant system. Some examples are: *jean* 'jeans,' *djinne* 'gin,' *botch* '(cigarette) butt,' *scratcher* 'to scratch,' *botcher* 'to botch, louse up,' *pitcher* 'to throw,' *ponnetcher* 'to punch (a time-clock),' *patcher* 'to patch,' *djobbe* 'job.' Algonquin French differs from Quebec French in one important respect. Rule (14) has been modified in this dialect so that the resulting affricates are alveo-palatal rather than alveolar.

(15) Algonquin French Affrication

$$\begin{bmatrix} t \\ d \end{bmatrix} \longrightarrow \begin{bmatrix} č \\ ǰ \end{bmatrix} / \underline{\quad} [- \text{cons}, + \text{high}, - \text{back}]$$

In all other respects the rule is unchanged. Notice, however, that the results of this rule are identical to the already existing affricates. Alongside of *chip* '(potato, poker) chip,' *cheap* 'stingy; of poor quality,' *djobbe* 'job', *juke-box* 'jukebox', there are words like *ǰir* (<dire), *pčit* (<*petite*), *sorčir* (<*sortir*). Furthermore, this affrication must be considered a rule because of alternations like [*parčir*] 'to leave', [*parte*] 'you (pl) leave'. Rule (15) is then a neutralization rule, since underlying *č* and *ǰ* occur in similar environments ([swɪ̌če], [skrače]). Algonquin French affrication is a rule which changes unmarked segments to marked ones and is (contra H & I) a neutralization rule.

This does not appear to be a unique case of this type. Fruitful areas of investigation are languages which have at various points in their history undergone a palatalization process only to have a second palatalization process come into the language, which has not yet been rendered opaque by subsequent developments. The Montagnais dialects (the eastern branch of the Cree complex of the Algonquian family) contain underlying *č* (or *c*) as a result of a Proto-Algonquian palatalization rule ($t \rightarrow č$) which has since become quite opaque. They subsequently underwent velar palatalization ($k \rightarrow č$; *č* has changed to *c* in some dialects, i.e., those that have *c* also as a result of the first palatalization). The exact status of velar palatalization in modern Montagnais is not clear and so cannot be considered a counter-example to H & I in the absence of further research.

Cajun and Acadien French have two palatalization processes: velar palatalization before some front vowels and dental palatalization before the palatal glide. These two processes are stated informally in (16).

(16) Cajun-Acadien French Palatalizations

a. Velar $\begin{bmatrix} k \\ g \end{bmatrix} \longrightarrow \begin{bmatrix} č \\ ǰ \end{bmatrix}$ / ____ front vowel

b. Dental $\begin{bmatrix} t \\ d \end{bmatrix} \longrightarrow \begin{bmatrix} č \\ ǰ \end{bmatrix}$ / ____ y

Note that the *y* drops after the application of (16b). Examples of the first process taken from Acadien include these: *deǰøle* < dégueuler 'vomit', *deǰize* < déguisé 'disguised', *či* < qui 'who'. Dental palatalization is illustrated in akaǰɛ̃ <Acadien, ǰø < dieu 'god', čɛ̃< tien 'yours'. The former process is quite opaque and probably does not function as a synchonic rule of these dialects. If this is so, palatalized velars are to be represented as such in underlying forms. The latter process, dental palatalization, appears to be more regular. If this proves to be the case, and more research is needed in this area, then dental palatalization would be a neutralization rule. This would constitute another violation of H & I's principle.

In this paper I have attempted to exemplify violations of H & I's principle: rules creating relatively unmarked segments which are allophonic (Algonquin) and rules creating relatively marked segments which are neutralizing (Algonquin French). I wish to emphasize that the fact that H & I's principles generally hold is completely beside the point. This fact follows from general notions of markedness such as those discussed in Chomsky and Halle (1968). It is clear that the sorts of principles proposed by H & I play no role in constraining the class of possible phonologies. The fact that Algonquin had no voicing contrast in word-initial position did not prevent an initial devoicing rule from arising in that language. The fact that the underlying alveo-palatal affricates existed in Algonquin French (perhaps also in Acadien-Cajun) did not block the entry of a subsequent palatalization rule.

The above examples also show how events occurring in the course of the history of a language may lead to seemingly peculiar synchronic states. Approaches to phonological structures based on principles of the sort discussed here (see also Sanders' contribution to this volume) appear hopelessly simplistic. Language change is triggered by a variety of factors. It is far from clear that these factors operate in harmony. Nor is it to be expected that they will produce uniform results. The failure of H & I's principle should come as no surprise.

I wish to thank my colleagues Debbie Clifton, Diane Daviault, Lynn Drapeau and Claire Lefebvre for their aid on certain points contained in this paper. They are, of course, not responsible for any faults that may be found therein.

CHAPTER THIRTEEN

Some Observations on "Substantive Principles in Natural Generative Phonology"

James W. Harris

Editor's Note: This paper is based on a draft of Hooper's paper submitted in advance of the conference. It should be noted, however, that Hooper's contribution to the volume represents a substantial revision which has no doubt benefited from Harris' remarks during the discussion period at the conference and which are summarized herein. Thus, quotations are necessarily taken from Hooper's earlier draft and do not necessarily reflect her present thinking.

Joan Hooper's 'Substantive principles in natural generative phonology' (henceforth HSP) touches on a wide range of facts and issues. To do justice to all of these would require that a "discussant" produce a document longer than HSP and far exceeding the limits imposed for the present volume. I have thus tried to organize these remarks so as both to reflect the relative weight Hooper assigns to her topics and to be compatible with space limitations.

I take it that Hooper considers the center of gravity of HSP to be her presentation, illustration, and refinement of the Semantic Transparency Hypothesis. This hypothesis embodies a "principle of analysis," presumably one of the substantive principles referred to in the title, which is said to be employed by "real speakers" as they construct their internalized grammars and which should be employed by linguists to "guide synchronic analyses of morphologically motivated alternations even where additional substantive evidence is not available." Hooper envisions that such analyses are to be provided by a theory of "natural morphology" of which the Semantic Transparency Hypothesis "is, unfortunately, only the beginning." Hooper sees no reason why the morphological theory she has in mind cannot be developed, since "great progress has been made recently in the investigation of natural processes of phonology, and in the development of substantive universal principles [of phonology]." We are cautioned, however, that "the principles borrowed from phonological analysis are totally inappropriate" for morphological analysis, and that valid principles of morphology "will be forthcoming . . . only when we stop treating morphology in terms of phonological criteria and start dealing with it as a meaning-based phenomenon."

We will return below to Hooper's view of the difference between morphology and phonology and of substantive universal principles of phonology. Let us first investigate the substantive content of the Semantic Transparency Hypothesis.

THE SEMANTIC TRANSPARENCY HYPOTHESIS

Hooper initiates her exposition of the Semantic Transparency Hypothesis with a diagram, which is reprinted for convenience as (1):[1]

	Primitive Category	Secondary Category
(1) Semantic Level	A	A + b
Level of Overt Manifestation	X	X + y

Hooper gives an explanation of (1) that can be quickly exemplified as follows: The forms *cat, foot* are overt manifestations (X) of the Primitive Category (A) "(singular) noun."[2] *Cat+s* and *feet* are manifestations (X+y) of the Secondary Category (A+b) "noun, plural." In the expression "X+y," "y" refers to some "mark," e.g., the addition of the morpheme -*s* in *cat+s,* application of a non-automatic rule in *foot/feet.* Crucially, the manifestly "marked" form is associated with the secondary semantic category rather than with the primary one.

Hooper realizes that the spirit (though not the letter) of the Semantic Transparency Hypothesis will be violated if a deletion rule is allowed to count as a "mark," i.e., as a "y" in "X+y." For example, the correlation of "marked" (resp. "unmarked") overt form with "marked" (resp. "unmarked") semantic category would be subverted if in some language plural nouns like *zat* were related by deletion to corresponding singular forms like *zats.*[3] Hooper therefore proposes as a "refinement" of the Semantic Transparency Hypothesis the restriction on (1) that "*y* may be an M[orpho]P[honemic]-rule, e.g., Umlaut or G-insertion, but *not* a deletion rule."

Hooper's "refinement" runs into trouble immediately. Consider English present tense verb inflection. If third person singular is taken, as it generally is, to be the Primitive Category, then, for example, *talks* would be "X" in (1); and in the Secondary Category manifestation *talk* (="X+y"), "X" would be *talks* and "y" would be a rule deleting -*s*. According to Hooper, "this analysis is wrong." Presumably no one would disagree with this judgment. But we now face a dilemma: the deletion analysis of *talk* violates the "refinement" of (1)—and is wrong anyway— yet, as we know, the unrefined version of (1) does not permit the manifestation of the Primitive Category (*talks*) to be more complex, in the appropriate sense, than that of the Secondary Category (*talk*). Hooper gets out of the dilemma by proposing a sort of fail-safe version of (1), which is reprinted as (2):

(2)

	Primitive Category	Secondary Category
Semantic Level	A	A + b
Level of Overt Manifestation	X + z	X + y

In the example at hand, then, "z" is the third singular marker -*s* of *talks,* and "y" is null. The relationship of (2) to (1) is that "(2) . . . is preferable to (1) just in case (1) would require that *y* be a deletion rule." We must apparently understand this to mean that if (1) does not require "y" to be a deletion rule, then (2) is not preferable to (1). That is, (1) and (2) are both valid, but the analyst (linguist or "real speaker") appeals to (2) only if forced to in the situation just described. In other words, we can have our cake (1), and, in an emergency, eat it too (2).

The trouble with the Semantic Transparency Hypothesis as Hooper formulates it—as incorporating both (1) and (2), as described—is that its empirical content is left unclear. We are told about "y" only that it can represent null but it cannot refer to a deletion rule. Notice that this stipulation does not follow from (1) or (2) but rather must be stated separately. We are told absolutely nothing about "z." Although Hooper provides a rich enough discursive context so that we can guess some of her intentions, the conditions that must be met by the terms in (1) and (2) are nowhere stated fully and explicitly. It is therefore simply wishful thinking to regard the Semantic Transparency Hypothesis as embodying a "substantive principle" of analysis or theory.[4]

Hooper's decision to weaken (1) deserves another look. Faced with the dilemma mentioned above, she might in principle have taken a number of positions—the English verb-inflection example is an irrelevant anomaly, third person singular is not the relevant Primitive Category (a possibility mentioned in a footnote), the proposed "refinement" of (1) should be dropped, the version of the Semantic Transparency Hypothesis represented in (1) should be scrapped in favor of a radically different alternative, and so on. Among these and other imaginable alternatives, the incorporation of (2) into the Semantic Transparency Hypothesis is one of the least desirable choices, since it results in a weakening of the hypothesis. It is curious then that Hooper provides no clear explanation for her selection of just this move.

We have so far glossed over another conspicuous weakness of the Semantic Transparency Hypothesis, one which Hooper acknowledges. This is that much remains to be learned about the distinction between "Primitive" versus "Secondary" categories. Suffice it to say at this point that the extent to which the Semantic Transparency Hypothesis lacks content can be appreciated only when the lack of clarity regarding this distinction is coupled with the absence of information, mentioned just above, regarding conditions that must be met by the terms on the level of overt manifestation.

To summarize. The Semantic Transparency Hypothesis finds its roots, as Hooper tells us, in the work of Kuryłowicz, Jakobson, and others (see HSP for bibliography). We owe Hooper a debt of gratitude for reminding us of this older work and of the relevance it may have for the current renascence of interest in morphology. I speculate that many linguists believe, as I do, that there is at least a grain of truth, and probably much more, in the notion "unmarked category" and related concepts. It is not obvious, however, that Hooper's new formulations carry us beyond the work from which they take their inspiration.

MORPHOLOGICAL VERSUS PHONOLOGICAL CRITERIA

Fundamental to Hooper's program is the distinction between what she terms "P-rules" and "MP-rules."[5] HSP repeatedly characterizes this distinction along the following lines: "Phonetically motivated processes

[=P-rules] are controlled by the physical facts of production (and per-haps perception), while morpho-syntactically motivated processes [=MP-rules] are governed by the cognitive and psychological processes that create meaning" P-rules "are all 'natural,' by which I mean they are all phonetically explainable synchronically", while "MP-rules are conditioned by semantic categories, [and] the principles which guide their formulation should be based on semantics not on phonology."

Before proceeding, a caveat is in order regarding Hooper's insistent use of such words as "meaning" and "semantic." Like the rest of us, she tends to use these terms to form a rubbish bin for anything that is hard to label otherwise. It is of course not Hooper's fault that there exists today no well-supported semantic theory and consequently no explicated con-tent to the words "meaning," "semantic," etc. It is nonetheless extremely destructive to Hooper's enterprise that she has couched her basic propo-sitions in such vague terms. This much is clear: whatever "semantic," etc., may ultimately turn out to be, Hooper does not use these words in HSP with the same intended referents they have in work that is generally taken to constitute the serious literature of semantics. In fact, so far as I can see, Hooper's "semantic" and "meaning based" could be replaced in nearly every instance by "morpho-syntactic" or simply "formal," with no loss of precision.

With this in mind, in order to appreciate the relation of the distinc-tion at issue to the Semantic Transparency Hypothesis, we turn to a direct examination of all of the major examples given in HSP as illus-tration and support of Hooper's contentions

> that the principles previously used in analyzing morpho-syntactically motivated alternations, the principles borrowed from phonological analysis are totally inappropriate, and must be replaced by principles based on meaning

and that

> because MP-rules are conditioned by semantic categories, it follows that the principles which guide their formulation should be based on semantics not on phonology. The Semantic Transparency formula should replace principles of analysis that are based on phonology.

Hooper's first major example illustrates that "there is no point in seeking phonologically motivated generalizations and explanations for MP-rules in a synchronic grammar". She uses the "well-worked examples" of stem-vowel alternations in Spanish verbs, e.g., *contár/*

cuénto 'count', *mentír/miénto/mintió* 'lie', *pedír/pído* 'request'. It is well known that the distribution of these alternations is "lexically arbitrary," as Hooper states, in the sense that it is quite unpredictable which verbs alternate this way and which don't. It should be equally clear that "semantics" or "meaning," whatever these are, play no role at all, and that morphological information is relevant only in the case of the alternation of high vowels with mid, not in the case of alternations involving the diphthongs *ue* and *ie*.[6] Indeed, the MP-rule which Hooper herself formulates for these alternations (Hooper 1976:159, rule (29)) is stated ENTIRELY in phonological terms, e.g., stress, vowel height, syllabicity. It seems then that Hooper is failing to distinguish LEXICAL conditions, which are relevant in this example, from MORPHOLOGICAL conditions, which are partially relevant, and SEMANTIC conditions, which are totally irrelevant. In sum, Hooper's own recent descriptive practice is not in accord with the principles suggested in the passage quoted just above. I do not wish to speculate how Hooper might resolve this discrepancy, but it is difficult to imagine how any generalizations concerning the data at hand could be related to "principles based on meaning" or "semantic categories."

Hooper's next example is also from Spanish and is adduced to provide further exemplification of the fact that "morphologically-conditioned rules are phonologically arbitrary, and that phonological considerations may play no role at all in their formulation." The data are the alternations illustrated in sets of forms like *comér/comémos/comímos/comiéron/cóme* (all forms of the stem meaning 'eat') and *vivír/vivímos/viviéron/víve* ('live'). Hooper cites the analysis of these alternations in Brame and Bordelois 1974 as an instance of illicit use of phonological considerations. When one looks at the rules Brame and Bordelois actually wrote, however, we see that they appeal to such morphological properties as [+ 3 conj], [+ theme], [+ S], [− present], in addition to the phonological properties "vowel," [− low], [+ high], [− stress], and so on. Hooper has written a rule to cover exactly the same alternations (1976:156, rule L), so that a comparison is available. We see that her rule appeals to such morphological properties as [− 3rd conj], [Th(eme)V(owel)], [present], and to phonological properties such as "vowel," [− low], [+ high], [− stress]. It is not obvious in what sense either of these analyses is any more or any less dependent on "phonological considerations" or "conditioned by semantic categories" than the other. There is an issue here, however, as examination of Brame and Bordelois 1974 shows, namely the question of to what degree formal abbreviatory notational devices can be employed to conflate the statement of phonological generalizations with the statement of morphological generalizations. But Hooper's presentation tends to obfuscate this issue rather than to clarify it, and this is not the place to pursue the matter.

Another example from Spanish, examined at some length from both synchronic and diachronic perspectives, purports to illustrate how the Semantic Transparency Hypothesis makes the correct choice of a morphologically based analysis over a phonologically based analysis of identical material. The data are sets of verb forms like *po*[n]*e* (indicative)/*po*[ŋg]*a* (subjunctive) 'put', and *cre*[s]*e* (indic.)/*cre*[sk]*a* (subj.) 'grow'. The question is: which is correct, a phonologically based analysis in which the velars *g, k* are deleted in indicative *po*[n]*e, cre*[s]*e* or a putatively meaning-based analysis in which *g, k* are inserted in subjunctive *po*[ŋg]*a, cre*[sk]*a?*[7] On the basis of the history of these forms, Hooper argues that in a synchronic analysis of the modern language, the velars must be inserted in *po*[ŋg]*a, cre*[sk]*a,* etc., rather than deleted in *po*[n]*e, cre*[s]*e,* etc. I think that this conclusion is correct and inescapable. Hooper also states, however, that the (incorrect) deletion analysis is "clearly the best analysis using phonological criteria." This is false. In Harris 1972 I gave a detailed argument showing that deletion analyses of the data in question are untenable.[8] Crucially, my arguments in favor of insertion over deletion were based entirely on phonological considerations. Since, therefore, the Semantic Transparency Hypothesis is not uniquely successful in predicting the correctness of insertion, this example contributes nothing one way or the other to the question at hand.

Hooper's final major example deals with vowel alterations in Portuguese verb forms.[9] This material is said to "illustrate clearly" that the Semantic Transparency Hypothesis reflects a strategy actually used in language acquisition. The developmental data cited do indeed suggest, as Hooper claims, an order of acquisition that is consistent with predictions derivable from the Semantic Transparency Hypothesis. This fact is not uninteresting but it shows very little if any useful degree of specificity. It could hardly fail to be the case that many acquisition strategies are consistent with something whose empirical content is as vague as that of the Semantic Transparency Hypothesis, as Hooper has refined it.

Hooper's further claims relating to the Portuguese material are more serious. She states that "until evidence appears which shows that the acquisition process includes a total revision of the child's underlying forms and rules before adulthood, so that child and adult grammars differ radically, we can hypothesize that adult grammars, like child grammars, are based on the Semantic Transparency Hypothesis." The considerable developmental literature accumulated over the last decades suggests that the acquisition process involves a series of successive approximations to adult grammars, and that some adjacent stages involve discontinuities that might well be characterized as "radical." Be this as it may, to proceed as Hooper seems to suggest would be heuristically disastrous, since it would simply guarantee that if child and adult grammars do differ radically, we would never discover this fact. A less dogmatic and heuristically more valuable procedure would be to approach the study of adult grammars unencumbered by strong preconceptions regarding the Semantic Transparency Hypothesis and child grammars. This way we stand a chance of finding out what their interrelationships actually are.

From what I have presented so far, the reader might well conclude that Hooper's so-called substantive principles regarding phonological and morphological criteria in linguistic analysis reduce to the quasi-tautology that we should write rules with phonological environments where phonological conditions are relevant, and we should write rules with morphological environments where morphological conditions are relevant. Such a conclusion, however, would be in error. I have kept in reserve Hooper's interesting and provocative "hypothesis that speakers, when presented with a choice, will prefer to construct a morphologically motivated analysis over a purely phonological analysis." The expression "when presented with a choice" refers to a situation in which it is impossible to determine on the basis of primary data alone whether phonological or morphological conditions are operative. The linguist's analog of this hypothesis is a "general principle that should guide synchronic analyses of morphologically motivated alternations even where additional substantive evidence is not available."[10] It goes without saying that these proposals are very interesting. There is some reason to believe, however, that they are too strong. I will give one example from Spanish, where the primary data are clear beyond the point of controversy. In standard dialects, the marker of imperfective aspect in past-tense verb forms is /ba/ in some forms and /a/ in others, for example:

(3) 1st conjugation   2nd/3rd conjugation
     pasá + ba 'passed'   caí + a 'fell'
     tomá + ba 'took'   viví + a 'lived'

Is the alternative *ba ~ a* phonologically or morphologically determined? The primary data are ambiguous, since the two types of conditioning factors are absolutely coextensive: in the first conjugation (morphological condition) the imperfective marker is always preceded by the low syllabic [a] (phonological condition); in other conjugations (morphological condition) the imperfective marker is always preceded by the high front syllabic [i] (phonological condition). Either of the rules (4a), (4b) will work:[11]

(4) a. b → Ø / [− 1 conj] + _____
    b. b → Ø / [i] + _____

Hooper's principle says that linguists, like "real speakers," must prefer (4a), the morphologically conditioned rule. But now consider how forms like those illustrated in (3) have evolved in the dialect of San Antoñito, a small town in the Sandía Mountains of New Mexico:[12]

(5) 1st conjugation   2nd/3rd conjugation
   pasá + ba   *cá*[y] + *ba*
   tomá + ba   *viví + a*

Standard *ca*[í]*a* has become *cá*[y]*ba;* similarly, *tra*[í]*a* 'brought' has become *trá*[y]*ba*. These are the only second conjugation stems in which the low vowel [a] precedes the pre-inflectional segment, and this segment has lost its syllabicity—an unremarkable phonological adjustment. Remarkably, along with this phonological adjustment, the imperfective marker has become /ba/. This suggests that the allomorphy *ba ~ a* of the imperfective marker is NOT controlled by morphological conditions—the stems of *cá*[y]*ba* and *trá*[y]*ba* do not cease to belong to the second conjugation, as is shown by forms in other paradigms—but rather by phonological conditions. Specifically, the allomorph /ba/ appears in these forms, in accordance with rule (4b) (or (ii)) of note 11), because it is preceded by non-syllabic [y] rather than by syllabic [i]. In sum, unless there is something wrong with this example, and its simplicity makes it hard to imagine what this might be, Hooper's principle makes the wrong prediction. The generation of "real speakers" that initiated the San Antoñito innovation must have analyzed the ambiguous primary data illustrated in (3) according to phonological rather than morphological criteria.

Of course there are, just as Hooper claims, cases in which language change does appear to follow Hooper's principle. What remains to be discovered is what revision of this principle, or what other principle, makes the correct prediction in every case.

SUBSTANTIVE PRINCIPLES OF PHONOLOGY

Hooper states that the "major claim of natural generative phonology is that speakers construct only generalizations that are surface-true and transparent." This claim is expressed in a principle known as the "True Generalization Condition," which "is meant to apply to MP-rules just as it applies to P-rules." Hooper does not provide an explicit statement of the True Generalization Condition in HSP, or, to the best of my knowledge, anywhere else. Thus if we are to attempt to understand the True Generalization Condition, we must turn to examples of its application, one of the most striking of which is found in Chapter 13 of Hooper 1976.

This example involves the well-known "epenthetic *e*" of Spanish, which is generally believed to be inserted under the conditions specified in (6).

(6) $\emptyset \rightarrow e \, / \, \#$_____s [+ consonantal]

This epenthesis process is phonologically governed, totally general, exceptionless, and extraordinarily hard to learn to suppress in foreign language acquisition. One would think it to be a perfect exemplar of a P-rule, in Hooper's terms. Yet rule (6) is excluded by the True Generalization Condition "because the rule requires that ALL [word-initial] sequences of /s/ + C have to be preceded by /e/" (1976:234). In other words, the True Generalization Condition requires that P-rules be biconditionally transparent, so to speak. But Spanish has countless words with a vowel other than *e* before initial *sC*, e.g. *astro, usted, hospital* [ospital]. Consequently rule (6) does not meet the biconditional requirement of the True Generalization Condition and is not a possible rule. As a result, in Hooper's natural generative phonological theory, "all [Spanish] words with initial /esC/ are entered in the lexicon with the /e/ present" (1976:234).[13] I underscore: the True Generalization Condition requires that there be no level of representation in which the so-called epenthetic *e*'s are not present.

Consider the consequences of this requirement for the (extremely productive) morphological process of diminutive formation in Spanish.

Two of the allomorphs of the diminutive suffix are distributed, in some dialects, according to the number of syllables of the base word, in certain classes of words. For example:

(7) Two-syllable base
   madre, dim: *madrecita*
           (**madrita*)
   saurio, dim: *sauriecito*
           (**saurito*)

   More than two-syllable base
   comadre, dim: *comadrita*
           (**comadrecita*)
   dinosaurio,
       dim: *dinosaurito*
               (**dinosauriecito*)[14]

Now consider these examples:

(8) *estudio,* dim: *estudiecito*
           (**estudito*)
   espacio, dim: *espaciecito*
           (**espacito*)

   preludio, dim: *preludito*
           (**preludiecito*)
   despacio, dim: *despacito*
           (**despaciecito*)

How can the apparently bizarre array of data in (8) be accounted for? One especially attractive description is based on the fact that words like *estudio* and *espacio*, though phonetically trisyllabic [es-tu-δyo] and [es-pa-syo], count as disyllabic for diminutive formation. More specifically, diminutive formation "looks at" the representations *stu-dyo* and *spa-syo* which lack the epenthetic *e* supplied by rule (6). But these representations and this rule are disallowed by the True Generalization Condition, as we have seen. The True Generalization Condition thus disallows a description which is not only attractive but is in fact the only non-ad hoc one that is likely to exist for data pertaining to one of the most productive word-formation processes found in any language. This fact should not be lightly dismissed in evaluating the True Generalization Condition.

EPILOGUE

These observations have been extremely critical of HSP. Such is the task, unpleasant though it may be, of an assigned "discussant," a sort of hired gun.

It should be clear that my criticisms have been directed largely at the quality of evidence and argumentation in HSP. I have nowhere intended to suggest that the "unmarked category" principle (of which the Semantic Transparency Hypothesis is a version) does not merit study, that there is no linguistically significant difference between phonologically and morphologically based generalizations, or that there exist no substantive universal principles of phonology. It is precisely because the issues involved are so important that we should expect arguments concerning them to be able to withstand the severest scrutiny. Although this expectation is sometimes disappointed in HSP, Hooper has to be commended for so persistently and effectively forcing us to reexamine and reevaluate time and again our most fundamental assumptions regarding the phonology and morphology of human languages.

NOTES

1. This formulation is taken from Baxter 1975, which Hooper characterizes as "the most comprehensive treatment of morphology in the framework we are working in here." I have not seen Baxter 1975, and thus rely entirely on HSP.

2. We glide over the question of whether the Primitive Category is, strictly speaking, "singular," "noun," "singular noun," or something else.

3. I provide a hypothetical example here because Hooper provides no allegedly correct one, hypothetical or real.

Bear in mind that the prohibition against deriving the manifestation of the Primitive Category (e.g. English *cat*) from that of the Secondary Category (e.g. *cats*) by deletion is already built into (1). Thus (1) excludes, for example, Bloomfield's (1933:217) analysis of French adjectives in which masculine (presumably the more basic semantic category), e.g., *petit* [*peti*], are derived by a "minus-feature" from feminines, e.g., *petite* [*petit*].

4. See also note 11.

5. There is considerable elaboration of the P-rule/MP-rule dichotomy in Hooper 1976.

6. Fuller discussion can be found in a number of sources, the most recent of which is Harris 1978.

7. Hooper seems to attribute the deletion rule she gives to Foley 1965. I am unable to find any such rule in my copy of Foley 1965. I find instead an analysis in which the velar of *cre*[sk]*e* becomes t^s because of the following front vowel, the resulting [st^s], becomes [ss], which becomes (long) [š], which becomes [s], giving *cre*[s]*e*. In any event, to refer to the sequence [sk]→. . .→ [s] as "deletion" is innocuous in the present context.

8. I argued specifically against the analyses of Foley 1965 and Saporta 1965, but it seems clear that the argument generalizes easily to any deletion analysis.

9. Hooper's discussion of the primary linguistic data and of the analysis in Harris 1974 is somewhat out of focus. This is not the place, however, to

clarify the facts of Portuguese, nor do I have any desire to defend particular details of Harris 1974. Redenbarger 1977 suggests, at the very least, that this study needs thorough reevaluation, but for reasons and in ways that have nothing to do with Hooper's arguments.

10. Inclusion of the words "morphologically motivated" begs the question at issue. Let us overlook this. What Hooper obviously means is that the linguist should always choose morphological over phonological conditions when the data are ambiguous.

11. Of course if morphophonological deletion rules are disallowed as Hooper proposes, (4a), (4b) have to be restated. This might be done in a number of ways. Following Hooper (1976:155, rule G) closely, let us propose (i) and (ii), respectively.

(i)   Imperf $\longrightarrow \begin{Bmatrix} a/[-1\ \text{conj}] + \underline{\hspace{1cm}} \\ ba \end{Bmatrix}$

(ii) Imperf $\longrightarrow \begin{Bmatrix} a/[i] + \underline{\hspace{1cm}} \\ ba \end{Bmatrix}$

The choice of (4a,b) versus (i), (ii) has nothing to do with the main thread of the argument at this point. It does, however, speak to the question of the adequacy of the Semantic Transparency Hypothesis. In the case at hand, which is the more marked overt manifestation, /ba/ or /a/? How can these realizations be associated with either a primitive or a secondary semantic category, since there is only one category, namely, imperfective aspect? The Semantic Transparency Hypothesis should presumably illuminate these questions, but it is difficult to see how Hooper's formulation of it even bears on the data under discussion.

12. Data from Bowen 1976.

13. Hooper does not explore what this treatment entails for alternating morphemes, as in *checoslovaco* but *eslovaco*, *inscribir* but *escribir*, etc.

14. *Saurio* is dissyllabic: [saw-ryo]. Thanks to Osvaldo Jaeggli for the nice example *saurio/dinosaurio* and for confirming the acceptability judgment in (7) and (8).

Incidentally, examples like those in (7) and (8) show that Hooper and Terrell 1976 grossly underestimates the complexity of diminutive formation in Spanish.

CHAPTER FOURTEEN

Comments

James D. McCawley

Editor's note: The title of this volume was to have been *Current Phonological Theories*. In response to McCawley's remarks at the conference and reiterated herein, the title was revised.

The plural in the title *Current Phonological Theories* is misleading, since it wrongly suggests that each of the nine major presentations at this conference dealt with a separate phonological theory. In general, the various presentations dealt with specific issues in phonology, with little overlap among the issues that different presentations took up. The disagreements among the participants appear to be not so much disagreements over specific issues as disagreements as to what issues are most worth discussing. Thus, it is hard to see how there could be any conflict between Goldsmith's position on the nature of phonological structures, Leben's position on the 'directionality' of derivations, Dinnsen's position on how the class of possible phonological rules is constrained, and Houlihan and Iverson's position on the relationship between the function of rules and the allophonic/morphophonemic distinction. Except for Donegan and Stampe's paper, which expounds a really comprehensive theory of phonology,[1] and to a lesser extent also Hooper's paper, the various papers presented not phonological theories but treatments of particular aspects of phonology that could in principle serve as parts of a broad range of possible phonological theories.

I will devote the remainder of my remarks here to taking up certain points raised by the three papers that I was specifically asked to discuss. My neglect of the other papers should not be taken as implying that I did not find them stimulating—only that the three covered here are the ones that I have read the most carefully.

I wish Leben had dealt with an important issue that has considerable significance for his approach, namely that of how one can tell what morphemic relationships exist and which of those relationships are mediated by rules. I have commented elsewhere (McCawley 1976, 1977) on the failure of generative phonology to provide any basis for determining when two words share a morpheme (e.g., Does any variety of generative phonology provide grounds for saying that *sign* and *signature* begin with the same morpheme but *moth* and *mother* do not?) or to consider the possibility that different morphemic identities may have different psychological status. Leben treats his 'upside-down' derivations as comprising the whole of phonology, rather than considering the possibility that they might correspond only to a specific kind of morphemic relatedness. Since Leben's derivations allow rules to 'apply' or not, depending only on whether their application allows for greater similarity in the underlying forms of the putatively related morphs, the most obvious function that they fulfill is simply that of an aid to perceiving the morphemic relationship in the first place: the rules simply tell one that certain differences between morphs can be ignored in deciding whether they can be identified. To say that there are rules having this function is not to say anything about whether there are other systems of rules with other functions. Leben's derivations provide an eminently reasonable proposal for how language-particular phonological rules could play a role in the perception of morphemic identity. However, I find it highly implausible to suppose that *all* phonological rules have the sort of optionality that his rules do, i.e., that they can apply or not, whichever makes the deeper representations of putatively identical morphs more alike. Thus I would find his treatment of *Christian,* etc. far more plausible if he were taking it as typical only of non-productive morphology and were taking productive phonological processes as subject to a different set of principles of rule application. I of course do not rule out the possibility of there being an overlap between the rules of productive phonology and the rules that figure in the identification of non-productively related morphs, and there would be considerable interest in the question of what learning in the one domain might be carried over into the other.

I should add that it is doubtful that all psychologically real morpheme identifications can be covered by rules (taking a 'rule' to be something that in principle could figure in derivations other than the one given). Whatever general facility human beings have for perceiving similarity surely plays a role in the perception of morpheme identity,[2] and I conjecture that there is nothing specifically phonological in one's perception of such morphemic relationships as that between [kīhówtēy] and [kwìksátik]. But what morphemic relations *are* learned on the basis of prior knowledge of rules, and how much uniformity is there in a linguistic community with regard to either what non-productive rules the various speakers know or what morphemic relationships they mediate? The notion that an orthodox generative phonologist is likely to invoke here, namely that of 'evaluation measure', is a red herring. An evaluation measure is supposed to provide a rate of exchange between rules and examples: each rule has a 'cost' that is offset whenever the number of examples to which it applies exceeds a certain threshold. But it gives no clue as to what examples should count as instances of a particular rule, e.g., it gives no clue as to whether *cholera* is a derivative of *coal,* with a derivation involving trisyllabic laxing. Moreover, as Stampe has pointed out, it is extremely implausible to suppose that on learning his n-th word to which a given rule would apply and thereby becoming able to afford the rule, a child rewrites his dictionary entries for the n-1 examples he had known before. The perception of morphemic relationships thus will often precede the learning of rules that could be taken as mediating the relationships. In McCawley (1976, 1977), I argue for a non-deterministic picture of language acquisition: there are numerous factors, some linguistic and some non-linguistic, affecting the likelihood of one's perceiving a morphemic relation or learning a rule, and the only relationship between the number of instances of a rule and whether one learns it is that the more chances you have to learn a rule, the greater the likelihood that you will learn it. I accordingly would expect that there would be a great amount of interspeaker variation with regard to the status of the rules and the examples that Leben cites: variation as to whether a speaker perceives two given words as related at all, variation as to whether a morphemic relation that he perceives is connected with any phonological generalization that he knows, and variation as to what exactly the phonological generalization is.

Anderson's discussion of curly brackets conflates two issues that should be kept apart: the issue of whether there are 'rules' that can be shown to function as units but which subsume separate cases that must be listed individually as in the curly bracket notation, and the issue of whether, if such rules exist, the curly brackets function as an 'abbreviatory device'. That these are separate issues can be seen from my argument (McCawley 1974) that there are rules appropriately formulated in terms of 'optional' segments but that the notation (parentheses) used

in formulating such rules is not an 'abbreviatory device,' since the rules
that the notation supposedly allows one to put together need not be possible phonological rules, e.g., a voicing assimilation rule *requiring* the
affected and conditioning segments to be separated by a glide is not a
possible rule, though a voicing assimilation rule *allowing* an optional
glide between the two segments is possible. I in fact am now inclined to
agree with Anderson that Finnish consonant gradation is appropriately
described in terms of a rule that gives the environment in which gradation takes place and lists (in curly brackets) all the different changes
that gradation comprises.[3] However, the plausibility that I see in the
gradation rule that Anderson describes comes from a conjecture as to
how consonant gradation might be acquired, and under this hypothetical
picture of language acquisition, the curly brackets would not be an abbreviatory device, since the child would learn the curly brackets without
ever learning the rules that the curly brackets supposedly abbreviated.
Specifically, I conjecture that Finnish children first learn that strange
things happen at the beginning of a short closed non-initial syllable and
that only gradually do they learn the details of those strange things. The
child would first learn a rule that could be formulated with an empty
pair of curly brackets, and only later would he learn what went inside
those curly brackets.

Under this conjecture, the Finnish child's first gradation rule would
be something that generative phonology has never countenanced: a rule
that does not say what happens. Nonetheless, such a rule could play an
important part in the child's language use: it would identify segments in
certain environments as potentially variants of other segments and would
thus make many morpheme identifications more readily accessible to
him than they otherwise would be. I note in this regard that under
Leben's approach there is no reason why rules in adult language might
not also be incomplete. For example, I do not find it at all implausible
to suppose that many speakers of English recognize morphemic relationships in terms of a rule $V \rightarrow [?]$ (i.e., something happens to a vowel),
a synchronic analogue of Voltaire's famous remark about etymology.

The notion of 'exegetic adequacy' that Anderson introduces is really
not a property of theories but rather of 'research programs' in the sense
of Lakatos (1970). A research program is a set of policies accepted
within a scientific community (or subcommunity) on what sorts of
questions members of that community should ask and what sorts of
answers they should seek. It is possible for different theories to be
combined with nearly identical research programs, since one can hold

that it is worthwhile to seek first a certain type of answer without necessarily subscribing to a theory that says that only that type of answer can be right; for example, you don't have to believe that sound change is conditioned only by phonological factors in order to believe that an analysis in terms of phonological factors should be sought first.[4] Many ostensible defenses of theories are really defenses of research programs. For example, when Bloomfield pointed with pride to the Swampy Cree data that confirmed his earlier reconstruction of Central Algonkian and when Chomsky (1972:198) spoke of the policy that "the formal devices of language should be studied independently of their use" as having been "fruitful," their remarks really said nothing about theories. In both cases their remarks amounted to the claim that many valuable results have been achieved when a certain type of answer has been sought. However, the proposition that many valuable results have been achieved in no way conflicts with the proposition that many valuable results have been systematically avoided and that many highly dubious results have been achieved. Testimonials to a research program are comments on the author's tastes rather than on any theory that may be attached to the research program: they say that the results achieved through the research program have been enough to keep him content, but they provide no basis for evaluating theoretical claims (such as the claim that sound change is conditioned only by phonological factors). It is misleading for Chomsky to describe the policy of studying formal devices independently of use as a 'hypothesis': a hypothesis says how the world is, not how researchers should investigate the world.

Goldsmith's autosegmental phonology allows one to preserve what was worthwhile in Lightner's (1965) now discredited analysis of vowel harmony, while avoiding the faults that led to its being discredited. Lightner treated Classical Mongolian vowels as underlyingly unspecified for gravity and had a morpheme feature [+ / − GRAVE] as part of the dictionary entry of each root. The [+ / − GRAVE] specification of a root conditioned the adding of its lower-case counterpart (i.e., [+ / − grave]) to all vowels that either belonged to the root or belonged to affixes attached to the root. Lightner's proposal gives no clue as to why, in Finnish, Hungarian, and Turkish, when vowel harmony is violated within a root, suffixes normally harmonize with the *last* non-neutral vowel of the root: if harmony is conditioned by a morpheme feature, there is no reason why the last vowel of a root should have any more privileged position as a conditioner of vowel harmony than does the first vowel. The autosegmental treatment allows roots that conform to vowel harmony to have a single specification for gravity or whatever the harmonic feature is, and does not require the proliferation of features that Lightner's treatment does (GRAVE ≠ grave), and the same principles that insure the spread of the single gravity feature onto both root and suffix vowels when the root conforms to vowel harmony will also insure that the last gravity specification spreads onto the suffixes when the root does not conform to harmony: all vowels have association lines, and association lines may not cross.[5]

There remain some problems with the autosegmental treatment of vowel harmony, however, particularly with regard to 'neutral vowels'. It is normally the last *non-neutral* vowel, not the last vowel, that conditions harmony, e.g., Finnish *dityrambi-na/*-nä*, where the suffix harmonizes with the /a/, skipping over the 'neutral' /i/ (/e/ is also 'neutral' in Finnish vowel harmony). Nonetheless, neutral vowels are not irrelevant to vowel harmony, since when a Finnish root contains only neutral vowels, the suffixes take front-vowel harmony, e.g., *kiel-tä*, partitive of *kieli* 'language,' evidently reflecting the frontness of neutral vowels. If neutral vowels are taken to have a frontness specification on the front-back tier of an autosegmental structure, then such forms as *pankki-na* 'as a bank' will involve crossing association lines: the line connecting the backness specification of the root to the ending will cross the line connecting the /i/ to its frontness specification. Lloyd Anderson (1975) discusses a number of instances in which vowel harmony indeed crosses over *non-neutral* vowels, e.g., *ambassadööri-na* 'as an ambassador', in which the suffix harmonizes not with the neutral /i/ nor the front /öö/ but with one of the preceding /a/'s. Anderson's solution to the problem of identifying the vowel with which a suffix harmonizes was to isolate a number of factors that affect vowel harmony and give an algorithm for determining which factor would prevail when they conflicted. Proximity was one of the factors (i.e., other things being equal, a vowel will harmonize with the vowel that is closest to it). Another was vowel quality: Anderson set up a hierarchy of strength with which different vowels condition vowel harmony, with /a/ at the top of the hierarchy, /ö/ in the middle, and /i,e/ at the bottom. In *pankki-na*, the strength of the /a/ as a conditioning factor overrides the proximity of the /i/, and in *ambassadööri-na* it overrides the proximity of the /ö/ and /i/. In words like *kiel-tä* there is nothing to override the proximity of the /e/, and the suffix takes front vowel harmony. Anderson's approach to vowel harmony could be recast in revisionist autosegmental terms by making the principle against crossing association lines relative rather than absolute: various segments and/or association lines would provide obstacles of different strength to crossing association lines rather than presenting impenetrable barriers.

I dispute one universal claim that Goldsmith makes, namely that "there are no association lines in the stored or underlying representation." In fact, as far as I can see, Goldsmith's (1975a) own treatment of Japanese accent involves "association lines in the underlying representation," in that the accent mark that Goldsmith allows in his underlying representations for pitch accent systems amounts to an association line: it indicates with which syllable a particular tone of the melody will be associated.

Finally, I would like to throw out a rather programmatic suggestion for autosegmental phonology, namely that the different tiers as well as the associations among them may be represented not only in discrete but also in continuous terms. In Goldsmith's present framework, tones must be associated with vowels (and not with interstices between vowels), and a sequence of tones must be realized as a contour tone. It is thus impossible to represent a downstep as an unrealized low tone between two high tones, and Goldsmith is forced to adopt a "Low-high simplification rule," which creates a "drop tone" out of an LH sequence associated with a single vowel. Suppose, however, that an HLH sequence were associated with two syllables in such a way that the first H was associated with the entire first syllable, the second H with the entire second syllable, and the L with the boundary between the two syllables, and suppose that the drop from an H to an L exceeds the rise from an L to an H. This association would cause the L to be unrealized as such but would leave it as part of the phonological structure and allow its presence to be manifested in the superposition of a small rise (L to H) on a large drop (H to L), which yields a small drop, i.e., downstep, at the syllable boundary in question. Such a generalization of the notion of "association" allows one to treat what Goldsmith calls "drop tones" as simply H's (which is in fact what they behave like in Igbo phonology) without having to resort to representations in terms of absolute pitch values as in the derivations suggested in such works as Schachter and Fromkin (1968):

> H L H
> → 5 2 4 (numerical indication of pitch level)
> → 5 4 4 (by assimilation) = H 'H H

The absolute pitch levels that figure in the inputs to the assimilation and deletion rules that give rise to downstep in Schachter and Fromkin's analyses are highly questionable, in that it is doubtful that any rule would be sensitive to specific pitch levels, e.g., there can't be a rule that raises all 2's (regardless of whether they are realizations of H's or of L's), though there can be a rule that raises an L to the pitch of a following H. The extended autosegmental treatment that I have just suggested allows one to have essentially the same assimilation and deletion rules that Schachter and Fromkin do (the assimilation rule extends leftward the domain associated with an H) and yet do the entire phonology with only L and H tones.

NOTES

1. The principal deficiency in coverage on the part of the Donegan-Stampe theory is in the realm of those things that, for them, are not strictly phonology but nonetheless interact with phonology. I am thinking particularly of what Stampe calls "rules" (as opposed to processes) and of such largely unanswered questions as "What in general can be the form and/or content of a rule?" and "How does the acquisition of rules fit into language acquisition in general?"

2. I thus find it a non-sequitur for Chomsky, after arguing convincingly that there is an innate faculty that is specific to the learning of language, to jump to the conclusion that that faculty bears the sole responsibility for *all* language learning by human beings. Whatever general faculties human beings possess for learning surely do not switch off whenever language is being learned. One possible side benefit to be obtained from research on teaching sign language to chimpanzees is an appreciation of *what* features of language require a learning faculty that is specific for language.

3. I thus reject my earlier unpublished analysis, in which consonant gradation voiced any stop at the beginning of a short closed non-initial syllable, and other rules deleted or changed the voiced stop under various conditions, e.g., *matto-n → matdo-n → mato-n; hampas → hambas → hammas; kylpy-n → kylby-n → kylvy-n*.

4. The connection between a research program and a theory can be extremely tenuous. For example, much research done in the 1960's on language acquisition was tied to a linguistic theory that says essentially nothing about language acquisition, namely the version of transformational grammar presented in Chomsky (1965). (The 'idealizations' in the scheme of language acquisition presented in Chapter 1 of Chomsky (1965) idealize away the subject matter of a theory of language acquisition: Chomsky's scheme treats language acquisition as if it were instantaneous and thus says

nothing about the developmental stages that the acquirer goes through.) The research program consisted in writing generative grammars for various instances of child language. It was a fruitful research program because it led many investigators to examine in detail many aspects of child language that had previously been ignored, and it contributed greatly to the development of theories of language acquisition. However, the theory of language acquisition that ostensibly was part of its theoretical foundations was in fact irrelevant to it.

5. Goldsmith's approach appears to force one to give up the Jakobsonian feature of gravity, since the gravity of consonants (labial or velar articulation) neither inhibits nor conditions the spread of the gravity of vowels.

CHAPTER FIFTEEN

Nonsegmental Phonology

Sanford A. Schane

Within standard generative phonology a phonological representation is depicted as a linear arrangement of segments, although each of the segments itself is composed of simultaneously occurring features. Phonological rules operate on such strings, deleting, inserting, or permuting segments, or changing one or more of their feature values. Because of its adherence to segment-sized units, the theory with its associated notational conventions has not always accommodated easily higher-level phonological constructs, such as the syllable, or 'suprasegmental' phenomena which may extend over a sequence of segments, such as pitch and stress contours. Recent proposals by Goldsmith, Selkirk, and myself have demonstrated the value of recognizing such nonsegmental entities and the necessity for formally incorporating them into phonological theory.

I

Some processes affecting syllable structure show that a segmental phonology does not always lend itself to the most insightful analysis and may even engender notational complexity. Consider, for example, the standard generative formulation of the processes which lengthen vowels in open syllables and shorten them in closed syllables.

(1) a. $V \rightarrow [+ \text{long}] / \underline{\hspace{1cm}} \begin{Bmatrix} CV \\ \# \end{Bmatrix}$

   b. $V \rightarrow [- \text{long}] / \underline{\hspace{1cm}} C \begin{Bmatrix} C \\ \# \end{Bmatrix}$

Hooper (1972) and Vennemann (1972b) have convincingly argued for the syllable boundary in phonological rules. Rules mentioning open and closed syllables becomes notationally simpler, as reference to unrelated disjoint environments is no longer required.

(2) a. V → [+ long] / ____ $ b. V → [−long] / ____ C$

Although the recognition of the syllable boundary is a step in the right direction, its status is no different from that of the other boundaries of generative phonology. It appears interspersed among the segments of the linear string.

There is reason to believe that the *syllable* should be regarded as a higher-level unit in its own right, separate from the segments of which it is composed, for it plays a significant role in determining certain phonological phenomena. A case in point is 'closed-syllable' adjustment in French, a process affecting the vowels [ə] and [e]. These vowels occur in open syllables; in closed syllables they both become [ɛ].

(3) a. geler   [žə̣le] 'to freeze'
    (il) gèle   [žɛ̣l] '(it) freezes'
    (il) gèlera   [žɛ̣l(ə)ra] '(it) will freeze'
    gel   [žɛ̣l] 'freezing'
(3) b. gérer   [žẹre] 'to manage'
    (il) gére   [žɛ̣r] '(he) manages'
    (il) gérera   [žɛ̣r(ə)ra] '(he) will manage'

To accommodate this alternation the standard generative rule must list three environments.

(4) ə, e → ɛ / ____ C { C # ə }

The first two contexts are typically cases where the consonant following ə or e closes the syllable. By employing the syllable boundary, we can easily restate these two environments as a single one. However, this reformulation cannot encompass the third context, where the following syllable contains schwa, as this environment by no means represents a typical closed syllable; hence, it necessitates a separate statement.

(5) ə, e → ɛ / ____ { C$ $Cə }

It would appear that the second part of the environment could perhaps be eliminated by allowing schwa deletion to apply first. Then the ə or e would truly be in a closed syllable. This ploy is not really effective, for in those styles where schwas are preserved, it is still the case that ə̣ and ẹ become [ɛ]—e.g., [žɛ̣ləra], [žɛ̣rəra].

It is well known that French schwa has peculiar properties. Selkirk (1978) accounts for the strange behavior of schwa by referring to higher-level constructs. She proposes that segments be grouped into syllables. A word will have as many syllables as it has vowels. (Every schwa belongs to its own syllable.) Syllables in turn are then grouped into yet higher-order units, called *feet*. Normally, a foot is composed of a single syllable. However, within a word a non-initial schwa does not form a foot by itself; rather, it is part of the same foot as the *preceding* syllable. But a schwa in the first syllable can constitute a foot. A French foot then may contain at most two syllables, in which case schwa appears as the second member and is considered to be subordinate. The words of (3a) are analyzed into feet, with brackets used to denote the domain of each foot.

(6) geler [žə̣] [le]
    (il) gèle   [žə̣lə]
    (il) gèlera   [žə̣lə] [ra]
    gel   [žə̣l]

We can now state the appropriate generalization for closed-syllable adjustment: ə and e become ɛ *when followed by something else within the foot,* whether a single consonant, a consonant cluster, or an entire subordinate syllable containing schwa.

(7) ə, e → ɛ / [C₀ _____ C X]

Selkirk also shows how the foot explains other processes associated with schwa: schwa deletion and stress assignment. The latter has traditionally been described as follows: The last vowel of the word is stressed, unless it is schwa, in which case stress will be on the penultimate. The following words, taken from (3), will have stress on the italicized vowel: gel*e*r, (il) g*è*le, (il) gèl*e*ra, g*e*l. The standard generative rule is:

(8)   V → [+ stress] / _____ C₀ (ə) #

A reformulation utilizing the notion of foot requires no mention of schwa. The new rule becomes: *Stress the last foot of the word.* (Whenever the final foot contains a subordinate schwa, stress will of course be assigned to the vowel of the dominant first member.)

(9)   [ ] → [+ stress] / _____ #

II

Suprasegmental phenomena also lend themselves to a treatment divorced from the consonants and vowels of the segmental string. Goldsmith (1976b and in this volume), in his 'autosegmental' phonology, demonstrates that tonal contours are not mere features of vowels but constitute a separate tier of representation to which phonological rules can appeal. Within his system every vowel bears at least one tone and every tone is assigned to at least one vowel. 'Association lines' match tones and segments.

(10) a. C V C V   b. C V C V C V   c. C V C
          | | \ / | /\
          H   L   H   L   H   L

In (10a) the first syllable carries a high tone and the second a low one, in (10b) a high contour is spread over the first two syllables, and in (10c) the syllable bears a 'falling' (high-low) tone.

Rules may apply separately to each tier without disrupting any of the entities on the other level, although the association lines may require reassigning. For example, assume that there is a process whereby a syllable without an inherent tone is affixed to the beginning of a word, such as (11) (= 10a).

(11) C V C V   ⟶   C V C V C V
        | | | |
        H   L   H   L

Since every vowel must bear at least one tone, the two tones will have to realign themselves to cover three syllables. Because association lines may not cross, the resulting contour would be that of (10b). By the same token, a deletion rule applying to segments need not touch any of the tonal contour. Imagine a rule deleting the final vowel of (10a).

(12) C V C V   ⟶   C V C
        | | | |
        H   L   H   L

As every tone must be assigned to some vowel, once again there will have to be realignment of association lines. The result will be a contour such as (10c).

Rules might also insert or delete tones without disrupting the sequence of vowels and consonants. The necessary realignments would be similar to those already illustrated. Or consider tonal assimilations. Let us assume that the second syllable of (10a) assimilates the tone of the preceding syllable. The resulting contour will be a high tone followed by a falling one.

(13) C V C V   ⟶   C V C V
        | | |/\|
        H   L   H   L

Goldsmith cites many interesting examples of these different possibilities. It is easy to see the advantages of his proposal and its facility
in handling the various processes, most of which are considerably more
complex than what has been discussed here. He also has some insightful
suggestions for extending the framework to other aspects of phonology,
such as vowel harmony.

III

Stress is another phenomenon amenable to a nonsegmental approach.
In Chomsky and Halle (1968) stress is a feature of vowels and the stress
rules assign integer values to this feature on the basis of properties of the
strings of segments. In Schane (1978) I propose a radically different
treatment, one where stress contours are represented as alternating patterns of strong (S) and weak (W) syllables.

(14)　　　SW　W S　　S W W　W S W　WSWW
　　a. solid, adore, Canada, Dakota, solidity
　　　　　S　WS　　S　WWSW　S　W S W　　　SW S WW
　　b. circulate, circulatory, adoration, California
　　　　　S W SW　S　　S　WS WS WW
　　c. parallelogram, artificiality

These data reveal certain surface constraints on the distribution of Ss and
Ws. We shall be concerned with two of these constraints.

(15)　a. *S S (Two Ss are never contiguous.)

　　　b. *# W W (A word may not begin with two Ws.)

Constraint (15a) entails that any two Ss must be separated by at least
one W. Hence, a word containing two Ss must have a minimum
of three syllables—e.g., S WS circulate. Constraint (15b) means that a word
may begin with at most one W—e.g., W SW Dakota, WWS WW *California. Thus, whenever two Ws occur they are always preceded by an S.

There are many examples of related forms with shifting stress configurations—e.g., *solid:solidity, adore:adoration,* etc. We shall view the
more complex form as composed morphologically of the simpler (base)
form with the addition of a derivational suffix. With the juxtaposition of
the suffix, it may happen that one of the constraints of (15) becomes
violated. The impermissible sequence will then have to be corrected.
The adjustments change the first element of the sequence—that is, if in
the course of a derivation two contiguous Ss should arise, the first one
will be changed to W, and conversely, if there should be an unpermitted
sequence of two Ws, the first one will become S.

(16) a. * S S   b. * # W W
             ↓   ↓
             W   S

In the following examples, observe what happens to a base form (line 1) when a suffix with its own accentual properties is added (line 2). The addition of the suffix creates sequences in violation of (15), which are then adjusted in conformity with (16) until no violations result.

First let us look at some examples where two Ss become juxtaposed, causing the first one to change to W. Consider the derivation of *circulatory*.

(17) circulate
      S WS   ] ory
      S WS   S W
      S WW   S W

The stress configuration of *circulate* is SWS, to which is added the suffix *-ory* with its pattern SW. The final S of *circulate*, because it is now immediately followed by the S of *-ory*, will be changed to W, and as a consequence its vowel will be reduced to schwa.

A slightly different example is *solidity*.

(18) solid
      SW   ] ity
      SS   WW
      WS   WW

To the base form *solid* (SW) is added the suffix *-ity*, which itself has the pattern WW. However, with this particular suffix S is assigned to the immediately preceding syllable. The initial syllable of *solid* must accordingly become W and its vowel will then reduce.

The other rhythmic constraint disallows words beginning with two Ws. Should such a situation arise, the first one will be changed to S. Note the derivation of *adoration*.

(19) adore
      W S   ] ation
      W S   S W
      W W   S W
      S W   S W

Here the base form *adore* (WS) is followed by the SW suffix *-ation*, and so there are two consecutive Ss. But the change of the first one to W now produces a word beginning with two Ws. As this sequence is unacceptable, the first W becomes S.

We have examined three different proposals for describing phonological data. Each of these approaches makes use of entities different
from the traditional segments of generative phonology. Selkirk's notion
of foot entails a higher-level construct, comprising one or two syllables,
where the syllables in turn are higher-order units composed of segments. Goldsmith envisages separate 'suprasegmental' (and by extension perhaps also 'subsegmental') sequences, constituting a distinct
phonological tier, yet in alignment with the segmental layer. I have advocated rhythmic patterns of alternating strong and weak syllables. All of
these proposals have a common trait: Phonological rules are able to
refer directly to these nonsegmental entities, thereby bypassing reference
to individual consonants and vowels. In each case there emerges a more
insightful account of particular phenomena, which, in the standard framework, are accommodated clumsily. This line of investigation represents
one of the truly exciting avenues of research currently unfolding within
phonology.

CHAPTER SIXTEEN

Remarks on Markedness

Linda R. Waugh

One of the most important issues in phonology, which was addressed directly by one of the papers in this volume (Houlihan and Iverson) and only indirectly by others, is that of markedness.[1] Markedness follows directly from the nature of opposition: opposition is a binary relation of mutual implication where the two poles of the opposition educe one another and where they are in a hierarchical arrangement vis-à-vis one another, which hierarchical arrangement is given by the terms marked and unmarked. Phonological elements, then, just as semantic elements, far from being disparate and equal, are hierarchically organized—they set up equivalences but they do not create equals. In both phonology and semantics, the marked term is opposed to the unmarked term by its constraining, focusing character, by its concentration on a certain characteristic. The constraining, focusing character of the marked term of any grammatical opposition is directed toward a more closely specified conceptual item—thus in the general meanings of coupled grammatical categories one of them signals a certain grammatical concept which the other one leaves unsignalled. In phonology, in the distinctive features, the marked term is opposed to the unmarked one by a closer concentration on a certain, whether positive or negative, perceptual sound property polar to that of the unmarked term; and accordingly it is characterized by a restrictive selection of contextual conditions of occurrence (whether a sequential or concurrent context). In this respect, then, in the obstruents, as was pointed out in Houlihan and Iverson, who based their remarks on implicational statements by Trubetzkoy (1969) and Jakobson (1968), voicing is marked whereas unvoicing is unmarked. Similarly, continuancy is marked in the obstruents (e.g., fricatives) whereas non-continuancy is unmarked (e.g., stops).

Aspiration (one of the forms of tenseness) is marked with respect to non-aspiration (laxness),[2] and so forth.

One thing which it is important to understand is that the concept of markedness applies at the level of features and not at the level of segments. In other words, if we say that /n/ is marked vis-à-vis /t/ then that is a shorthand for saying that /n/ is markedly nasal while /t/ is non-markedly oral (non-nasal). In other words, if one were to ask whether /k/ is marked or unmarked, the question would have no sense, for /k/ is marked for being compact (velar) but unmarked for being non-continuant, non-nasal. Similarly, to ask what the marked counterpart of /t/ is has no sense because /n/ is its marked counterpart with respect to nasality, /d/ its marked counterpart with respect to voicing, /p/ and /k/ its marked counterparts with respect to gravity and compactness respectively, and so forth.

The ways in which these statements have been formulated reveals another characteristic of markedness—it is context-sensitive. It is not the case, for instance, that voicing is marked everywhere, but rather that it is marked in obstruents but unmarked in vowels. Thus, /+ voice/ in the concurrent context of /+ consonantal/ is marked whereas /+ voice/ in the concurrent context of /+ vocalic/ is unmarked. Other examples of context-sensitivity include the markedness of compactness in consonants—/k/ and /t̆/[3] are marked as against /t/ and /p/—while compactness in vowels is unmarked—/a/ vs. /u/, /i/. Similarly, tenseness is marked in consonants and unmarked in vowels.

These two context-sensitive types of markedness point up another important phenomenon—namely that the distinction between vowel and consonant is a fundamental one. Markedness values are often reversed within the two systems. (But not always—nasality is marked both in vowels and in consonants.) And even within one of these two major categories markedness reversals can occur: thus in the consonants, within the unmarked diffuse consonants, gravity is marked—the bilabial stop is marked in contradistinction to the dental stop. However, within the compact consonants, gravity is unmarked: the velar stop is unmarked in contradistinction to the palatal stop. With respect to this it should be pointed out that markedness relations have often been based on the order of acquisition of features in child language and this has sometimes been adduced as evidence for the unmarkedness of the bilabial stop (i.e., gravity with diffuseness) vs. the dental stop (i.e., acuteness with diffuseness). However, if one looks at consonantal systems around the world, it is generally the dental series which is the more elaborated, i.e., the less focused, and the more frequent in terms of lexical and text frequency.

A further characteristic which is important in terms of markedness is the difference between distinctiveness and redundancy. In English and French, for example, stops and fricatives (e.g.,p,f,t,s,k,š vs. b,v,d,z,g,ž) are distinctively opposed as tense to lax (as shown by, e.g., Malécot 1970, 1977 and Fischer-Jørgensen 1954, 1972), while voiceless vs. voiced is redundant. The redundant nature of the latter is particularly apparent in cases of assimilation where tense~lax remains as distinctive and voiced~voiceless is assimilated: cf. French *acheter* with tense and voiceless [š] vs. *à jeter* with lax and voiceless [ž]. In French in certain contexts there may be voicing of the 'unvoiced' stops or devoicing of 'voiced' stops, but since tense~lax is the distinctive opposition, the pairs are still differentiated. In English, the tenseness of the tense stops, for example, is implemented by various phonetic correlates—aspiration, length, intensity, etc.—depending on its position in the word. (In general, the tense stop is stronger the closer it is to 'strong position'—either word-initial or syllable-initial before the stressed vowel.) And this is corroborated by the fact that its lax opposite is correspondingly weaker in all of these positions. The phonemes /p/, /t/, /k/ then are markedly tense (and redundantly voiceless)— and all of their specific phonetic manifestations are as it were rule-governed. In certain Swiss German dialects the only distinction is tense~lax, with both phonemes basically voiceless. Russian, on the other hand, displays a voiced~voiceless distinctive opposition with only minimal reinforcement by tense~lax. In such cases, it is also important to realize that the markedness values are again reversed. In languages with a voiced~voiceless opposition, it is voicing which is marked while in languages with a tense~lax opposition it is tenseness which is marked. This is borne out not only by child language studies, implicational universals, frequency counts, historical changes, assimilative effects, etc., but also by what happens in languages which use both oppositions autonomously with a three-termed system. In such languages, it is the marked combination of marked tenseness with marked voicing which is unused; i.e., such languages have unmarked laxness with unmarked voicelessness unmarked laxness with marked voicing, and marked tenseness with unmarked voicelessness: p_____pʰ.

$$\begin{array}{ccc} \text{p} & \rule{2cm}{0.4pt} & \text{p}^{\text{h}} \\ & \diagdown \diagup & \\ & \text{b} & \end{array}$$

Only rarely does a four-term system occur: p————pʰ. It is such data

$$\begin{array}{ccc} \text{p} & \rule{2cm}{0.4pt} & \text{p}^{\text{h}} \\ | & & | \\ \text{b} & \rule{2cm}{0.4pt} & \text{b}^{\text{h}} \end{array}$$

which show that Voice Onset Time (so-called VOT), while helpful in discerning certain phonetic differences between languages, is not a primitive since it often combines the effect of voiced~voiceless with tense~lax.

In some cases, however, it is not clear which feature is distinctive and which is redundant—and then it is the combination (or syncretism) of the two features which is distinctive; there is no direct marked~unmarked relation. Such examples include the typical five-vowel system with two acute non-flat vowels, two grave flat vowels, and one compact vowel:

i   u
  e   o
    a

For some languages, but not all, it is the syncretism of acuteness and non-flatness which is distinctively opposed to the syncretism of gravity and flatness. In languages with bifurcations of such systems—i.e., with flat acute vowels and/or non-flat grave vowels—it becomes clear that in flat vowels acuteness is marked while in grave vowels non-flatness is marked. Furthermore, the /a/ (the unmarked vowels) of such systems is neither acute nor flat. In such cases, then, there is an equipollent opposition between the acute (marked) non-flat (unmarked) and grave (unmarked) flat (marked):

Neither series is unmarked vis-à-vis the other.

Cases like these syncretisms also result when one of the features in question is distinctive and the other redundant. In the examples mentioned above, a lax and thus unmarked stop is redundantly voiced (marked) whereas the tense and thus marked stop is redundantly voiceless (unmarked). Likewise, the optimal stop (unmarked for being non-continuant) is non-strident (marked) whereas the optimal fricative (marked for being continuant) is strident (unmarked). Bifurcations of these combinations into strident non-continuants (affricates) or non-strident continuants (weak fricatives) are rarer in languages of the world. Apparently, the differential marking of the phonemes—their syncretism—is perceptually and systematically more salient and thus unmarked.

There is also a tendency in language for the non-accumulation of marks, i.e., for the superposition of markedness on unmarkedness. This is borne out by the data on the scission of the syncretism of the tenseness feature and voicing feature mentioned above: the doubly marked /dʰ/ (voiced and tense) is rarely found. Furthermore, the marked compact consonants only rarely are subdivided into grave vs. acute (velar vs. palatal) while the unmarked diffuse consonants are so subdivided, near-universally or perhaps universally. In other words, if the two features are autonomous (both distinctive), very often three-way systems are found and the phoneme which is lacking is that which exhibits the accumulation of marks. Furthermore, no system evidences the accumulation of marks (e.g., a /dʰ/) without the other three possibilities. And no system displays the opposition grave ~ acute in compacts without at the same time having the opposition grave ~ acute in the diffuse phonemes. The (marked) nasal consonants tend to be less elaborated than their (unmarked) non-nasal counterparts (especially the stops). Moreover, nasality is almost universally distinctive in the (unmarked) consonants, whereas it is much more rarely distinctive in the (marked) vowels. And there is a general tendency for consonantal systems to be more elaborated (i.e., to use more features distinctively) than vocalic systems.

The work of Thomas Gamkrelidze and Irina Melikišvili has established that for obstruents the opposition of voiced and voiceless is most prevalent in the (unmarked) dentals, whereas the labials (marked for gravity) may have only the voiced series and the velars (marked for compactness) may have only the voiceless series. Such typological observations await explanation from the systematic analysis of markedness effects in combinations.

With respect to the relation of markedness and neutralization, it is not always the case that the unmarked segment always stands in the place of neutralization. In French, for example, while both [e] and [ɛ] can occur in open syllables, only [ɛ] can occur in a closed syllable,[4] thus producing alternations of the sort *premier* ~ *première*. Yet, in the vowels, tenseness is unmarked (as shown by the prevalence of the typical five-vowel system) while laxness is marked. Thus, while there is a tendency to have the unmarked in the place of neutralization, such is not always the case. Furthermore, German, in at least some of its dialects, has the following inventory:

	-s-	-s#
#z-	-z-	

Thus, in both initial and final position, the tense ~ lax opposition is neutralized (or better, an 'incomplete' phoneme occurs, being deprived of the tense ~ lax opposition, with the lax contextual variant of this incomplete phoneme in initial position and the tense variant in final position.). In addition, as it happens, the non-distinctively tense -s# may correlate with both the distinctively tense -s- or the distinctively lax -z-, depending on the morpheme—in other words, the neutralization has grammatical consequences. Furthermore, the interrelation between markedness, productivity and neutralization should not be seen in absolute terms. In Russian, before /e/ there is productive neutralization of the opposition between palatalized and non-palatalized consonants: only the palatalized (sharp-marked) series regularly occur. Non-palatalization is a marker of foreignisms, of special vocabulary like interjections, acronyms, names of letters of the alphabet, etc. In other words, it performs a special, stylistic function. The regular, productive way of making a foreign word native or of situating a word within the normal stock of vocabulary of Russian is through the use of a palatalized consonant before /e/. Non-palatalization signals that the word is of special status, while palatalization does not. Thus, before /e/ the marked (sharp) consonants occur; the presence of the unmarked (non-sharp) consonants is a marker of the special status of the word itself. Markedness then assumes an important role—in particular, it is only in such grammatically marked elements as interjections, foreignisms, acronyms, or alphabet names that the combination of the unmarked non-palatalized consonant + /e/ occurs.

It seems to me then that further research in phonology will most profitably take into account the problem of markedness, as well as the very interesting question of the interrelation between markedness in sound systems and markedness in grammatical systems.

NOTES

1. For a discussion of markedness, see Trubetzkoy (1969 and 1976), Waugh (1976), and Jakobson and Waugh (forthcoming). Compare Chomsky and Halle (1968).
2. I use the features as defined in Jakobson and Halle (1971).
3. I am using [t̆] to symbolize a palatal (i.e., compact acute) stop.
4. For those speakers of French who have [e] ∼ [ɛ] in, e.g., future vs. conditional (*j'aurai* vs. *j'aurais*) but do not have [ɛ] vs. [ɛ:]: (*faite* v.s *fête*).

Bibliography

Allen, W.S. 1962. *Sandhi*. The Hague: Mouton.

Andersen, Henning. 1972. "Diphthongization." *Language* 48:11–50.

Anderson, L. B. 1975. "Phonetic and Psychological Explanations for Vowel Harmony, Especially in Finnish." Ph.D. dissertation, University of Chicago.

Anderson, Stephen R. 1969. "West Scandinavian Vowel Systems and the Ordering of Phonological Rules." Ph.D. dissertation, Massachusetts Institute of Technology.

Anderson, Stephen R. 1972. "U-umlaut and Skaldic verse." In *A Festschrift for Morris Halle*, edited by S. Anderson and P. Kiparsky. New York: Holt, Rinehart and Winston.

Anderson, Stephen R. 1974. *The Organization of Phonology*. New York: Academic Press.

Anderson, Stephen R. 1975. "On the interaction of phonological rules of various types." *Journal of Linguistics* 11:39–62.

Anderson, Stephen R. 1976a. "On the conditioning of Icelandic *u*-umlaut." *Language Sciences* 40:26–27.

Anderson, Stephen R. 1976b. "Icelandic *u*-umlaut: an exchange of views." *Language Sciences* 42:31–34.

Anderson, Stephen R. 1976c. "Nasal consonants and the internal structure of segments." *Language* 52:326–44.

Anderson, Stephen R. 1977. "Historical change and the ordering relation in phonology." In *Recent Advances in Historical Phonology*, edited by J. Fisiak. The Hague: Mouton.

Anderson, Stephen R. Forthcoming, a. "Tone features." In *Tone: A Linguistic Survey*, edited by V. Fromkin. New York: Academic Press.

Anderson, Stephen R. Forthcoming, b. "Problems and perspectives in the description of vowel harmony." In *The Proceedings of the CUNY Vowel Harmony Symposium*, edited by R. Vago.

Anderson, Stephen R., and Wayles Browne. 1973. "On keeping exchange rules in Czech." *Paper in Linguistics* 6.4:445–82.

Anwar, M. S. 1974. "Consonant devoicing at word boundary and assimilation." *Language Sciences* (October): 6–12.

Aronoff, M. 1976. "Word formation in generative grammar." *Linguistic Inquiry Monographs* 1. Cambridge: MIT Press.

Austerlitz, R.; Eric Hamp.; and F.W. Householder. 1966. *Readings in Linguistics* II. Chicago: University of Chicago Press.

Austin, William. 1957. "Criteria for phonetic similarity." *Language* 33: 538–44.

Bach, E. 1968. "Two proposals concerning the simplicity metric in phonology." *Glossa* 2:128–49.

Bailey, Charles-James N. 1974. "Variations resulting from different rule ordering in English phonology." In *New Ways of Analyzing Variation in English,* edited by C.-J. Bailey and R. Shuy, pp. 211–52. Washington, D.C.: Georgetown University Press.

Baudouin de Courtenay. 1895. *Versuch einer Theorie phonetischer Alternationen.* In *A Baudouin de Courtenay Anthology,* translated by E. Stankiewicz. Bloomington: Indiana University Press, 1972.

Baxter, A. R. W. 1975. *Some Aspects of Naturalness in Phonological Theory.* London: Oxford University Press.

Baz, José María. 1967. "El habla de la tierra de Aliste." *Revista de Filología Española* [Madrid], Suppl. 82.

Bazell, C. E. 1954. "The Choice of Criteria in Structural Linguistics." In *Linguistics Today (Word 10),* edited by A. Martinet and U. Weinreich, pp. 6–15. New York: Linguistic Circle of New York.

Bedell, George. 1974. "Morpheme Structure Conditions in Pāṇini." *Descriptive and Applied Linguistics,* Bulletin of the International Christian University Summer Institute of Linguistics, 7.

Bloch, B. 1948. "A set of postulates for phonemic analysis." *Language* 24:3–46.

Bloomfield, Leonard. 1917. *Tagalog Texts.* University of Illinois Studies in Languages and Literature 3.2–4.

Bloomfield, Leonard. 1933. *Language.* New York: Holt.

Bloomfield, Leonard. 1939. "Menominee Morphophonemics." In *Études Phonologiques dediées à la mémoire de M. le Prince Trubetzkoy. Travaux de Cercle Linguistique de Prague* 8:108–15.

Boas, F., and E. Deloria. 1941. *Dakota Grammar.* Washington D.C.: National Academy of Sciences.

Bond, Zinny S. 1969. "Constraints on production errors." In *Papers from the Fifth Regional Meeting of the Chicago Linguistic Society,* edited by R. I. Binnick, et al, pp. 302–305. Chicago: Chicago Linguistic Society.

Bowen, J. D. 1976. "Structural analysis of the verb system in New Mexican Spanish." In *Studies in Southwest Spanish,* edited by J. D. Bowen and J. Ornstein, pp. 93–124. Powley, Mass.: Newbury House.

Boyd-Bowman, Peter. 1960. *El Habla de Guanajuato.* Mexico: Imprenta Universitaria.

Brame, Michael K. 1974. "The cycle in phonology: stress in Palestinian, Maltese and Spanish." *Linguistic Inquiry* 5:39–60.

Brame, Michael K., ed. 1972. *Contributions to Generative Phonology.* Austin: University of Texas Press.

Brame, Micheal K., and Ivonne Bordelois. 1974. "Some controversial questions in Spanish phonology." *Linguistic Inquiry* 5:282–98.

Braune, Wilhelm. 1967. *Althochdeutsche Grammatik,* revised by Walther Mitzka. 12th ed. Tübingen: Max Niemeyer Verlag.

Buiskool, H. E. 1939. *The Tripādī.* Leiden: E. J. Brill.

Burrow, Thomas. 1955. *The Sanskrit Language.* London: Faber and Faber.

Burrow, Thomas. 1965. *The Sanskrit Language.* London: Unwin and Unwin.

Campbell, A. 1959. *Old English Grammar.* London: Oxford University Press.

Canfield, Delos Lincoln. 1962. *La pronunciación del español en América.* Bogotá: Instituto Caro y Cuervo.

Chen, Matthew Y. 1973. "On the formal expression of natural rules in phonology." *Journal of Linguistics* 9:223–49.

Chen, Matthew Y. 1974a. "Natural phonology from the diachronic vantage point." In *Papers from the Parasession on Natural Phonology,* edited by A. Bruck et al., pp. 43–80. Chicago: Chicago Linguistic Society.

Chen, Matthew Y. 1974b. "Metarules and universal constraints in phonological theory." In *Proceedings of the XIth International Congress of Linguists,* edited by L. Heilmann. Bologna. September 1972 meeting.

Cheng, Robert L. 1977. *Economy and Locational Information in Phonology.* Bloomington: Indiana University Linguistics Club.

Chomsky, Noam. 1955. *The Logical Structure of Linguistic Theory.* New York: Plenum Press.

Chomsky, Noam. 1957. *Syntactic Structures.* The Hague: Mouton.

Chomsky, Noam. 1964. "Current issues in linguistic theory." In *The Structure of Language: Readings in the Philosophy of Language,* edited by J. A. Fodor and J. J. Katz, pp. 50–118. Englewood Cliffs, N.J.: Prentice-Hall.

Chomsky, Noam. 1965. *Aspects of the Theory of Syntax.* Cambridge: MIT Press.

Chomsky, Noam. 1967. "Some general properties of phonological rules." *Language* 43:102–28.

Chomsky, Noam. 1972. *Studies on Semantics in Generative Grammar.* The Hague: Mouton.

Chomsky, Noam, and Morris Halle. 1965. "Some controversial questions in phonological theory." *Journal of Linguistics* 1:97–138.

Chomsky, Noam, and Morris Halle. 1968. *The Sound Pattern of English.* New York: Harper and Row.

Clements, G.N. 1976a. "Vowel harmony in non-linear generative phonology: The autosegmental theory (I)." Unpublished. Harvard University.

Clements, G.N. 1976b. "The autosegmental treatment of vowel harmony." In *Phonologica 1976,* edited by W. Dressler. Innsbruck Beiträge zur Sprachwissenschaft, vol. 19, forthcoming.

Clements, G.N. 1976c. "Hungarian vowel harmony." In *Proceedings of the Seventh Meeting of the Northeast Linguistics Society,* edited by Kegl, Hash, and Zaenen.

Collinder, Björn. 1969. *Survey of the Uralic Languages.* 2d ed. Stockholm: Almqvist and Wiksell.

De Chene, Brent, and Stephen Anderson. 1977. "On compensatory lengthen-
    ing." Presented at Linguistic Society of America, 1977 annual meeting.
Deferrari, Harry A. 1954. *The Phonology of Italian, Spanish, and French.*
    Washington, D.C.: Roy J. Deferrari. (Ann Arbor: Edward Brothers,
    Inc.)
Dell, François. 1970. "Les Règles phonologiques tardives et la morphologie
    dérivationelle du français." Ph.D. dissertation, Massachusetts Institute
    of Technology.
Dinnsen, Daniel A. 1976a. "On the explanation of rule change." *Glossa*
    10.2:175–99.
Dinnsen, Daniel A. 1976b. "Some preliminaries to atomic phonology." In
    XII Regional Meeting of the Chicago Linguistic Society, edited by S.
    Mufwene, C. Walker, and S. Steever, pp. 133–44. Chicago: University
    of Chicago.
Dinnsen, Daniel A. 1977a. "Some formal and empirical issues in atomic
    phonology." In *Communication and Cognition,* in press. To be reprinted
    in *Phonology in the 1970's,* edited by D. L. Goyvaerts. Antwerp: Story-
    Scientia, forthcoming.
Dinnsen, Daniel A. 1977b. "A functional explanation of dialect difference."
    Language Sciences 46:1–7.
Dinnsen, Daniel A., and A. Koutsoudas. 1975. *On the Explanation of Rule
    Reordering.* Bloomington: Indiana University Linguistics Club.
Dinnsen, Daniel A., and Fred Eckman. 1976. "The atomic character of
    phonological processes." Paper presented at the IIIrd International
    Phonology Meeting, Vienna. In *Phonologica 1976,* edited by W. Dressler.
    Innsbruck Beiträge zur Sprachwissenschaft, vol. 19, pp. 133–37.
Dinnsen, Daniel A., and Fred R. Eckman. 1977. *Some Substantive Uni-
    versals in Atomic Phonology.* Bloomington: Indiana University Lin-
    guistics Club. Also in *Lingua* 45:1–14.
[Donegan] Miller, Patricia. 1972. "Some context-free processes affecting
    vowels." In *Ohio State University Working Papers in Linguistics* 11, pp.
    136–67.
[Donegan] Miller, Patricia. 1973a. "Bleaching and coloring." In *Papers from
    the Ninth Regional Meeting,* edited by Claudia Corum et al., pp. 386–
    97. Chicago: Chicago Linguistic Society.
[Donegan] Miller, Patricia. 1973b. "Chain shifts, reported mergers and
    natural ordering in phonology." Paper delivered at Linguistic Society
    of America winter meeting, San Diego.
[Donegan] Miller, Patricia. 1974. "Southern discomfort." Paper delivered
    at Linguistic Society of America winter meeting, New York.
Donegan, Patricia Jane. 1976. "Raising and lowering." In *Papers from the
    Twelfth Regional Meeting,* edited by S. Mufwene et al., pp. 145–60.
    Chicago: Chicago Linguistic Society.
Donegan, Patricia Jane. 1978. "On the Natural Phonology of Vowels:
    Processes and Systems." Ph.D. dissertation, Ohio State University.
Donegan, P., and D. Stampe. 1977a. "On the description of phonological
    hierarchies." *CLS Squibs.* Chicago: Chicago Linguistic Society, in press.

Donegan, Patricia Jane, and David Stampe. 1977b. "The syllable in phonological and prosodic structure." For Conference on Segment Organization and the Syllable, Boulder, Colorado.

Donegan, Patricia, and David Stampe. 1977c. "Old Sam Peabody: verbal imitations of birdsong." Paper read at Linguistic Society of America, Summer Meeting, University of Hawaii.

Donegan, Patricia Jane, and David Stampe. In press. "The Syllable in Phonological and Prosodic Structure." Paper given at the Conference on Segment Organization and the Syllable, Boulder, Colorado, 1977.

Dressler, Wolfgang. 1972. *Allegro-regeln rechtfertigen Lentoregeln: Sekundäre Phoneme des Bretonischen.* Innsbruck: Institüt für Sprachwissenschaft.

Edmundson, T., and J.T. Bendor-Samuel. 1966. "Tone pattern of Etung." *Journal of African Linguistics* 5:1–6.

Edwards, Mary Louise. 1973. "The acquistion of liquids." *Ohio State University Working Papers in Linguistics* 15:1–54.

Einarsson, Stefán. 1945. *Icelandic.* Baltimore: The John Hopkins Press.

Eliasson, S. 1975. "On the issue of directionality." In *The Nordic Languages and Modern Linguistics,* vol. 2, edited by K. -H. Dahlstedt, pp. 421–44. Stockholm: Almqvist and Wiksell.

Eliasson, S. 1977. "Inferential aspects of phonological rules." In *Phonologica 1976,* edited by W. Dressler. Innsbrucker Beiträge zur Sprachwissenschaft, vol. 19, forthcoming.

Elimelach, B. 1976. "A tonal grammar of Etsako." *Working Papers in Phonetics 35.* Los Angeles: University of California at Los Angeles.

Espinosa, A. M. 1946. "Estudios sobre el español de Nuevo Méjico, Parte II, Morfología." In *Biblioteca de Dialectología Hispanoamericano,* II, edited by A. Rosenblat. Buenos Aires: Facultad de Filosofía y Letras de la Universidad de Buenos Aires, Instituto de Filología.

Ferguson, C.A. 1963. "Assumptions about nasals: a sample study of phonological universals." In *Universals of Language,* edited by J.H. Greenberg, pp. 53–60. Cambridge: MIT Press.

Feyerabend, P. 1970. "Consolations for the specialist." In *Criticism and the Growth of Knowledge,* edited by I. Lakatos and A. Musgrave. New York: Cambridge University Press.

Feyerabend, P. 1975. *Against Method.* London: NLB.

Firth, J.R. 1957. *Papers in Linguistics.* London: Oxford University Press.

Fischer-Jørgenson, E. 1954. "Acoustic analysis of stop consonants." *Miscellanea phonetica* 2:58ff.

Fischer-Jørgenson, E. 1972. "Kinesthetic judgment of effort in the production of stop consonants." *Annual Report of the Institute of Phonetics of the University of Copenhagen* 6:59.

Foley, J. 1965. "Spanish Morphology." Ph.D. dissertation, Massachusetts Institute of Technology.

Foley, J. 1967. "Spanish plural formation." *Language* 43:486–93.

Foley, J. 1972. "Rule precursors and phonological change by meta-rule." In *Linguistic Change and Generative Theory,* edited by R. P.

Stockwell and R. K. S. Macauley, pp. 96–100. Bloomington: Indiana University Press.

Fodor, J. A, and J. J. Katz, eds. 1964. *The Structure of Language.* Englewood Cliffs, N.J.: Prentice-Hall.

Fouché, Pierre. 1927. *Études de Phonétique Générale. Publications de la Faculté des Lettres de l'Université de Strasbourg* [Paris], Fasc. 39.

Fromkin, Victoria A. 1971. "The non-anomalous nature of anomalous utterances." *Language* 47:27–52.

Gamkrelidze, T. 1975. "On the correlation of stops and fricatives in a phonological system." *Lingua* 35:231–61.

Goldsmith, John. 1974. "English as a tone language." *Communication and Cognition,* in press.

Goldsmith, John. 1975a. "An autosegmental typology of tone and how Japanese fits in." In *Proceedings of the Fifth Meeting of the North East Linguistics Society,* edited by E. Kaisse, pp. 172–82.

Goldsmith, John. 1975b. "Tone melodies and the autosegment." In *Proceedings of the Sixth Conference on African Linguistics,* pp. 135–47. Ohio State Working Papers, no. 20, R. Herbert, ed.

Goldsmith, John. 1976a. "An overview of autosegmental phonology." *Linguistic Analysis* 2:23–68.

Goldsmith, John. 1976b. *Autosegmental Phonology.* Bloomington: Indiana University Linguistics Club.

Goldsmith, John. In preparation, a. "A review of Firthian prosodic analysis."

Goldsmith, John. In preparation, b. "Syllables without [+syllabic]."

Goldsmith, John. In preparation, c. "Counterfeeding in Igbo."

Goodman, Nelson. 1951. *The Structure of Appearance.* Cambridge: Harvard University Press.

Goodman, Paul. 1971. *Speaking and Language: Defense of Poetry.* New York: Random House.

Grammont, M. 1933. *Traité de phonétique.* Paris: Librairie Delagrave.

Green, M.M., and G.E. Igwe. 1963. *A Descriptive Grammar of Igbo.* Berlin: Academie-Verlag.

Greenberg, Joseph H. 1963. "Some universals of grammar with particular reference to the order of meaningful elements." In *Universals of Language,* edited by Joseph H. Greenberg. Cambridge: MIT Press.

Greenberg, J. H. 1966. *Language Universals.* The Hague: Mouton.

Greenberg, J. H. 1969. "Some methods of dynamic comparison in linguistics." In *Substance and Structure of Language,* edited by Jaan Puhvel, pp. 147–203. Berkeley: University of California Press.

Greenberg, J. H., and J. J. Jenkins. 1964. "Studies in the psychological correlates of the sound system of American English, I-II." *Word* 20:157–77.

Gussmann, E. 1976. "Recoverable derivations and phonological change." *Lingua* 40:281–303.

Gussmann, E. In press. "Implications of the vowel-zero alternations in Polish." *Linguistic Inquiry* 9.

Haber, Lyn R. 1975. "The muzzy theory." In *Papers from the Eleventh*

Regional Meeting, edited by R. E. Grossman et al., pp. 240–56. Chicago: Chicago Linguistic Society.

Hale, Kenneth. 1973. "Deep-surface canonical disparities in relation to analysis and change: an Australian example." In *Current Trends in Linguistics, 11,* edited by T.A. Sebeok et al. The Hague: Mouton.

Halle, M. 1959. *Sound Pattern of Russian.* The Hague: Mouton.

Halle, M. 1961. "On the role of simplicity in linguistic description." In *Structure of Language and its Mathematical Aspects. Proceedings of the Twelfth Symposium in Applied Mathematics,* edited by R. Jakobson, pp. 89–94. Providence: American Mathematical Society.

Halle, M. 1962. "Phonology in generative grammar." *Word* 18:54–72. Reprinted in *The Structure of Language: Readings in the Philosophy of Language,* edited by J. A. Fodor and J. J. Katz. Englewood Cliffs, N.J.: Prentice-Hall, 1964.

Haraguchi, S. 1976. *The Tone Pattern of Japanese: An Autosegmental Theory of Tonology.* Tokyo: Kaitakusha.

Harms, R.T. 1968. *Introduction to Phonological Theory.* Englewood Cliffs, N.J.: Prentice-Hall.

Harms, Robert T. 1973. *Some non-rules in English.* Bloomington: Indiana University Linguistics Club.

Harris, James W. 1969. *Spanish Phonology.* Cambridge: MIT Press.

Harris, James W. 1970. "A note on Spanish plural formation." *Language* 46: 928–30.

Harris, James W. 1972. "Five classes of irregular verbs in Spanish." In *Generative Studies in Romance Languages,* edited by J. Casagrande and B. Saciuk, pp. 247–71. Rowley, Mass.: Newbury House.

Harris, James W. 1974. "Evidence from Portuguese for the 'Elsewhere Condition' in phonology." *Linguistic Inquiry* 5:61–80.

Harris, James W. 1978. "To theories of non-automatic morphophonological alternations." *Language* 54:41–60.

Harris, Z. 1944. "Simultaneous components in phonology." *Language* 20: 181–205.

Hastings, A. 1974. *Stifling.* Bloomington: Indiana University Linguistics Club.

Hockett, C.F. 1955. *A Manual of Phonology.* Memoir 11, *International Journal of American Linguistics,* 21:1.

Holden, Kyril. 1976. "Assimilation rates of borrowings and phonological productivity." *Language* 52:131–47.

Hooper, Joan B. 1972. "The syllable in phonological theory." *Language* 48:525–40.

Hooper, Joan B. 1974. *Aspects of Natural Generative Phonology.* Bloomington: Indiana University Linguistics Club.

Hooper, Joan B. 1975. "The archisegment in natural generative phonology." *Language* 51:536–60.

Hooper, Joan B. 1976. *An Introduction to Natural Generative Phonology.* New York: Academic Press.

Hooper, Joan B. 1977. "Substantive evidence for linearity: vowel length and nasality in English." In *Papers from the Thirteenth Regional Meeting of the Chicago Linguistic Society,* edited by Woodford Beach et al.

Hooper, Joan B., and T. Terrell. 1976. "Stress assignment in Spanish: a natural generative analysis." *Glossa* 10:64-110.

Houlihan, K. 1975. "The Role of Word Boundary in Phonological Processes." Ph.D. dissertation, University of Texas.

Houlihan, Kathleen, and Gregory K. Iverson. 1977. "Phonological markedness and neutralization rules." Paper presented at the summer meeting of the Linguistic Society of America, Honolulu. In *Minnesota Working Papers in Linguistics and Philosophy of Language* 4:45-58.

Householder, F.W. 1965. "Phonological theory: a brief comment." *Journal of Linguistics* 2:99-100.

Householder, F.W. 1971. *Linguistic Speculations.* New York: Cambridge University Press.

Householder, F. W. 1972. "Vowel overlap in Azerbaijani." In *Papers in Memory of Pierre Delattre,* edited by A. Valdman, pp. 229-30. The Hague: Mouton.

Householder, Fred W. 1974. Review of R. P. Stockwell and R. K. S. Macaulay, eds., *Linguistic Change and Generative Theory. Language* 50:555-68.

Howard, Irwin. 1972. "A directional theory of rule application in phonology." *University of Hawaii Working Papers in Linguistics* IV, 7.

Hudson, G. 1974. "The representation of non-productive alternations." In *Proceedings of the First International Conference on Historical Linguistics,* 2, edited by J. Anderson and C. Jones, pp. 203-29. Amsterdam: North Holland.

Hudson, Grover. 1975. "Suppletion in the Representation of Alterations." Ph.D. dissertation, University of California, Los Angeles.

Hyman, L.M. 1975. *Phonology: Theory and Analysis.* New York: Holt, Rinehart and Winston.

Hyman, Larry M. 1977. "Phonologization." In *Linguistic Studies Offered to Joseph Greenberg,* edited by Juilland Alphonse, pp. 407-18. Saratoga, California: Anma Libri.

Hyman, L. M., and R. G. Schuh. 1974. "Universals of tone rules: evidence from West Africa." *Linguistic Inquiry* 5:81-115.

Imanishi, E. C. 1975. "O Processo de Metafonia Nos Verbos." Master's thesis, Pontifícia Universidade Católica de Campinas.

Isačenko, A. V. 1972. "Rol, usečenija b russkom slovoobrazovanii." *International Journal of Slavic Linguistics and Poetics* 15:95-125.

Iverson, G. K. 1974. "Ordering Constraints in Phonology." Ph.D. dissertation, University of Minnesota.

Iverson, G. K. 1976. "A guide to sanguine relationships." In *The Application and Ordering of Grammatical Rules,* edited by A. Koutsoudas. The Hague: Mouton.

Jakobson, R. 1928. "The concept of the sound law and the teleological criterion." In *Časopis pro moderní filologii XIV.* Prague. Reprinted in *Selected Writings* 1:1-2. The Hague: Mouton, 1962.

Jakobson, R. 1932a. "Phoneme and phonology." In Secondary Supplementary

Volume to *Ottův slovník naučný*. Prague. Reprinted in *Selected Writings* 1:231–33. The Hague: Mouton, 1962.

Jakobson, R. 1932b. "Zur Structur des russischen Verbums." Reprinted in *Selected Writings* 2:3–15. The Hague: Mouton, 1971.

Jakobson, R. 1939. "Signe zero." In *Milanges de Linguistique Offerts a Charles Bally*. Geneve. Reprinted in *Selected Writings* 2:211–19. The Hague: Mouton, 1971.

Jakobson, Roman. 1942. "Kindersprache, Aphasie, und allegemeine Lautgesetze." In *Selected Writings* 1:328–401. The Hague: Mouton, 1962. Translated by A. Keiler as *Child Language, Aphasia, and Phonological Universals*. The Hague: Mouton, 1968.

Jakobson, R. 1948. "Russian conjugation." Reprinted in *Selected Writings* 2:119–29. The Hague: Mouton, 1971.

Jakobson, R. 1965. "Quest of the essence of language." In *Selected Writings* 2:345–59. The Hague: Mouton, 1971.

Jakobson, R., C. G. M. Fant, and M. Halle. 1951. *Preliminaries to Speech Analysis*. Massachusetts: MIT Press.

Jakobson, R., and Morris Halle. 1971. *Fundamentals of Language*. The Hague: Mouton.

Jakobson, R., and L. R. Waugh. Forthcoming *The Sound Shape of Language*. Bloomington: Indiana University Press.

Jensen, John T., and Margaret Stong-Jensen. 1976. "Ordering and directionality of iterative rules." In *The Application and Ordering of Grammatical Rules*, edited by A. Koutsoudas, pp. 104–19. The Hague: Mouton.

Jespersen, O. 1964. *Language: Its Nature, Development, and Origin*. New York: W.W. Norton.

Johnson, C. Douglas. 1970. "Formal aspects of phonological description." In *POLA Reports*, Second Series, II. Berkeley: University of California Linguistics Department. (Reprinted in *Monographs on Linguistics Analysis* 3. The Hague: Mouton, 1972.)

Jones, Daniel, and Dennis Ward. 1969. *The Phonetics of Russian*. New York: Cambridge University Press.

Jones, W.E., and J. Laver. 1973. *Phonetics in Linguistics*. London: Longmans.

Joos, Martin, ed. 1963. *Readings in Linguistics I*. 3rd ed. New York: American Council of Learned Societies.

Joos, Martin, ed. 1966. *Readings in Linguistics I*. 4th ed. Chicago: University of Chicago Press.

Jordan, R. 1974. *Handbook of Middle English Grammer: Phonology*, translated and revised by E. A. Crook. The Hague: Mouton.

Kahn, Dan. 1976. "Syllable-based Generalizations in English Phonology." Ph.D. dissertation, Massachusetts Institute of Technology.

Kaye, J. D. 1974. "Opacity and recoverability in phonology." *The Canadian Journal of Linguistics* 19:134–49.

Kaye, J. D. 1975. "A Functional Explanation for Rule Ordering in Phonology." In *Papers from the Parasession on Functionalism*, pp. 244–52. Chicago: Chicago Linguistics Society.

Kean, Mary-Louise. 1974. "The strict cycle in phonology." *Linguistic Inquiry* 5:179–204.

Keel, William D. 1976. "Phonological variation and change in the dialects of Northeast Switzerland." Paper presented at the Mid-America Linguistics Conference, University of Minnesota, Minneapolis.

Keel, William D. 1977. "Phonological Variation and Complement Rule Addition." Ph. D. dissertation, Indiana University.

Keel, William D., and T. Shannon. 1976. "On gradual generalization." Paper presented at the Minnesota Regional Conference on Language and Linguistics, Minneapolis. Also in *Glossa* 11:125–38.

Kenstowicz, Michael. 1976. "Rule application in pregenerative American phonology." In *The Application and Ordering of Grammatical Rules,* edited by A. Koutsoudas, pp. 259–82. The Hague: Mouton.

Kenstowicz, Michael, and Charles Kisseberth. 1971. "Unmarked bleeding orders." In *Studies in the Linguistics Sciences* 1:8–28. Champaign-Urbana: University of Illinois Department of Linguistics. Reprinted in *Studies in Generative Phonology,* edited by C. Kisseberth, pp. 1–12. Edmonton, Alberta: Linguistic Research, Inc.

Kenstowicz, Michael, and Charles Kisseberth. 1973. "The multiple application problem in phonology." In *Studies in Generative Phonology,* edited by Charles W. Kisseberth, pp. 13–41. Champaign, Illinois: Linguistic Research, Inc.

Kenstowicz, Michael, and Charles Kisseberth. 1977. *Topics in Phonological Theory.* New York: Academic Press.

King, Robert D. 1969a. "Push chains and drag chains." *Glossa* 3:3–21.

King, Robert D. 1969b. *Historical Linguistics and Generative Grammar.* Englewood Cliffs, N.J.: Prentice-Hall.

King, Robert D. 1973. "Rule insertion." *Language* 49:551–78.

Kiparsky, Paul. 1965. "Phonological Change." Ph.D. dissertation, Massachusetts Institute of Technology.

Kiparsky, Paul 1968a. *How Abstract Is Phonology?* Bloomington: Indiana University Linguistics Club.

Kiparsky, P. 1968b. "Linguistic universals and linguistic change." In *Universals in Linguistic Theory,* edited by E. Bach and R. Harms, pp. 171–202. New York: Holt, Rinehart and Winston.

Kiparsky, P. 1971. "Historical linguistics." In *A Survey of Linguistic Science,* edited by W.O. Dingwall, pp. 576–649. College Park: University of Maryland Linguistics Program.

Kiparsky, Paul. 1972. "Metrics and morphophonemics in the Rigveda." In *Contributions to Generative Phonology,* edited by Michael K. Brame, pp.171–200. Austin: University of Texas Press.

Kiparsky, P. 1973a. "Phonological representations." In *Three Dimensions of Linguistic Theory,* edited by O. Fujimura, pp. 5–56. Tokyo: TEC.

Kiparsky, Paul. 1973b. "Elsewhere' in phonology." In *A Festschrift for Morris Halle,* edited by S.A. Anderson and P. Kiparsky. New York: Holt.

Kiparsky, P. 1976. "Abstractness, opacity, and global rules." In *The Applica-*

tion and Ordering of Grammatical Rules, edited by A. Koutsoudas, pp. 160–86. The Hague: Mouton.

Kisseberth, C.W. 1970. "On the functional unity of phonological rules." *Linguistic Inquiry* 1:291–306.

Kisseberth, Charles. 1972. "Cyclical rules in Klamath phonology." *Linguistic Inquiry* 3:3–33.

Kisseberth, Charles W. 1973. "Is rule ordering necessary in phonology?" In *Papers in Honor of Henry and Renée Kahane,* edited by B. Kachru et al., pp. 418–41. Urbana: University of Illinois Press.

Kisseberth, Charles W. 1976. "The interaction of phonological rules and the polarity of change." In *The Application and Ordering of Grammatical Rules,* edited by A. Koutsoudas, pp. 41–54. The Hague: Mouton.

Klausenburger, Jurgen. 1976a. "(De)Morphologization in Latin." *Lingua* 40:305–20.

Klausenburger, Jurgen. 1976b. "French linking phenomena: a natural generative analysis." Paper presented at the summer meeting of the Linguistic Society of America, Oswego, N.Y.

Klausenburger, Jurgen. 1977. "The relevance of Kruszewski's theory of morphophonology today." Ms. University of Washington, Seattle.

Koutsoudas, A., ed. 1976. *The Application and Ordering of Grammatical Rules.* The Hague: Mouton.

Koutsoudas, Andreas; Gerald Sanders; and Craig Noll. 1971. *On the Application of Phonological Rules.* Bloomington: Indiana University Linguistics Club. Also in *Language* 50(1974):1–28.

Kruszewski, M. 1881. *Über die Lautabwechslungen.* Kazan.

Kuipers, Aert. 1960. *Phoneme and Morpheme in Kabardian.* The Hague: Mouton.

Kuryłowicz, J. 1949. "La nature des procès dits 'analogiques.'" *Acta Linguistica* 5:121–38. Reprinted in *Readings in Linguistics* II, edited by R. Austerlitz, Eric Hamp, and F.W. Householder, pp. 158–74. Chicago: University of Chicago Press, 1966.

Kuryłowicz, J. 1968. "The notion of morpho(pho)neme." In *Directions for Historical Linguistics,* edited by W. P. Lehman and Y. Malkiel. Austin: University of Texas Press.

Labov, W. 1972. "The internal evolution of linguistic rules." In *Linguistic Change and Generative Theory,* edited by R. Stockwell and R. Macaulay, pp. 101–71. Bloomington: Indiana University Press.

Labov, W.; M. Yaeger; and R. Steiner. 1972. *A Quantitative Study of Sound Change in Progress.* Philadelphia: NSF Report.

Ladefoged, Peter. 1975. *A Course in Phonetics.* New York: Harcourt, Brace, Jovanovich, Inc.

Lakatos, I. 1970. "Falsification and the methodology of scientific research programs." In *Criticism and the Growth of Knowledge,* edited by I. Lakatos and A. Musgrave, pp. 91–196. London: Cambridge University Press.

Langacker, Ronald W. 1969. "Mirror-image rules II: lexicon and phonology." *Language* 45:844–62.

Langendoen, D.T. 1968. *The London School of Linguistics*. Cambridge: MIT Press.

Lashley, K.S. 1951. "The problem of serial order in behavior." In *Cerebral Mechanisms in Behavior*, edited by L. A. Jeffress, pp. 112–56. New York: John Wiley and Sons.

Lass, Roger. 1976. *English Phonology and Phonological Theory*. New York: Cambridge University Press.

Leben, W. 1973. "Suprasegmental Phonology." Ph.D. dissertation, Massachusetts Institute of Technology.

Leben, W. R. 1974. "Rule inversion in Chadic: a reply." *Studies in African Linguistics* 5:265–78.

Leben, W. 1977a. "Studies in Suprasegmental Representation of Tone." Stanford University. Unpublished.

Leben, W. R. 1977b. "Parsing Hausa plurals." In *Papers in Chadic Linguistics*, edited by P. Newman and R. M. Newman. Leiden: Afrika Studiecentrum.

Leben, W.R., and O. W. Robinson. 1977. "Upside-down phonology." *Language* 53:1–20.

Lee, Gregory. 1975-76. "Natural phonological descriptions." *University of Hawaii Working Papers in Linguistics* 7.5:85–125; 8.3:25–61.

Lee, Gregory. 1976. "Interpretative phonological rules." *University of Hawaii Working Papers in Linguistics* 8.3:11–24.

Lee, Gregory, and Irwin Howard. 1974. "Another mouthful of divinity fudge." In *Papers from the Parasession on Natural Phonology*, edited by A. Bruck et al., pp. 220–32. Chicago: Chicago Linguistic Society.

Liberman, M. 1975. *The Intonational System of English*. Ph.D. disertation, Massachusetts Institute of Technology. Bloomington: Indiana University Linguistics Club.

Liberman, M., and A. Prince. 1977. "On stress and linguistic rhythm." *Linguistic Inquiry* 8:249–336.

Lightner, T. M. 1965. "On the description of vowel and consonant harmony." *Word* 21:244–50.

Linell, Per; Bengt Svensson; and Sven Öhman. 1971. *Ljudstruktur: Inledning till fonologin och särdragsteorin*. Lund: Gleerups.

Lovins, Julie. 1973. "Loanwords and the Phonological Structure of Japanese." Ph.D. dissertation, University of Chicago. Published by Indiana University Linguistics Club, Bloomington.

Lovins, J. 1974. "Why loan phonology is natural phonology." In *Papers from the Parasession on Natural Phonology*, edited by T. Bruck et al., pp. 240–50. Chicago: Chicago Linguistic Society.

Lyons, J. 1962. "Phonemic and non-phonemic phonology: some typological reflections." *International Journal of American Linguistics* 28:127–33. Reprinted in *Phonetics in Linguistics: A Book of Readings*, edited by Jones and Laver, pp. 229–39. London: Longmans, 1973.

McCarthy, J. 1977. Paper presented to the fifth North American Conference of Afro-Asiatic Linguistics, Ithaca, N.Y., April 24–25. Mimeographed.

McCawley, James D. 1971. "On the role of notation in generative phonology."

In *The Formal Analysis of Natural Languages,* edited by M. Gross, M. Halle, and M. Schützenberger, pp. 51–62. The Hague: Mouton.

McCawley, J. D. 1974. Review of Chomsky and Halle, *The Sound Pattern of English. International Journal of American Linguistics* 40:50–88.

McCawley, J. D. 1976. "Some ideas not to live by." *Die neueren Sprachen* 75:151–65.

McCawley, J. D. 1977. "Acquisition models as models of acquisition." In *Studies in Language Variation,* edited by R. Fasold and R. Shuy, pp. 51–64. Washington, D.C.: Georgetown University Press.

Major, Roy C. 1977. "Phonological differentiation of a bilingual child." *Ohio State University Working Papers in Linguistics* 22:88–122.

Malécot, A. 1970. "The lenis-fortis opposition: its physiological parameters." *Journal of the Acoustical Society of America* 47:1588–92.

Malécot, A. 1977. *Contribution à l'étude de la force d'articulation en français.* The Hague: Mouton.

Malkiel, Y. 1974. "New problems in Romance interfixation (I)." *Romance Philology* 28:304.

Malone, J. L. 1970. "In defense of non-uniqueness of phonological representations." *Language* 46:328–35.

Mańczak, Witold. 1958. "Tendances générales des changements analogiques." *Lingua* 7:298–325, 387–420.

Mandelbaum, David, ed. 1949. *Selected Writing of Edward Sapir.* Berkeley and Los Angeles: University of California Press.

Martin, Samuel E. 1951. "Korean phonemics." *Language* 27:519–33.

Martinet, A. 1955. *Économie des changements phonétiques.* Berne: A. Francke.

Mascaro, Joan. 1976. "Catalan Phonology and the Phonological Cycle." Ph.D. dissertation, Massachusetts Institute of Technology.

Mattoso Cámara, J., Jr. 1972. *The Portugese Language,* translated by Anthony J. Naro. Chicago: The University of Chicago Press.

May, R., and J. Goldsmith. 1975. "Tone Sandhi in Sanskrit." Unpublished.

Melikišvili, I. 1972. *Otnošenie markirovannosti v fonologii* (uslovija markirovannosti v. klassje šumnyx fonem). (In Georgian with Russian summary.) Tbilisi.

Menn, L. 1977. "Autosegmental child phonology: first pass." Paper presented to Harvard Workshop on Autosegmental Phonology.

Miller, D. Gary. 1976. "On mirror-image rules." *Linguistic Inquiry* 7:383–88.

Miller, Wick. 1965. *Acoma Grammar and Texts.* UCPL 40. Berkeley: University of California Press.

Mitchell, T.F. 1962. *Colloquial Arabic.* London: English Universities Press.

Moll, Francisco de Borja. 1952. *Gramatica Historica Catalana.* Madrid: Editorial Gredos.

Moon, Yang-Soo. 1974. "A Phonological History of Korean." Ph. D. dissertation, University of Texas.

Morin, Yves-Ch., and Joyce Friedman. 1971. "Phonological grammar tester: underlying theory." In *Natural Language Studies,* no. 10. Ann Arbor: University of Michigan Phonetics Laboratory.

Moulton, William G. 1954. "The stops and spirants of Early Germanic." *Language* 30:1–42.

Moulton, William G. 1962. *The Sounds of English and German.* Chicago: The University of Chicago Press.

Neeld, R. 1973. "Remarks on palatalization." *Ohio State University Working Papers in Linguistics* 14:37–49.

Newman, P. 1972. "Syllable weight as a phonological variable." *Studies in African Linguistics* 3:301–23.

Newton, Brian. 1971. "Ordering paradoxes in phonology." *Journal of Linguistics* 7.31–53.

Norman, L. J. 1973. "Rule addition and intrinsic order." *Minnesota Working Papers in Linguistics and Philosophy of Language,* pp. 135–60.

Norman, L. J. 1976. "Bidirectional rules and nonextrinsic ordering." In *The Ordering and Application of Grammatical Rules,* edited by A. Koutsoudas, pp. 122–50. The Hague: Mouton.

Ohala, John. 1974. "Phonetic explanation in phonology." In *Papers from the Parasession on Natural Phonology,* edited by A. Bruck et al, pp. 251–74. Chicago: Chicago Linguistic Society.

Ohso, M. 1972. "A phonological study of some English loan words in Japanese." *Ohio State University Working Papers in Linguistics* 14:1–26.

Ostler, Nicholas. In press. "Autosegmental theory and Japanese accent-spread." In *Proceedings from the Eighth Meeting of the North East Linguistics Society.*

Passy, P. 1890. *Étude sur les changements phonétiques et leurs caractères généraux.* Paris: Librairie Firmin-Didot.

Pike, Kenneth. 1943. *Phonetics.* Ann Arbor: University of Michigan Press.

Polomé, Edgar C. 1967. *Swahili Language Handbook.* Washington, D.C.: Center for Applied Linguistics.

Poppe, N. 1970. *Mongolian Language Handbook.* Washington: Center for Applied Linguistics.

Postal, P.M. 1968. *Aspects of Phonological Theory.* New York: Harper and Row.

Pratt, G. 1911. *Grammar and Dictionary of the Samoan Language.* 4th ed. Malua, Western Samoa: Malua Press.

Pullum, G.K. 1976. "The Duke of York gambit." *Journal of Linguistics* 12:83–102.

Quilis, Antonio, and Joseph A. Fernández. 1973. *Curso de fonética y fonología españolas.* Madrid: Consejo Superior de Investigaciones Científicas.

Quine, W. V. 1953. *From a Logical Point of View.* Cambridge: Harvard University Press.

Read, C. 1975. *Children's Categorizations of Speech Sounds in English.* Research report no. 17, National Council of Teachers of English. Urbana: NCTE.

Redenbarger, W. J., 1977. "Portuguese vowel harmony and the 'Elsewhere Condition'." Paper read at the 1977 Linguistic Symposium on Romance Languages, Cornell University.

Ringen, Catherine. 1972. "On Arguments for Rule Ordering." *Foundations of Language* 8:266–73.

Robinson, O. W. 1976. "A 'scattered' rule in Swiss German." *Language* 52:148–62.

Robinson, O.W. In press. "Rule ordering in a parsing model of phonology." *Communication and Cognition*.

Rohlfs, G. 1966. *Grammatica storica della lingua Italiana e del suoi dialetti.* Torino: Giulio Einaudi.

Rosenblat, A. 1946. *Biblioteca de dialectología hispanoamericano,* II. Buenos Aires: Facultad de Filosofía y Letras de la Universidad de Buenos Aires, Instituto de Filología.

Ross, J. R. 1972. "A reanalysis of English word stress." In *Contributions to Generative Phonology,* edited by M. K. Brame. Austin: University of Texas Press.

Rubach, J. 1977. *Changes of Consonants in English and in Polish.* Warsaw: Zaklad narodowy imienia ossolinskich wydawnictwo polskiej akademii nauk.

Rudes, Blair. 1976. "Lexical representations and variable rules in natural generative phonology." *Glossa* 10:111–50.

Sadock, J. M. 1973. "Word-final devoicing in the development of Yiddish." In *Issues in Linguistics: Papers in Honor of Henry and Renee Kahane,* edited by B. B. Kachru et al., pp. 290-97. Urbana: University of Illinois Press.

Sag, Ivan. 1974. "The Grassmann's law ordering pseudoparadox." *Linguistic Inquiry* 5:591–607.

Sag, Ivan. 1976. "Pseudosolutions to the pseudoparadox: Sanskrit diaspirates revisited." *Linguistic Inquiry* 7:4.

Saltarelli, M. 1970. "Spanish plural formation: apocope or epenthesis?" *Language* 46:89–96.

Sanders, G. 1971. "On the symmetry of grammatical constraints." In *Papers from the Seventh Regional Meeting of the Chicago Linguistic Society,* pp. 232–41. Chicago: Chicago Linguistic Society.

Sanders, G. 1972. *Equational Grammar.* The Hague: Mouton.

Sanders, G. 1974a. "On the notions 'optional' and 'obligatory' in linguistics." *Minnesota Working Papers in Linguistics and Philosophy of Language* 2:145–86. Revised version in *Linguistics* 195:5–47.

Sanders, Gerald A. 1974b. "The simplex feature hypothesis." *Glossa* 8:141–92.

Sanders, G. 1976. "A functional typology of elliptical coordinations." Bloomington: Indiana University Linguistics Club. Revised version in *Current Themes in Linguistics,* edited by F. Eckman, pp. 241–70. Washington, D.C.: Hemisphere Publishing Corp, 1977.

Sapir, Edward. 1915. "Notes on Judeo-German phonology." *The Jewish Quarterly Review,* n.s. 6:231–66. Reprinted in Mandelbaum (1949: 252–72).

Sapir, E. 1921. *Language.* New York: Harcourt Brace.

Sapir, Edward. 1925. "Sound Patterns in Language." *Language* 1:37–51. Reprinted in Joss (1963:19–25).

Sapir, Edward. 1929. "Male and female forms of speech in Yana." In Mandelbaum, ed., 1949:206–12.

Sapir, E., 1933. "The psychological reality of phonemes." *Journal de Psychologie Normale et Pathologique* 30:247–65. Reprinted in *Selected Writings of Edward Sapir,* edited by D. G. Mandelbaum, pp. 46–60. Berkeley: University of California Press, 1949.

Saporta, S. 1965. "Ordered rules, dialect differences and historical processes." *Language* 41:218–24.

Saporta, S., and H. Contreras. 1960. "The validation of a phonological grammar." *Lingua* 9:1–15.

Saussure, F. 1949. *Cours de linguistique générale.* Paris: Payot.

Schachter, Paul, and V. Fromkin. 1968. "A phonology of Akan: Akuapem, Asante, and Fante." *Working Papers in Phonetics* 8. UCLA Phonetics Laboratory.

Schane, S. A. 1968a. *French Phonology and Morphology.* Cambridge: MIT Press.

Schane, S. A. 1968b. "On the non-uniqueness of phonological representations." *Language* 44:709–816.

Schane, S. A. 1971. "The phoneme revisited." *Language* 47:503–21.

Schane, S.A. 1973. *Generative Phonology.* Englewood Cliffs, N.J.: Prentice-Hall.

Schane, S. A. 1974. "There is no French truncation rule." In *Linguistic Studies in Romance Languages,* edited by R. J. Campbell, M. G. Goldin, and M. C. Wang, pp. 89–99. Washington, D. C.: Georgetown University Press.

Schane, Sanford A. 1977. "The rhythmic nature of English word stress." Colloquium presented at December 1977 meeting if the Linguistic Society of America, Chicago.

Schourup, L.C. 1973a. "A cross-language study of vowel nasalization." *Ohio State University Working Papers in Linguistics* 15:190–221.

Schourup, L. C. 1973b. "Unique New York Unique New York Unique New York." In *Papers from the Ninth Regional Meeting of the Chicago Linguistic Society,* edited by C. Corum et al., pp. 587–96. Chicago: Chicago Linguistic Society.

Schuh, R. G. 1972. "Rule inversion in Chadic." *Studies in African Linguistics* 3:379–97.

Schuh, R. G. 1974. "A comment on 'Rule inversion in Chadic: a reply.' " *Studies in African Linguistics* 5:279–80.

Schultz-Lorentzen, C. W. 1945. *A Grammar of the West Greenland Language.* Copenhagen: C. A. Reitzel.

Sebeok, Thomas; Henry Hoenigswald; and Ronald Longacre, eds. 1973. *Current Trends in Linguistics,* 11. The Hague: Mouton.

Selkirk, Elizabeth O. 1978. "The French foot: on the status of 'mute' *e.*" *Studies in French Linguistics,* 1:141–50. Proceedings of the Conference on Current Issues in French Phonology, Indiana University, September 28–29, 1977.

Semiloff-Zelasko, H. 1973. "Syncope and Pseudo-Syncope." In *Papers from the Ninth Regional Meeting of the Chicago Linguistic Society,* pp. 603–14. Chicago: Chicago Linguistic Society.

Shibatani, Masayoshi. 1973. "The role of surface phonetic constraints in generative phonology." *Language* 49:87–106.

Shuy, Roger, and C.-J. Bailey, eds. 1974. *Toward Tomorrow's Linguistics.* Washington, D. C.: Georgetown University Press.

Sievers, E. 1901–1905. *Grundzüge der Phonetik.* Leipzig: Breitkopf und Härtel.

Sigurd, Bengt. 1972. "Linearization in phonology." In *Phonologica 1972,* edited by W. Dressler and P. V. Mareš, pp. 185–208. Munich: Wilhelm Fink Verlag, 1975.

Skousen, Royal. 1975. *Substantive Evidence in Phonology: The Evidence from Finnish and French.* The Hague: Mouton.

Smith, Neilson V. 1973. *The Acquisition of Phonology.* New York: Cambridge University Press.

Solá, D. F., and Gary J. Parker. 1964. *The Structure of Ayacucho Quechua.* Ithaca: Cornell University Press.

Stampe, David L. 1965. "Recent work on Munda linguistics I." *International Journal of American Linguistics* 31:332–41.

Stampe, D. 1968a. "Yes, Virginia, . . ." Paper read at the Fourth Regional Meeting of the Chicago Linguistic Society.

Stampe, David. 1968b. "On some recent views of linguistic theory." Paper read at the Linguistic Society of America winter meeting, New York.

Stampe, D. 1969. "The acquisition of phonetic representation." In *Papers from the Fifth Regional Meeting, Chicago Linguistic Society,* pp. 443–54.

Stampe, David. 1972a. "On the natural history of diphthongs." In *Papers from the Eighth Regional Meeting,* edited by P. M. Peranteau et al., pp. 578–90. Chicago: Chicago Linguistic Society.

Stampe, David. 1972b. "How I spent my summer vacation." Ohio State University. Mimeographed. Revised as 1973b.

Stampe, David. 1973a. "Speech as music." Paper read at the Linguistic Society of America Winter Meeting, San Diego.

Stampe, David. 1973b. "A Dissertation on Natural Phonology." Ph.D. dissertation, University of Chicago. Revision of 1972b.

Stampe, David. 1973c. "On chapter 9." In *Issues in Phonological Theory,* edited by M. Kenstowicz and C. Kisseberth. The Hague: Mouton.

Stampe, D. Forthcoming. *Natural Phonology.*

Stankiewicz, Edward, trans. 1972. *A Baudouin de Courtenay Anthology.* Bloomington: Indiana University Press.

Stanley, Richard. 1967. "Redundancy rules in phonology." *Language* 43: 393–436.

Stanley, Richard. 1972. "Boundary markers in phonology." In *A Festschrift for Morris Halle,* edited by S. Anderson and P. Kiparsky. New York: Holt, Rinehart and Winston.

Steyaert, M. 1976. "Verb reduplication in Dakota." *Minnesota Working Papers in Linguistics and Philosophy of Language* 3:127–43.

Steyaert, M. 1977. "Theoretical implications of voicing neutralisation in Dakota obstruents." Paper presented at the Linguistic Society of America summer meeting, Honolulu, Hawaii.

Stoel-Gammon, Caroline. 1976. "Metaphony in Portuguese: analysis and acquisition." Paper presented at the Colloquium on Hispanic and Luso-Brazilian Linguistics, Oswego, N. Y.

Swadesh, Morris. 1934. "The Phonemic Principle." *Language* 10:117–29. Reprinted in Joos (1966:32–37).

Sweet, H. 1877. *Handbook of Phonetics*. Oxford: Clarendon Press.

Thrainsson, H. 1978. "On the phonology of Icelandic preaspiration." Unpublished.

Trager, George L. 1934. "The phonemes of Russian." *Language* 10:334–44.

Tranel, B. 1977. "On the source of non-alternating nasal vowels in Modern French." *Glossa* 11:74–105.

Trubetzkoy, N. S. 1969. *Principles of Phonology,* translated by Christiane A. M. Baltaxe. Berkeley: University of California Press.

Trubetzkoy, N. 1976. *Letters and Notes*. The Hague: Mouton.

Tucker, A.N., and E.O. Ashton. 1942. "Swahili phonetics." *African Studies* 1:77–103, 161–82.

Twaddell, W. Freeman. 1935. "On defining the phoneme." In *Language, Monograph 16.* Reprinted in Joos (1966:55–80).

Twaddell, W. Freeman. 1938. "A note on Old High German umlaut." *Monatshefte für deutschen Unterricht* 30:177–81. Reprinted in Joos (1966:85–87).

Unbegaun, B.O. 1957. *Russian Grammar*. Oxford: Clarendon Press.

Vago, Robert. 1977a. "In defense of extrinsic ordering." *Journal of Linguistics* 13:25–41.

Vago, Robert, 1977b. "On the revised simultaneous application theory." In *Papers from the Thirteenth Regional Meeting of the Chicago Linguistic Society,* forthcoming.

Velten, H. V. 1943. "The growth of phonemic and lexical patterns in infant language." *Language* 19:281–92.

Vennemann, Theo. 1971. "Natural generative phonology." Paper presented at the Annual Meeting of the Linguistic Society of America, St. Louis.

Vennemann, Theo. 1972a. "Rule inversion." *Lingua* 29:209–42.

Vennemann, Theo. 1972b. "On the theory of syllabic phonology." *Linguistische Berichte* 18:1–18.

Vennemann, Theo. 1974a. "Phonological concreteness in natural generative grammar." *Toward Tomorrow's Linguistics,* edited by R. Shuy and C.-J. Bailey, pp. 202–19. Washington D.C.: Georgetown University Press, 1974.

Vennemann, Theo. 1974b. "Restructuring." *Lingua* 33:137–56.

Vennemann, Theo. 1974c. "Words and syllables in natural generative grammar." In *Parasession on Natural Phonology,* pp. 346–74. Chicago: Chicago Linguistic Society.

Walsh, Thomas. 1976a. "On the characterization of certain sound changes in Romance." Paper presented at the Sixth Symposium on Romance Languages and Linguistics, Montreal.

Walsh, Thomas. 1976b. "On complement rules and drag chains." Paper presented at the Minnesota Regional Conference on Language and Linguistics, Minneapolis.

Wang, William S-Y., and Matthew Y. Chen. 1975. "Sound change: actuation and implementation." *Language* 51:255–81.

Waugh, L.R. 1976. *Roman Jakobson's Science of Language*. Lisse: de Ridder Press.

Whitney, William Dwight. 1879. *A Sanskrit Grammar*. Leipzig: Breitkopf and Härtel.

Wilkinson, R. 1976. "Tunen tone changes and derived phonological contrast." *Language* 51:561–75.

Williams, E. 1976. "Underlying tone in Margi and Igbo." *Linguistic Inquiry* 7:463–84.

Winteler, J. 1876. *Die Kerenzer Mundart des Kantons Glarus in ihren Grundzügen dargestellt*. Leipzig: C. F. Winter'sche Verlagshandlung.

Wolfram, W., and R. Fasold. 1974. *Study of Social Dialects in American English*. Englewood Cliffs, N.J.: Prentice-Hall.

Zwicky, A.M. 1972a. "Note on a phonological hierarchy in English." In *Linguistic Change and Generative Theory*, edited by R. Stockwell and R. Macaulay. Bloomington: Indiana University Press.

Zwicky, Arnold M. 1972b. "The strategy of generative phonology." *Phinologica 1972*, edited by W. Dressler and F. V. Mareš, pp. 151–68. Munich: Wilhelm Fink Verlag, 1975.